MANAGEMENT
RESEARCH

SAGE has been part of the global academic community since 1965, supporting high quality research and learning that transforms society and our understanding of individuals, groups and cultures. SAGE is the independent, innovative, natural home for authors, editors and societies who share our commitment and passion for the social sciences.

Find out more at: **www.sagepublications.com**

MANAGEMENT RESEARCH

4th EDITION

Mark Easterby-Smith,

Richard Thorpe and

Paul Jackson

Los Angeles | London | New Delhi
Singapore | Washington DC

Los Angeles | London | New Delhi
Singapore | Washington DC

SAGE Publications Ltd
1 Oliver's Yard
55 City Road
London EC1Y 1SP

SAGE Publications Inc.
2455 Teller Road
Thousand Oaks, California 91320

SAGE Publications India Pvt Ltd
B 1/I 1 Mohan Cooperative Industrial Area
Mathura Road
New Delhi 110 044

SAGE Publications Asia-Pacific Pte Ltd
3 Church Street
#10-04 Samsung Hub
Singapore 049483

Editor: Kirsty Smy
Development editor: Amy Jarrold
Editorial assistant: Ruth Stitt
Production editor: Rachel Eley
Marketing manager: Ben Sherwood
Cover design: Francis Kenney
Typeset by: C&M Digitals (P) Ltd, Chennai, India
Printed and bound in Great Britain by Ashford Colour
Press Ltd

First edition published 1991
Second edition published 2001
Reprinted 2002, 2003, 2004, 2005
Third edition published 2008
Reprinted 2008, 2009, 2010, 2011 (twice)

This fourth edition published 2012

Library of Congress Control Number: 2011940502

British Library Cataloguing in Publication data

A catalogue record for this book is available from
the British Library

MIX
Paper from
responsible sources
FSC® C011748
www.fsc.org

ISBN 978-0-85702-116-8
ISBN 978-0-85702-117-5 (pbk)

SUMMARY OF CONTENTS

CONTENTS

1 Introducing management and business research   1

2 The philosophy of management research   16

3 Designing management research   36

4   The politics and ethics of management research   75

5   Reviewing the literature   101

6   Creating qualitative data   125

7   Framing qualitative data   161

ABOUT THE
AUTHORS

MARK EASTERBY-SMITH is Professor of Management Learning at Lancaster University Management School. He has a first degree in Engineering Science and a PhD in Organizational Behaviour from Durham University. He has been an active researcher for over 30 years with primary interests in methodology and learning processes. He has carried out evaluation studies in many European companies, and has led research projects on management development, organizational learning, dynamic capabilities and knowledge transfer across international organizations in the UK, India and China.

He has published numerous academic papers and over ten books including: *Auditing Management Development*, Gower, 1980; *The Challenge to Western Management Development*, Routledge, 1989; *Evaluation of Management Education, Training and Development*, Gower, 1994; *Organizational Learning and the Learning Organization*, Sage, 1998; *The Handbook of Organizational Learning and Knowledge Management*, 2nd edn, Wiley, 2011.

At Lancaster he has been variously, Director of the School's Doctoral Programme, Director of the Graduate Management School and Head of Department. Externally he spent several years as a visiting faculty member on the International Teachers' Programme, acting as Director when it was held at the London Business School in 1984. During the early 1990s he was national co-ordinator of the Management Teaching Fellowship Scheme funded by the UK's Economic and Social Research Council (ESRC), which was responsible for training 180 new faculty members across UK management schools. He is a former member of the ESRC Post-graduate Training Board and was President of the British Academy of Management in 2006 and Dean of Fellows from 2008.

RICHARD THORPE is Professor of Management Development and Pro Dean for Research at Leeds University Business School. His early industrial experience informed the way his ethos has developed. Common themes are: a strong commitment to process methodologies and a focus on action in all its forms; an interest in and commitment to the development of doctoral students and the development of capacity within the sector; a commitment to collaborative working on projects of mutual interest. Following a number of years in industry, he joined Strathclyde University as a researcher studying incentive payment schemes. This led to collaboration on *Payment Schemes and Productivity*, Macmillan, 1986. In 1980 he joined Glasgow University where he widened his research interests to include small firm growth and development as well as making regular contributions to the Scottish Business

School's Doctoral Programme. In 1983 he attended the International Teachers' Programme in Sweden where he met Mark and embarked on a PhD under Mark's supervision. Collaboration continued through the 1990s with the ESRC Teaching Fellowship Scheme. In 1996 he was instrumental in establishing the Graduate Business School at Manchester Metropolitan University and in 2003 joined the ESRC Training and Development Board. There, he was involved in establishing the training guidelines for both doctorate and professional doctorate provision and more recently in initiatives to address capacity building in management and business. In 2003 he contributed to the ESRC's Evolution of Business Knowledge programme, his research interests including: performance, remuneration and entrepreneurship, management learning and development and leadership and he has published (with others) a number of books including: *Remuneration Systems*, Financial Times/Prentice Hall, 2000, *Management and Language: The Manager as Practical Author*, Sage, 2003, *Dictionary of Qualitative Management Research*, Sage, 2008, *Performance Management: Multidisciplinary Perspectives*, Palgrave, 2008 and more recently the *Gower Handbook of Leadership and Management Development*, 2010. He was President of the British Academy of Management in 2007 and is currently Dean of Fellows.

PAUL R. JACKSON is Professor of Corporate Communications at Manchester Business School. He has a first degree in Psychology from the University of Sheffield and an MSc in Applied Statistics from Sheffield Polytechnic (now Sheffield Hallam University). His first university post was as a research assistant in studies on impression formation, where he decided that it was worth learning how to write programs in Fortran so that the computer could do the tedious work of adding up and he could do the interesting bits. His research interests have included lab studies of impression formation, large scale surveys of the impact of unemployment on psychological health, longitudinal field studies of the effects of empowerment and work design on employee health and performance, employee communication and teamworking, mergers and social identity.

He has published widely in journals such as the *Academy of Management Journal*, *Journal of Applied Psychology*, *British Medical Journal*, *Human Relations*, *Journal of Occupational Health Psychology* and *British Journal of Management*. His books include: *Developments in Work and Organisational Psychology: Implications for International Business* (Amsterdam: Elsevier, 2006); *Psychosocial Risk Factors in Call Centres* (London: HSE Publications, 2003); *Change in Manufacturing: Managing Stress in Manufacturing*, HSE Publications, 2001; *Organisational Interventions to Reduce the Impact of Poor Work Design* (London: HSE Publications, 1998).

Over the years he has undertaken various roles including Director of Doctoral Programmes at the University of Sheffield and, at UMIST, Head of the Division of Marketing, International Business and Strategy as well as designing the doctoral training programme at MBS. He has been teaching research methods to undergraduate, Masters and doctoral students since 1975 and has contributed to books on research methods teaching as well as workshops for students and teachers on behalf of the British Academy of Management.

PREFACE TO THE 4TH EDITION

The first edition of this book appeared in 1991, at a time when there were very few management research methods books on the market. It quickly became established as the leading text because it covered all of the essential ground, yet was not too long or intimidating. Students and staff liked it because it tackled difficult issues, but avoided either trivializing them, or making them unnecessarily complex. The success of the book was attested by the sales figures, and by the fact that it has become the most highly cited management methodology book in the world according to Google Scholar.

The second edition was published in 2002, and this included a substantial updating of the material since methodology had become a hot topic during the intervening years, and there were many new methods and approaches to management research which needed to be covered. The market had also begun to change significantly, since research methods were starting to be taught at undergraduate level. This resulted in a modest repositioning of our book, but also stimulated the appearance of strong competitors in the market.

The third edition maintained the continuity in the sense that it provided comprehensive treatment of philosophies and methods, plus coverage of both qualitative and quantitative techniques; but it also introduced some radical departures both in terms of content and design. The most significant change was that we strengthened the treatment of quantitative methods, running from the basic techniques for collecting and analysing quantitative data, up to multivariate analysis and structural equation modelling. In keeping with our desire to avoid complications, we covered the principles of analytic methods without introducing complicated algebra. We claimed in the third edition that this part of the book now provided advanced statistics without tears!

In this fourth edition we use full colour, and have added more boxed examples from our own experiences and from those of our students. We have rethought some of the material on philosophy and research design and have extended the coverage of qualitative analysis, particularly with the use of computer assisted methods. The exercises, which are based on our own extensive methodology teaching, have been updated in response to student feedback, and we have retained the companion website, which contains further guidance for teachers, plus exercises and tests for students. Finally, we have added a system of icons based around the metaphor of research being like a tree that sucks up nutrients (data, ideas and experiences) from the ground and then converts them into leaves and fruits (reports, publications and theses). Without wanting to labour the metaphor exhaustively, we use the icons to illustrate some of the points and as a general orientation tool.

ACKNOWLEDGEMENTS

This book is based on the personal research experience of the authors, but thanks should also go to a number of students and colleagues. Both have contributed to this edition in a number of ways, through their encouragement as well as their ideas. We have tried to reflect their suggestions as far as possible in the text.

Our students have taught us a great deal and we have included a number of their examples. We would like to thank Chavi Chen, Gerard Duff, Ray Forbes, Suzanne Gagnon, Jean Clarke, Anya Johnson, Mohamed Mohamud, Lee Beniston, Kendi Kinuthia, Paul Grimshaw, Anna Zueva, Brian Simpson, Julie Schönfelder, Sanaz Sigaroudi and Geetha Karunanayake.

Colleagues have also assisted us by reading through the transcripts, making comments and suggesting ideas and to them we are extremely grateful. These include Lisa Anderson, Joep Cornelissen, Ann Cunliffe, Ardha Danieli, Susan Baker, Ashish Dwivedi, David Holman, Robin Holt, Ossie Jones, Efthimios Poulis and Christine Reid. Jean-Claude Usunier provided a valuable critique of the first edition of the book from a European perspective, and this led to a French translation of the book which is now in its second edition. Joanne Larty helped with the references, and Mirjam Werner in our third edition and Daniella Fjellstrom in this fourth edition provided an invaluable service in assisting with the preparation and organization of the manuscript.

Our editor at Sage for the first edition was Sue Jones. She provided us with the initial inspiration, and since then Rosemary Nixon, Kiren Shoman, Natalie Aguilera and Delia Alfonso offered encouragement, and occasionally hectored us. Our minders for this fourth edition have been Kirsty Smy and Alan Maloney.

The authors are grateful to Sage for permission to include extracts from R. Thorpe and J. Cornelissen (2003) 'Visual media and the construction of meaning', Chapter 4 in D. Holman and R. Thorpe (eds), *Management and Language*.

Finally, we would like to thank our families for their tolerance while this book was being written and rewritten – we hope they will consider the outcome to be worth the effort.

ABOUT THIS BOOK

REALISM

NOMINALISM

Ontology

VARIOUS 3RD WAYS

Ontology | Epistemology | Methodology | Methods and Techniques

We use the metaphor of a tree to represent how the research process unfolds. The key elements of the tree are the roots, the trunk and branches, the leaves, and the fruit – and each of these parallels an aspect of conducting research.

The *roots* symbolize the research traditions within particular disciplines as well as the experiences of past researchers from particular fields. These perspectives, understandings, ideas and beliefs are drawn up (as the tree draws nutrients from the soil) to form the basis of the researcher's ideas in relation to such things as design, methods and forms of analysis.

The *trunk* transports the nutrients from the roots through the branches to the leaves and fruit; it also provides strength and shape to the tree. Here we use a simplified cross-section of the trunk to symbolize four main features of a research design. The inner ring (or heartwood) is the densest part of the trunk, and we use it to represent *ontology*, the basic assumptions made by the researcher about the nature of reality. The next ring represents *epistemology*, the assumptions about the best ways of inquiring into the nature of the world. The third ring from the centre represents *methodology*, or the way research techniques and methods are grouped together to provide a coherent picture. And the fourth ring represents the individual *methods and techniques* that are used for data collection and analysis. The four rings are named and ordered in this way, because the most visible parts of research projects are the methods and techniques used for data collection and analysis and represented by the outer ring. The three inner rings are increasingly hidden from the external observer, yet each makes a critical contribution to the strength, vitality and coherence of the research project.

Moving up and along the branches, the leaves and fruit form the tree's canopy. The leaves collect energy from sunlight, and represent the collection and analysis of data within a research project. It is the collection of research data which stimulates new ideas and enables the evaluation of existing theories. Here we distinguish between three main kinds of data based on the underlying epistemology (second ring in the trunk), according to whether they are essentially positivist, constructionist, or hybrid approaches. To provide differentiation we indicate the positivist approaches in orange, constructionist approaches in green, and hybrid approaches in a combination of these colours.

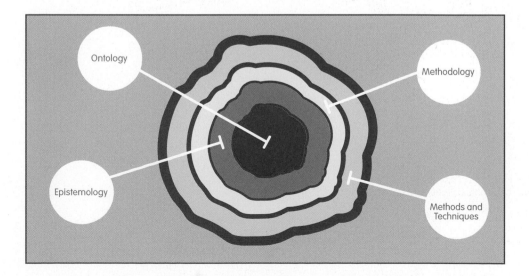

In the final chapter of the book we focus on the *fruit* of the tree which represents the way the research is written up and communicated to third parties. Here we show the coherence between the outputs of the research, and the ontology, epistemology, methodology and methods which underpin any research. In this way, the views and values adopted by the researcher from the early stages of the framing of the research, the design of the research project and the collection of the data are coherently connected and linked.

Within the chapters which follow we have placed a number of these icons in key locations. This is not intended to be exhaustive in the sense that everything is necessarily covered by the icons; nor are we seeking to explain everything through the use of these icons. Our intention is mainly to use them in the light sense as an organizer and as a reminder of the origins of some of the ideas being discussed.

Key of symbols

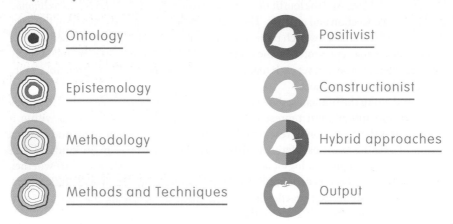

Ontology

Epistemology

Methodology

Methods and Techniques

Positivist

Constructionist

Hybrid approaches

Output

COMPANION WEBSITE

Be sure to visit the Companion Website at www.sagepub.co.uk/easterbysmith to find a range of teaching and learning material for both lecturers and students including the following:

For Lecturers

1. Instructor's manual: A manual is provided on the website with teaching notes and links to additional material.
2. PowerPoint slides: PowerPoint slides for each chapter for use in class are also provided. The slides can be edited by instructors to suit teaching style and needs.

For Students

1. Author podcast: A video of the authors talking about their textbook and its unique features.
2. Online readings: Links to full-text journal articles and book chapters which are related to each chapter.
3. Links to relevant websites: Direct links to related websites including financial databases.
4. Dataset and notes: A complete dataset is provided to allow you to practice data analysis with helpful notes from the authors.
5. Glossary: A glossary is provided online to allow you to check definitions even when you are away from your book.

INTRODUCING MANAGEMENT AND BUSINESS RESEARCH

1

LEARNING OBJECTIVES

 To appreciate how views of management and its research have evolved over time.

 To understand what is distinctive about management research.

 To gain insights into the personal and situational factors that affect success in doing research.

To appreciate different modes of management and business research and how they link to different levels of study.

INTRODUCTION

This book provides comprehensive coverage of research methods in management and business research. It is written for people who have to conduct projects and research studies as part of educational qualifications, which can range from undergraduate to doctoral levels. It is also intended for consultants and others who need to conduct research as part of their normal work. The book covers both the practical techniques for conducting research, and the philosophies and assumptions underlying these techniques. This introductory chapter starts with some reflections on the nature of business and management research, we then provide guidance on the skills and resources required to conduct good research, and we finish with an outline of the content and presentation of the book as a whole.

THE NATURE OF MANAGEMENT AND BUSINESS RESEARCH

We cover methods relevant to both management and business research because there is a great deal in common between the two areas. Indeed the differences are relatively small and cover things such as style, setting and emphasis. Thus management research may concentrate on the nature and consequences of managerial actions, often taking a critical edge, and covers any kind of organization, both public and private. On the other hand business research is more likely to focus on determinants of corporate performance, with an emphasis on private sector organizations. Given these differences we use the two terms interchangeably in the book, but on occasions where there is a significant difference we explain the implications.

There are three features of management and business research that have influenced the structure and content of this book. The first is a long-standing tension between the use of qualitative and quantitative methods in conducting research, and the fashion has swung back and forth over the last few decades between the two. When our first edition was published in 1991, quantitative methods were in the ascendancy, with an emphasis on hypotheses, measurement and statistical analysis. At that time we tried to redress the balance in favour of qualitative methods. Increasingly there is acceptance that we need both qualitative and quantitative methods to answer some of the major questions of management research; consequently the third edition provided extensive treatment of quantitative methods to a more advanced level, and this fourth edition looks more at the logic for mixing methods within the same studies. The philosophical logic for choice of methods is covered in Chapter 2, and guidance on the use of qualitative and quantitative methods form the core of the book from Chapters 6 to 10.

A second feature is the ongoing debate about whether management research should lead to developments in **academic theory**, or whether it should lead to solutions of practical problems. The former, referred to as **pure research**, conjures the image of the white-coated scientist studying companies and their employees from a distance; the latter, known as **applied research**, suggests researchers in grey suits or overalls working with managers and employees to understand the strategies and practices. The arguments for and against each style of research and the practical consequences of their implementation are reviewed in Chapter 3.

The third feature is that management research is usually political. This is because most studies take place within formal organizations that have distinct boundaries which are controlled from within. Hence access to companies and employees depends on senior managers being convinced that the potential benefits will outweigh the costs. They may require a say in how the results will be used and disseminated, and there is always the danger of research data and results being used out of context to strengthen the case of one group against another. Researchers can also come under pressure to provide positive stories about the companies they study, often as a condition for being allowed further access. This means that the researcher should be prepared to confront ethical issues, and to navigate complex political relationships. In Chapter 4 we provide guidance on these matters.

WHAT IS MANAGEMENT?

There are many views about what constitutes 'management'. Early civilizations demonstrated the ability to organize large scale activities that were efficient and effective: the Egyptians built the pyramids, the Chinese built the Great Wall and the Mesopotamians learned to irrigate the land to wall their cities. All these feats required a high degree of co-ordination, and although many had captive labour forces, there must have been sophisticated organization of their work. Formal records of production management techniques can be traced back to Mencius (372–289 BC). This Chinese philosopher dealt with models and systems, and pointed to the advantages of the division of labour, putting the concepts rediscovered over 2000 years later into perspective.

The modern use of the term 'management' derives from the USA, with the requirement for business and entrepreneurial skills in the early twentieth century when American industries and railroads were developing very rapidly (Lawrence, 1986). From these beginnings, management was put forward as an important subject that could, and should, be taught in business schools. The establishment of business schools led to greater systematization of techniques and knowledge, although much of this was based on the principles that managers had distilled from their own experiences. Two of the dominant figures during this period were Taylor (1947), who developed rational systems to simplify the organization of work and link rewards directly to effort, and Fayol ([1916] 1950) who classified the main functions that managers should perform, such as: planning, organizing, co-ordinating and controlling. Although this **classical** view of management has much face validity, later researchers were to show that these functions did not resemble what managers actually did in their work (Mintzberg, 1973), nor did it provide an adequate account of how they might get the best results out of their subordinates.

An early critique of the classical view was the **human relations** school, which demonstrated that workers were not necessarily motivated by rational incentives, and that they were more likely to be productive if managers took personal interest in them (Roethlisberger and Dickson, 1939), or if they were given more responsibility in their jobs (Herzberg, Mausner and Snyderman, 1959). Moreover these researchers suggested that a key role for managers was to get employees to accept changes and improvements in the workplace, and this would be accomplished most easily if they got them closely involved in decision-making processes (Coch and French, 1948). The focus of this work was therefore on the non-rational aspects of human behaviour in organizations.

During the 1960s a view was developed that the key to effective management was the ability to take rational decisions, even under conditions of uncertainty (Simon, 1959; Cyert and March, 1963). This **decision theory** emphasized the techniques that could be used to analyse the impact of external factors on corporate strategy, and ways of reaching adequate decisions under conditions of uncertainty, even if they were not completely ideal. Quantitative methods of analysis and model-building still dominate the curricula of many business schools, especially in the USA and France.

The classical view has also been attacked by researchers such as Stewart (1967), Mintzberg (1973), Kotter (1982) and Hales (1986) who, as we have indicated above, found almost no evidence of managers behaving as they are supposed to do. Instead of standing back and directing enterprises strategically, most managers, even top ones, spend most of their time talking to people; they work long hours at an unrelenting pace; their work patterns are varied, fragmented and reactive; and there is rarely any time for planning ahead and anticipating crises. Consequently, those who follow the **work activity** view argue there is little point in trying to get them to behave according to the classical text books. Rather, managers should be helped to deal with the realities of their jobs through managing their own time and becoming more skilled at leading and negotiating with others.

The second line of attack came from employers, who suggested that the emphasis on analytic techniques is of limited value, and may even be harmful to companies. They argued that it was more important for managers to be entrepreneurial, to exhibit leadership, to provide collective visions and to mould the culture and values of the organization (Porter and McKibbin, 1988). This line has given rise to a view of management as a set of **competencies** which represent the skills that need to be demonstrated in the course of effective managerial work (Boyatzis, 1982; Silver, 1991; Evers and Rush, 1996).

During the 1990s there was an increase in the literature based on **critical management theory**. This came from various sources, including postmodernism, which rejects the rationality that is so strongly embedded in the idea of management (Hassard and Parker, 1993), social constructionism, which emphasizes that the most important part of management involves making sense of ambiguous and complex situations through conversations and dialogue (Weick, 1995; Cunliffe, 2002b) and critical theory, which tends to see management as an agent in maintaining wider power differences in society (Fournier and Grey, 2000). This has been largely a theoretical critique, and to date there have been few attempts to articulate appropriate methodologies for conducting empirical research into management from a critical perspective, other than Alvesson and Deetz (2000).

The view that has developed over the last decade is based on **process theory**, the idea of management as a process. This emphasizes learning processes, the creation and management of organizational knowledge (Nonaka and Takeuchi, 1995; Scarbrough, 2008), and the importance of power and politics underlying knowledge legitimation (Lawrence et al., 2006; Buchanan and Bryman, 2007). At a wider level there are links to strategic perspectives including absorptive capacity (Todorova and Durisin, 2007), the focus on change leading

TABLE 1.1　Seven perspectives on management

Views of Management	Period of Dominance	Key Features	Type of Theory
Classical	1910–1950	Functional activities	Normative
Human Relations	1940–1970	Motivating people and managing change	Normative
Decision Theory	1950–1970	Optimizing decisions	Analytic
Work Activity	1970s	What managers do	Descriptive
Competencies	1980s	Skills required for effective performance	Normative
Critical	1990s	Social construction and politics	Analytic
Process	2000s	Learning and strategizing	Analytic and Normative

to dynamic capabilities (Winter, 2003), and the idea of strategy as practice (Jarzabkowski, Balogun and Seidl, 2007).

The seven views summarized in Table 1.1 are by no means the only views about what management is, or should be; but they are important historically. It should also be apparent that these include different types of theory. Some are **normative**, in the sense that they specify what or how managers should do their work; some are **descriptive**, because they try to describe what managers do in practice; and some are **analytic**, because they take a particular theoretical perspective which emphasizes some aspects of work, at the expense of others.

In the context of the present book, there are three main implications from the above review. First, although we have presented the story chronologically, all seven perspectives co-exist and significant research is still being conducted within each one of them. Second, the perspectives here are illustrative rather than exhaustive; there are plenty of other perspectives that lead to a wide range of questions for management and business research. Third, the research methods are likely to vary considerably according to the view that the researcher takes of the focus of enquiry. If she is working within the decision theory school, she will seek to manipulate quantitative data that can simulate processes or predict the best courses of action; if she adopts the work activity view of management, then she might choose observational methods that provide a structured description of managerial activities and roles within real organizations; and if she is interested in management as a socially constructed activity, then she is more likely to be interested in gathering stories, narratives and conversations about management.

A key point here is that there are many different ways of conducting research into management and business, and one of the main aims of the book is to provide guidance on the criteria for choosing different methods. Chapters 2 and 3, in particular, provide both frameworks and advice to aid the research design process.

EXERCISE
1.1

Management perspectives and research foci

For each of the seven perspectives of management described above, summarize in one sentence the way that research is most likely to be conducted. Work in small groups. We have already provided hints above for three of them.

- Classical
- Human relations
- Decision theory
- Work activity
- Competencies
- Critical
- Process

SKILLS AND RESOURCES FOR MANAGEMENT AND BUSINESS RESEARCH

There are both tacit and explicit skills involved in research. Although it is possible to develop formal skills and knowledge through training, these tacit skills can only be fully acquired through trial and error, and through working with others who are able to pass on their skills. This is where the relationship with the tutor or supervisor is very important, and if one gets the chance to work on a project with experienced researchers, this can be very valuable.

In this section we have listed what we believe to be the important qualities of researchers. These are based partly on our own experiences and partly on external sources such as the ESRC guidelines for research methods training (ESRC, 2009). We have classified the resulting personal qualities according to whether they comprise knowledge, skills or personal attributes. This classification is based substantially on Burgoyne and Stuart's (1976) work into the attributes of effective managers, because we think there are close parallels between managing and researching. The skills and knowledge areas are progressively more specific to the conduct of research. These are 'core' qualities, which are important in any form of research, and are listed in Exercise 1.2.

EXERCISE
1.2

Rating skills and qualities

Rate yourself on each quality using the following 1 to 4 scale:

4   Possess to a high degree

3   Possess to a moderate degree

2   Possess to a limited extent

1   Have virtually none of these

(Continued)

(Continued)

Knowledge/awareness	Skills and abilities	Personal qualities
1 Different assumptions about the world ☐	7 Planning, organizing and managing one's own time ☐	13 Self-awareness ☐
2 Qualitative and quantitative research methods ☐	8 Searching libraries and online data sources ☐	14 Clarity of thought ☐
3 Range of research designs ☐	9 Interviewing and observation ☐	15 Sensitivity to events and feelings ☐
4 Immediate subject of study ☐	10 Analysing and interpreting data ☐	16 Emotional resilience ☐
5 Related subjects and disciplines ☐	11 Arguing views orally and in writing ☐	17 Creativity ☐
6 Key networks and contacts in chosen research area ☐	12 Gaining support and co-operation from others ☐	18 Learning from experience ☐
Total ☐	Total ☐	Total ☐

If you have managed to rate yourself on the above qualities, then any ratings below 3 may be cause for concern (with the possible exception of item 5). What to do about any apparent deficiencies is, of course, a different matter. As a generalization: knowledge can be acquired by reading and talking, or by attending courses; skills can be acquired through practising them, either in a simulated or a real environment; and personal qualities can be acquired, with much difficulty, through life or educational experiences. This book certainly cannot offer everything. It provides a reasonable coverage of items 1, 2, 3, 8, 9 and 10; and it touches on 6, 7, 12, 13 and 18. As for the rest, they may be acquired most easily by working with other researchers, in the form of apprenticeship suggested by Turner (1988).

Beyond a certain point, however, specialization begins to creep in. One form of specialization depends upon whether the researcher is following a primarily quantitative or qualitative path. Those following the quantitative path will need to have high levels of skill in areas such as survey design, sampling methods and statistical analysis; those following the qualitative path may need to be skilled at conducting in-depth interviews, making field notes, coding and interpreting transcripts, and so on. But there is a trend towards more mixing of subjects and methodologies as will be explained further in later chapters. Thus quantitative subjects may be tackled with qualitative methods, as in behavioural accounting; and qualitative subjects can be tackled with quantitative methods, such as frequency counts in textual analysis. In Chapters 6 to 10 we give extensive guidance on the choice and application of qualitative and quantitative methods.

Support and supervision

Supervision is important both to provide technical guidance and as a structure for the research activity. On taught courses tutors will normally work with small groups of students. These can be organized either in action learning sets where the members will be looking at different topics but taking the opportunity both to support each other and to learn from their experiences, or as group project teams where members are working together on the same task. In the case of group projects there is the added challenge of having to work as a team, which requires division of roles and co-ordination. We discuss further some of the challenges of team working in Chapter 4.

For those working towards research-based degrees such as MPhil or PhD the relationship with the supervisor is crucial. In contrast to taught courses, there is usually an opportunity to negotiate about supervision, so it is worth knowing something about the success rate of a supervisor. Phillips (1984) studied the characteristics of successful supervisors. In addition to having relevant specialist knowledge, she identified practical aspects of the relationship: the better supervisors tend to set regular, and realistic, deadlines, although they do not interfere too much with the detail of the work. A responsive style seems most appropriate if the researcher is to be encouraged to become autonomous and independent, and it helps if the supervisor is prepared and willing to respond quite rapidly to any problems or to written work. Availability is very important, and for this reason the star researcher with a string of brilliant publications, but who is never available for consultations, may not necessarily be the best supervisor! Ideally there should be mutual commitment between the two parties, and this can sometimes be formalized as a supervision contract.

From our own experiences, the supervisor role can be quite tough, too, because students often move beyond the existing knowledge of the supervisor during the course of the project. In the case of a doctoral thesis this is almost an inevitable consequence of the requirement for originality in a PhD thesis. But also in postgraduate and undergraduate dissertations, which involve tackling broad-based problems, the work will often fall outside the specialist area of the supervisor who therefore has to rely on generic supervisory skills such as asking challenging questions or pointing the student to alternative sources of expertise. There is also a delicate balance to be struck between providing critical feedback that highlights weakness in a piece of work, and providing praise and encouragement in order to motivate the student.

In addition to tutors and supervisors it is worth considering alternative sources of emotional support. One of the best forms of support can come from colleagues, either through naturally occurring friendships, or through constructing a 'support set' – a group of four or five researchers committed to meeting regularly every few weeks to discuss their research progress and problems. It helps if the members of this set are working in related fields. The set may have a tutor (or set advisor) who can help with organization, and possibly provide specialist advice and support. The members of the set should be able to use it to 'bounce' ideas off each other and, particularly for those who are researching part-time, to provide contact with others who may be going through similar experiences of doubt, confusion and disillusionment as themselves. Furthermore it is important to recognize the potential for support outside one's immediate institution. In particular, those wishing to develop academic careers will need to develop links within the broader community through attending conferences, and this is another area where the supervisor should be able to help.

Problems with supervision

Find out the procedures you have to follow in your institution if you are having difficulties with your supervisor. This information should be easily accessible on your institution's intranet. Remember supervisory problems are matters of serious concern and should be dealt with as soon as possible to avoid the situation escalating.

Style and creativity

In the previous section we explained why support is a key factor in the successful completion of research work. Here we focus more on ways of ensuring that the research will be of good quality and will contain some originality. We argue that this is determined largely by the personal style and approach adopted by the researcher.

A fascinating study into the personal factors that contribute to discoveries in medicine is provided by Austin (1978), an American neurosurgeon, who had become dissatisfied by the trite explanations provided by scientists about how great discoveries occur. He identified three factors that seem to underlie the 'blind luck' that is apparent in many discoveries:

- First, the researcher needs to be *in motion*. Nobody trips over anything while sitting down. The greater the curiosity, resilience and persistence of the researcher, the more likely he or she is to find something of significance.

- Second, he or she needs to have a *prepared mind* and be ready to see new relationships and solutions. This means being aware of past research that has been conducted through searching the literature and talking to other researchers, while at the same time being prepared to think outside existing frameworks and knowledge.

- Third, there needs to be *individualized action*. This means encouraging distinctive, even eccentric, hobbies and lifestyles. In particular, the researcher should try to take a broad interest in people and other disciplines. Creativity is often born from associations and links made across traditional boundaries.

The illustration that Austin uses is the discovery of penicillin by Alexander Fleming in 1928. In an interview after the Second World War, Fleming commented that the discovery of penicillin was almost entirely a matter of luck: 'like winning the Irish Sweepstake'. But Austin shows that this was not only a matter of blind luck. Fleming, by all accounts, was a tireless researcher; his great aim being to discover a new antiseptic, and even after the penicillin discovery he was extremely busy making and selling antibacterial vaccines. Thus he was a man who was continuously *in motion*.

But it was his *prepared mind* that enabled him to note the effect on colonies of bacteria when a stray spore of a rare mould fell by accident onto his culture dish. Nine years earlier he had discovered the bacterial enzyme Lysozyme when, 'whilst suffering from a cold, his own nasal drippings had found their way into a culture dish. He noted that the bacteria round the mucus were killed and astutely followed up the lead' (Austin, 1978: 74). The parallels between these and other experiences would be easy to perceive. *Individualized action* enters into the story because Fleming was a keen swimmer and water polo player. He had chosen to train and work at the old St Mary's Hospital not because of the excellence of its scientific facilities, but because it had a good swimming pool. The laboratories were basic, badly equipped, cold and 'contaminated by organisms swirling in and out of the London fog' (Austin, 1978: 92). This made them a particularly good breeding ground for bacteria and stray spores! In this example it is possible to see how natural chances can be enhanced, and Austin suggested that major discoveries are most likely to take place when several factors coincide. This is what he calls the 'unifying observation' of the Fleming effect.

Unfortunately not all researchers are destined to make major discoveries. The bulk of research is much more humdrum. This is true both for the social and natural sciences. Many sociologists have carried out detailed studies of the way that the natural sciences progress, and the consensus is that it is a gradual process, with much hard graft and very few genuine breakthroughs. Latour and Woolgar (1979) demonstrated in a classic study of a biological laboratory how scientific 'facts' emerged through a process of debate, which was linked to the career strategies and progress of individual researchers. Similarly, the study by Law (1994) into the management and organization of a particle physics research laboratory shows the impact of factors such as funding, politics and status hierarchies on the way scientific knowledge is produced and recognized. He also commented reflexively on his debates with colleagues and various changes of heart in the course of doing his own research study. These issues will be considered in more depth in Chapters 3 and 4.

LEVELS AND OUTCOMES OF MANAGEMENT RESEARCH

As suggested at the outset, this book is intended to aid research at different levels, including undergraduate, postgraduate and doctoral degrees, and funded research projects. We also mentioned the distinction between pure and applied forms of research. In this section we extend the pure/applied distinction in relation to the different outcomes of research, and then discuss how they may link to different levels of research.

One of the key features of *pure research* is that its results are openly disseminated through books, articles, conference papers or theses, addressed mainly at an academic audience. Dissemination is seen as a major responsibility for the researcher, and career progress for academics depends on getting the fruits of their work placed in the most prestigious journals, which is seen as proof of the quality of the work. *Applied research* is intended to lead to the solution of specific problems, and usually involves working with clients to identify important problems and deciding how best to tackle them. There are a number of variants of applied research including: **best practice research**, where other 'leading' companies are surveyed in order to assess how they have tackled, or solved, the same problem (Burgoyne and James, 2006); **action research**, which involves making changes within an organization or its parts in order to understand the dynamic forces within it; and **engaged research**, which requires close collaboration between academics and practitioners (Van de Ven and Johnson, 2006).

The results of applied research always need to be reported to the client, who is likely to evaluate the quality of the research in terms of its usability. But there is always the potential to publish the results of applied research in practitioner or professional journals provided the results can be shown to have wider significance, although this possibility often raises questions of commercial confidentiality and the need to maintain good relationships with the initial client. In Chapter 4 we discuss in more detail issues such as ethics, confidentiality and the control of information.

The pure/applied distinction is similar to the ideas of Gibbons et al. (1994) who describe two forms of research: **mode 1** research, which concentrates on the production of knowledge by detached scientists working from single disciplines and focusing on theoretical questions and problems; and **mode 2** research, which is often trans-disciplinary and is characterized by the production of knowledge through direct engagement with social practice and problems. Some scholars argue that management research should follow the latter approach with an emphasis on practical application (Tranfield, 2002), others suggest a compromise position where both theoretical and practical work is required, which is sometimes characterized as **mode 1½** research (Huff, 2000).

Different types of research also tend to be linked to different levels. At *undergraduate* levels, research is likely to be specific and bounded, either as an assignment from tutors or as a question posed by a client. Common tasks include small market research studies, or interview-based studies of employee attitudes, and hence an emphasis on applied research is most likely. In most cases a single method will be used and this may also be specified in advance. The opportunities for choice are mainly around how a method is used and how results are interpreted and communicated. In most cases undergraduate research projects are conducted in teams because this creates economy of scale from a teaching point of view. It also means that significant projects can be undertaken in a short period of time, and students should benefit from combining their skills when working as teams.

Research conducted as part of a *postgraduate* degree will normally have greater scope, and more time will be available. Again, applied research is likely to dominate, with evaluation research being one of the easiest options. This involves looking at some system or practice that already exists and making recommendations for how it might be changed and improved. If the project seeks to create or learn from organizational change it will assume features of action research. Involvement in change can lead to rich and interesting results, and it may be a valuable experience for people seeking work in consultancy.

Doctoral dissertations need to produce theoretical contributions with some degree of originality, and this suggests that they need to contain significant elements of pure research. Although doctoral studies may include both applied and action research, the theoretical contribution is a necessary condition for the award of a doctorate. These contributions may include the discovery of new ideas, the invention of new procedures and methods, the replication of existing studies in new contexts, or the application of new theoretical perspectives to existing research questions.

Funded projects are usually conducted by experienced researchers, but face many of the same choices as projects conducted for university degrees. Required outputs will depend on the expectations of the funding body: if funding is provided by a company there may be an emphasis on applied research, and if it is a research council then there will be an emphasis on pure research.

We summarize in Table 1.2 the main links between types and levels of research. We will discuss in more detail in the next three chapters the many factors, both political and

TABLE 1.2   Types of research most likely to be associated with different levels

	Undergraduate Level	Postgraduate Level	Doctoral Level	Funded Projects
Applied Research	**	**	*	**
Action/evaluation Research	*	**	*	*
Pure Research		*	***	***

*TYPE OF RESEARCH OCCASIONALLY ASSOCIATED WITH SPECIFIC LEVEL OF STUDY.
**TYPE OF RESEARCH OFTEN ASSOCIATED WITH SPECIFIC LEVEL OF STUDY
***TYPE OF RESEARCH MOST COMMONLY ASSOCIATED WITH SPECIFIC LEVEL OF STUDY.

philosophical, which can influence the way research is designed and conducted in practice. We also review in Chapter 11 both strategies for demonstrating a 'contribution', and how the evaluation criteria might vary with different contexts.

The examples above have all assumed that research will involve the collection of **primary data** directly by the researchers. The value of primary data is that it can lead to new insights and greater confidence in the outcomes of the research, which is very useful for students wishing to use their research experiences as a basis for subsequent careers in management or consultancy practice. Consequently it is normally expected that dissertations at undergraduate, postgraduate and doctoral levels will include some primary data.

However, some subjects such as economics and finance rely more on public or corporate financial data and statistics. This is known as **secondary data**, and the skill of the researcher is demonstrated by exploring new relationships and patterns within this existing data. Another form of secondary data is represented by published literature, and all research studies need to demonstrate familiarity with existing literature both to ensure that the research is not merely repeating something that has already been done, and to provide an opportunity to build on what has been done before. In Chapter 5 we discuss both sources and strategies for using secondary data, especially in the form of literature surveys, which are commonly used to underpin primary data collection.

IS MANAGEMENT RESEARCH DISTINCTIVE?

At the start of this chapter we outlined three features of management research that have influenced the shape and content of this book. Here we identify three other features that give a distinctive flavour to management research, particularly in contrast to some of the other social sciences.

First, the practice of management is largely *eclectic*: managers need to be able to work across technical, cultural and functional boundaries, and they need to be able to draw on knowledge developed by other disciplines such as sociology, anthropology, economics, statistics and mathematics. The dilemma for the researcher, then, is whether to examine management from the perspective of one discipline (mode 1), or whether to adopt a trans-disciplinary approach (mode 2). The former is often seen to be the safer course for those who wish to gain respectability from academic peers, whereas the latter is more likely to produce results that are of use to practising managers. Moreover, the danger of eclectic approaches to research is that they may incorporate underlying assumptions that are incompatible with each other, which is why we devote the next chapter to reviewing the philosophical underpinnings of research approaches and methods.

Second, managers and other employees tend to be highly *educated*. Most managers have undergraduate or MBA degrees, and many specialists, particularly in research-oriented companies, have PhDs – thus they have similar educational backgrounds to the researchers who would study them. This means that they will be more likely to appreciate the value of research-based knowledge, and have clear views about the appropriate directions of research. It also means that researchers cannot assume that they have the premium on expertise, and this opens up the possibility of the joint production of knowledge – combining the insights and expertise of both managers and researchers. Of course, this challenges traditional assumptions about the objectivity of researchers, and presents intriguing problems about the ownership of scientific knowledge.

Third, there is often an expectation that research will lead directly to *action*. The expectation comes both from employees and managers in exchange for offering access and support, and from funding agencies that look for potential economic benefits from management research. This has led to a variety of ways whereby researchers engage with both practice and practitioners, as will be discussed in the next section.

We summarize the features that make management research distinctive in Table 1.3. Admittedly each is not unique to management research: the problem of multiple disciplines exists in educational research; the wider dissemination of higher education means that the expertise of lay people must be recognized in many fields, including health research; and the link to action is apparent in design sciences. But the combination of all three at the same time within management research suggests that some of the traditional assumptions and practices in social research may well need rethinking. This is what we do in this book, and it is something that is being taken further in the Sage Series on Management Research.

TABLE 1.3 Implications of distinctive features of management research

Key Features	Implications for Management Researchers
Management research methods are eclectic	Researchers need to be aware of different underlying assumptions.
Managers and employees are highly educated	Managers will have academic interest in research process/results and may want to contribute to the direction of work.
Action is a frequent outcome of management research	Research results may both derive from, and lead to, practical action. Both traditional analytic research and action research are legitimate activities.

CONCLUSION

In this opening chapter we have discussed a number of ways of understanding management, we have also considered what makes management research distinctive both in form and in the demands it places on the researcher, and we have reviewed the skills and support that the researcher is likely to require to achieve successful outcomes. Some key points/lessons that we have wanted to emphasize in this chapter are:

 The diversity of perspectives on management and business research.

 The need to negotiate and maintain adequate support.

 The importance of self-awareness and development of personal skills.

 The need for awareness of politics and underlying assumptions in management research.

This volume is intended to be self-sufficient in a number of ways. It provides extensive coverage and guidance in relation to: philosophical and political perspectives (Chapters 2 and 4); designing studies and reviewing literature (Chapters 3 and 5); generating and analysing both qualitative (Chapters 6 and 7) and quantitative data (Chapters 8 to 10); and writing and communicating research results (Chapter 11). This coverage should be sufficient for most research projects at undergraduate and postgraduate levels. Naturally, additional techniques may be appropriate in some specialized areas of research and we provide guidance on further reading about these. The book also provides basic grounding for the first year of doctoral training, although doctoral students will also need to refer back to original sources, and to develop their own critiques of methods and underlying philosophies.

The book is furthermore intended to be self-sufficient pedagogically. That is, we provide a range of examples and exercises across all the chapters, which can be used for individual review and for group discussion in classrooms. There are additional exercises in the accompanying website (www.sagepub. co.uk/easterbysmith), and this provides further guidance to teachers in using these exercises with different groups of students. We are also developing an organic metaphor for the processes of research: this is the idea of a tree that absorbs nutrients from the ground which it distributes through the trunk and into the leaves and fruit. We will introduce this progressively, starting with the next chapter.

EXERCISE
1.4

Schools of thought about management

We have described seven views of management above, but there are others, such as 'mushroom management' (where you keep everyone in the dark and every now and then you open the door and drop a pile of shit on them!). Working in small groups share your experiences of managing or being managed: use this to invent a new label, or school of thought, about management. Be prepared to explain and justify to other groups.

FURTHER READING

Grey, C. (2005) *A Very Short, Fairly Interesting and Reasonably Cheap Book About Studying Organizations*. London: Sage.

As it says on the label, this book provides a succinct overview of theories of management and organization, and it is reasonably priced. It adopts a critical view in the sense that it has a slight preference for the perspectives of those who are managed, rather than the managers themselves.

Marshall, S. and Green, N. (2007) *Your PhD Companion: A Handy Mix of Practical Tips, Sound Advice and Helpful Commentary to See You Through Your PhD*, 2nd edn. Oxford: Cromwell Press.

Mintzberg, H. (2005) *Managers Not MBAs: A Hard Look at the Soft Practice of Managing and Management Development*. San Francisco: Berrett-Koehler.

Henry Mintzberg made his reputation from demonstrating the inadequacy of classical views of management and the nature of managerial work. This book continues his argument that managers are less in need of the analytic skills taught on traditional MBAs, and more in need of process and intercultural skills. In particular, it looks at ways in which managers can best learn these skills and abilities.

THE PHILOSOPHY OF MANAGEMENT RESEARCH

2

LEARNING OBJECTIVES

 To understand the different philosophical assumptions 'hidden' beneath management research and to appreciate the strengths and weaknesses of each.

To appreciate how different philosophical assumptions influence criteria for judging research quality.

To enable readers to surface and identify their own philosophical assumptions.

INTRODUCTION

> 'It is a capital mistake to theorise before one has data'.
> ARTHUR CONAN DOYLE

The relationship between data and theory is an issue that has been hotly debated by philosophers for many centuries. Failure to think through such philosophical issues, while not necessarily fatal, can seriously affect the quality of management research, and they are central to the notion of research design. The aim of this chapter is therefore to consider the main philosophical positions that underlie the designs of management research – in other words, how do philosophical factors affect the overall arrangements that enable satisfactory outcomes from the research activity?

There are at least three reasons why an understanding of philosophical issues is very useful. First, it can help to clarify research designs. This not only involves considering what kind of evidence is required and how it is to be gathered and interpreted, but also how this will provide good answers to the basic questions being investigated in the research. Second, knowledge of philosophy can help the researcher to recognize which designs will work and which will not. It should enable him or her to avoid going up too many blind alleys and should indicate the limitations of particular approaches. Third, it can help the researcher identify, and even create, designs that may be outside his or her past experience. It may also suggest how to adapt research designs according to the constraints of different subject or knowledge structures.

Arguments, criticisms and debates are central to the progress of philosophy. It is unfortunate that within the social sciences such debates sometimes take the form of denigrating the other point of view, or of completely ignoring its existence. We believe that it is important to understand both sides of an argument because research problems often require eclectic designs that draw from more than one tradition. Thus we try to provide a balanced view of the different philosophical positions underlying research methods and designs here; to do this we have had to return to some of the original sources of these positions. Therefore the chapter starts by reviewing some key debates among philosophers of the natural sciences and social sciences. Then we explore these philosophies further, and review a number of alternative positions.

THE PHILOSOPHICAL DEBATES

Most of the central debates among philosophers concern matters of **ontology** and **epistemology**. Ontology is about the nature of reality and existence; epistemology is about the best ways of enquiring into the nature of the world. Scientists and social scientists generally draw from different ontological and epistemological assumptions when developing their methodologies for conducting research. Sometimes they do this consciously and deliberately; more often they simply follow the traditions passed on by those who trained them. For example, most of the time medical researchers can simply follow the procedures of scientific research when developing new drugs, and they rarely need to reflect on the nature of the human soul – unless of course they are using human embryos to conduct research into the therapeutic value of stem cell treatments. In which case the differing views about when human 'life' begins are very important.

Similarly, social researchers often follow the traditions of their training without dwelling on more fundamental issues. We think this is a shame. Awareness of philosophical

TABLE 2.1   Ontology, epistemology, methodology and methods and techniques

Ontology	Philosophical assumptions about the nature of reality.
Epistemology	A general set of assumptions about ways of inquiring into the nature of the world.
Methodology	A combination of techniques used to inquire into a specific situation.
Methods and Techniques	Individual techniques for data collection, analysis, etc.

assumptions can both increase the quality of research and contribute to the creativity of the researcher. Furthermore, there is much confusion among researchers about the distinction between terms such as epistemology and ontology, and hence in this section we will try to establish some clarity around these terms.

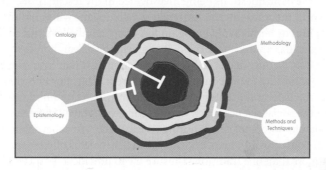

The essence of ontology, epistemology, methodology and **methods and techniques** is summarized in Table 2.1, and in the icon above we illustrate the relationship between these four terms using the metaphor of a tree as explained at the end of the last chapter. In this case it is the trunk of a tree that has four rings. It is the outer ring, the bark, which represents the methods and techniques adopted in a research project, such as interviews and questionnaires. These are the most obvious and visible features of a project, but they depend on decisions and assumptions about methodology, epistemology and ontology which lie behind the scenes, and which are progressively less visible. So we will start with ontology, represented by the central core, or heartwood of the tree, and then we will work outwards. Since the second half of the book is concerned with the choice and application of individual methods we will concentrate in this chapter on ontology, epistemology and methodology.

 ## ONTOLOGY: FROM REALISM TO NOMINALISM

The first term, ontology, is the starting point for most of the debates among philosophers. Although there are strong parallels between the debates within the natural sciences and the social sciences, there are also differences. Thus among philosophers of *natural science* the

debate is between **realism** and **relativism**. There are several varieties of realism. A traditional position emphasizes that the world is concrete and external, and that science can only
progress through observations that have a direct correspondence to the phenomena being
investigated. This extreme position has been modified by philosophers of science in recent
decades who point out the difference between the laws of physics and nature, and the knowledge or theories that scientists have about these laws. This position is labelled by Bhaskar as
transcendental realism, which assumes that 'the ultimate objects of scientific inquiry exist
and act (for the most part) quite independently of scientists and their activity' (1989: 12).

The next position along the continuum (see Table 2.2) is **internal realism**. This assumes that
there is a single reality, but asserts that it is never possible for scientists to access that reality
directly, and it is only possible to gather indirect evidence of what is going on in fundamental
physical processes (Putnam, 1987). A nice illustration is provided by the 'bubble chamber',
which was developed in the 1950s to track the paths of sub-atomic particles during experiments.
The bubble chamber is a tank filled with an unstable transparent liquid such as superheated
hydrogen; as these high energy particles pass through the chamber they boil the liquid, leaving
a track of tiny bubbles, which can be photographed immediately. Thus the bubbles provide a
visible record of the activity of sub-atomic particles, which cannot otherwise be 'seen' directly.
The problems of observation at this level were summarized more formally by the Indeterminacy
Principle, formulated by Werner Heisenberg in 1927, which states that, 'The more precisely the
position is determined, the less precisely the momentum is known in this instant, and vice versa'.
Thus it is never possible to obtain full and objective information about the state of a body because
the act of experimentation itself will determine the observed state of the phenomenon being
studied. Any attempt to measure the location of an electron will, for example, affect its velocity.

TABLE 2.2 Four different ontologies

Ontology	Realism	Internal Realism	Relativism	Nominalism
Truth	Single truth.	Truth exists, but is obscure.	There are many 'truths'.	There is no truth.
Facts	Facts exist and can be revealed.	Facts are concrete, but cannot be accessed directly.	Facts depend on viewpoint of observer.	Facts are all human creations.

Internal realism does accept, however, that scientific laws once discovered are absolute and
independent of further observations. The position of *relativism* goes a stage further in suggesting
that scientific laws are not simply out there to be discovered, but that they are created by people. It has
been strongly influenced by the work of Latour and Woolgar (1979) who have studied the way scientific ideas evolve within research laboratories and noted the amount of debate and discussion that
takes place about how to explain observed patterns and phenomena. People hold different views,
and their ability to gain acceptance from others may depend on their status and past reputation.
Thus the 'truth' of a particular idea or theory is reached through discussion and agreement between
the main protagonists. Furthermore, Knorr-Cetina (1983) points out that the acceptance of a
particular theory, and hence the 'closure' of a scientific debate, may be highly influenced by the
politics of business and commercial resources.

EXAMPLE
2.1

The Intergovernmental Panel on Climate Change published a series of reports in 1990 which argued that global warming represented a very serious threat to human civilization. But their own data also showed a period of global warming about 1000 years ago, when vineyards were widespread in Britain. This opened a question about whether current signs of global warming are caused by CO_2 emissions from fossil fuels burnt by humans, or whether they are just part of natural cycles of global climate change.

The current debate about climate change is a good example of the potential for debate around the significance of 'scientific' evidence (see Example 2.1). Although the same evidence is potentially available to all protagonists, no single piece of evidence is accepted as definitive by all, and both supporters and sceptics of the climate change hypothesis tend to select evidence that specifically supports their own views. In addition there are very strong entrenched interests – oil companies, environmentalists and national governments – which see their political and economic interests bound up with one or another outcome from the debate. The relativist position assumes that there may never be a definitive answer to the climate change debate, just different accommodations as the interests of different groups interact with the gradual accumulation and acceptance of scientific evidence. We shall return to some of these political and ethical issues in Chapter 4.

Realist scientists have responded vigorously to the relativist challenge by arguing that even if scientists work through social and political networks, the truth of scientific laws is quite independent of the process of discovery. Richard Dawkins, the biologist, famously comments that even the most dedicated relativist does not believe, when flying at 40,000 feet in a Boeing 747, that the laws of physics which hold the jet in the air are mere constructs of the imagination (Irwin, 1994).

Within *social science* there have been similar debates, although primarily between the positions of internal realism, relativism and **nominalism**. Of course, within the social sciences, we are interested in the behaviour of people rather than inanimate objects. And this leads to debate about whether the assumptions and methods of natural science are appropriate to be used in the social sciences (Blaikie, 2007). The answer in our view depends both on the topic of enquiry and the preferences of the individual researcher. Therefore concepts such as social class and racial discrimination can be treated as real phenomena, which exist independently of the researcher and which have real consequences for the life chances and career success of people of different classes or gender. In both cases it can be difficult to agree what these concepts mean or how to measure them, but such disagreements do not alter the reality of their consequences. This indicates the *internal realist* position.

From a *relativist* ontology it is accepted that social class and racial discrimination are defined and experienced differently by different people, and this will depend greatly on the classes or races to which they belong and the contexts or countries in which they live. Thus there is no single reality that can somehow be discovered, but many perspectives on the issue. The relativist position assumes that different observers may have different viewpoints and as Collins (1983: 88) says, 'what counts for the truth can vary from place to place and from time to time'.

The position of nominalism goes further by suggesting that the labels and names we attach to experiences and events are crucial. Postmodern authors, such as Cooper and Burrell (1988), envisage social life as paradoxical and indeterminate, and argue that social reality is no more than the creation of people through language and discourse (Cunliffe, 2001). From this position there is no truth, and the interesting questions concern how people attempt to establish different versions of truth. Thus, the idea of 'social class' is often used as an explanation of why some people (and families) are systematically more successful than others. For some it provides a critique of the way privilege is maintained through educational and employment institutions, for others it may provide a justification of the superiority or some classes (or castes) over others. Similarly, following the racial discrimination line, the label 'institutional racism' provided a sharp critique of the internal practices of the Metropolitan Police following their botched investigation into the murder in London of the black teenager Stephen Lawrence in 1993.

These four ontological positions are summarized below in Table 2.2.

We can illustrate these different positions with two examples, one physical and the other social. First, consider the game of snooker. A realist view of snooker would concentrate on mapping the locations, trajectories and ricochets of different balls, and how the rules of snooker lead to games being won or lost. The internal realist would see a more complex picture: balls do not necessarily follow the principles of classical mechanics: they may be spun or jumped, different tables will behave in different ways, and the technical abilities of players will affect the outcome. Moving to the relativist position, we would focus less on the mechanics of the game, and more on the strategies of the players, and how they manoeuvre the balls to gain advantage over opponents. From a nominalist perspective, the focus could be on the way the rules evolve over time, on who controls the finances of the professional game, or the way careers are forged.

The second example, which is more relevant to business, is the notion of corporate profit. A realist view will assume that there is a single figure which represents the difference between income and expenditure, and that the accounts posted by companies at the year-end are normally accurate. The internal realist will see a more complex position: the boundaries may be permeable with acquisitions and divestments taking place during the previous year, highly diverse activities may be woven into single threads, and decisions will be taken about how to divide ongoing activities between one year and the next. Thus the profit figure posted will be just an approximation of the 'true' profit of the company. From a relativist position it would be recognized that profit is just one indicator of corporate health and other indicators, such as sales growth, innovation rates or stock market valuations may be equally relevant – with no one view taking precedence. The nominalist perspective will draw attention to the way profit figures are constructed from many operational decisions about what to show or hide, and at corporate levels may well be manipulated to ensure that directors maximize their annual bonus payments.

EPISTEMOLOGY: POSITIVISM VERSUS SOCIAL CONSTRUCTIONISM

As indicated above, epistemology is about different ways of inquiring into the nature of the physical and social worlds. It has formed the ground for a sustained debate among social scientists, which has focused around the respective merits of two contrasting views of how social science research should be conducted: **positivism** and **social construction-ism**.[1] Each of these positions has to some extent been elevated into a stereotype, often by the opposing side. Although we can draw up comprehensive lists of philosophical assumptions and methodological implications associated with each position, there is no single philosopher who ascribes to all aspects of one particular view. Indeed, occasionally an author from one side produces ideas that belong more neatly to those of the other side.

Also when we look at the actual practice of research, as we shall see below, even self-confessed extremists do not hold consistently to one position or the other. And although there has been a gradual trend from positivism towards constructionism since the early 1980s, there are many researchers, both in management and social science research, who deliberately combine methods from both traditions. We elaborate on these two traditions below.

Positivism

The key idea of positivism is that the social world exists externally, and that its properties should be measured through objective methods, rather than being inferred subjectively through sensation, reflection or intuition. The nineteenth-century French philosopher, Auguste Comte (1853: 3), was the first person to encapsulate this view, saying: 'All good intellects have repeated, since Bacon's time, that there can be no real knowledge but that which is based on observed facts'. This statement contains two assumptions: first, an ontological assumption, that reality is external and objective; and second, an epistemological assumption, that knowledge is only of significance if it is based on observations of this external reality. This has a number of implications, although not all of them were proposed by Comte (see Table 2.3).

It is worth repeating that these propositions are not simply the view of any single philosopher; they are a collection of points that have come to be associated with the positivist viewpoint. Some 'positivists' would disagree with some of these statements. Comte, for example, did not agree with the principle of reductionism. Wittgenstein argued strongly in his early work that all factual propositions can be reduced to elementary propositions that are completely independent of one another. But in his later work he challenged his earlier view on the grounds that elementary propositions, such as colours, could still be logically related to each other (Pears, 1971). So philosophers within one school not only disagree with each other; they may also disagree with themselves over time.

The view that positivism provides the best way of investigating human and social behaviour originated as a reaction to metaphysical speculation (Aiken, 1956). As such, this philosophy has developed into a distinctive **paradigm** over the last 150 years. The term 'paradigm' came into vogue among social scientists, particularly through the work of Kuhn (1962) who used it to describe the progress of scientific discoveries in practice, rather than how they are subsequently reconstructed within text books and academic journals. Most of the time, according to Kuhn, science progresses in tiny steps, which refine and extend what is already 'known'. But occasionally experiments start to produce results that do not fit into existing theories and patterns. Then, perhaps many years later, a Galileo or Einstein

---

[1] We use this term, rather than the expression 'social constructivism', which is preferred by Guba and Lincoln (1989) and Knorr-Cetina (1983).

TABLE 2.3 Philosophical assumptions of positivism

- *Independence*: the observer must be independent from what is being observed.
- *Value-freedom*: the choice of what to study, and how to study it, can be determined by objective criteria rather than by human beliefs and interests.
- *Causality*: the aim of the social sciences should be to identify causal explanations and fundamental laws that explain regularities in human social behaviour.
- *Hypothesis and deduction*: science proceeds through a process of hypothesizing fundamental laws and then deducing what kinds of observations will demonstrate the truth or falsity of these hypotheses.
- *Operationalization*: concepts need to be defined in ways that enable facts to be measured quantitatively.
- *Reductionism*: problems as a whole are better understood if they are reduced into the simplest possible elements.
- *Generalization*: in order to move from the specific to the general it is necessary to select random samples of sufficient size, from which inferences may be drawn about the wider population.
- *Cross-sectional analysis*: such regularities can most easily be identified by making comparisons of variations across samples.

proposes a new way of looking at things, which can account for both the old and the new observations. It is evident from these examples, and from the illustration given in Chapter 1, that major scientific advances are not produced by a logical and incremental application of scientific method. They result from independent and creative thinking that goes beyond the boundaries of existing ideas. The result of this is a 'scientific revolution', which not only provides new theories, but which may also alter radically the way people see the world, and the kind of questions that scientists consider are important to investigate. The combination of new theories and questions is referred to as a new paradigm.

Social constructionism

The new paradigm that has been developed by philosophers during the last half-century, largely in reaction to the application of positivism to the social sciences, stems from the view that 'reality' is not objective and exterior, but is socially constructed and given meaning by people. The idea of social constructionism then, as developed by authors such as Berger and Luckman (1966), Watzlawick (1984) and Shotter (1993), focuses on the ways that people make sense of the world especially through sharing their experiences with others via the medium of language. Social constructionism is one of a group of approaches that Habermas (1970) has referred to as interpretive methods. We will touch on these, and a number of other approaches, in the course of this and the following chapter.

What, then, is the essence of social constructionism? First, it is the idea, as mentioned above, that 'reality' is determined by people rather than by objective and external factors. Hence the task of the social scientist should not be to gather facts and measure how often certain patterns occur, but to appreciate the different constructions and meanings that people place upon their experience. The focus should be on what people, individually and collectively, are thinking and feeling, and attention should be paid to the ways they communicate with each other, whether verbally or non-verbally. We should therefore try to understand and appreciate the different experiences that people have, rather than search for external causes and fundamental laws to explain behaviour. Human action arises from the sense that people make of different situations, rather than as a direct response to external stimuli.

The methods of social constructionist research can be contrasted directly with the eight features of classical positivist research. They are summarized in Table 2.4. Again, it should be emphasized that these represent a composite picture rather than the viewpoint of any single author.

The implications of holding these different views may be seen, for example, in the way researchers can study managerial stress. The positivist would start with the assumption that occupational stress exists and then would formulate measures of stress experienced by a large number of managers in order to relate them to external causes such as organizational changes, interpersonal conflicts or critical performance reviews. Measures of stress could be based on standardized verbal reports from the managers or on physiological factors such as blood pressure. The social constructionist would be interested in the aspects of work that managers consider 'stressful', and perhaps in the strategies that they develop for managing these aspects. He or she would therefore arrange to talk with a few managers about their

TABLE 2.4   Contrasting implications of positivism and social constructionism

	Positivism	Social Constructionism
The observer	must be independent	is part of what is being observed
Human interests	should be irrelevant	are the main drivers of science
Explanations	must demonstrate causality	aim to increase general understanding of the situation
Research progresses through	hypotheses and deductions	gathering rich data from which ideas are induced
Concepts	need to be defined so that they can be measured	should incorporate stakeholder perspectives
Units of analysis	should be reduced to simplest terms	may include the complexity of 'whole' situations
Generalization through	statistical probability	theoretical abstraction
Sampling requires	large numbers selected randomly	small numbers of cases chosen for specific reasons

jobs, about the aspects they find more, or less, difficult, and would attempt to gather stories about incidents that they had experienced as stressful.

LINKING ONTOLOGY, EPISTEMOLOGY AND METHODOLOGY

It should be clear by now that there is a link between epistemology and ontology, with positivism fitting with realist ontologies, and constructionism fitting with nominalism. We also introduce here a distinction between stronger and more normal versions of positivism and constructionism. With regard to positivism, this follows the distinction introduced by the Oxford philosopher A.J. Ayer ([1936] 1971: 50) between statements that are respectively either directly, or only indirectly, verifiable. The idea of 'normal' constructionism refers to those who construct their own knowledge, while accepting the existence of independent, objective knowledge; whereas strong constructionism assumes that there is no difference between individual and social knowledge (Ernst, 1996).

The correspondence is therefore summarized in Table 2.5, where positivism and constructionism are linked to internal realist and relativist ontologies, while strong positivism and strong constructionism are linked to the realist and nominalist ontologies. However, we

TABLE 2.5 Methodological implications of different epistemologies

Ontologies	Realism	Internal Realism	Relativism	Nominalism
Epistemology	Strong Positivism	Positivism	Constructionism	Strong Constructionism
Methodology				
Aims	Discovery	Exposure	Convergence	Invention
Starting points	Hypotheses	Propositions	Questions	Critique
Designs	Experiment	Large surveys; multi-cases	Cases and surveys	Engagement and reflexivity
Data types	Numbers and facts	Numbers and words	Words and numbers	Discourse and experiences
Analysis/ interpretation	Verification/ falsification	Correlation and regression	Triangulation and comparison	Sense-making; understanding
Outcomes	Confirmation of theories	Theory testing and generation	Theory generation	New insights and actions

no mix although headings quite broad

take the argument further by suggesting that with the weaker versions of both epistemologies, there are overlaps in these positions, and the methodologies that follow from them combine different features of each. The table therefore summarizes the main methodologies under the four main positions, and we explain these further below.

In the *strong positivist* position it is assumed that there is a reality which exists independently of the observer, and hence the job of the researcher is to discover the laws and theories that explain this reality. This is most readily achieved through the design of experiments that eliminate alternative explanations and allow key factors to be measured precisely in order to verify or falsify predetermined hypotheses. On the other hand, less strong versions of positivism accept that reality cannot be accessed directly. The research therefore needs to infer the nature of this reality indirectly through conducting surveys of large samples of individuals, activities or organizations. Data will normally be expressed in quantitative form, but this may be supplemented by qualitative data. This should enable patterns and regularities in behaviour to be identified, thus allowing propositions to be tested and new ideas to be developed. Even so, it is only a matter of probability that the views collected will provide an accurate indication of the underlying situation.

From the *constructionist* position, the assumption is that there may be many different realities, and hence the researcher needs to gather multiple perspectives through a mixture of qualitative and quantitative methods and to gather the views and experiences of diverse individuals and observers. This is sometimes described as **triangulation**, based on the idea that a ship's navigator wishing to identify his or her position (before the invention of GPS) would take compass bearings on three different landmarks and would then draw lines on the chart from these points thus producing a small triangle that would indicate the position of the vessel.

The story from the *strong constructionist* perspective is different again because it assumes there is no pre-existing reality, and the aim of the researcher should be to understand how people invent structures to help them make sense of what is going on around them. Consequently, much attention is given to the use of language and conversations between people as they create their own meanings. Researchers following this path are encouraged to be critical of the way meanings can be imposed by the more powerful on the less powerful. Furthermore, the recognition that the observer can never be separated from the sense-making process means that researchers acknowledge that theories which apply to the subjects of their work must also be relevant to *themselves*. Such reflexive approaches to methodology are recognized as being particularly relevant when studies are considering power and cultural differences (Anderson, 1993; Easterby-Smith and Malina, 1999; Cunliffe, 2003).

EXERCISE
2.1

Spot the epistemology!

Researchers normally betray their epistemology in the language they use. Here are seven brief statements of the aims of different papers. Which is which? What clues did you spot?

1   'We advance research on absorptive capacity by extending and empirically validating the conceptual distinction between potential and realized absorptive capacity' (Jansen, Van den Bosch and Volberda, 2005: 1000).

(Continued)

(Continued)

2   'This paper develops a holistic model of the overall process, by integrating knowledge oriented, routine oriented, and social/context of perspectives' (Hong, Easterby-Smith and Snell, 2006: 1027).

3   'This article contributes to the study of managerial agency in the absorption of new knowledge and skills … Empirical data are drawn from a longitudinal study of a …' (Jones, 2006: 355)

4   'We (also) examine the influence of tacit and explicit knowledge on IJV performance. We find that relational embeddedness has a stronger influence on the transfer of tacit knowledge than it has on the transfer of explicit knowledge' (Dhanaraj et al., 2004).

5   'These findings can be explained by elements of JCT and social exchange theory. As expected, when both LMX quality and empowerment were low the most negative outcomes resulted, and in general, when both variables were high the most positive outcomes resulted' (Harris, Wheeler and Kacmar, 2009: 397).

6   'Organizational routines are ubiquitous, yet their contribution to organizing has been underappreciated. Our longitudinal, inductive study traces the relationship between organizational routines and organizational schemata in a new research institution' (Rerup and Feldman, 2011: 577).

7   'This brings me to a discussion of the credibility performance of agency-client relations. In some respects the very structure of a corporation can be seen in how it arranges performances … Like an individual, a corporation may be seen as a performer …' (Moeran, 2005: 917).

STRENGTHS AND WEAKNESSES OF THE MAIN TRADITIONS

Here we summarize some of the strengths and weaknesses of each position. This should help the researcher to choose which methods and aspects are most likely to be of help in a given situation. In the case of quantitative methods and the positivist paradigm, the main strengths are that they can provide wide coverage of the range of situations, they can be fast and economical and, particularly when statistics are aggregated from large samples, they may be of considerable relevance to policy decisions. On the debit side, these methods tend to be rather inflexible and artificial; they are not very effective in understanding processes or the significance that people attach to actions; they are not very helpful in generating theories; and because they focus on what is, or what has been recently, they make it hard for the policy-maker to infer what changes and actions should take place in the future. In addition, much of the data gathered may not be relevant to real decisions even though it can still be used to support the covert goals of decision-makers.

The strengths and weaknesses of the *social constructionist* paradigm and associated qualitative methods are fairly complementary. Thus they have strengths in their ability to look at change processes over time, to understand people's meanings, to adjust to new issues and ideas as they emerge, and to contribute to the evolution of new theories. They also provide a way of gathering data, which is seen as natural rather than artificial. There are, of course, weaknesses. Data collection can take up a great deal of time and resources, and the analysis and interpretation of data may be very difficult, and this depends on the intimate, tacit knowledge of the researchers. Qualitative studies often feel very untidy because it is harder to control their pace, progress and end points. There is also the problem that many people, especially policy-makers, may give low credibility to studies based on apparently 'subjective' opinions.

It is tempting, then, to see the relativist position as a useful compromise, which can combine the strengths, and avoid the limitations, of each. But it is not that simple: the *relativist* position is distinct and has its own strengths and weaknesses. The main strengths are that: it accepts the value of using multiple sources of data and perspectives; it enables generalizations to be made beyond the boundaries of the situation under study; and it can be conducted efficiently, for example, through outsourcing any survey work to specialized agencies. The weaknesses are that: large samples are required if results are to have credibility, and this may be costly; the requirement for standardization means it may not be able to deal effectively with the cultural and institutional differences found within international studies; and it may be hard to reconcile discrepant sources of data that point to different conclusions.

TABLE 2.6 Strengths and weaknesses of different epistemologies

	Strengths	Weaknesses
Strong Positivism	If it works it can provide highly compelling conclusions.	Hard to implement social experiments and to control for alternative explanations of results. Focus may be very narrow.
Positivism	Can provide wide coverage. Potentially fast and economical. Easier to provide justification of policies.	Inflexible and artificial. Not good for process, meanings or theory generation. Implications for action not obvious.
Constructionism	Accepts value of multiple data sources. Enables generalizations beyond present sample. Greater efficiency including outsourcing potential.	Access can be difficult Cannot accommodate institutional and cultural differences. Problems reconciling discrepant information.
Strong Constructionism	Good for processes, and meanings. Flexible and good for theory generation. Data collection less artificial.	Can be very time consuming. Analysis and interpretations are difficult. May not have credibility with policy-makers.

OVERVIEWS OF OTHER PHILOSOPHIES

Up to this point, we have reviewed the fundamental philosophical positions that underlie the practice of management research. We have discussed and evaluated them openly in order to provide options for the researcher depending on the situation and his or her interests. However, there are also a number of discrete philosophical positions, which have been worked out as coherent schools of thought and which, to some extent, exclude other positions. We have already mentioned critical realism in passing, and this will be one of a number of positions to which numbers of social researchers will adhere. Hence it seems important to explain a little more about these philosophical frameworks since they represent relatively coherent ways of thinking, which are promoted by influential proponents. In this section, we cover, in alphabetical order: critical realism, critical theory, feminism, hermeneutics, postmodernism, pragmatism and structuration theory.

Critical realism

Over the last two decades **critical realism** has been adopted by a number of management and organizational researchers because it provides a compromise position between the stronger versions of positivism and constructionism. It starts with a realist ontology, which recognizes social conditions (such as class or wealth) as having real consequences whether or not they are observed and then incorporates a relativist thread, which recognizes that social life is both generated by the actions of individuals, and also has an external impact on them (Ackroyd and Fleetwood, 2000).

A key feature of critical realism is the idea of a 'structured ontology', which differentiates between three levels: the *empirical* domain, which comprises the experiences and perceptions that people have; the *actual*, which comprises events and actions that take place whether or not they are observed or detected; and the *real*, which comprises causal powers and mechanisms that cannot be detected directly, but which have real consequences for people and society (Bhaskar, 1978: 13). These three domains correspond roughly to three of our ontological positions, respectively relativism, internal realism and realism.

Two other features are important in critical realism. First is the idea that causality exists as potential, rather than the automatic correlation of events that is normally associated with strong positivism. Second is the idea, drawn partly from critical theory, that many of these underlying mechanisms do not work in the interests of ordinary people and employees, and that greater awareness of their underlying causes will provide potential for emancipation from their effects.

The implications for management research are therefore that it has an agenda which may be critical of the status quo, and also that it recognizes and differentiates between different levels of phenomena, leading to an eclectic approach to research methods. There are relatively few research studies that have adopted the methods of critical realism whole-heartedly, but many draw on its ideas to structure processes of data collection and analysis.

Critical theory

Critical theory started as an intellectual movement, also known as the Frankfurt School, which sought to critique the effects of society and technology on human development. The key figure in this movement is Habermas (1970) who argues that society leads to inequalities and alienation; yet this is invisible to people who do not realize what is taking place. He therefore argues that there is a degree of irrationality in capitalist society which creates a false consciousness regarding wants and needs. Thus people are seduced into wanting consumer products that they don't really need.

Habermas also identifies clear differences between the natural and social sciences: the former being based on sense experiences, and the latter on communicative experiences. This means that although understanding in the natural sciences is one-way (monologic), where scientists observe inanimate objects, in the social sciences communication should be two-way (dialogic), with both researchers and the researched trying to make sense of the situation. Hence he suggests that it is only through dialogue that social scientists will be able to work effectively. Another important point introduced by Habermas (1970) is the idea that knowledge is determined by interests and that very often it is the more powerful people in society who determine what is regarded as 'true'. Consequently, truth should be reached through discussion and rational consensus, rather than being imposed by one group over another.

Critical theory has several implications in management and organizational research. It casts a sceptical eye on the motives and impact of powerful groups and individuals, which in an emancipatory way shows a concern for the interests of the least powerful members. Of course awareness of the way that knowledge is determined by political processes is of increasing relevance – especially within the so-called knowledge intensive organizations.

Feminism

Feminism is critical of the status quo, but from a very specific angle: that women's experiences have been undervalued by society and by scientific enquiry. From a philosophical view it contains a strong critique of science on the grounds that women's perspectives have been ignored by most scientific enquiry, in at least five aspects (Blaikie, 2007): there are very few women employed within science; there is gender bias in the definition of research problems; there is bias in the design and interpretation of research; there are too many rigid dualisms in male-dominated science; and science is not as rational and objective as it claims to be. Furthermore it is claimed that similar processes operate in the social sciences especially with structured interviews, which create a status difference between the interviewer and respondent, even when the interviewer is a woman (Cotterill, 1992). In particular it is emphasized that external knowledge is impossible and we must therefore understand human behaviour from within, through understanding the experiences of women themselves.

There is also an emancipatory agenda to feminism, although in relation to (social) science, there is a split between epistemologies known as 'feminist empiricism' and 'feminist standpoint'. The former assumes that the problem is not with science itself, but with the way it is conducted, therefore there is a need to rectify the norms and procedures of the natural sciences and the social sciences so that they incorporate a gendered perspective. The feminist standpoint, on the other hand, is more radical. It suggests that social science and its methods are fundamentally flawed, and it needs to be completely rethought. In particular, it needs to include issues of power dynamics and gender differences, and should make a far greater use of subjective experiences and the procedures of **reflexivity**.

The relevance of feminism to management research is not only that it provides a spotlight on the historical and continuing inequalities of women working in most organizations, but it also provides sensitivity to other areas of discrimination within organizational life, which may be caused by other factors such as race or age.

Hermeneutics

Although **hermeneutics** were originally developed by Protestant groups in seventeenth-century Germany as a means of interpreting the Bible, the theory still has some relevance to management research. Essentially it provides insight into ways of interpreting textual material, which can comprise both formal written texts and spoken words that can be recorded. Two of the best-known proponents of hermeneutics are Gadamer (1989) and Ricoeur (1981).

Gadamer is particularly concerned about the context within which texts are written. He points out that contemporary interpretations of earlier texts are influenced by the culture in which the interpreter is located, so in order to understand a particular text one must try to understand what is going on in the world of the writer at the time that the text is written. Ricoeur argues that when reading any text there is bound to be a gap between the author and the reader due to temporal differences – which he refers to as 'distanciation'. Ideally, there needs to be some kind of discourse between the author and the reader at the same point in time, but in the case of historical texts this is no longer possible. We therefore have to be aware that there may be no single, and correct, interpretation of a particular text, because both the writing and the reading will be context-dependent.

From the viewpoint of management research, some of the insights from hermeneutics have obvious relevance if the researcher wishes to analyse corporate documents such as annual reports. In this case, instead of, for example, conducting a content analysis of statements about the environment in annual reports for 1980, 1990 and 2000, one would need to analyse references in each report separately in relation to the social, economic and political context at each point of time. Thus the analysis would be between context-based observations, rather than simple additions and enumerations of mentions.

Postmodernism

Postmodernism first came to wide academic attention with the English publication of Jean-François Lyotard's (1984) book, *The Postmodern Condition*, although the term had been used intermittently in relation to literary criticism since 1926 (Chia, 2008). A loose cluster of other, mainly French, philosophers have been associated with the development of ideas around postmodernity, including Derrida (1978) and Foucault (1979).

There are three key ideas to postmodernism. First, it provides a critique of scientific progress, suggesting that it is not necessarily a good thing. Thus scientific progress is discontinuous and contested, rather than being linear and continuous. Lyotard, for example, examines the impacts of computerization on the control of knowledge, and demonstrates how technology enables many large corporations to become more powerful than states. Second, it is associated with a somewhat experimental movement in architecture and the arts, which seeks to redress the excesses of modernism, for example the bleak concrete architecture of the 1960s. Thus postmodern architecture tends to be very eclectic, drawing upon different traditions and ideas, and therefore avoiding the large-scale regularity of modern architecture. Third, as we have discussed above, it contains an ontological position, which is opposed to realism, though it is sometimes dismissed as supporting relativism and mere nihilism.

There are several implications for management research. First, the opposition to systematic control and regularity leads to an emphasis on flux and flexibility. Thus, postmodernists do not see organizations as static and monolithic, and this makes their perspective particularly appropriate for studying organizational dynamics and change. Second, the opposition to realism places an emphasis on the invisible elements and processes of organizations, including tacit knowledge and the informal processes of decision-making. Finally, postmodernism retains a critical edge and is sceptical about the role and motivation of large industrial organizations, and questions whether they are of lasting value to society.

Pragmatism

Pragmatism originated in the writings of early twentieth-century American philosophers, particularly William James ([1907] 1979) and John Dewey (1916). It is often seen as a compromise position between internal realism and relativism: it does not accept that there are pre-determined theories or frameworks that shape knowledge and truth; nor can people construct their own truths out of nothing. The key point is that any meaning structures must come from the lived experience of individuals. Dewey, in particular, talks about the need to balance concrete and abstract on one hand, and reflection and observation on the other.

Perhaps it is no coincidence, since Dewey was an educationalist, that pragmatism has had a significant impact on theories of learning within organizations. The Kolb Learning Cycle (Kolb, 1984) adopts a pragmatic approach, suggesting that learning takes place as a continual movement from concrete experience, to reflective observation, to abstract conceptualization, to active experimentation and back to concrete experience. It is also consistent with the original thinking of James that organizational theorists have adopted elements of pragmatism because it offers a synthesis between features often regarded as irreconcilable dualisms, such as positivism and anti-positivism (Brandi and Elkjaer, 2008).

Pragmatism is a valuable perspective in management research because it focuses on processes that are particularly relevant to studies of knowledge and learning, and its impact on methods can be seen in the tradition and methods of grounded theory, which we will discuss in some detail in the next chapter.

Structuration theory

Structuration theory is most associated with the work of Anthony Giddens (1984), where he develops the idea of 'duality of structure', in that structure and agency should not be regarded as pre-ordained. Instead, he suggests that structures are created and recreated through social action and the agency of individuals, and structure then guides and constrains individual agency. Hence, there is a continual interaction between social structure and social action.

Philosophically, he is at pains to point out that the laws of science and social science are fundamentally different, because the former are potentially universal, while the latter depend upon the context (including both structure and action) in which things are taking place. He is also concerned about the use of language, pointing out that words are not precisely 'representational', and their use depends on agreement about their meaning, which may be the product of debates and reinterpretations. Because language is essentially problematic he therefore advocates that social scientists should try to avoid specialist language, because it potentially obscures and creates confusion for outsiders. In order to communicate insights from social science he suggests that social scientists should attempt to use common sense language in the normal course of their work.

From the viewpoint of management research, structuration theory has relevance to understanding the relationships between employees and the organizations within which they work, or between communications and the information systems that are supposed to facilitate them. In other words, it can throw light on aspects of organizations where there is some kind of structural duality.

Overview

In figure 2.1 we provide a sketch of how these six philosophies relate to each other against the basic ontological dimension introduced earlier in this chapter. The positions are intended to be indicative rather than precise mappings.

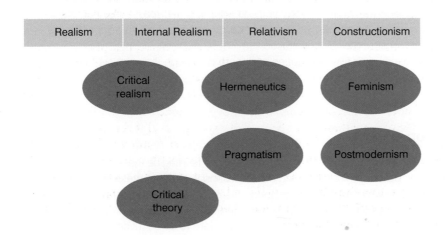

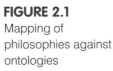

FIGURE 2.1

Mapping of philosophies against ontologies

CONCLUSION

In this chapter we have concentrated on philosophies that underlie management research, and our main aim has been to help the reader identify philosophical assumptions underlying other people's work, and to understand how they might influence and assist his or her own research endeavours. At this point we can emphasize four key points/lessons:

 All researchers hold philosophical assumptions, although these are often tacit rather than explicit positions.

 Researchers need to be aware of their own philosophical assumptions.

 The strongest philosophical contrast is between realist and nominalist ontologies.

 There is often correspondence between ontologies, epistemologies and methodologies.

So far, the discussion has been inevitably theoretical. In the next chapter we will start to work on how these philosophical positions influence specific research methods, and will provide a number of illustrations and practical exercises to assist in developing your own research plans or designs.

EXERCISE 2.2

Identifying one's own philosophical positions

Write down a very brief description of some research that you are planning to do, or might do, including a title, the main question and how you would do it (one sentence for each). Consider (a) what ontology you are adopting (i.e. realist, internal realist, relativist or nominalist); and (b) what epistemology you are likely to adopt (strong/weak positivist or strong/weak constructionist).

Share/exchange with two colleagues and try to challenge the analysis that each provides.

EXERCISE 2.3

A balloon debate

The idea of a 'balloon debate' is that contestants have to imagine that they are travelling in a hot air balloon which is running out of fuel and is about to crash into a mountain. In order to save the lives of the majority, it is decided that one person must be tipped out of the basket. Each person in the basket therefore has to argue why they would represent the greatest loss to society if they were to be sacrificed.

(Continued)

(Continued)

Within the balloon debate each person normally has to argue the case for a famous person or an ideology. In this exercise we suggest that groups argue the case for one of the philosophical positions outlined above. So, divide into groups of four or five people. Each group should:

- Pick one general philosophical position described in the penultimate section (i.e. critical theory, feminism, hermeneutics, etc.).

- Summarize its main features.

- Draw out methodological implications for researching a question or issue.

- Make the case to the rest of the class for why this is a valuable philosophy/ method and why it should not be thrown out of the balloon.

After each group has presented, groups must identify one of two philosophies that should remain in the balloon (no self-nominations or tactical voting!)

FURTHER READING

Ackroyd, S. and Fleetwood, S. (eds) (2000) *Realist Perspectives on Management and Organizations*. London: Routledge.
   A useful collection of readings that cover both the theoretical assumptions of critical realism and their applications to organizational research in different contexts, such as medicine, and high technology companies. Authors emphasize different features of critical realism and do not follow a single party line.

Alvesson, M. and Deetz, S. (2000) *Doing Critical Management Research*. London: Sage.
   One of the few books that articulates what 'critical' management research looks like, and how it can be conducted, for example, through increasing sensitivity to the aspects of organization life that normally lie hidden. Also provides a much deeper review of critical theory and why it is important.

Blaikie, N. (2007) *Approaches to Social Enquiry*, 2nd edn. Cambridge: Polity Press.
   This book provides an excellent overview of different philosophical approaches to social research, with particular attention to the question of whether the research methods in the natural sciences are appropriate for the social sciences. It is quite comprehensive and very useful, provided you are prepared to put in the effort!

Hassard, J. and Parker, M. (eds) (1993) *Postmodernism and Organizations*. London: Sage.
   Since postmodernism is such a wide and disparate field, it is probably best to start with edited collections. This book is one of a number of edited works on postmodernism, but has the advantage that it focuses on the relevance and application of postmodernism to organization and management theory. Contributors include many of the leading European management scholars with expertise in postmodernism.

DESIGNING MANAGEMENT RESEARCH

3

LEARNING OBJECTIVES

 To appreciate how research philosophies impact on research designs.

 To understand what is regarded as (good) theory within each tradition.

 To be able to critique others' research designs.

 To be able to develop and justify one's own research design.

INTRODUCTION

As suggested in the previous chapter, research designs are about organizing research activity, including the collection of data, in ways that are most likely to achieve the research aims. Let us start with an example. In 1985 Kenneth Lay (see Figure 3.1, a police mugshot from 2004) founded Enron after merging Houston Natural Gas and InterNorth. The company expanded very rapidly first as an energy company and then through diversification, so that by mid-2000 its stock was valued at over $60 billion. But on 2 December 2001 it filed for bankruptcy following the failure of a rescue bid from a rival company. It quickly emerged that the company had systematically developed accounting practices that had inflated revenue while keeping debts and liabilities off the books. Not only had these practices been fostered by Lay and his colleagues at the top, but also the global consultancy firm Arthur Anderson, which had regularly audited Enron, had failed to report any problems.

FIGURE 3.1
Businessman Kenneth Lay

This raised major implications about the efficacy of accepted practices for auditing corporate accounts. Imagine that you wish to conduct empirical research into the changes in corporate accounting practices following this scandal. In the previous chapter we outlined an ontological dimension containing the positions of realism, internal realism, relativism and nominalism. Following each of these positions in order, your research design might involve: (1) conducting a review of new legislation and accountancy practices published over the period 2002–2005; (2) sending out a postal questionnaire to 200 members of the Chartered Institute of Management Accountants; (3) arranging to interview one accountant from each of 20 different organizations including companies and consultancies; or (4) getting a job for a year in the accounting department of a US energy company.

Each of these brief statements includes at least three decisions about research designs. In (1) there is a decision to focus on two categories of written documents published over a specific period of time; in (2) the decision is to design a questionnaire, which will be mailed to a specific number of people who belong to one professional association; in (3) the aim is to gather views from a medium sample of people likely to have different perspectives and experiences; and in (4) the decision is to invest personal time in observing accountancy practices in a US company within a specific industry. Each of these decisions specifies courses of action in preference to other options. For example, the focus on published sources precludes internal corporate documents; the decision to mail the questionnaire precludes face-to-face interviews; the decision to interview only one person from each company precludes multiple perspectives from any company; and the decision to work in one company precludes obtaining direct data from other companies.

This is the essence of research design: it is about making choices about what will be observed, and how. But each of these designs is incomplete, and there are many other choices to be made, and features to be specified. A research design is a statement written, often before any data is collected, which explains and justifies what data is to be gathered, how and where from. It also needs to explain how the data will be analysed and how this will provide answers to the central questions of the research.

In this chapter we explain: what a research design is; the main choices that need to be made; how research designs vary according to the underlying philosophical position; and how the quality of research designs can be judged. In the later chapters of the book we will be looking in detail at techniques and methods for gathering and analysing qualitative and quantitative data; though questions of research design need to be resolved before gathering (much) data.

EPISTEMOLOGY AND RESEARCHER ENGAGEMENT

There is a second dimension implicit in the Enron example, which concerns the role of the researcher in each of the research designs outlined above. In the first case, since the focus is on documents in the public domain, the researcher remains quite detached from the source of the investigation. In each of the subsequent examples, he or she is likely to become increasingly involved with the people who influence the evolution and implementation of accounting practices. This defines a second major dimension of choice for the researcher, which is the degree of engagement with the object of the research. It is similar to the pure/applied research distinction, where the former tries to maintain the independence and objectivity of the researcher, and the latter encourages greater engagement and interchange between the researcher and the research setting. In this section we will build up a model that presents these two dimensions as orthogonal axes of a matrix (see Figure 3.2).

We sometimes find it useful to take the analogy of fictional detective work to symbolize the differences in research designs that can be depicted by the resulting matrix. In the horizontal dimension, which represents contrasting epistemologies, we can contrast the scientific approach of Sherlock Holmes with the more intuitive style of the Agatha Christie character, Miss Marple. Whereas Holmes relies on detailed observation of physical evidence, and the process of logical deduction about the circumstances of the crime, Miss Marple acts as an insider to the scene of the crime and makes use of the intuitive feel about the characters involved. Sherlock Holmes therefore represents the positivist side, and Miss Marple represents the constructionist side.

We can also identify characters who personify the vertical dimension in Figure 3.2. Thus, the other famous Agatha Christie character, Hercule Poirot, is a classic example of the detective who is totally untouched and unruffled by the mayhem that inevitably surrounds his

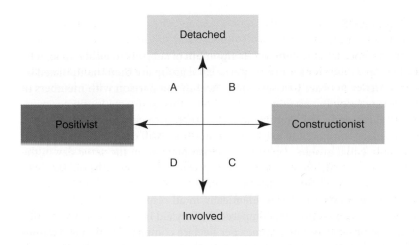

FIGURE 3.2
Epistemology and
research style

progress through high society. His only concern is his apparent inability to solve the crime immediately, although it is his superior intellect, those 'little grey cells', that always enable him to get there in the end (and well before Superintendent Jaap). Poirot stands in sharp contrast to many of the Hollywood detectives who operate very close to the world of the criminals they hunt, and who regularly provoke violent exchanges with their quarries. Clint Eastwood's portrayal of Dirty Harry provides an example of a cop who acts first and thinks later – in contrast to the effète intellectual style of Hercule Poirot who is all brain and no action.

Of course, the poles in Figure 3.2 represent extreme positions, and because it is relatively rare for research designs to be purely one or another we will now focus on the space between them, essentially the quadrants, which we have labelled A, B, C and D. We also need to emphasize that the horizontal dimension is a continuum between strong positivism on the left hand side, and strong constructionism on the right hand side. In the next two sections we give examples of typical methodologies that fit into each of these quadrants, although we have grouped them as primarily positivist or constructionist methodologies. There are also some methods and designs that bridge across quadrants, or combine elements of constructionism and positivism. We refer to these as mixed methods, and we will cover these in the third section.

POSITIVIST RESEARCH DESIGNS (QUADRANTS A AND D)

As we noted in the previous chapter, positivist methods usually incorporate the assumption that there are true answers, and the job of the researcher is either to start with a hypothesis about the nature of the world, and then seek data to confirm or disconfirm it, or the researcher poses several hypotheses and seeks data that will allow selection of the correct one. The ideal methodologies for doing this are experimental and quasi-experimental methods, and we will describe the key principles of each below. We then look at survey methodologies, which are generally associated with positivism in the sense that they are looking for patterns and causal relations, which are not directly accessible.

Experimental designs

Classic experimental method involves **random assignment** of subjects to either an experimental or a control group. Conditions for the experimental group are then manipulated by the experimenter/researcher in order to assess their effect in comparison with members of the control group who are receiving no unusual conditions. This approach dominates natural science and medical research. For example in agriculture, if researchers want to know the effect of a new fertilizer compared to existing products they will divide the same batch of seed into two or more equal groups. The seeds are then planted on the same day in the separate sections of the same field. The new fertilizer is spread on Section 1, the old fertilizer on Section 2, and perhaps no fertilizer is spread on Section 3.

From that day on, all sections are treated identically in all respects, and on the day of harvesting the yields from each section are compared. If the yield from Section 1 is significantly different from the other two, say 8 tonnes per hectare compared to 6 and 4 tonnes respectively, we may conclude that the difference is only due to the new fertilizer. Of course, this raises the question of how big the difference needs to be in order for it to be considered 'significant', and this is one of the issues that we tackle later in Chapter 9.

Possibly the most famous experimental studies in the field of management were the Hawthorne experiments conducted by Elton Mayo at the General Electric Hawthorne Plant in Illinois between 1927 and 1932. One experiment involved the relocation of six women (the experimenters selected the first two, who were each asked to select two more) into a room separate from the rest of the employees who assembled telephone relays. Their working conditions were modified systematically in order to establish whether there was any link between physical conditions and productivity. An observer was located in this room making notes of what was happening and also keeping them informed about progress of the experiment and listening to their ideas and complaints.

Over a period of many months changes were made including shortening the working day, introducing increasing amounts of breaks into the day, and eventually providing a hot meal in the middle of the morning shift. With each change, productivity increased, which would suggest a correlation between productivity and the easing of working conditions. However, at the end of the experiment they returned conditions to the situation at the outset, expecting productivity to decrease to the initial level – but it increased once more. This observation led to the development of **human relations theory** (see Chapter 1) which stressed that positive relationships between employees and their supervisors were more significant than the physical circumstances of their work as predictors of productivity.

EXERCISE
3.1

Questions for discussion about the Hawthorne experiment

1   What is the primary question/hypothesis of the researchers?

2   What are the key features of the research design?

3   In what ways does the Hawthorne experiment diverge from classical experimental design?

There are three important implications from the Hawthorne experiment: first, that the most significant findings emerged because the experiment went *wrong*, in the sense that the expected results were not obtained; second, that the design, including the return to the original condition, was very systematic. These features reflect the ideas of Austin about what leads to scientific breakthroughs as discussed in Chapter 1. Third, it has raised awareness of the **experimenter effect** whereby human behaviour will be affected, and potentially 'distorted', by the presence of an observer

The main *advantages* of experimental research designs are that they encourage clarity about what is to be investigated, and should eliminate as many alternative explanations because the random assignment ensures that the experimental and control groups are identical in all respects, except for the focal variable. It is also easier for another researcher to replicate the study, and hence any claims arising from the research can be subjected to public scrutiny. The *disadvantages* are practical and ethical. With medical research there is always the danger that volunteers will be harmed by drug tests; hence stringent ethical guidelines have been developed, which are now filtering into social science and management research (see Chapter 4). Also, when dealing with people and business situations it is rarely possible to conduct true experiments, especially with randomization. For example, if a company wants to assess the value of an elite highflier career development scheme, it cannot simply assign managers at random to the scheme because the managers themselves will be aware of what is happening, and there will also be strong ethical, performance related and employment law objections to this arbitrary assignment. For this reason, quasi-experimental methods have been developed in order to circumvent the problem of random assignment.

Quasi-experimental designs

A key feature of **quasi-experimental design** is the use of multiple measures over time in order to reduce the effects of control and experimental groups not being fully matched (Shadish, Cook and Campbell, 2002). Individuals are not allocated randomly to the treatment group and the control group, but rather allocation takes place on some other criterion, usually by using intact groups. As a result, the **validity** of inferences from this type of design depends critically on how equivalent the two groups actually are. Since equivalence cannot be guaranteed in this type of design, some statisticians insist that they be called **non-experimental designs**; although in practice many forms of quasi-experimental design can allow relatively strong inferences in settings where true experiments would be impossible to achieve.

One of the most common methods is the 'pre-test/post-test comparison design'. For example, the effects of a leadership course on a group of managers might be evaluated by measuring the managers' attitudes and behaviour before and after the course, and by comparing the differences with those from a similar group of managers who did not attend the course but who completed identical tests at the same times.

This design is illustrated in Figure 3.3, although there are substantial problems when using it in real organizations. For example, the design assumes that 'nothing' happens to the control group during the period that the treatment (course attendance) is being

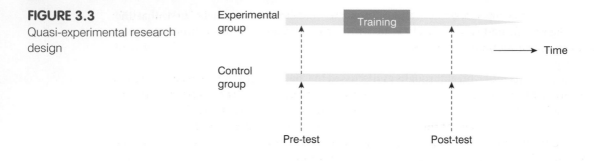

FIGURE 3.3
Quasi-experimental research design

given to the experimental group. This is a naive assumption, as Easterby-Smith and Ashton (1975) found, when attempting to evaluate a project-based management development programme held at Durham University Business School. While the 'chosen few' were away on the course, several members of the control group seized the opportunity to improve relationships with their bosses and strengthen their political standing in the company, thus harming the career prospects of a number of managers who had attended the course.

Quasi-experimental methods share some of the advantages of full experimental methods such as clarity, transparency and repeatability. However, as we have indicated above, they have problems accommodating the politics and agency of human beings in work settings. And there are also other subtle problems with pre-test and post-test designs because changes over time may be a consequence of measurement itself (a **testing effect**). The first measurement may get respondents to reflect on their initial answers, and this can lead to them answering differently the next time – not because of the intervention itself, but because they have been measured before. Thus, the process of measurement itself becomes a kind of intervention, but one that cannot easily be directly assessed. Returning to Figure 3.2, the aspiration of quasi-experimental methods is to conduct research without affecting the people under study, which would locate it in Quadrant A. But as we have seen, the necessary level of detachment is often difficult to sustain.

Survey research design

The dominant epistemology underlying survey research methods is positivism. As explained in the previous chapter, this assumes that there are regular patterns in human and organizational behaviour, although they are often difficult to detect and extremely difficult to explain due to the number of factors and variables that might produce the observed result. Consequently, survey research tends to use cross-sectional designs with large samples, which enable multiple factors to be measured simultaneously and hence potential underlying relationships to be examined.

There are three main types of survey that seek to take a detached viewpoint: factual, inferential and exploratory studies. Factual surveys can also be used in an engaged way, where they are established as survey feedback processes. The three main types generally fit with Quadrant A, whereas engaged factual surveys fit into Quadrant D. We will briefly describe and illustrate each type here. More detailed information on the technical design of surveys can be found in Chapter 8.

Factual surveys are most often associated with opinion polls and market research, and involve collecting and collating relatively 'factual' data from different groups of people. Thus, in order to assess market share or loyalty we might be seeking to identify what percentage of the population of Southampton entered either Sainsbury's or Tesco's supermarket at least once in the previous week. This is reasonably factual data, which could be gathered by a postal questionnaire or **structured interviews**; however, it could be affected by people's ability to recall what they did in the previous week, and possibly by **social desirability** factors where they claim loyalty to one supermarket over another in order to project a particular image of themselves to the researcher.

A common use of factual surveys within companies is **survey feedback**. This involves distributing a questionnaire to all employees asking for their views on the management of the organization, the quality of communications, their job satisfaction, feelings of security, etc. Data is then aggregated by department, level or job category and results are discussed in public. This puts pressure on management to change systems, procedures and their own behaviour in order to get 'better' results next year.

Inferential surveys predominate in academic management research, particularly in the fields of strategy, marketing and organizational psychology. They are aimed at establishing relationships between variables and concepts, whether there are prior assumptions and hypotheses regarding the nature of these relationships. Inferential surveys generally assume an internal realist ontology, although epistemologically they involve a weaker form of positivism than experiments. The usual starting point for inferential surveys is to isolate the factors that appear to be involved, and to decide what appears to be causing what. This means that researchers have to identify the main **dependent variables** and **predictor variables:**[1] it is the latter that are assumed to be causing the former.

In Figure 3.4, we are suggesting (hypothesizing) that the predictor variables of salary, leadership and responsibility have an impact on the dependent variable, motivation at work. In order to test this hypothesis it would be necessary to define ways of measuring each of these variables, generally through a small number of items in a questionnaire, and this would need to be completed by a sample of employees in one or more places of work. Naturally, this requires that the measures of the four variables are accurate, and that the sample is appropriate in terms of size and constitution in order to test the hypothesis: we discuss how to do this in more detail in Chapter 8. Moreover, the four factors identified in Figure 3.4 could be examined in more detail. For example, one might be interested in the interactions between some of the variables, such as whether

---

[1]The term **independent variable** is often used instead of predictor variable. We prefer the latter term because in practice, even independent variables tend to be related to each other, and therefore use of the term is misleading.

FIGURE 3.4

Possible predictors of
motivation at work

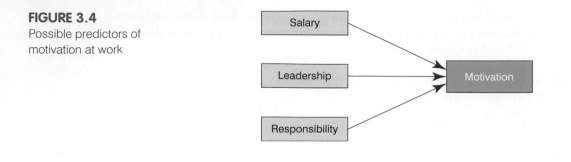

some forms of leadership result in greater responsibility being distributed around the workforce; or one might be interested in whether some of the arrows might work in other directions, so that a highly motivated workforce would lead to particular styles and strategies of leadership. These are some of the relationships that can be analysed, particularly with more complex models, through the use of structural equation modelling (see Chapter 10). Studies of this kind are often known as **cross-sectional surveys** because they involve selecting different organizations, or units, in different contexts, and investigating how other factors, measured at the same time, vary across these units.

Similarly, Lyles and Salk (1996) were interested in the conditions that led to greater transfer of knowledge from foreign parents into international joint ventures. So they selected a sample of 201 joint ventures that were regarded as small or medium-sized across four manufacturing industries in Hungary. Through comparing indicators of performance across the whole sample, they were able to conclude first that there was a strong link between knowledge transfer and performance, and second that this transfer was most likely to take place when the foreign and domestic parents had equal (50/50) equity stakes in the new venture. The sample size of 201 was sufficient for them to demonstrate that the results were statistically significant, but one of the key problems for researchers using cross-sectional designs is to know how large the sample needs to be.

Exploratory surveys Geert Hofstede's (1980/1984) study of national cultural differences provides an example of an exploratory survey. He attempted to develop a universal set of principles against which any culture can be measured – in the hope that this would provide a basis for predicting the behaviour of individuals and organizations in almost any country. However, he did not start with an explicit set of hypotheses; rather, he had a large number (about 216,000) of questionnaires completed by employees of IBM with regard to their views and values, and he was looking for patterns in the data. This he did by using **cluster analysis** and factor analytic techniques (see Chapter 10). His four dimensions – power distance, individualism/collectivism, uncertainty avoidance and masculinity – emerged from his data, and by demonstrating that they fitted reasonably well with prior research into this topic, he was able to substantiate his claim to the importance of these four dimensions.

Which variable is which?

EXAMPLE
3.1

Chen's doctoral thesis examined how workers in virtual teams doing different tasks used instant messaging to support their work. Her respondents were all Chinese language speakers in China or Taiwan; and some of them worked with people in the same location (building or city) while others worked with colleagues in other countries (such as Canada, USA, Germany).

Instant messaging is not a variable because everyone in the study used it; but other communication technologies (such as email, videoconferencing and face-to-face meetings) are variables because some people use them while others do not. Similarly dual language use (Chinese and English) is not a variable because the whole sample spoke both languages.

The focus of the study was on what led people to switch communication media or languages, and this therefore was the *dependent* variable. The *predictor* variables were task characteristics, indices of relationship quality (how well people knew each other), and whether they worked in the same or different locations.

Source: Chen, C.-Y. (2008) 'How virtual teams use media to manage conflict'. Unpublished PhD thesis, University of Manchester.

Validity of positivist designs

Experimental methods are particularly concerned to ensure that results provide accurate reflections of reality. They distinguish between internal and external validity with the former relating to *systematic* factors of bias and the latter being concerned with how far the conclusion can be generalized across other types of person, settings and times.

The aim of experimental designs is to maximize **internal validity**, and this requires the elimination of plausible alternative explanations for any differences observed between groups. That is why full experiments require random assignment to control and experimental groups, and efforts are then made to ensure that the subsequent experiences of the two groups are identical in all respects, except for the focal variable. But there are many threats to internal validity including history (experiences of the two groups diverge in some unexpected way), maturation (group members get older or other life changes take place) or mortality. The latter can be a problem in medical research where people literally die before the experiment is completed, and in organizational studies people may vanish from the research because they move jobs, leave the company or lose interest. Threats to internal validity are systematic rather than random; and they tend to focus on factors that cloud the interpretation of differences between groups in change over time.

External validity is about generalizability of results beyond the focal study. In the physical sciences we assume that Newton's Laws of Motion will have equal validity whether applied in New York, Bogota, Xi'an or on Mars. If they do not apply in the same way everywhere, then there should be a clear way of understanding how they vary in different circumstances. Thus Albert Einstein predicted through his Theory of Relativity that bodies do not follow Newton's Laws when they are moving at relative velocities near to the speed of light, and that light does not travel in straight lines when subject to strong gravitational forces. The latter prediction was confirmed by observations of the total eclipse of the sun in 1919 (see Example 3.2).

EXAMPLE 3.2

Relativity and the 1919 total eclipse of the Sun

Probably the most important eclipse in the history of science occurred on 29 May 1919. Just six months after the end of the First World War, British astronomers used it to test a new idea that came from Germany in 1915. Expeditions of astronomers photographed the eclipse in difficult tropical conditions in Brazil and on the African island of Principe. At the time, the Sun was in front of a useful cluster of stars, the Hyades. The astronomers compared the relative positions in the sky near the Sun with the positions of the same stars as previously photographed in the night sky.

The proposition was that gravity affected light, space and time itself, and as a result the Sun would deflect starlight passing by it. Changes in the apparent location of stars in the sky, seen close to the Sun during a total eclipse, could confirm the idea. It was predicted that for stars almost in line with the Sun, the shift in apparent position would be slightly less than two seconds of arc, or a few ten-thousandths of a degree. The 1919 measurements confirmed that the Sun bent the light rays by roughly the right extent – less than predicted in Principe, more than predicted in Brazil.

Source: www.esa.int/esaSC/SEM7I9R1VED_index_0.html.

However, in order to demonstrate external validity, management research designs need to demonstrate a number of features. First, they need to demonstrate that the results observed are not just a product of the selection of individuals or organizations. Sometimes the people who volunteer to take part in research are open minded and keen to help; sometimes they will put themselves forward because they have strong opinions or 'axes to grind'. Managers will often 'volunteer' employees to take part in research because they believe they will show the organization in a positive light, and will not offer individuals who are likely to be critical; or they will allow access to the organization because they hope research will add legitimacy to a new innovation or policy that they wish to promote. These issues of access and sampling are discussed further in later chapters (Chapters 4 and 8), but the key point to remember is that selection should avoid sources of bias as far as possible.

Other threats to external validity come from the setting and history. In the first case, the results of a piece of research in the health service may be difficult to generalize to an automobile manufacturer. Similarly, research conducted in large organizations may not apply to small organizations; and there is also increasing awareness that research conducted in one national setting may not apply to other national settings. With regard to history, it is important to note that patterns and relationships observed in one era may not apply in another era. For example at the present time, with the emergence of new economies such as China and India as global economic forces, the theories about the behaviour of financial markets that were developed during the era of US dominance are now having to be rewritten. Similarly, a study on reward systems conducted in one country where the supply of skilled labour is plentiful might not be relevant in another country where there is a marked shortage of skilled labour.

Quasi-experimental study on autonomous workgroups

EXERCISE
3.2

Wall, Kemp, Jackson and Clegg (1986) conducted a quasi-experimental study of the long-term effects of implementation of autonomous workgroups on job satisfaction in a manufacturing environment, and this study serves to illustrate ways in which strong inferences can be drawn by utilizing natural comparisons within an organization.

Research design

There were four conditions and three measurement occasions, as shown in the table below. Condition A, the main experimental group, included all day shift employees in a new factory who from the outset of production worked under a system of autonomous workgroups (where groups organized themselves without any formal supervision). Within the overall research design, condition B served initially as a non-equivalent control group and later as a second experimental group. It included all employees on the evening shift at the new factory who made the same products using the same machinery as their day shift colleagues. For the first 12 months of the study their work was conventionally organized: employees were allocated to particular tasks, and a supervisor who reported to a shift manager had control over all aspects of production. After 12 months of production at the new factory, however, the company decided to extend autonomous group working to this evening shift, largely at the request of the employees themselves. At this point, condition B became a second experimental group.

Conditions C and D were two further non-equivalent control groups, representing day and evening shifts in a factory elsewhere in the organization where jobs had conventional designs. The products and technology were very similar to those in the Greenfield site: the same overall company policies were in force, and pay levels were equivalent.

Three measurement occasions were planned for the Greenfield site after 6, 18 and 30 months of production, and two measurement occasions for the conventional site corresponding to the first two occasions at the first site. However, the final data collection for condition D was rendered impossible as the evening shift at the conventional factory was discontinued.

(Continued)

(Continued)

Summary of research design

				Time$_1$	Time$_2$	Time$_3$
Condition A	Greenfield	Day shift	x	**O**	**O**	**O**
Condition B	Greenfield	Evening shift		O	x **O**	**O**
Condition C	Conventional	Day shift		O	O	–
Condition D	Conventional	Evening Shift		O	–	–

x indicates the introduction of autonomous group working; O indicates measurement under conventional working; **O** indicates measurement under autonomous group working.

Discussion questions

1   What are the main threats to validity in this design, and how have the researchers tried to deal with these?

2   What additional checks would you carry out to ensure that the four groups are, and remain, as equivalent as possible throughout the study?

3   What general pattern of results would lead you to conclude that autonomous work groups lead to higher job satisfaction?

4   Can you see other potential comparisons that can be made with this set of data (the authors identified six)?

Since *survey designs* are informed by internal realist ontology, the issues of validity are reasonably similar to those of strong positivist studies. Thus, there is a major concern about whether the instruments and questionnaire items used to measure variables are sufficiently accurate and stable. Most of this is done through pre-testing instruments before the actual research is carried out, and hence measures of **reliability** are important because they assesses whether an instrument will produce the same score for each occasion that it is used. There is also the question of external validity: whether the patterns observed from the sample data will also hold true in other contexts and settings. And again, the technicalities of assessing reliability and validity with survey data will be discussed further in Chapter 8.

CONSTRUCTIONIST RESEARCH DESIGNS (QUADRANTS B AND C)

Constructionist research designs are linked to the relativist and nominalist ontologies. They start from the assumptions that there is no absolute truth, and that the job of the researcher should be to illuminate different truths and to establish how various claims for truth and reality become constructed in everyday life. Hence it is not surprising that there is a wide range of methodologies which fit within the constructionist paradigm. Here we cover some of the main methodologies – action research and co-operative inquiry, archival research, ethnography, and narrative methods – which are primarily based on constructionist designs. In the subsequent section we will look at methods that often bridge the epistemological divide, notably case method, grounded theory and so-called mixed methods.

Action research and co-operative inquiry

One of the key assumptions of positivism, and of natural scientific methods, is that the researcher should be objective, maintaining complete independence from the object of study. In the social sciences, where claims of the researcher's independence are harder to sustain, many people have tried to turn this apparent problem into a virtue. This is the tradition of **action research**, which assumes that social phenomena are continually changing rather than static. With action research, the researchers are often part of this change process itself. The following two beliefs are normally associated with action research designs:

1 The best way of learning about an organization or social system is through attempting to change it, and this therefore should be an objective of the action researcher.

2 The people most likely to be affected by, or involved in implementing, these changes should as far as possible become involved in the research process itself.

Some forms of action research appear to follow the principles of positivism, for example by attempting to change the organization from the outside and then measuring the results. Kurt Lewin (1948), who originated the action research tradition, used experimental designs when investigating the efficacy of different ways of getting housewives to change their nutritional habits during the Second World War (see Example 3.3).

An early example of action research

During the Second World War, Kurt Lewin and his associates experimented with groups of American housewives to see if they could be persuaded to serve unpopular types of meat, such as beef hearts, sweetbreads, and kidneys to their families. They used two methods to try to persuade them to change their habits. In the first case, a lecturer gave an attractive talk to members of the group on the dietary and economic value of using these meats, and offered some good recipes. In the second case, the same information was provided to the housewives; but they were invited to discuss the information and at the end to indicate by a show of hands whether they intended to serve the new meats. In a follow-up study it was found that only 3 per cent of the members of the lecture groups served one of the meats, compared with 32 per cent for the discussion/decision groups.

Similar results were obtained when persuading mothers to give orange juice and cod liver oil to their infants, although in these cases the discussion/decision method was only found to be twice as effective as the lecture method.

Source: Krech, Crutchfield and Ballachey (1962: 229–30).

EXAMPLE
3.3

Kurt Lewin's studies were, however, different from traditional experimental research because there was an emphasis on changes in behaviour, and his housewives were active participants in deciding whether or not to change. The weakness with his initial experimental design was that it did not allow him to discover *why* the changes took place. This required subsequent experiments and qualitative studies in order to build up deeper understanding of why behaviour changed under these different circumstances. Given the strong emphasis on intervention as part of the research process, and the focus on debate and discussion, these later studies fit within Quadrant C in Figure 3.1.

Involvement in the research process is taken a stage further in what has come to be known as **co-operative inquiry** (Reason, 1988; Heron, 1996). This has been developed for researching human action mainly at individual and community, rather than at organizational levels. It starts with the idea that all people have, at least latently, the ability to be self-directing, to choose how they will act and to give meaning to their own experiences. It fits with stronger versions of constructionism, and rejects traditional positivist methods where people are studied as if they were objects under the influence of external forces. Co-operative inquiry not only focuses on the experiences and explanations of the individuals concerned, it also involves them in deciding in the first place what questions and issues are worth researching. Thus the 'subjects' become partners in the research process.

A study of the development of Afro-Caribbean entrepreneurs in the West Midlands adds a further dimension. Ram and Trehan (2010) have worked for five years with a group of eight entrepreneurs. The group meets on a monthly basis and determines its own agenda, and more importantly, controls its own membership. The primary goal for the entrepreneurs is to gather ideas and develop strategies from their interaction with other owners, which will enable them to grow their businesses (none of the businesses are in competition with each other). The academics are present at these meetings in the roles of process consultant, facilitator and researcher; they are also given access to company documents and conduct interviews with group members. This approach, known as **critical action learning** is driven largely by group members and takes place within a social and political context. The academics thus become partners in the problem-solving of the group, and contribute particularly through surfacing the feelings and emotions of members.

Archival research

It is not always necessary to gather new data when conducting research. An enormous amount of data already exists in the public domain as corporate and government reports, and the statistical and financial databases that can be accessed online. Our focus here is mainly on textual information and its analysis, which we call **archival research**. Given the focus on words and on existing texts, this type of research fits with Quadrant B in Figure 3.1.

One of the favoured sources of archival data in business and management research are the annual reports from companies where statements from chief executives review achievements from the past year and outline plans and priorities for the next year. Analysis of the language used over time can demonstrate, for example, the emerging concern among large companies about environmental issues, or increasing emphasis being placed on employee engagement. By analysing policy statements produced by central and local government in the UK between1997 and 2008 O'Reilly and Reed (2010) were able to follow the changing rhetoric about the desirable behaviour of public sector managers over this period (see Example 3.4).

EXAMPLE
3.4

An archival study

O'Reilly and Reed (2010) analysed 29 'high level' government documents published between 1997 and 2000, which focused on the management of the public sector. They searched these documents for strings of text containing <profession>, <manag> and <leader>. By looking at the frequency of usage they were able to show how the discourse of leadership, which emphasizes change and reform, has started to take over from the older 'New Public Management' discourse of managerialism, which emphasized efficiency and performance.

Ethnography

The key principle of **ethnography** is that the researcher should 'immerse' him or herself in a setting, and become part of the group under study in order to understand the meanings and significances that people give to their behaviour and that of others. It is thus a strong form of constructionism. Most outsiders who are new to an organization or group will encounter things that they do not understand. These are what Agar (1986) calls 'breakdowns': events or situations where the researcher's past experience gives no help in understanding what is going on. This breakdown therefore represents something unique about that organization, and which was previously unknown to the researcher. For example, most groups have 'in-jokes', based on experiences shared only by members of the group. In order for an outsider to make sense of the breakdown provided by an in-joke it will be necessary to track back to the original experiences (Roy, 1952; Collinson, 2002). The breakdown provides a kind of window into exploring aspects of the experiences and meaning systems of groups and organizations. It will only be possible to resolve the breakdown when the researcher has understood these meaning systems.

Another important distinction is between what are known as **emic** and **etic** perspectives. These two terms were first coined by the American linguist Kenneth Pike (1954): *emic* refers to the sounds within a language which can only be distinguished by speakers of that language; and *etic* refers to features of a language that are easily identified by outsiders, but are largely inaudible to people who speak that language. For example, the four Chinese tones are *emic* because they cannot easily be distinguished by a non-Chinese speaker, yet are absolutely critical to understanding the language. On the other hand, most native English speakers are unaware that their speech is seen (from an *etic* perspective) as tight-lipped and monotonic by French and Italian speakers.

The distinction has also led to the view that better insights can be gained into management and organizations through combining insider and outsider perspectives. Thus, Bartunek and Louis (1996) advocate methods which involve research teams that combine people working inside the organization with people working from the outside. Using methods like this the ethnographer has the opportunity to challenge and extend conventional wisdom, and to generate new insights into human behaviour. However, in many organizations it can be difficult to conduct full ethnographic research because of access restrictions although it is often possible to combine observation of meetings with interviews of participants. We provide an example of a contemporary study in the aerospace industry in Example 3.5, which shows both the limitations on access and potential that researchers have to influence their informants. In Chapter 6 we develop the idea of **participant observation** further. The emphasis of involvement of the researcher in the research setting, combined with the strong constructionist element locates ethnography within Quadrant C in Figure 3.1.

EXAMPLE
3.5

A study of organizational decision-making

Winston Kwon and colleagues were interested in the way managers used discourse and rhetoric in meetings to influence strategic decisions. They conducted interviews and observations over a two-year period with senior managers in a large aerospace company. Regular team meetings and conferences were observed over a six-month period and all key participants were interviewed before and after the observation period. Due to other commitments of the researchers and constraints imposed by the company they were not able to be present all the time, and hence access was intermittent. They were also asked to provide non-evaluative feedback about their observations to the company, and on several occasions this feedback led managers either to change, or clarify, decisions that they thought they had already made.

Source: Kwon, Clarke and Wodak (2009).

Narrative methods

Another group of constructionist research designs have been given the general label of **narrative methods** (Boje, 1995; Czarniawska, 1998; Boje, 2001; Daiute and Lightfoot, 2004). These contain both ontological and epistemological elements. The ontological view suggests that stories and myths form a central element of organizational reality, and therefore organizational research, which ignores stories is necessarily incomplete. The epistemological position is that by collecting organizational stories the researcher will gain insights into organizational life which could not be reached by more conventional means. This may involve participant observation where the researcher can become part of the process of constructing and transmitting stories, or they may be collected through interviews by asking people for the stories that they have heard about particular events (see Example 3.6).

In essence, the method relies on literary theory (Hatch, 1996), and hence both the position of the narrator and the role of the analyst are very important.

A narrative-based study

EXAMPLE
3.6

Humphreys and Brown (2008) investigated the way corporate social responsibility (CSR) was introduced as an important function within a financial services company. The authors, consistent with our definition above, saw stories and narratives as central to the way managers and employees make sense of what was going on in the company. But their research design also involved the collection of stories from key actors involved in the establishment of corporate social responsibility within the company. From the analysis of semi-structured interviews with 64 employees they identified three major themes/narratives associated with CSR: idealism and altruism, economics and expedience, and ignorance and cynicism – which summarized the conflicting perspectives on CSR in that company.

One of the criticisms of narrative methods is that they do not offer much that is distinctive or additional to 'normal' qualitative research. Nevertheless, they do have a number of strengths: they provide a holistic perspective on organizational behaviour; they are particularly useful in developing social histories of identity and development; they are useful in helping to examine relationships between individuals and the wider organization; and they introduce values into the research process. Returning to the map in Figure 3.1, narrative research may be seen as more detached (Quadrant B) if the collection of existing stories is emphasized, or more involved (Quadrant C) if the researcher plays a role in encouraging people to invent new stories that illustrate their feelings.

Validity of constructionist designs

There is much concern about how to assure and demonstrate the quality of constructionist designs, although authors rarely use the term 'validity'. In a classic paper, Golden-Biddle and Locke (1993) identify three key criteria:

- authenticity;
- plausibility;
- criticality.

Authenticity involves convincing the reader that the researcher has a deep understanding of what was taking place in the organization; *plausibility* requires the research to link into some ongoing concern/interest among other researchers; and *criticality* encourages readers to question their taken-for-granted assumptions, and thus offer something genuinely novel. More recently Amis and Silk (2008), in discussing 'non-foundationalist' qualitative research, suggests that good research within the constructionist tradition should be partisan, taking the side of the less powerful members of society and organizations, and supporting a 'moral-sacred' philosophy. Thus quality would be indicated by the presence of the audience in the text, the sharing of emotional experience, stressing political action, taking sides, moving people to reflect and act, and providing collaborative, reciprocal, trusting and friendly relations with those studied.

Another perspective is provided by David Silverman (2000) who argues for a more objective stance (and hence a weaker form of social constructionism) because there are few safeguards to prevent researchers from picking evidence out of the mass of data to support their particular prejudices. In order to defend themselves against charges of 'anecdotalism' he suggests several principles, including refutability, constant comparison, comprehensive data treatment and tabulations. *Refutability* involves looking for examples that might disconfirm current beliefs; *constant comparison* follows the principles of grounded theory (see below) in looking for new cases and settings, which will stretch the current theory; *comprehensive data treatment* involves carrying out an initial analysis of all of the data available before coming up with conclusions; and *tabulations* imply greater rigour in organizing data, and accepting that it can also be useful to add up the occurrence of phenomena sometimes.

Our own view is that the results of constructionist research should be believable, and they should be reached through methods that are transparent. Thus it is very important for the researcher to explain how he or she gained access to the particular organization, what processes led to the selection of informants, how data was created and recorded, what processes were used to summarize or collate it, how the data became transformed into tentative ideas and explanations, and how he or she felt about the research.

CASE METHOD AND GROUNDED THEORY

There are several methods that, despite having a single label, can be used in quite different ways by different proponents. This is particularly true with **case method** and **grounded theory**. Although the dominant texts about case method come from the positivist end, the method can also be designed in ways consistent with relativist and constructionist perspectives. On the other hand, grounded theory was designed as a constructionist alternative to positivist methods, yet some respected versions now contain positivist elements.[2]

Case method

Essentially the case study looks in depth at one, or a small number of, organizations, events or individuals, generally over time. There is a very extensive literature on the design, use and purposes of case studies. In the management field authors tend to coalesce around those who advocate single cases and those who advocate multiple cases. Advocates of single cases generally come from a constructionist epistemology; those who advocate multiple cases usually fit with a more positivist epistemology.

Robert Yin is the best-known exponent of case method in the social sciences (Yin, 2002). His concern is that case studies are vulnerable to a number of criticisms from more *positivist*

---

[2]Our focus here is on single methods, which may be interpreted and practised in significantly different ways. This is distinct from 'mixed methods', which involve using combinations of different data collection methods and types for the same study (see Creswell, 2003).

researchers. In particular, it is suggested that they do not have the rigour of natural scientific designs; they rarely allow generalizations to be made from specific cases to the general population; and they produce huge piles of data, which allow researchers to make any interpretations they want. In response to these criticisms, he suggests that all case studies should have clear designs produced before any data is collected, and these designs should cover: the main questions or propositions, the **unit of analysis**, links between data and propositions, and procedures for interpretation of data. He is anxious to demonstrate that case studies may contain the same degree of validity as more positivist studies, and therefore his exposition of the method contains both rigour and the application of careful logic about comparisons.

The contrasting position, which is informed by a *constructionist* epistemology, is much less concerned with issues of validity, and more concerned with providing a rich picture of life and behaviour in organizations or groups. Robert Stake (2006) writes about qualitative case studies, and distinguishes between *instrumental* and *expressive* studies. The former involves looking at specific cases in order to develop general principles; the latter involves investigating cases because of their unique features, which may, or may not, be generalizable to other contexts. An example would be Andrew Pettigrew's research into organization development within the chemical company ICI during the 1970s and early 1980s. In those days ICI was the most powerful manufacturing company in Britain, so there was naturally a lot of interest in understanding how they were managing and developing themselves. In that respect, the study was expressive, but there was also an instrumental element since Pettigrew was interested in understanding the phenomenon of organization development, and ICI was regarded as one of its leading proponents. His research involved numerous interviews with key actors in the company over several years, and this provided a longitudinal element to his research, which enabled him better to understand both the contextual and historical settings of the company (Pettigrew, 1985a).

From a similar perspective, Nikkolaj Siggelkow (2007) provides a spirited defence of cases arguing that they are particularly valuable for demonstrating the importance of particular research questions, for inspiring new ideas and for illustrating abstract concepts. He also points out that even single cases can provide very convincing tests of theory by quoting the famous 'talking pig' example. Thus we only need to produce a single talking pig to demonstrate the error of the popular idea that pigs are incapable of intelligent speech. The logic being that we only need one example of an anomaly to destroy a dominant theory – as in the case of Einstein's refutation of Newton's theory. And although we are unlikely to identify a 'talking pig' organization, there are many examples where single cases can be uniquely interesting – for example, the company that does significantly better (or worse) than all others in the same industry, or the entrepreneur who builds a fortune from small beginnings.

A longitudinal case study

A study conducted by Prieto and Easterby-Smith (2006) explored the links between dynamic capabilities and knowledge management through a case study of the evolution of a single company over several years. Because the researchers were

(Continued)

(Continued)

interested in dynamic capabilities – which are by definition about continuous change – it made sense to observe processes over time so they could examine how, for example, the introduction of knowledge sharing routines led to greater strategic flexibility. Accordingly, the researchers spent time observing management meetings, talking with participants at meetings and interviewing other managers. They also followed information exchanges with partner organizations by conducting visits to their sites; repeating interviews with key informants; and feeding back emerging insights to senior managers to 'validate' their interpretations and to stimulate further insights.

Questions

1   How would you justify that this research was 'valid'?

2   What possibilities are there for generalizing the findings from this research?

3   Do questions about validity and generalizability make any sense in this instance?

A few points are important about constructionist studies. First, they are based on direct observation and personal contacts, generally through interviews. Second, they take place within single organizations, but then involve sampling from numbers of individuals. Third, the collection of data takes place over a period of time and may include both live observations and retrospective accounts of what has happened. Thus the unit of analysis is either the individual, or specific events such as the exchange of a piece of knowledge, or strategies employed to transfer or retain control of knowledge.

There is also an intermediate position, which has been developed particularly through the work of Kathy Eisenhardt (Eisenhardt, 1989; Eisenhardt and Groebner, 2007). This view draws inspiration from both the positivist and constructionist positions, and has been adopted widely by researchers using case method, particularly in North America. She is eclectic in her advice about methodology: using designs that are established at the outset, but then being flexible about their adaptation; recommending data collection through using multiple methods; and conducting both within case and across case analysis.

Above all, Eisenhardt is concerned about building theory from case based research, and this takes the form of developing hypotheses. She recommends that hypotheses can be formed, or shaped, through three main stages. The first stage involves sharpening up the basic constructs, and this is essentially an iterative process of moving back and forth between the constructs and the data. The second stage involves verifying that emergent relationships between constructs fit with the evidence from each case. In this respect she comments that: 'Each case is analogous to an experiment, and multiple cases are analogous to multiple experiments' (Eisenhardt, 1989: 542). The third stage involves comparing the emergent theory/concepts/hypotheses with the existing literature. In particular, she suggests paying attention to literature that is contradicted by the evidence, both because any evidence of having ignored contradictory findings is likely to reduce confidence in the final conclusions, and because the highlighting of contradictory conclusions is likely to make the original contribution from the research most explicit.

Comparative case study design

EXAMPLE 3.7

In a comparative study of investment decisions in Chinese and UK companies (Lu and Heard, 1995) case studies of 16 decisions in 8 companies were compared and contrasted in order to establish the cultural and institutional variations in business decision-making between China and the UK. The study involved collecting both qualitative and quantitative data, including extensive site visits to companies in both China and the UK. Each UK company was matched, in terms of size and industry, with the equivalent Chinese company. This allowed for a number of comparisons, between different industries, and between China and the UK, which led to new insights. For example, in the latter case the researchers noticed that the mean time between the interception and implementation of a major investment decision (approximately £100 million) was virtually identical in both China and the UK (approximately 3.4 years). This significantly contradicted theory of the time, which suggested that decision-making in China was far slower than in the UK. Of course, with the benefit of hindsight it is now possible to now see how fast Chinese companies have been developing over the last two decades; but this study was one of the first to demonstrate the speed of economic development in China.

Although the variations in case study design and application are complex and sometimes blend into each other, we summarize in Table 3.1 some of the main distinctions in the use and application of case method at three points along the epistemological continuum.

TABLE 3.1 Key features of case method informed by different epistemologies

	Positivist (Yin)	Positivist and Constructionist (Eisenhardt)	Constructionist (Stake)
Design	Prior	Flexible	Emergent
Sample	Up to 30	4–10	1 or more
Analysis	Cross-case	Both	Within case
Theory	Testing	Generation	Action

Grounded theory

Grounded theory was first formulated by Glaser and Strauss (1967). They saw the key task of the researcher as being to develop theory through 'comparative method', which means looking at the same event or process in different settings or situations. For example, the researcher might be interested in the workings of performance appraisal interviews and would therefore study a number of interviews handled by different managers, in different departments or in different organizations. As a result of the studies it might be noticed that most appraisal interviews either focus on reviewing performance in relation to last year's objectives, or they focus on future goals and how the subordinate may be helped to achieve these. They might then be labelled as 'judgemental' or 'developmental' interviews, and the distinction would represent a *substantive theory* about appraisal interviews.

However, the theorizing could be taken further. For example it might be observed that neither form of interview has much effect on individual performance, nor on the relationships between the managers and their subordinates. Then we could conclude that both forms of interview are simply organizational rituals, which have the function of demonstrating and reinforcing hierarchical power relations. This would be the beginning of a more generalized *formal theory* about power and organizational rituals. Glaser and Strauss consider both substantive and formal theory to be valuable, and they propose two main criteria for evaluating the quality of a theory. First, it should be sufficiently *analytic* to enable some generalization to take place; at the same time it should be possible for people to relate the theory to their own experiences, thus *sensitizing* their own perceptions.

It is important to note that 'I'm doing grounded theory!' should not be used as a justification for doing some vaguely qualitative research without any clear view of where it is supposed to lead. Grounded theory contains precisely articulated methods and presuppositions. The problem is, as Locke (1997) explains, that methods have evolved and developed since their initial exposition, and at the heart of this was a rather acrimonious debate between

TABLE 3.2 Agreed features of grounded theory

Grounded Theory	
Must:	● fit the substantive area; ● be understandable and useable by actors; ● be sufficiently complex to account for variation.
Key analytical operations are:	● cycle of theoretical sampling; ● constant comparisons; ● evolving theory, *leading to…* ● theoretical saturation.

TABLE 3.3 Points of disagreement between Glaser and Strauss

	Glaser	Strauss (and Corbin)
Researcher Roles	Maintain distance and independence.	Active interrogation of data.
Theory	Emerges from data itself.	Arises from theorist/data interaction.
Ontology	World is 'out there'.	Reality and experience are constructed.
Pre-understanding	Avoid literature from immediate area.	Flexible approach. Insights from many sources.

Barney Glaser and Anselm Strauss.[3] In essence, Glaser now believes that researchers should start with no pre-suppositions, and should allow ideas to 'emerge' from the data (Glaser, 1978, 1992); whereas Strauss recommends familiarizing oneself with prior research and using structured, and somewhat mechanistic, processes to make sense of the data (Strauss, 1987; Strauss and Corbin, 1998). The implication is that the researcher should be aware that there are different versions of grounded theory, and hence needs to articulate his or her own position when writing up the research. These differences are summarized in Table 3.3.

The debate is extended further by Cathy Charmaz (2000), who characterizes the methods of both Glaser and Strauss as 'objectivist'. Her complaint is that both authors separate the researcher from the experiences of the subjects of the study. She also feels that the recommendations from Strauss and Corbin (1998) about detailed analysis of transcripts, including line-by-line analysis and 'fracturing of data', reduces the ability to represent the whole experience of individuals involved. In her view, a constructionist should recognize, 'that the viewer creates the data and ensuing analysis through interaction with the viewed' (Charmaz, 2000: 523). As such she is located a little further in the constructionist direction than Strauss because she emphasizes the interaction between the researcher and the researched, rather than between the researcher and the data.

In order to make sense of these differences, we need to look both at the ontology and epistemology of the authors. Ontologically, Glaser comes across as a realist, or possibly an internal realist; whereas both Strauss and Charmaz have a more nominalist ontology, because they assume that the social world is created through the interaction of actors. Epistemologically, Strauss, who was significantly influenced by Corbin (personal communication) adopts a weak positivist position, which emphasizes systematic and reductionist approaches to the analysis of data. Glaser, on the other hand, promotes a more relaxed epistemology, insisting that the data should be analysed in its entirety, and should not be reduced to discrete elements. In

---

[3]We understand that Glaser and Strauss did meet up and resolve their differences shortly before the untimely death of Anselm Strauss (personal communication).

some respects this is similar to the constructionist perspective of Charmaz, though she goes further in emphasizing the primacy of the stories and experiences of her research subjects.

Before completing this section, it is important to note that the methods of grounded theory have been developed mainly within educational and health settings where the 'white coat brigade' can have relatively easy and flexible access to data and cases. But access is far more difficult within commercial organizations, and researchers are rarely given the freedom to select their samples on theoretical grounds – hence some of the assumptions of grounded theory have to be amended further to deal with this kind of situation (Locke, 2001). Organizational researchers have to accept the interviewees assigned to them by powerful organizational members who act as gatekeepers (see the discussion on strategies for gaining research access in Chapter 4); there are also limits imposed in terms of timing, topics and the use of data. This often requires a number of compromises to be made in terms of research design, as can be seen from the reflections of Suzanne Gagnon in Exercise 3.4 about her study of identity formation among highflying managers in two different international organizations.

EXERCISE 3.4

How grounded is this? A letter from a doctoral student

Hi Mark

I started with a general area for study – the interplay of personal and organizational identities in multi-nationality, multicultural organizations (how important is organizational culture in such settings, and why? What identities do people see themselves as having in these settings, and why?)

Once having been in the sites for some time and gathered some data through interviews, I found that *identity regulation* was a term (perhaps even a central category in Strauss' and Corbin's words) that had explanatory power; I got this term from the literature, having continued to iteratively study the literature and the data, while continuing to gather data.

My 'sample' was more or less set from the beginning (all participants on two management development programmes), so in this sense I did not use theoretical sampling. However, I did add questions and change emphases in the interviews as I proceeded.

Whether I reached theoretical saturation, I am not fully sure. In a sense it was more a question of talking to everyone, and then sampling the data (with some follow-up and changes to subsequent questioning and focus, as above).

I see this as a kind of 'theory elaboration' rather than deduction per se. But there is definitely a deductive side to it. It may also be the case that I come up with my own theory (hope so), especially, perhaps, in comparing results across the two cases.

That's as far as I can go at the moment. What do you think? How grounded is this?

Suzanne

Questions

1   How grounded is this?

2   Should she be sticking more closely to GT principles, and if not, why not?

MIXED METHODS

In recent years there has been growing interest in the use of research methods that draw from both positivist and constructionist epistemologies, and which combine both qualitative and quantitative methods in the same study. This has been stimulated by several influential books published around a decade ago (Creswell, 2003; Tashakkori and Teddlie, 2003) and more recently by the founding of the specialist *Journal of Mixed Methods Research* in 2007.

There has also been a debate between proponents of mixed methods and those who are sceptical about their value. Those in favour argue that by using a range of different methods within the same study the researcher will increase the validity and generalizability of results and the potential theoretical contribution; the sceptics point to practical limitations such as the competence of researchers in conducting different methods, and to possible contradictions between the paradigms underlying different methods.

There are many variants of mixed methods in social research, but the key idea is that they involve combinations of qualitative and quantitative methods for data collection and analysis. We will therefore start by discussing the choices with regard to data collection, then we consider different strategies for analysis, and finally we consider some of the arguments for and against the use of mixed methods.

Designs for data collection

There are two main considerations in the design of studies that use both qualitative and quantitative methods to conduct research: *sequencing* and *dominance*. Sequencing refers to whether one method goes before the other, and if so which goes first. Dominance is a matter of whether one method uses significantly more time and resource than the other, or whether they are roughly balanced in importance. These considerations are summarized in Table 3.4 below.

By combining these choices we can identify three distinct designs, which incorporate both quantitative and qualitative methods. We call these handmaid, partnership and compensatory designs.

With *handmaid* designs the key point is that one method serves the needs of the other. There is usually a definite sequence in the use of methods, and naturally one method dominates the other. The most common format is the qualitative pilot study based on interviews or direct observation, which is used to develop, and maybe test, the items for the main

TABLE 3.4 Choices in designing mixed methods research

Design Features	Alternatives to Consider
Sequencing of methods	Qualitative first, or quantitative first, or both at the same time
Dominance of methods	Predominantly qualitative, or quantitative, or balanced

study, which involves a questionnaire survey. Here the questionnaire survey is dominant, and the pilot study serves no function in the final result of the work, other than helping the researchers to design a questionnaire that is likely to yield accurate and reliable data.

There are also contemporary examples of the reverse process, where a survey is used to identify a small number of 'interesting' cases for in-depth investigation, and then the survey results are largely ignored in the final results. For example Macpherson et al. (2010) conducted a survey based on single interviews with 92 entrepreneurs. From this sample they identified three critical cases where they conducted repeated interviews over a year in order to establish how various artefacts (such as knowledge management software, benchmarking and problem-solving forums) contributed to the learning processes of the SME. In this case it is the qualitative study that dominates the published paper, with the survey merely in the background. Similarly, Detert and Edmondson (2011) investigated why employees usually fail to speak their minds to those in authority through a four-stage design. In the first stage they conducted interviews in one company to identify the implicit theories from employees about why it was unwise to speak up; and the second stage used an open survey questionnaire circulated to 185 managers in different organizations to test the generalizability of these theories. Stages three and four then developed and validated quantitative survey instruments, which could be used to examine the phenomenon on a much larger scale.

Partnership designs typically involve combining more than one method, such as a questionnaire survey and interviews, where both assume similar importance in the study. For example, entrepreneurial behaviour can be investigated by interviewing a small sample of entrepreneurs about their origins, motives, strategies, successes and failures, supplemented by a questionnaire containing similar questions sent out to a larger sample. When combined, the interview data will contain greater detail, clarifications and added explanations; the questionnaire data will contain shorter answers, possibly more focused, but will be able to cover responses from a wider range of entrepreneurs who could be divided into subgroups to explore possible differences according to family history, levels of funding, types of technology, etc.

Compensatory designs combine qualitative and quantitative studies where each is used to make up for the weaknesses of the other. Typically qualitative studies are seen as weak on generalization, and quantitative studies are weak at explaining why the observed results have been obtained. Thus there is a growing trend in leading US publications such as the *Academy of Management Journal* for quantitative studies that establish statistical relationships between variables to be supplemented by quotations from substantial numbers of interviews focusing on the mechanisms and processes, which may provide explanations of the observed results.

Analysis

Another form of mixed methodology can be introduced at the analysis stage. Although qualitative and quantitative data are normally analysed within their respective traditions, there is also the possibility of 'cross dressing'. Thus quantitative data can be analysed in qualitative ways, or qualitative data can be analysed in quantitative ways. The most common form of the latter is when frequency counts are made of the use of particular words, phrases or themes from a sample of interview transcripts. The study by O'Reilly and Reed (2010) (see Example 3.4) provides an example of qualitative archival data in the form of government policy documents being analysed quantitatively for the occurrence of particular words and expressions. Slightly less common is when quantitative data is analysed by techniques such as factor analysis, and **principal components analysis** (see Chapter 10), which look for patterns that are largely hidden. Techniques such as the **repertory grid** technique (see Chapter 7) involve starting with qualitative data, which then becomes quantified and analysed statistically, and the result is then interpreted qualitatively.

Arguments for and against mixed methods

As we have outlined above, there are many reasons why mixed methods are regarded as a good thing: they have the potential to throw new perspectives on research questions, to increase the credibility of results, to demonstrate generalizability, and to provide deeper insights that explain why things take place. But there are also plenty of reasons for being cautious about their wholesale adoption. We summarize some of these pros and cons below in Table 3.5 based on the arguments of Jick (1979); Tashakkori and Teddlie (2003); and Bryman and Bell (2007).

There is, however, a more fundamental critique of the use of mixed methods, which hangs on the notion of paradigm incommensurability (Burrell and Morgan, 1979; Morgan and Smircich, 1980). The argument is that it is unwise to combine different paradigms within the same study because the different underlying assumptions mean that it will not be possible to join the two parts of the study together. At the extreme this can produce a **semi-detached design**, because like two semi-detached houses, they are physically linked together, yet there is no adjoining doorway between the two parts of the house.

TABLE 3.5 Pros and cons of mixed methods

Arguments for Mixed Methods	Arguments against Mixed Methods
They: • increase confidence and credibility of results; • increase validity; • stimulate creative and inventive methods; • can uncover deviant dimensions; • can help synthesis and integration of theories; • may serve as a critical test of competing theories; • can combine confirmatory and exploratory research at the same time; • present greater diversity of views; • provide better (stronger) inferences.	• Replication is difficult. • The research design must be relevant to the research question. • They provide no help if you are asking the wrong questions. • They take up more resources than single method studies. • Their use requires a competent overall design. • The researcher needs to be skilled in the use of both methods. • It is not helpful if one method simply provides window dressing for the other (an extreme version of the handmaid design discussed above).

The weakness of the incommensurability argument is that it assumes that paradigms are always distinct and that there can be no overlaps. Recent thinking about paradigms suggests that boundaries are more fluid than originally portrayed (Cunliffe, 2011), and hence it may be acceptable to combine paradigms up to a point. In our view the limits can be defined by the continuum presented in Figure 2.1, where it is possible to combine adjacent ontologies and epistemologies within a mixed methods study, but increasingly problematic when combining more distant positions. For example, a positivist study might demonstrate that 80 per cent of corporate performance could be predicted by three variables – size, market share and growth rate. But when combined with an ethnographic study exploring the micro-politics of constructions of corporate performance, this would not contribute in any way to identifying the remaining 20 per cent in the predictive formula. It would be more likely to undermine the credibility of the main study by arguing that the concept of 'performance' is a sham.

The use of mixed methods can often lead to contradictory results. If the ontologies are very different there will be no way of resolving the confusion. However, if they are close enough then resolution may be possible, as illustrated in Example 3.8.

Problems with mixed methods

Morgan Tanton and Mark Easterby-Smith carried out a comparative evaluation study of two executive management programmes (Courses A and B), held in two different business schools (respectively, Institutions A and B). Observations during the course, and qualitative data obtained from follow-up interviews, showed quite clearly that Course A was superior to Course B, but the quantitative data in the form of student ratings about the two courses showed clearly that Course B was preferred to Course A. Was this discrepancy caused by the methods used, or could it highlight some unusual features of the two courses being examined?

To resolve this dilemma we showed the survey results to participants and asked for their explanations. First, participants commented that they were cautious when filling in multiple choice rating forms, because they could never be sure what the data would be used for; therefore, they usually avoided unduly negative responses. Second, the course designs and institutional settings affected the criteria that participants used for evaluating the two courses. In Institution A the emphasis was on the longer term application of what had been learnt; in Institution B the emphasis was on the immediate quality of sessions conducted within the classroom. Thus it was not surprising that the rating forms which were completed at the end of the course showed one pattern; whereas follow-up interviews conducted some months later showed another pattern. In this case it was possible to combine the two sets of data because the survey and interviews were respectively backed by internal realist and relativist perspectives, and both parts shared a common research question.

Finally, we can note that much of the interest in mixed methods comes from those on the positivist side of the spectrum, who hold at least an internal realist view of the world, on the grounds that added data and more perspectives will enable them to get closer to the intangible objects of their enquiries. And cynics might say that positivists need to incorporate more constructionist methods to make up for the shallowness of their traditional methods!

Summary

We accept that in some circumstances mixed methods can be advantageous, but think it is important that a clear rationale for their use is worked out in advance, and care needs to be taken to ensure that the methods are reasonably compatible. There is always a danger in using mixed methods just because they might add to the overall credibility of the research, because the *ad hoc* combination of different kinds of study means that neither may be done properly. As Bryman and Bell (2003: 493) comment: 'multi-strategy research should not be considered as an approach that is universally applicable or as a panacea'.

COMMON DESIGN DILEMMAS

In this section we identify five areas that require decisions when formulating research designs, irrespective of the ontology or epistemology that informs the study. These are:

- identifying the unit of analysis;
- universal theory or local knowledge;
- theory or data first;
- cross-sectional or longitudinal;
- verification or falsification.

Identifying the unit of analysis

The **unit of analysis** is the entity that forms the basis of any sample. Thus, samples may be formed from one or more of the following: countries, cultures, races, industrial sectors, organizations, departments, families, groups, individuals, incidents, stories, accidents, innovations, etc. In positivist forms of research, including multiple case studies informed by an internal realist perspective, it is important to be clear about the unit of analysis in advance, because this is the basis for collating data that will subsequently be analysed. It is not essential in constructionist forms of research, but with highly unstructured data it can help to provide an initial guidance for analysis. In the above example from our research, which compared decision-making between China and the UK (Example 3.7), the unit of analysis was the company, but there was a subsidiary unit of analysis (what is sometimes referred to as an **embedded case**), which was the investment decision. Hence it is possible to have more than one unit of analysis provided the theoretical aims of the research justify this, but it is not advisable to have too many.

Universal theory or local knowledge?

One of the key principles of scientific methods and positivist knowledge is that theories and observations made in one context should be applicable to other defined contexts. As we have discussed above, being able to provide assurances of **generalizability**, or external validity, are critical features both of experimental designs and the statistical procedures that are employed to interpret realist research data. In these cases, as with the guidance of Kathy Eisenhardt on case method, the objective is to produce **universal theories**.

On the other hand, a number of scholars argue that **local knowledge** is more significant. For example, according to post-colonial theory many theories of race, economic development and culture are constructs of scholars in Western countries, which typically cast non-Western culture and institutions as being somehow inferior to their own (Said, 1978). Similarly, from feminist theory there is a strong view that many of the dominant theories of social behaviour are blind to the effects of gender and patriarchy (Ahmed, 1998). In both cases the argument is that any generalized statement about the social world is likely to contain within it assumptions that mask relations of power between those who formulate theories and those to whom they are applied. Moreover, there is a strong view that significant social theory should be understood in relation to the context whence it is derived.

Local knowledge is also important for management and organizational research. First, it is suggested that the practical knowledge used by managers is essentially contextually bound, and is learnt through engaging in practice (Cook and Brown, 1999; Rouleau, 2005). If this is the case then it follows that for research to have theoretical value it should focus on these local practices – which may well be unique to that situation. Second, some people argue that managerial behaviour is culturally relative, including both national and organizational cultures (Boyacigiller and Adler, 1991). Hence researchers should formulate their ideas separately within each cultural context, and should not try to generalize across cultures.

For example, it has been accepted for some time that models derived from Western management research are unlikely to be relevant in Asian contexts, as Nor (2000) found in his study of Malaysia, because of Malaysia's unique cultural, political and institutional circumstances. Over the last decade there has been much interest in the development of entrepreneurial capabilities in Asian countries such as China, Vietnam, Malaysia and India. It is increasingly accepted that the cultural and institutional differences between these countries are such that local theories to explain entrepreneurial behaviour are necessary in each country (Taylor, 1999; Hobday and Rush, 2007).

Theory or data first?

The third choice is about which should come first: the theory or the data? Again this represents the split between the positivist and constructionist paradigms in relation to how the researcher should go about his or her work. The Straussian view of grounded theory assumes that pre-conceptions are inevitable. After all, it is common sense to assume that someone will not be interested in a research topic or setting without knowing something in advance about it. Hence he argues that the researcher should make him or herself aware of previous work conducted in the general field of research before starting to generate his or her own theory.

Recent developments in organizational research have led to a wide range of designs, some of which extend the range of fieldwork methods, and others which provide intermediate positions between the two extremes. In a recent research project looking at absorptive capacity within European companies, Easterby-Smith et al. (2008) became increasingly aware that the relationship between theory and data needs to be an interactive process. When researchers observe something that seems surprising or novel in a company, it is important to go back to the literature in order to see whether anybody else has remarked on it. Similarly, when a new paper gets published it may have a direct impact on the ongoing collection and interpretation of data.

Cross-sectional or longitudinal?

Cross-sectional designs, particularly those which include questionnaires and survey techniques, generally belong to positivist traditions. As we have noted earlier, they have undoubted strengths in their ability economically to describe features of large numbers of people or organizations. But a major limitation is that they find it hard to describe processes over time and to explain *why* the observed patterns are there. Thus, although Lyles and Salk (1996) were confident that balanced equity stakes led to the highest chance of knowledge transfer, their study itself could not explain what mechanisms or processes led to knowledge being transferred.

In order to understand processes of change over time it is necessary to adopt longitudinal designs. From the positivist side these include quasi-experimental methods because repeated measurements are taken over time, but it is more often associated with constructionist research, where repeated visits are made to the same individual or companies over months or years, or when the researcher conducts an ethnographic study working continuously in the same location.

Verification or falsification

This final decision is slightly different from the four preceding ones since it is not linked to resolving the broader debate between positivist and constructionist views. However, it is very important both for researchers and for managers, as we will explain below. The distinction between **verification** and **falsification** was made by Karl Popper (1959) as a way of dealing with what has become known as Hume's 'problem of induction'. This is the philosophical problem that, however much data one obtains in support of a scientific theory it is not possible to reach a conclusive proof of the truth of that law. Popper's way out of this problem is to suggest that instead of looking for confirmatory evidence one should always look for evidence that will *disconfirm* one's hypothesis or existing view (as in the 'talking pig' example above). This means that theories should be formulated in a way that will make them most easily exposed to possible refutation. The advantage then is that one only needs one instance of refutation to falsify a theory; whereas irrespective of the number of confirmations of the theory, it will never be conclusively proven.

The example often given to illustrate this approach takes as a start the assertion that: 'all swans are white'. If one takes the verification route, the (non-Australian) researcher would start travelling around the country accumulating sightings of swans, and provided that he or she did not go near a zoo, a very high number of white sightings would eventually be obtained, and presumably no black sightings. This gives a lot of confidence to the assertion that all swans are white, but still does not conclusively prove the statement. If, on the other hand, one takes a falsification view, one would start to search for swans that are *not* white, deliberately looking for contexts and locations where one might encounter non-white swans. Thus, our intrepid researcher might head straight for a zoo, or perhaps book a flight to Western Australia where most swans happen to be black. On making this discovery, the initial hypothesis would be falsified, and it might then have to be modified to include the idea that 'all swans have either white or black feathers'. This statement has still what Popper calls high 'informative' content because it is expressed in a way that can easily be disproved; whereas a statement like 'all swans are large birds' would not be sufficiently precise to allow easy refutation.

Much of the debate about verification and falsification fits within the positivist view because ideas of 'truth' and 'proof' are associated mainly with that paradigm. But there are also important lessons that the constructionist might take from this discussion. For example, Alvesson and Deetz (2000) advise 'critical sensitivity', and Reason (1988) advocates 'critical subjectivity', which involves recognizing one's own views and experiences, but not allowing oneself to be overwhelmed and swept along by them. If the idea of falsification is to be applied more fully to constructionist research then one should look for evidence that might confirm or contradict what one currently believes to be true.

This advice not only applies to researchers but also to managers who are concerned to investigate and understand what is taking place within their own organizations. Most managers are strongly tempted to look for evidence that supports the currently held views of the world. This is not surprising if they are responsible for formulating strategies and policies within a context that is very uncertain, and hence they will be looking for evidence that demonstrates that their strategies were correct. The logical position that follows from the above argument is that, even if *disconfirmatory* evidence is unpopular, it is certainly both more efficient and more informative than confirmatory evidence. Moreover, if managers adopt the falsification strategy and fail to come up with evidence that disconfirms their current views, then they will be able to have far more confidence in their present positions.

CONTRIBUTING TO THEORY

Good research designs need to have some link to theory. In the case of student projects and dissertations it is generally necessary to *use* theory, whereas for doctoral theses and papers in academic journals it is necessary to demonstrate a *contribution* to theory. This is not as daunting as it might seem, and in this section we elaborate on the types and purposes of theory, and explain how they can be incorporated into research designs.

The term 'theory' often has negative connotations. Someone might report back on a lecture saying, 'It was all a lot of theory!' meaning that it was either difficult to understand or just plain boring. Or someone might react to a new idea saying, 'Well that's all right in *theory*, but …', meaning that although the idea sounds plausible, it would not work in practice. So, in this case theory is seen as the opposite of practice. On the other hand there is the well-known saying, 'There is nothing so practical as a good theory' (Lewin, 1948). In order to unscramble this confusion we offer distinctions between everyday and academic theory, the latter subdividing further into middle-range and grand theories.

Everyday theory refers to the ideas and assumptions we carry round in our heads in order to make sense of everyday observations. For example, if you observe an old man walking down the street arm in arm with a young woman you might conclude that they were grandfather and granddaughter. In order to reach this conclusion you might hold two assumptions about family relations – that grandparents often live close to their family members and that grandparents often have very close relations with their grandchildren. If the man is leaning slightly on the woman, then it would strengthen the grandfather–daughter hypothesis; but if the man's walk was very unsteady this might suggest a new theory, that they are patient and nurse. On the other hand, if the man is well dressed and the woman is conspicuously glamorous, an alternative hypothesis might suggest itself: that the man is a wealthy philanderer and the woman is a mistress or 'trophy' wife.

Although everyday theories enable people to make sense out of specific events or situations, **academic theories** tend to look for higher levels of generalization. Following the above example for just a moment, in order to explain what was going on, a sociologist might draw on theories about the power of male patriarchy, palliative care for the elderly, or the evolution of the institution of marriage. The distinction between **middle-range theories** and **grand theories** is a matter of scale and formality. An example of the former would be the key idea of absorptive capacity: that the ability of an organization to absorb new external knowledge depends on whether it already possesses related knowledge (Cohen and Levinthal, 1990). It is middle-range because it is a generalizable proposition that can potentially be tested empirically.

On the other hand grand theories tend to be more abstract and contain whole edifices of assumptions that are often not testable. The theory of psychoanalysis is one example because it provides a self-contained set of ideas to explain human behaviour. Similarly Personal Construct Theory (PCT) contains a set of propositions starting with the fundamental postulate that, 'A person's processes are psychologically channelled by the way they anticipate events', which is linked to a series of corollaries about human sense-making and communications (Kelly, 1955; Bannister and Fransella, 1971). In the management field, elements of PCT have been used to make sense of group decision-making and strategy formulation (see Chapter 7). A number of the integrated philosophies summarized at the end of Chapter 2, such as critical theory or structuration theory, are grand theories in the way we have described them here.

Where researchers are seeking to build theory, this is normally at the level of middle-range theory, and is an incremental process. Thus recent work on absorptive capacity has argued that Cohen and Levinthal's (1990) model of absorptive capacity is too rational and unduly focused around R&D, and consequently more attention needs to be paid to political and systemic processes (Todorova and Durisin, 2007). This leads to a question about how we can evaluate the quality of theories, or theoretical contributions, and how can we distinguish a good contribution from one that is less good? The answer is that some criteria are fairly obvious: good theories need to be simple, have good explanatory power, and be relevant to issues that need explaining. But beyond this the evaluation of contribution is largely a matter of judgement among people who already know the field quite well, which is why peer review is normally used to evaluate the theoretical contributions of research proposals and academic papers. We will be returning to these issues at various points later in the book, especially in Chapter 11.

CONTRASTING VIEWS ON VALIDITY AND RELIABILITY

There is an underlying anxiety among researchers of all persuasions that their work will not stand up to outside scrutiny. This is very understandable since research papers and theses are most likely to be attacked on methodological grounds, and one of the key justifications for doing 'research' is that it yields results that are more accurate and believable than common everyday observations.

The technical language for examining this problem includes terms such as validity, reliability and generalizability. But as we have indicated above, these mean different things within different research traditions. In Table 3.6 (see page 71) we therefore summarize how these terms are discussed from the philosophical viewpoints of positivism, relativism and constructionism.

The implication of Table 3.6 is fairly obvious: that depending upon where people stand on the epistemological continuum, they are likely to use different criteria for judging the quality of research. This will affect how they design and conduct their own studies and how they assess the quality of others' work particularly when they are acting as examiners, reviewers or just colleagues.

RESEARCH DESIGN TEMPLATE

We have argued throughout this chapter that research designs should take account of epistemology, and hence formal research designs need to focus on different issues. In Table 3.7 (see page 71) we list some of the main headings that need to be covered within each epistemology. The key point about this table is that a research proposal will need to consider different issues and to use different language according to where the researchers, and more importantly any external assessors, stand.

The way to use this template is to decide which epistemology is most appropriate to your research study and then follow the questions down the relevant column.

TABLE 3.6 Four perspectives on validity, reliability and generalizability

Viewpoint	Strong Positivist	Positivist	Constructionist	Strong Constructionist
Validity	Do the measures correspond closely to reality?	Do the measures provide a good approximation to the variables of interest?	Have a sufficient number of perspectives been included?	Does the study clearly gain access to the experiences of those in the research setting?
Reliability	Has the design eliminated all alternative explanations?	Will the measures yield the same results on other occasions?	Will similar observations be reached by other observers?	Is there transparency about data collection and interpretation?
Generalizability	To what extent does the study confirm or contradict existing findings in the same field?	How probable is it that patterns observed in the sample will be repeated in the general population?	Is the sample sufficiently diverse to allow inferences to other contexts?	Do the concepts and constructs derived from this study have any relevance to other settings?

TABLE 3.7 Research design template

Epistemology	Strong Positivist	Positivist	Constructionist	Strong Constructionist
Background	What is the theoretical problem and what studies have been conducted to date?	What is the theoretical problem and what studies have been conducted to date?	What are the ongoing discussions among researchers and practitioners?	What are the ongoing discussions among researchers and practitioners?
Rationale	What is the main gap in existing knowledge?	What are the main variables, and how are they related to one another?	What perspectives have been covered and what are missing?	What are the limitations in the discussions so far?

(Continued)

TABLE 3.7 (Continued)

Epistemology	Strong Positivist	Positivist	Constructionist	Strong Constructionist
Research Aims	Specify testable hypotheses.	List main propositions or questions.	Identify the focal issue or question.	Explain how the research will add to the existing discussion.
Data	Define variables and determine measures.	Define dependent and independent variables and determine measures.	Explain and justify a range of data collection methods.	Identify main sources of data. How will interviews be recorded/transcribed, etc.?
Sampling (see Chapter 8)	Explain how group selection and comparison will eliminate alternative explanations.	Justify sample size and explain how it reflects the wider population.	How will the sample enable different perspectives to be included?	Explain sampling strategy. Will it be opportunistic, emergent, comparative, etc.?
Access (see Chapter 4)	How are experimental subjects to be recruited?	How can responses to questionnaires etc. be assured?	What is the strategy for gaining access to individuals, organizations?	How will insights from co-researchers be combined?
Ethics (see Chapter 4)	Is participation voluntary?	Could results be used to harm any participants?	Will the interests of individuals and organizations be protected?	How 'open' is the research? Will there be any deception?
Unit of Analysis	Differentiate between control, experimental groups, etc.	Specify whether individuals, groups, events or organizations.	How will units/ cases be compared with each other?	What are the entities that are to be compared with each other?
Analysis (see Chapters 7, 9 and 10)	Statistical procedures for examining differences between groups.	Statistical procedures for examining relationships between variables.	Arrangements for coding, interpreting and making sense of data.	How will co-researchers be involved in sense-making?

(Continued)

TABLE 3.7 (Continued)

Epistemology	Strong Positivist	Positivist	Constructionist	Strong Constructionist
Process	Explain stages in the research process.	Explain stages in the research process.	Explain what can be pre-planned and what can be open-ended.	Provide realistic timing including adequate provision for contingencies.
Practicalities (see Chapters 6 and 8)	How will groups be recruited? Where will experiments take place?	Who will gather data? How will it be recorded/stored? Who will analyse it?	How will researchers share observations? Who will do transcriptions, etc.?	How will co-researchers be engaged?
Theory	How will hypotheses be tested?	In what ways will the results add to existing theories?	Will the research build on existing theory or develop new concepts?	Will the research build on existing theory or develop new concepts?
Outputs (see Chapter 11)	Where will the research results be published?	What is the dissemination strategy?	What is the dissemination strategy?	How will insights be shared with colleagues and collaborators?

CONCLUSION

In this chapter we have discussed some of the key philosophical debates underlying research methods in the social sciences, and we have looked at the implications these have for the design of management research. Some key points are:

 There is a clear dichotomy between the positivist and social constructionist worldviews, but the practice of research involves a lot of compromises.

 Each position has its own language and criteria for evaluating research designs.

 There is considerable diversity of methods and designs, especially within the constructionist research tradition.

 Differences in opinion about research methods are often underpinned by ontological differences.

(Continued)

(Continued)

The worldview held by an individual researcher or institute is an important factor, which affects the choice of research methods. But there are other factors, too. Senior academics can exert pressure on junior colleagues and students to adopt methods that they favour. Governments, companies and funding organizations can exert pressure on institutions to ensure that the aims and forms of research meet with their interests. The politics of research are complex, and researchers neglect them at their peril. That is why we have chosen to devote the next chapter to a discussion of these issues.

EXERCISE
3.5

Discussion questions (for small group in class)

Classify the following according to whether you consider them to be ontologies, epistemologies, methodologies or methods: grounded theory; unobtrusive measures; narrative; case method; ethnography; critical realism; participant observation; experimental design; falsification; theoretical saturation. If it is a weak association put * into the corresponding box, ** for a moderate association, and *** for a strong association. Explain your reasoning. (Note: many of them could be more than one thing.)

	Ontology	Epistemology	Methodology	Method
Grounded theory				
Unobtrusive measures				
Narrative				
Case method				
Ethnography				
Critical realism				
Participant observation				
Experimental design				
Falsification				
Theoretical saturation				

FURTHER READING

Boje, D. (2001) *Narrative Methods for Organizational and Communication Research*. London: Sage.
An authoritative book on the use of stories as a source of understanding of organizational life. It provides eight different ways of making sense of stories using the idea of 'anti-narrative', which recognizes that organizational stories are not necessarily complete, that they can be fragmented and can vary with the times and purposes of the story-teller.

Charmaz, K. (2006) *Constructing Grounded Theory: A Practical Guide Through Qualitative Analysis*. London: Sage.
A good textbook that introduces grounded theory, and then leads through the steps in conducting grounded theory analysis. Charmaz argues for adopting a constructionist approach, and starts to distance herself from the more positivist leanings of the founders of grounded theory.

Locke, K. (2001) *Grounded Theory in Management Research*. London: Sage.
This is an excellent overview of the origins of grounded theory including the differences of opinion between Glaser and Strauss, the key methods and approaches as currently practised, and the specific adaptations that may be required when conducting organizational or management research.

Shadish, W.R., Cook, T.D. and Campbell, D.T. (2002) *Experimental and Quasi-Experimental Designs for Generalised Causal Inference*. Boston, MA: Houghton Mifflin
An updated version of the classic book on experimental forms of social research.

THE POLITICS AND ETHICS OF MANAGEMENT RESEARCH

4

LEARNING OBJECTIVES

 To be able to identify stakeholders, evaluating the interests of beneficiaries and recognizing those potentially at risk.

 To review different strategies and methods for gaining access in different contexts.

 To develop awareness of personal and organizational ethics.

To develop judgement in dealing with 'grey' ethical issues, and the ability to argue pros and cons.

INTRODUCTION

One of the myths about research is that it is an 'ivory tower' activity. According to this view, research is carried out by independent scholars dedicated to the pursuit of knowledge. Questions and issues are defined as interesting according to the current state of knowledge and the curiosity of the researcher's intellect. It is doubtful whether there was ever much truth behind this myth. Scholars have regularly got themselves into trouble for following beliefs that were politically unpopular. Socrates was condemned to drink a cup of hemlock because he did not seem sufficiently respectful of current Athenian divinities; and Galileo was forced to recant his belief, which was based on careful observation of sunspots and planetary orbits, that the earth moved around the sun. In China the first Qin emperor is reputed to have buried alive some 400 scholars because he did not like their opinions.

Although many academics have tried in the past to maintain their independence it has never been altogether possible to separate **scholarship** from politics. But what do we mean by 'politics'? Our basic premise is that it concerns the power relationships between the individuals and institutions involved in the research enterprise, plus the strategies adopted by different actors and the consequences of their actions on others. Crucial relationships may be between student and supervisor, funder and grant holder, authors and journal editors, companies and research institutes, project leaders and research assistants, researchers and managers, or between managers and their bosses. Influence within these relationships may be exerted over: what is to be researched, when, by whom; how information is to be gathered and used; and how the products of research are to be evaluated.

In this context it is important to emphasize two major differences between management and business research and other forms of social and psychological research. First, 'management' is essentially about controlling, influencing and structuring the awareness of others. It is the central process whereby organizations achieve the semblance of coherence and direction. As we pointed out in Chapter 1, this process is political, and various authors have commented on the same point (Pettigrew, 1985b; Hardy, 1996; Buchanan and Badham, 2008). Although management and business are not the only arenas where politics is important, it does mean that political issues will rarely be absent from the research process.

The second difference is linked, and it starts with the observation that empirical research in the social sciences is usually carried out on members of society who are less powerful than the researchers. That is why psychologists conduct their experiments on students rather than on professors, and sociologists tend to focus on people who are relatively powerless due to their low social or economic status. It is 'the mad, the bad, and the ill' who have received most attention from social researchers in the past (Slater, 1989). This is no accident, for the more powerful members of society generally have both the awareness and the means to protect themselves from the prying eyes and tape recorders of researchers. It is rare to find researchers who have succeeded in studying powerful members of society without adopting methods of deceit, concealment or subterfuge.

When conducting research into management and business, the subjects of research are very likely to be more powerful than the researchers themselves. Furthermore, most organizations are both tightly structured and controlled, so that gaining access to the corporate boardroom, for example, is exceedingly difficult. Managers are usually in a position where they can easily decline to provide information for researchers; they are also adept at handling face-to-face interviews and at managing interactions with strangers. In such circumstances they are fully aware of the significance of information and the importance of determining what use it might be put to, and by whom. So, in the case of managerial research the boot is firmly on the other foot.

Therefore we begin this chapter with a discussion of the political factors that can influence the nature and direction of research. The second part focuses on some of the problems of gaining access to organizations, and offers suggestions about how this can be handled. The third part considers some of the ethical dilemmas encountered in fieldwork, particularly those resulting from strategies to gain access, and which are contingent upon the utilization of data.

POLITICAL INFLUENCES ON THE RESEARCH QUESTION

Most positivist researchers are not keen on self-disclosure, because the admission of personal motives and aspirations might be seen to damage the image of independence and objectivity that they are at pains to cultivate. Hence they rarely explain precisely where their ideas and questions have come from.

Fortunately things are beginning to change, for two reasons. First, because social studies of the development of scientific knowledge (Latour and Woolgar, 1979) have started to show that the formal view of scientific progress is at variance with what most scientists do in practice. Second, because there is a growing acceptance among social scientists of the need to be reflexive about their own work, and this has led to more autobiographical accounts of research in practice (Czarniawska, 1998). Consequently there is less reliance on traditional 'linear' models of scientific progress.

Although it is recognized that a thorough knowledge of prior research is very important, it is rare for good research ideas to be derived directly from the literature. Indeed, qualitative researchers often develop *post hoc* theoretical rationales for their work, which are explained when the thesis, or learned paper, is submitted (Golden-Biddle and Locke, 2007). Our argument in this chapter is that there are many other factors which can influence the kind of questions that are seen as worthy of research, and that these include both the personal experiences of the researcher, the attitudes and influence of external stakeholders, and the broader context within which he or she works and studies. These factors are summarized below in Figure 4.1. We do not regard this as a mechanistic model; we see research ideas evolving in an incremental way through a continual process of negotiation with these factors.

Before tackling each of these factors in turn we would like to offer a simple model, which we have found useful in making sense of the politics of research. This is based on the classic study by Boissevain (1974) of social networks, especially in the Sicilian Mafia, where he identified two distinct roles played by participants: brokers and patrons. *Brokers* are social 'fixers' who use their secondary resources, such as information and a wide range of contacts, in order to achieve their ambitions. *Patrons* have direct control over primary resources such as people and money. But when they need information or the resolution of a problem they

FIGURE 4.1

Sources of political
influence

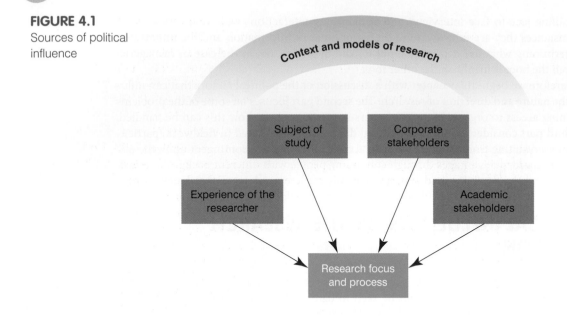

turn to brokers who have the contacts and a past record of solving problems. A skilful broker will also specify a tariff that is only part of the real cost – so that when the transaction is made he will have built up further goodwill with the patron. This will in turn increase the broker's overall credit for future problem-solving.

While we would not wish to suggest a direct correspondence between the worlds of Mafiosi and business researchers, there are a number of parallels. In the research world, senior academics and tutors can act as brokers because they know the way round the system, and are known by others. They may be able to arrange for access to a particular organization; clarify and negotiate assessment criteria, to advise on how to obtain funds from research councils; identify appropriate external examiners, or to make links with journal editors who are most likely to be interested in a particular paper. Within companies, training and human resource managers can often act as brokers because, although they have little formal power, they usually have a wide range of contacts at all levels of the organization. Successful researchers can also develop brokerage skills. Thus personnel managers are more likely to help provide access to their company if they think the researcher may be able to provide them with something in return – whether it be expertise, credibility or other contacts.

The experience of the researcher

Motivation   Personal background affects what the researcher can see: experience acts both as a sensitizer and as a filter for the researcher. The motivations of individual researchers may be quite varied. As Platt (1976) has shown, many researchers in the early stages of projects are unclear about their aims and goals; others may have more precisely defined career goals, political aims or agendas to create change in their own institutions and environments. When it comes to fieldwork, personal background, including social class, will affect the ease with which the researcher can gain access to different settings, and this may also pre-determine responses from different client groups. Those who conduct research on workers rarely get round to investigating managers, and vice-versa. This may be for ideological reasons, or merely for personal and social ease.

Management and business research is done by lone scholars, and increasingly by teams, both as student project groups and as teams of funded researchers. These arrangements can provide added advantages through combining people with different backgrounds and interests, and the flexibility and synergy that this can create. A team that balances perspectives, backgrounds and skills may be much more effective than individuals at conducting research. Teams can also be established to take advantage of the insider/outsider perspective. This, as explained in the previous chapter, follows the ethnographic principle that insiders will be able to see and understand things that will make no sense to outsiders, while outsiders will notice things that may have become quite invisible to insiders. Sometimes a student project group will gain access to a company because, say, the mother of one of the students is a senior manager there. Similarly the growth of executive MBAs and part-time Masters programmes has also resulted in many students carrying out research into aspects of their own organizations. Not only does this help with access, but they may also have direct experience of the issues they are investigating. So up to a point, their insights are likely to be deeper than those of researchers who arrive from outside the organization.

Team dynamics   However, political and other problems can arise within teams. In our own research we have found that the internal dynamics of a team can be affected by external pressures. In Mark Easterby-Smith's UK/China decision-making project the research team contained both Chinese and UK nationals, but the researchers sometimes found that UK companies to which they were seeking access would only talk to the UK staff and would not respond to any communications from Chinese staff. This may seem surprising nowadays in view of the enormous economic power of China, but back in 1990 people were locked into racial stereotypes. Even though we resisted these external pressures they still affected internal relationships, and they also created difficult decisions about who was most appropriate to carry out interviews in the companies (Easterby-Smith and Malina, 1999).

In a classic paper Hyder and Sims (1979) analyse the tensions between grant holders who are awarded the funds, and research officers who are hired to carry out the work. They suggest that the relationship can become difficult for three main reasons. First, there are different timescales: grant holders are generally tenured academics, while research staff on fixed-term contracts are chronically insecure. Second, in terms of commitment, research staff are likely to be doing little else than working on the project while grant holders will have many other responsibilities and commitments. Third, most grant holders develop conflicting expectations of their research officers, expecting them on the one hand to be general factotums and dogsbodies, and on the other to be creative contributors to the research enterprise.

Barwise et al. (1989) also encountered the latter issue in the context of a multidisciplinary investigation of strategic investment decisions. Although the project was conceived and 'sold' to the funders by three senior staff, it was carried out by a half-time researcher who was recruited specifically for the project. The senior academics initially treated the researcher as their 'eyes and ears', but about half way through the project they were forced to recognize that she had developed a greater understanding of the project than they, and that she now had a major contribution to make both in the interpretation of data and in the overall direction of the project. This recognition meant that they just managed to avoid the researcher becoming an alienated worker.

There is much potential for conflict here. The power of grant holders lies in their control of funds and their potential influence on the future career of the researcher. The researcher's power, on the other hand, lies in intimate knowledge of the research process and the potential to withhold co-operation. Thus both parties are in a position to exert influence throughout the project, although the relative balance of this might vary as the project evolves. And things often come to a head when arrangements are made to start publishing the results, unless clear rules can be agreed in advance, which are generally seen as fair to all parties. This is also a growing problem for research students where there is an expectation of one or two papers emerging from the thesis possibly with joint authorship from the supervisor. It is worth clarifying expectations early in the research period – a good principle is that author order is determined by who does most of the work, and no one should expect a 'free ride'!

Academic stakeholders

The relationship between supervisors and research staff or students is a key power dynamic. But there are many other dynamics within the academic world. Research councils exert influence on the direction of research through control of funds; disciplinary associations determine quality criteria in their own fields; journal editors, referees and conference organizers act as final arbiters of academic quality; and senior academics control career rewards. In almost all circumstances, members of the academic community operate with a high degree of probity and professionalism; nevertheless, given the amount of competition for relatively few prizes, there are bound to be criteria and processes which are not totally transparent. Our aim in this section of the chapter is to make these criteria and processes more visible.

Funding bodies   Academic funding bodies cannot entirely ignore the agendas of their political masters. These often require some explicit links to be made between research funding and national well-being. Consequently, in a number of countries, Research Councils have adopted policies of targeting resources towards specific initiatives that may generate sufficient critical mass to provide rapid development of theories and practical applications. Research proposals therefore stand greater chance of funding if they can demonstrate how they are meeting the priorities of their respective Councils. At the present time, political pressures in the UK are demanding that government-funded research should demonstrate usefulness, which means that user engagement and impact are now essential elements of research proposals. Even in the case of charities, which should not be affected by national political pressures, funding needs to be consistent with the objectives of the charity, as laid down by boards of trustees, and hence it is important to check out policy statements (and perhaps scrutinize the range of projects already funded by the agency) while crafting any proposals for funding. Like it or not, the days of 'blue skies research' are over.

But there is also a danger if funding becomes *too* responsive to political priorities and pressures, because research results may be used by one group directly to harm another group, and it is very easy for researchers to become compromised in the process. An extreme example of this is the work carried out by scientists in Nazi Germany on concentration camp inmates. The majority of those involved appeared to be highly principled, as scientists, and strongly denied any anti-Semitism. Yet in a review of a careful study of surviving evidence, Billig (1988: 476) comments:

> In Murderous Science, we see academics continually writing grant applications, guessing what projects the controllers of the funding agencies will be considering socially useful: is it the Gypsies, or the degenerates, or the ability to withstand cold, which will bring the grants this year?

He who pays the piper not only calls the tune, but can also define what a good tune is. One hopes that exercises such as these would never take place in or around modern organizations. But the personal and social consequences of losing a power struggle, or a job, can be very profound indeed. Researchers should therefore be very wary of the ends that they may be serving, whether wittingly or unwittingly, and this is why increasing attention must be given to ethical issues, as we will see later in this chapter.

Funding bodies always receive more proposals than they can accommodate. Proposals in the UK are given an *alpha* rating if the independent referees consider them to be technically worthy of funding, but the ESRC only has funds for around 20 per cent of the alpha-rated proposals. Thus decisions about the awards often have to take other information into account. Chief among these are whether the researcher has a good 'track record' of prior funded research, whether he or she is known to those involved in making the decision, and whether the research appears to be aligned with current funding council priorities. For those with international reputations and many years' of successful research experience, this is an advantage; but for the newcomer it is a major obstacle to getting started on funded research. Hence we offer below some advice to newcomers wishing to get their feet on the ladder.

- Start with modest-sized proposals.[1]
- Make the best use of your own experience through highlighting any related work or publications you may have.
- Get known by key people in the field by going to conferences and submitting papers for publication.
- Take the opportunity to attend workshops that provide guidance on crafting proposals.[2]

---

[1]Most research councils have schemes that fund relatively small grants (say, up to £100,000) which are available exclusively to younger researchers who have never received grants before.
[2]The British Academy of Management runs excellent workshops on grant applications every year.

● Make use of networks, possibly by submitting proposals jointly with people who are already established, and by sending drafts to potential referees. In both of these cases, senior colleagues may be able to act as brokers by establishing initial contacts, or they may be willing to collaborate directly.

Supervisors and institutions   For those working on projects or research degrees, the main pressures come from supervisors, colleagues and gatekeepers. At the undergraduate level, supervisors will normally use their personal contacts in local firms to identify viable projects. They will be concerned to ensure that the project meets the requirements of the company because they will be hoping to source projects in future years from the same company. Research degree supervisors may have different concerns: they will be keen to ensure that the research stays fairly close both in terms of content and methodology to their own research interests (and competence). If the research is being conducted for a doctoral degree, the supervisor will increasingly be anxious about whether the work will be completed successfully within a given time; this is because both academic departments and whole institutions are now being judged upon completion rates for research students and will have funding withdrawn if the four-year completion rate falls below 60 or 70 per cent. The consequence of this is that both institutions and supervisors are tending to tighten up on guidelines and procedures – by reducing the maximum length of a thesis to 80,000 words, and by introducing regular review mechanisms.

The rise of professional doctorates in subjects such as education, psychology, social administration and business has added another dimension to the system. In our view they offer a distinct opportunity for working on the relationship of theory to practice. In the early days they were largely ignored by the traditional academic community, and universities were able to invent their own criteria and practices. But more recently entry qualifications, research training requirements, assessment criteria and overall standards have been tightened up with more consistency between institutions. Students are encouraged to produce their results for both academic and practitioner audiences through conference presentations and journal articles. Given that the majority of students on professional doctorates study part-time, supervisory support systems have to be appropriate to their needs, recognizing that most study at a distance. In general, it is expected that professional doctorates should be equivalent to PhDs, although they need to demonstrate that they contribute to both theory and practice.

House style   Most academic departments have their own house styles, which support and encourage particular kinds of work, whether quantitative or qualitative, and there is also much pressure on departments to prioritize their research interests. This can make it hard to find the right supervisors and examiners. The ideal external examiner not only needs to share the same research philosophy as the candidate, but also needs to know a lot about the subject of investigation. It is advisable in most cases to start looking for potential external examiners at a fairly early stage in a research degree. This helps to focus the research project, because it requires the candidate to be clear about the boundaries of the field in which he or she is operating, and also to know who are the key movers and shakers in the field. Although the supervisor will need to approach the external examiner, it is important that the candidate is able to provide a list of potential examiners. If the candidate does not have such a list, it is a worrying sign because it suggests he or she may not be sufficiently on top of the field.

Conferences As we have mentioned above, conferences provide a valuable form of contact within the academic community, and it is essential for anyone doing a doctorate to get onto the right conference circuits. Most conferences are not too competitive, and will accept papers on the basis of one- or two-page abstracts; those that are more competitive, such as the US or British Academy of Management, will usually give preferential treatment to doctoral students. The benefits of conference participation should be obvious, but here is a list of points: they provide visibility for you and your ideas; they enable you to get feedback on papers that you will subsequently submit to journals; they enable you to identify others working in your own field; they give access to early copies of publications that may not appear in journals within two or three years; and they help you to spot potential external examiners. In addition, conferences act as recruitment fairs, explicitly in the USA and implicitly in the UK. Gibson Burrell (1993: 75) provides an entertaining account of how the system works at the Academy of Management Conference:

> Doctoral candidates, looking for university positions, are glaringly obvious in the hotel lobbies. The males dress in blazers and grey trousers, the women in blue suits. Prestigious professors dress in Bermuda shorts and sandals. One's position in the hierarchy therefore is marked by dress, so the 'smarter' the attire, the lower is one's standing.

We offer this quote partly for those who agonize over what to wear at conferences – the message being to dress down rather than up – but also to highlight aspects of power within the academic game, which is often expressed through (not so subtle) symbols. And if you are tempted to wear Bermuda shorts and Hawaiian T-shirts, remember that they should be well ironed.

Sometimes edited books and journal special issues are initiated at conferences, and conference organizers often take on the editorial roles for these publications. Although peer review is normally used to support decisions, one of the easiest ways of getting included in such publications is to offer to co-edit the proceedings. You too can become a gatekeeper! But this is by no means the end of the road, because conference proceedings and book chapters only achieve modest ratings in the increasingly hierarchical world of academic publishing. The gold standard is the academic journal, and this is where some of the strictest hierarchies operate.

There are two simple ways of judging in advance the standing of an academic journal. First, submission and rejection rates indicate how much demand there is to get into the journal. Top journals will have rejection rates of over 95 per cent, lesser journals may be around 50 per cent. Journals that take almost everything will not be considered as serious journals (but then they are unlikely to publish their rejection rates). Second, the citation index *ISI* **Web of Knowledge** produces annual rankings of journals based on the frequency with which papers from a given journal are cited by papers published in other respectable journals (see http://wok.mimas.ac.uk/). These rankings use 'impact factor' as the key criterion. This is calculated as the number of citations appearing in *ISI* journals during the target year that refer to papers published in the focal journal during the two previous years, divided by the total number of papers published in the focal journal during the two previous years.

EXAMPLE
4.1

Calculating the 2010 impact factor for *Journal of Management Studies*

Number of citations			Number of articles		
to articles published in:	2009	122	published in:	2009	50
	2008	294		2008	59
	Sum:	416		Sum:	109
Calculation: Divide citations to recent articles by number of recent articles					
	416 ÷ 109 = 3.8				

Journals with impact factors over 3.00 are generally considered 'world class'; those between 1.5 and 3.0 are seen as very good international journals; those between 0.5 and 1.5 are respectable international journals, and those below 0.5 are in danger of relegation. Of course, interpretation of these ratings depends greatly on where your favourite journals fall, and it is also important to look at trends over several years since these ratings can be quite volatile!

Beyond that, one must make up one's own mind, by reading past papers in the journal, or by submitting something to it. If you want to get something published quickly or easily then start with one of the more lowly journals. Top journals have much greater lead times, often running into several years. This is not because they are slow or inefficient, more that they will be dealing with a very large volume of material and they will be very exacting in their standards. For example, a paper that Mark Easterby-Smith published in the *Academy of Management Journal* (Easterby-Smith and Malina, 1999) was initially submitted in March 1996 (and that was based on earlier conference papers given in 1993 and 1995). The initial rewrite offer from *AMJ* arrived 11 weeks after submission and contained eight single-spaced pages of comments and advice from the editor and referees. Over the next two years the paper went through four rewrites, and on each occasion the guidance from the editorial office ran to four or five pages. Thus by the time the paper was accepted in July 1998 the length of comments from the editorial office was greater than the eventual length of the paper. On occasions such as this, as Golden-Biddle and Locke (2007) comment, one starts to wonder whether the referees should be included as co-authors of the paper!

As we said at the outset of this section, it is important for people carrying out academic management research to understand some of the hidden rules and procedures, because these may determine whether they are eventually successful. Despite efforts to be fair and transparent, these hidden rules and procedures are inevitable. In general it is easier for

North Americans to get accepted in North American journals, and for Europeans to get accepted in European journals, because of the institutional and human networks that support these journals. US journals tend to prefer quantitative papers based on survey data; European journals often prefer qualitative papers based on in-depth case studies. But there are always exceptions to these rules, and therefore it is important to be alert and not to accept stereotypes too easily.

Corporate stakeholders

We use the term 'corporate' loosely here, to include companies, public organizations and others generally within the user community. These are becoming very significant because they are both sponsors and users of management research. Many companies invest heavily in executive education, sponsoring managers to attend MBAs and other programmes, and most of these involve projects conducted within the sponsoring organization. There is also growing interaction between companies and universities through enterprise development networks, knowledge transfer partnerships, and the sponsorship of consulting/research projects for both undergraduates and postgraduates.

Undergraduate projects

EXAMPLE
4.2

At Lancaster University undergraduates on the Bachelor of Business Administration carry out consulting projects with local companies, which involve tackling live problems concerning human resources, marketing or internationalization. These run for about ten weeks and require both practical presentations for the companies and academic reports for the university. In the course of these projects, students have to appreciate and deal with many issues. They have to learn to manage their own time and make effective use of their own resources; they have to take responsibility for managing the relationship with the company, gaining the support both of the initial sponsor and key actors; they have to help the company work out what it actually wants from them, and then deliver it; and they have to strike a balance between producing useful consulting reports and providing good academic support for their recommendations.

In the case of postgraduate projects, there are several potential sets of expectations. A production manager attending a part-time MBA might, for example, want to set up a three-month project in the marketing department. This means that the main stakeholders will include: the project sponsor in the marketing department, the academic supervisor, the training department that has organized sponsorship in the first place and the manager. Again, there is often tension between the sponsor who wants a solution to a problem, and the academic supervisor who will be looking for a well-argued case that uses recent literature and is supported by tangible evidence. Sometimes it is necessary to write two separate reports. Occasionally the two sets of expectations can be met with one seamless report that blends academic theory with practical action. Alternatively there is the 'sandwich' model where the client report is prefaced by an academic introduction and literature review, and then followed by a methodological and substantive critique.

One residual consideration is whether research that is conducted for corporate clients will become 'contaminated' because of the funding relationship. There are two ways in which this might happen. As we have already noted, funders are likely to exert some influence on the direction of research and the kinds of questions that are considered to be significant. But this is likely to be the case with all forms of funded research, whether following a positivist or constructionist approach, and we think that the differences due to the presence or absence of corporate funding are merely a matter of degree. The other form of contamination may come from people within the organization deliberately feeding information into the project, which is likely to support their political agendas.

Again, the same thing can happen with any kind of organization, for example a school or a hospital, whether or not there is also a funding relationship. Given that contamination inevitably arises from political factors, the question is how best to deal with it? Our view is that these political factors and their consequences should not be kept hidden; but they should be incorporated explicitly into the reports of the research process. The researcher's own interests, the process of gaining access or funds from organizations, or discussions about dissemination of results: these may all be relevant. Thus we would advise researchers to keep regular records not only of formal research data, but also to chronicle their own views and moods, and the processes of organizing and conducting the research. Further, we think it important that researchers are prepared to reflect critically on all of these influences on their research, and to make these thoughts available to others. As we mentioned in Chapter 2 this requires an element of reflexivity – which should increase, rather than decrease, the credibility of the results.

The subject of study

The subject or topic of study may also exert considerable influence on the nature and direction of the research enterprise. By the 'subject' we mean the problems or issues to be considered – rather than the people and data that will be looked at within the study. Each academic discipline, whether it be mathematics, engineering, sociology or organizational theory, tends to have a number of key debates and issues at any one time. There is also a tendency among researchers to follow fads and fashions with regard to both method and focus (Calhoun, Starbuck and Abrahamson, 2011).

For example, in the early 1990s when the first edition of this book was published some of the fashionable debates stimulated by academic management researchers in Europe were: postmodernism, ethics and critiques of the enterprise culture. A decade later some of the hottest areas were the knowledge economy, globalization and e-commerce. Now there is particular interest in the rising economies of India and China, dynamic capabilities and innovation. There are clear advantages to situating one's work close to the mainstream: others will be interested in the subject, debates will be lively, and there will be conferences and special issues of journals being commissioned on the topic. On the other hand, there will be a lot of competition for space and to establish ownership of new ideas. And the fashion may also turn, so that unless the research topic is defined in a flexible way there is a danger of being stranded with good ideas and materials that excite no further interest.

A 'strategic' approach may be to try to spot issues that are currently regarded as mundane, in the hope that they will suddenly pick up interest. This is another reason for working the conference circuit to find out what the 'industry leaders' think will be important issues for the future. At a wider level, though, the focus on fashion may result in other important or 'ordinary' issues being overlooked. Very often it is the ordinary and commonplace that can be most revealing. Ryave and Schenkein (1974), for example, describe a study of the relatively trivial topic of how people walk. Their results show how a number of social rules can be identified with regard to space, control and propriety – which are by no means mundane, and which have direct relevance to architecture and the design of public spaces.

If the research is to be carried out in a corporate setting it is always worth talking to managers and other employees to find out what they consider to be the emergent issues for them. Often practitioners are ahead of mainstream academics in identifying key problems and relevant solutions. Sometimes this can lead to tension between corporate sponsors and academic supervisors around the questions they consider to be important. But there are plenty of examples of the appropriate combination being achieved. One of our research students was asked by her sponsoring company to investigate how appraisal systems were working in practice in different parts of the company. The researcher was able to answer this practical question to the satisfaction of the company. At the same time she was able to use data from her interviews to show how organizational systems, such as appraisals, are a product of wider cultural value systems in those parts of the organization; and conversely how such systems are a channel for the transmission and articulation of value systems, particularly as defined by senior members of the organization.

Collaborative research project with engineering companies

EXAMPLE
4.3

The Knowledge and Information Management (KIM) project was funded by the Engineering and Physical Science Research Council (EPSRC) between 2006 and 2009. It involved teams from 11 universities looking at the social and technical problems of information management within engineering companies that were seeking to add a significant service element to the products that they sell. The project had a steering committee comprising representatives of 16 companies, which provided general guidance on the direction and potential outputs of the project.

There were many forms of collaboration here: between universities, between engineers and social scientists, between companies and universities, and between companies (some of which are normally in direct competition with each other). Sponsoring companies were able to exert influence by allowing research access only to those projects that had potential to contribute to the business; but they also contributed significantly to the quality of the academic debates by making presentations at the universities, and organizing workshops and seminars on their own sites (see www-edc.eng.cam.ac.uk/kim/).

Thus there is no particular reason why academic and practical goals should not be achieved simultaneously; indeed, as in Example 4.3, we have found that many practitioners will become enthusiastically involved in theoretical debates created from the academic perspective. Such managers are not only likely to be familiar with academic debates about culture and values; they also wish to contribute substantially to these debates. This increasingly leads to the possibility of managers, sponsors and gatekeepers being seen as collaborators in the research process itself.

Context and models of research

We now come to the effect of the broad context within which the research is taking place. By 'context' we include both the national setting and the extent to which resources and attitudes are likely to be supportive of research. We will then look at four different models of the role of the researcher. These are not derived theoretically from philosophical positions, as in the last two chapters, but based on observations of different forms of research in practice.

The national setting is important both because of the way resource availability affects what is possible, and because different countries and cultures may have different views regarding what constitutes 'good' research. David Hickson (1988) provides a nice description of the contrasting resources that he found when conducting research in oil-rich Alberta, compared to his subsequent experiences of research at the University of Bradford, which was at that time reeling from severe government cutbacks. Also, Derek Pugh's (1988) account of the early period of the Aston research programme sounds almost unrecognizable today. Thus he and his team were able to spend a whole year reading books and discussing what the focus of their research would be, with no expectation during the first year that they should collect any data or produce preliminary reports.

The case for the localization of management research is argued by Davila (1989) on the grounds that North American models of research, which require large samples and substantial data analysis, are largely irrelevant both methodologically and substantively in the context of Latin America. He advocates paying far more attention to case studies, which can draw more extensively upon local culture and problems – many of these problems being quite different from those considered significant in more highly developed countries. Teagarden et al. (1995) also found that US research methods could not be applied uniformly in their major cross-national study of HRM practices. The potential for co-operation from companies and managers varied greatly between countries, and it was simply not possible to adhere to the rigorous criteria for sampling and data collection that they had assumed from the USA. Thus we believe that it is important for the researcher to be at least aware of the constraints and opportunities posed by the context within which he or she is currently working.

This leads us to propose four archetypical research models, which although they are not comprehensive, offer different ways of tackling contextual variations. The first is what we call the *military* model, which involves: teams of people; substantial preparation and planning; some differentiation of roles between those who design the research, those who gather data and those who make sense of the data. This is most appropriate in a resource-rich environment as in the case of the work of Pugh and his colleagues at Aston, or Hickson and his colleagues in Alberta. It does mean that substantial resources can be focused on solving major problems, as with the KIM project described above, but there are also downsides to the military model because large hierarchical teams can find it hard to operate within the unpredictability of the research environment – and these need to be managed carefully.

Whereas the workers in the military model are generally hired for the job, in the second model, the *private agent*, one is more likely to find research students and lone academics. This involves individuals operating independently, developing their own ideas using their own resources, and making the best of whatever opportunities are available. Occasionally there may be an element of co-ordination, or networking, among the lone researchers through the Internet and conference links. Institutions that run doctoral programmes may also establish arrangements whereby students, although conducting their research quite independently, are also members of action learning sets that provide support and guidance to each other. Indeed the existence of academic communities of sufficient size is one of the necessary conditions for government funding of research studentships in the UK.

A third possibility is the *team* model, which lies between the two previous models. It involves teams of three to seven people, either students or funded researchers, working together on the particular project or problem. In these cases there is considerable interdependence between the team members, and there needs to be both flexibility and specialization in the roles that members adopt. For example, one person may specialize in maintaining relationships with companies or research settings, another may specialize in handling and analysing data, another may specialize in logistics and group ordination, etc. The team approach is probably most appropriate for dealing with conflicting expectations and tight deadlines.

A final, and somewhat controversial, possibility is the *investigative* model. This starts from the assumption that powerful organizations and individuals will always try to control and repress research conducted on themselves, and hence some deception is both legitimate and necessary. This implies that researchers should be opportunistic, they should use any means necessary to gain access and gather data, and they should publish their findings quickly regardless of consequences. One of the main proponents of this model, sometimes known as conflict methodology, is Douglas (1976). Beynon's classic study of life on and around the assembly line at the Ford plant in Liverpool also had elements of investigative journalism in it (Beynon, 1973). But this subsequently attracted the comment from the company that:

TABLE 4.1 Summary of archetypical research models

Military Model	Large, complex projects conducted by funded researchers, with considerable planning and internal structure.
Private Agent Model	Research students or lone academics pursuing a single project.
Team Model	Groups of students or funded researchers working on a common project.
Investigative Model	Investigations into potential wrong-doing or exploitation which is semi (or totally) covert.

'It's extreme left-wing propaganda . . . we don't think it merits serious discussion as it's not a serious attempt at sociology or education'. There is much sympathy for the investigative model because it can expose fraud, injustice, the misuse of power and organizational myths. But there are also concerns because of the potential backlash and the effect it may have on the opportunities for future researchers who might wish to gain access for non-investigative reasons.

All four of these models to some extent pre-determine the kind of research questions that can, and should, be investigated in their respective cases. Thus one might expect grand theoretical issues to emerge from the military model, the private agent to be focusing on detailed and small-scale processes and issues, the team would be working collaboratively with companies, and the investigator would concentrate on exposing wrongdoings.

POLITICS OF ACCESS

In this section we consider the politics that are involved in gaining access to research sites. We distinguish between *formal* access, which involves gaining permission from senior management to gather data from within the organization, and the *informal* process of gaining access to people and documents. Similar to Buchanan, Boddy and McCalman (1988), we would argue for an opportunistic approach. Most researchers seriously underestimate the amount of time and patience that can be required to gain this initial access. In the following paragraphs we provide some 'war stories' of how hard it can be, and offer some advice on how access may be eased. The good news is that there seems to be a growing acceptance of the value of in-company projects – possibly because a growing number of middle managers have now been through business schools themselves. Consequently they are not so likely to be threatened, and they may be genuinely interested in what is being investigated.

It is extremely difficult to gain access to companies out of the blue (sometimes called 'cold calling'). In our experience it is essential to start with some kind of personal contact, however tenuous. If one's supervisor or institution does not have the right links then it is often worth trying the relevant trade or professional associations, or using contacts in related organizations. We have found associations to be very helpful here, and they rarely object to being mentioned as the source of the contact – because, of course, brokerage is the lifeblood of most trade and professional associations (see Example 4.4).

Once the initial contact has been made by phone, letter or email, the gatekeeper is likely to consider two questions: (1) is this individual worth supporting, and (2) will it be possible to 'sell' to others whose co-operation is being requested? The latter question hangs on a consideration of whether the potential benefits will outweigh the likely costs, or potential risks, of the project. Given that information about costs and benefits will be very imprecise it usually helps at this stage if:

- the project has potential relevance and benefit to the organization;
- the time and resources requested are minimal;
- the project appears not to be politically sensitive; and
- the individuals concerned and their institution have a good reputation.

EXAMPLE
4.4

Trade associations and access

Selen Kars wanted to explore dynamic capabilities in medium-sized Turkish companies. She decided to focus on three different sectors – olive oil, motor components and tourism – which represented increasing degrees of dynamism. Within each sector she needed matched pairs where two companies should be as similar to each other in all respects, except that one would have a reputation with the industry for being particularly innovative, and the other would be well known for sticking with 'traditional' methods. Accordingly, she visited the national industry association for each sector, and they both helped her to identify companies that fitted her criteria and then provided introductions to the chief executives.

However, projects can still go wrong. In a recent ESRC funded project on the evolution of business knowledge (www.ebkresearch.org/people.html) the research design required us to gain access to four distinct companies. Within the first six months of the project we obtained access, and had commenced fieldwork, in the first three – and these all yielded valuable data and stories. We also gained an official letter of invitation from the fourth company, IBM, but before we were able to arrange the first meeting our sponsor, who had written the letter, abruptly left the company. Three months later at a dinner, Mark happened to sit next to a senior manager from IBM, and she agreed to provide another introduction. We attended a meeting and presented our proposals to a new group of managers, but were informed a few weeks later that IBM had taken a policy decision to engage in research links with a very small list of universities, and ours was not on that list.

A few months later he discovered that a Lancaster alumnus was working as PA to the UK managing director of IBM. She offered to organize a meeting with the top man, which meant that we might be able to outflank the earlier policy decision. Unfortunately, a week before the meeting IBM announced an international structural reorganization, which threatened the role of the UK managing director, and hence the meeting was cancelled. By this time we were three months from the end of the project and it was too late to replace IBM with another company. The moral of this story is that it is always important to plan for contingencies: don't count your chickens, and keep something in reserve!

The principle of reciprocity is important: the more the company gives, in time or money, the more it expects in exchange. Another feature that is common to the above examples is that the initiative usually comes from the researcher, and organizational brokers may then be used to reach the patrons. However, there are occasions when patrons themselves may wish to initiate some research. At least six reasons for sponsoring research are common, and these are summarized in Table 4.2.

As we have suggested above, official access is only the start of the story: the next problem is to obtain co-operation and trust inside. This depends mainly on the researcher's skills in dealing with what are sometimes very complex interpersonal relationships. In our experience these relationships are complex because of political issues within the organization, and we divide these into micro-issues, which are about relationships with individual managers, and macro-issues, which are to do with the wider political conflicts.

TABLE 4.2 Common reasons for sponsoring organizational research

To tackle a known problem.
To gain support for a new idea.
To demonstrate the success of a recent project.
To help the individual or unit defend against attack.
To act as a sounding board.
To support research for its own sake.

At a *micro-political* level it is important to be able to develop a co-operative relationship with each informant. With most managers the relationship begins when you try to negotiate an appointment either directly or through an assistant. Most managers will be protective over their time and will also be making assessments of the personal costs and benefits of co-operating. Some managers will get interested in the topic during the interview and will want to keep talking, others will give very short replies, and you will wonder how you are going to get through the allotted hour. We will discuss the dynamics of interview situations in more detail in Chapter 6; but for the time being we note some of the typical problems for researchers.

EXAMPLE
4.5

Internal blockages to access

Barbara Czarniawska (1998) provides a fascinating account of her experiences in Warsaw, where she had obtained agreement to conduct a ten-day observational study of the director of finance of the city council. Most of this period seemed to be taken up with the director finding excuses not to talk to her, or to exclude her from meetings. Even when the director, in a moment of helpfulness, tried to arrange for Barbara to meet the deputy mayor she only managed a passing contact and never managed to schedule an actual interview.

Czarniawska (see Example 4.5) is a senior professor with an international reputation, so perhaps it was hard for the director to resist her openly. With younger researchers more direct 'put downs' may be used. One technique is for the interviewee to cross-examine the interviewer at the outset in order to establish that he has very little relevant experience of the organization or context that he is apparently studying, and is very naive about the realities of anything outside the academic environment. Having established who is really in control of the interaction, the senior manager may then be prepared to sit back for 40 or 50 minutes and respond honestly to questions.

Even experienced researchers occasionally get caught out by this tactic. Beynon (1988) provides a nice example of a senior National Coal Board manager attacking the credibility of an expert academic witness involved in a colliery enquiry by asking such direct questions as 'Are you qualified to manage a coalfield?', 'What practical management experience have you had in operating?', 'Have you any personal knowledge of selling to commercial buyers?' This form of discrediting the external expert provides a very effective form of corporate defence, and perhaps the minor 'put downs' given to researchers by senior managers may be an anticipatory form of defence just in case the 'wrong' results are produced by the study.

When it is a *macro-political* problem, the researcher often becomes trapped between two major groups or factions. When Mark Easterby-Smith was researching for his PhD he had been asked by the works manager of a major chemical plant to conduct a study into the consequences of a large plant closure. This exercise had apparently been handled very successfully and had led to the voluntary redundancy of over 1000 workers, without any overt industrial relations strife occurring. About a week after starting the study he noticed that people were starting to become less available for interview, and people with access to personnel records were suddenly too busy to deal with requests. He was, however, very much reassured to be invited to lunch one day with a general manager from that site: discussion ranged over the research project that had recently started, and the manager showed much interest in some initial observations. It was later the same day that Mark met one of the personnel managers from the site who informed him regretfully that a meeting had been held that same morning to discuss the research project, and that one person had been very insistent that the project be stopped – this was the general manager with whom he had just had lunch.

This was unexpected, since nothing had been mentioned at lunchtime. It was even more surprising that the personnel manager thought there was nothing exceptional about this behaviour. It later emerged that the decision to ban the project was the focal point in a major battle between the works manager and the general manager with regard to the appropriate management style on the site. The former was backing a rather paternalistic line of management, and the results of the study would no doubt have helped him in his argument. His protagonist was arguing for a much harder form of managerialism, and unfortunately for the research project it was an argument that the latter won. Like many organizational researchers faced with similar problems, Mark was forced to complete the study by interviewing people in their homes, and by using networks of internal contacts provided for another project who would accept some surreptitious questioning about the closure themselves.

The lesson from these political examples is that the researcher needs to be aware of conflicts that may be far deeper and more complex than will be evident to a relative newcomer in the organization. We can offer three pieces of advice on how to deal with such politics. First, try to identify one or two 'key informants' who may be prepared to help in a disinterested way. They need to be generally well informed but not directly concerned with the issues under investigation. Informants may be able to advise on whom to talk to, and they should be able to explain why things are, or are not, happening. Second, deliberately look for people who have different perspectives on key issues. Talk further to them and others in order to understand *why* they hold different views. Third, always assume that there is more than meets the eye. People may withhold information because they think it is not important, or irrelevant, or they may genuinely have forgotten things. In organizations that have a policy of moving people around every two years, the collective memory may be very short.

The departmental officer may be the only person who knows that your topic has already been researched and written up twice in the last five years.

EXERCISE
4.1

Role-play about access

Your group has the possibility of being given access to a local Internet company, which sells broadband and associated services to small- and medium-sized businesses across the country. The task is to conduct fieldwork into 'leadership' and you need to complete a number of interviews in a real organization in order to complete your assignment. The initial contact with the company is through the training manager, and she has arranged for a meeting with the chief executive to discuss the possible research. The meeting will take place on-site, and the chief executive has a busy schedule. He has also indicated that he would like to see just two members of the team on this first instance.

Roles

● *Student 1, student 2*. Their aim is to gain access on behalf of their colleagues for a project that both fits their academic needs and is also ethically acceptable.

● *Chief executive*. He is prepared to provide access providing the project uses minimal resources/time, offers some potential benefit to the company, and carries absolutely no risks for the company or individuals within it.

● *Training manager*. She is a former employee of the university at which the students are studying, but her own position in the company is slightly insecure.

● *Other group members*. Should act as observers during the role-play and as facilitators of the debrief afterwards.

Role-playing process

The chief executive is in control of the meeting throughout. He has given himself 15 minutes in which to make a decision about whether or not to let the students in.

Timescale

● 15 minutes: preparation. Student reps; CEO and training manager; observers to discuss in separate groups their agendas and how they will handle/monitor the role-play.

● 15 minutes: role-play.

● 20 minutes: debrief. To be chaired/facilitated by the observers. Try to cover: pre-meeting strategies of different parties; degree of satisfaction with the outcome; what was unexpected; general lessons learnt about the process of access.

ETHICS

There are ethical issues bubbling under the surface of many of the examples we have given above. In this section we provide an analytic structure for thinking about ethical issues in the management field, and review the ongoing debate for and against the provision of ethical codes and procedures.

Management researchers, and their professional associations such as the British Academy of Management, and the (American) Academy of Management, have been relatively relaxed about the provision of ethical codes. But there is growing pressure from other academic disciplines, such as medicine and psychology for all universities to adopt definite ethical codes and practices, and there is growing coherence, especially in the social sciences, around a common set of principles. Bell and Bryman (2007) conducted a content analysis of the ethical principles of nine professional associations in the social sciences. They identified ten principles of ethical practice, which were defined by at least half of the associations. These principles are summarized in Table 4.3.

Essentially, the first seven of these principles are about protecting the interests of the research subjects or informants; the last three are intended to ensure accuracy, and lack of bias, in research results. These are of particular concern in the medical sciences because of the danger that experiments might be conducted that would bring genuine harm to participants, and also because of the enormous financial muscle of commercial funding bodies such as drug companies, which might well seek to influence results in directions that would give an advantage to their products.

TABLE 4.3 Key principles in research ethics

1	Ensuring that **no harm** comes to participants.
2	Respecting the **dignity** of research participants.
3	Ensuring a fully **informed consent** of research participants.
4	Protecting the **privacy** of research subjects.
5	Ensuring the **confidentiality** of research data.
6	Protecting the **anonymity** of individuals or organizations.
7	**Avoiding deception** about the nature or aims of the research.
8	Declaration of affiliations, funding sources and **conflicts of interest**.
9	**Honesty and transparency** in communicating about the research.
10	Avoidance of any **misleading** or false reporting of research findings.

The circumstances of management and business research are largely similar, but are distinct in one important respect, which we have already mentioned. Although the interests of informants still need to be protected, it can no longer be assumed that the researcher is in the all-powerful position held by clinical and social researchers. Indeed, when research is conducted into companies, it is the researcher who is often the least powerful party to the transaction. While researchers should normally protect interests of the organizations they are investigating, there may be times when they come across illegal or unethical behaviour within the organizations themselves – and some people would argue that this should be published in a way that will expose the organization. This means that in the area of management research, it becomes difficult to establish hard-and-fast ethical principles, and good practice requires considerable judgement from the researcher.

The most likely ethical dilemma may therefore be to betray the confidences given by employees, when one is cross-examined by more senior managers. Informants who are politically adept often read a great deal into the question that the interviewer is asking. For example, on one occasion Mark happened to be interviewing the director of a national investigatory organization about the longer term effects of a particular management development programme. He happened to ask a carefully focused question about how the reward system was working, to which the director immediately came back with, 'I take it you have been talking to John Dawson about that . . . Well in that case . . .'. Even though they may not be professionally trained as investigators, managers will often be able to work out the nature and sources of information already collected by researchers who are sufficiently unfamiliar with the detailed political context of the organization to be aware of the significance of the questions that they are asking.

Two particular ethical issues frequently concern organizational researchers. The first arises from the use of participant observation research methods, which, as Ditton (1977) says, are essentially deceitful. That is, if you are participating in a situation, and at the same time observing and recording (perhaps later) what has taken place, you cannot avoid some deception about your real purposes. Our preference is to be as open as possible when people ask challenging questions about the purpose of the research, for two main reasons. First, because they may well be interested in the nature of the research and might have valuable insights into what you are investigating; and second, because if they suspect that you are holding information back they are most unlikely to be co-operative if you ask for their help. Trust is important.

The second ethical issue is around the control and use of data obtained by the researcher. In most cases he or she has control and ownership of the data, and therefore must exercise due ethical responsibility by not publicizing or circulating any information that is likely to harm the interests of individual informants, particularly the less powerful ones. There is an interesting story, however, where this particular assumption was neatly turned upon its head. A senior academic happened to be interviewing a member of the British Royal Family, and at the end of the interview he offered to have the tape transcribed and to send a transcript to the interviewee who could then strike out any passages to which he objected. Whereupon the Royal Person stretched out a hand saying 'No. I shall retain the tape and will let you have the portions that I am prepared to have published'.

Finally, there is an on-going debate about the value, or otherwise, of ethical codes in relation to research. It is argued that at least some codes need to be made explicit in order to ensure that people are alerted to some of the likely ethical dilemmas that they may face. Such codes should also provide some kind of sanction in cases of blatant abuse and exploitation. But there is a problem here. As Snell (1993) points out, ethical issues are extremely complex. They involve not only the dynamics of power but also the competing claims of different ideologies. The danger is that ethical guidelines will not only be too rigid and simplistic to deal with real cases; they will also contain the biases that are inherent in one or another ideological position.

Mason (1996) and Bell and Bryman (2007) make similar points about ethical codes being generally written in abstract terms, aimed at preventing serious and unambiguous cases of abuse. The problem is that most of the ethical issues faced by the researcher are small-scale, incremental and ambiguous. Mason argues that researchers should operate as thinking, reflective practitioners who are prepared to ask difficult questions about the ethics and politics of their own research practice on a regular basis.

UTILIZATION OF RESEARCH

The link between research and action is often very weak, and many people find this extremely disappointing. Researchers themselves are only too aware of this feeling when they find that the fruits of several years' labour are gratefully accepted by the sponsoring organization, and are simply filed away in a dust-proof cabinet.

To some extent this disappointment could simply be a result of different people having different expectations from research. Within the academic world, the expectations are fairly specific. Good research should lead to contented corporate sponsors, to successful PhDs (completed within target dates), to the publication of articles in refereed journals, and to the timely production of end-of-grant research reports. Getting published in the appropriate academic journals is still very important for the career advancement of academics, and the main political problems are related to debates, cliques and paradigms within the academic world (as we have discussed earlier in this chapter). But most academic journals have a very limited circulation outside academia, and commercial sponsors are not often concerned about what is likely to be published in these outlets as a result of studies that they have sponsored. The same cannot be said for publication of reports and books, as Punch (1986) found out to his cost (see Example 4.6).

Dangers of signing away publication rights

EXAMPLE
4.6

Maurice Punch conducted some research into the Dartington Hall Trust, an educational charity. At the outset of his research he was persuaded to sign a piece of paper in which he committed himself only to publish with prior permission of the Trust. Initially he regarded this as a mere formality, and therefore he was greatly surprised when the document was used to prevent publication of a book about Dartington Hall School. Given the importance of publications to academic careers, Punch realized that his own career was effectively being blocked by what he regarded as the intransigent position of the organization he had studied. Conversely Dartington Hall felt that publication of Punch's findings would undoubtedly do harm to the school, and therefore that he should be stopped in his tracks.

Source: Punch (1986: 49–70).

The advice of Punch, then, is that the researcher should *never* sign away his or her rights of publication, and this view is also strongly supported by social scientists such as Bulmer (1988). On the other hand, we agree with Buchanan, Boddy and McCalman (1988) who take the more pragmatic line that organizational clients have a right to receive reports from those who research them, and that they should be allowed to comment upon the reports before they are published. This collaborative approach should enable both the quality of final reports to be improved, and may also contribute to the maintenance of positive relationships between researchers and clients. It also makes it more likely that the company will agree to being identified by name, which seems preferable to a pseudonym.

One way of resolving this dilemma is to consider the research models discussed above. Those adopting the *military* model will wish to have clear agreements about issues such as access, confidentiality and publication rights agreed well in advance. At the other end of the scale it is important that the *investigative* researcher does not sign anything that could be used in evidence against him or her. The two other models, *private agent* and *team* research, would represent intermediate cases between these two extremes. If agreements are to be reached in these cases they should ideally specify both the right that the researcher has to publish, as well as the right of the client to monitor and control certain kinds of output.

Issues of implementation and utilization become more serious with practical and applied forms of research. When working directly for clients or patrons, as in evaluation research, we have found it very important to tie the research closely to the question that the sponsors or clients want to have answered. This is not a one-off process, but depends on a considerable amount of discussion and negotiation between the needs of the client and the capabilities of the researcher (Easterby-Smith, [1986] 1994). Many clients already have a fairly good idea of the likely results from a research study *before* they commission it, and therefore the researcher should pay particular attention to the possibility of disproving what the client thinks to be the case. This way the clients might learn something new.

The problem of utilization is not confined only to academic research. Innovatory projects conducted within organizations can have just as much difficulty being accepted and implemented. One of the ways that the fast-moving company 3M deals with this problem is to formalize the role of sponsor – usually a senior manager who is prepared to champion a particular idea or project. As Nonaka (1988: 14) comments: 'Before a daring and promising idea can stand on its own, it must be defined and supported by a sponsor willing to risk his or her reputation in order to advance or support changes in intra-company values'.

What remains crucial is the relationship between the researcher and the client: this needs to be open and honest rather than sycophantic, and above all there should be a reasonable degree of mutual trust. Where the degree of mutual trust is limited we have noticed a marked tendency for clients and sponsors to try to push researchers into more of a 'technician' role where the researcher is expected to gather data, often quantitative, within a framework defined by the client. Interpretation of the data is then under the control of the client rather than the researcher.

To some extent we have assumed above that the responsibility for utilization and consequent action lies with the clients or patrons. In the case of policy-orientated research it is by no means as simple because one may be dealing with rather complex bureaucracies or political systems. In the case of research geared towards national (social) policy, Finch (1986) points to two distinct traditions, and assumptions, about the appropriate way of using such research. On the one hand there is the **social engineering model**, which sees research as a linear and rational process where research studies are commissioned so that their results feed into specific decisions and supply the missing facts to enable decision-makers to take the right course of action. On the other hand there is the **enlightenment model,** which sees implementation as an incremental process with lots of diffuse viewpoints being introduced from different levels of the social system, hence providing an indirect link between the research and policy implications. The former model makes full use of quantitative methods, and the latter has a preference for qualitative methods.

As one might expect, most governments and sponsoring agencies prefer to use the social engineering kind of research because it gives them more control over what will take place. But the problem with the largely quantitative studies implied by this model is that they can only describe the situation as it is now, or as it was in the past; they can give very little guidance on what should take place in the future, and this is a limitation when research is supposed to be aiding policy formulation. This is where the more democratic enlightenment model can help to some extent by providing a much wider range of options and ideas in order to guide future action.

CONCLUSION

At this point we can identify some general implications for the researcher.

 It is important to recognize that power and political issues will be significant even when they are not obviously present.

 There are no easy answers, nor solutions, to the political web. It exists in the form of ideologies, of personal interests, of power differences and of ethical dilemmas.

 The researcher needs both clarity of purpose and much flexibility in tackling problems.

 Clarity of purpose can come from self-awareness of one's own interests and assumptions about the world, and these can be incorporated into reflexive accounts.

We have discussed the issues of ontology, epistemology, research design, politics and ethics in the last three chapters. In the next part of the book we consider the range of methods and techniques that are at the disposal of the researcher. We stress consistently that these should not be seen as entirely free-standing; but they should be subordinated to the considerations of purpose and philosophy, which have been outlined above.

Political dilemmas in conducting student project (group discussion)

You have to do an in-company project as part of the assessment for your degree. Your tutor has arranged access to a local supermarket to investigate the quality of customer relations, and the contact, who is deputy manager, has suggested that you talk to members of two departments: one appears to be very successful, and the other is regarded as problematic. Here are some possible scenarios. What would you do?

1   When you arrive for the initial meeting with the deputy manager you are informed that she has been called on urgent business to the regional head office and cannot see you.

2   When you meet the deputy manager she asks you to sign a non-disclosure agreement.

3   During a one-to-one interview with a checkout assistant she comments that there have been incidents of sexual harassment in her department. What do you do with this information, if anything?

4   After conducting a number of interviews in both departments the deputy manager asks you for your opinion of the qualities of both supervisors.

5   During the project, one team member persistently fails to pull his weight. How do you deal with this?

FURTHER READING

Bell, E. and Bryman, A. (2007) 'The ethics of management research: an exploratory content analysis', *British Journal of Management*, 18 (1), 63–77.
   The authors suggest that management researchers face ethical issues that are distinct from those encountered by other social science researchers. They provide a review of ethics codes formulated by nine social scientific associations, and argue that reciprocity is a central principle for management research.

Buchanan, D. and Badham, R. (2008) *Power, Politics and Organizational Change: Winning the Turf Game*. London: Sage.
   This edition, which focuses on how managers can act as internal change agents, emphasizes the contexts in which they initiate and achieve change. It provides an accessible overview of organizational politics, which is useful for the researcher both in conducting and implementing research.

REVIEWING THE LITERATURE

5

LEARNING OBJECTIVES

 To appreciate what a literature review in management and business research entails and why it is necessary.

 To understand how to evaluate critically different sources of information and know how to write literature reviews.

 To be able to identify research gaps in the literature and know how to develop new theories.

INTRODUCTION

This chapter considers how students at different levels, who are starting to investigate a topic, can discover what is already known within a particular field and to identify gaps in the literature for their own study. Whether it is for taught or research postgraduate students, MBA or MSc level, a literature review is an essential part of the study. The main difference between the different levels of study is that the time constraints and the depth of the literature review vary.

The review should provide students with a basic understanding of how the topic has developed over time and what remains to be investigated. Anyone starting a research topic must be aware of the existing theories and research in the field. A literature review deals not only with the traditional sources such as textbooks and journal articles, but also may include knowledge gained from other communities of practice such as consultants and official bodies. A large amount of data can be found on the Internet, both to identify books and articles, but also to find electronic resources and newspapers. It is important for (management) researchers to be in touch with a range of perspectives and sources, whether these are internal or external, public or private.

The first part of this chapter reiterates the importance of being familiar with the literature in the researcher's field of study. The second part outlines how to get access to the information required and how to undertake a bibliographical search to find the data needed for a literature review. The third part discusses how the material collected might be recorded and organized noting those electronic aids that have emerged to assist this process. The fourth part indicates how a search activity might be framed, using examples from a **systematic review**, while the final part offers some conclusions and tips for those undertaking a literature review.

WHAT IS A LITERATURE REVIEW AND WHAT IS ITS PURPOSE?

A literature review has a number of features. The first essential characteristic is the need for the reviewer to give a rigorous but rational explanation of what is being reviewed. By engaging with and critiquing previous studies, the researcher needs to strike a balance that simultaneously displays criticality with regard to the assumptions, theories and methods used while at the same time acknowledging the insights and strengths of the studies. Second, literature reviews should be written in a descriptive manner that progressively builds towards the focal research topic. This includes identifying gaps in the extant literature, or interacting conversations in which you would like to take part. A third feature is that many reviews continue throughout a research project rather than being conducted only at the beginning of a study. The review remains an ongoing process, which requires refinements and modifications as the study progresses. This is due in part to empirical findings that might lead the research in a new direction and therefore require adjustments to the parameters of the topic, and also because new findings emerge all the time and the research needs to reflect these and be as up-to-date as possible.

One definition of a literature review is:

> The selection of available documents (both published and unpublished) on the topic, which contain information, ideas, data and evidence written from a particular standpoint to fulfil certain aims or express certain views on the nature of the topic and how it is to be investigated, and the effective evaluation of these documents in relation to the research being proposed. (Hart, 1998: 13)

A process of evaluation should identify where the gaps in prior studies exist and this will help the researcher locate their investigation in a broader context. Silverman (2000: 227) highlights a number of questions a literature review raises and which need to be considered:

- What do we already know about the topic?
- What do you have to say critically about what is already known?
- Has anyone else ever done anything exactly the same as what is proposed?
- Has anyone else done anything that is related?
- Where does your work fit in with what has gone before?
- Why is your research worth doing in the light of what has already been done?

A good literature review will ensure that the research undertaken fits in with the existing wider research within the focal area. It is a research activity all in itself and contributions can be made to knowledge on particular subjects simply through the literature review. Published reviews of literature can be seen in specialist review journals such as the *International Journal of Management Reviews*, *Academy of Management Review* or *Psychological Review*. These act as invaluable resources for those wishing to gain an overview of existing studies in a particular field.

In conducting reviews balance needs to be struck in two areas. First, between adopting a clear focus on the topic in hand, and opening the boundaries to include other literatures outside the focal area. Second, the review needs to provide both clear and comprehensive descriptions of key/relevant literature and a critique that covers the strengths and weaknesses of prior research. This will aid in the identity of the main research gap(s).

PREPARATION FOR THE LITERATURE REVIEW

A clear aim and getting started

The first thing is to have the aim of the literature review clear. After this is established, there are numerous ways in which a literature search can be done but it should always follow the aim of the research. A clear aim will make sure the literature review stays focused.

For years, the most obvious place to begin was the library. JAI Press is one example that compiles a series of sources of research in various disciplines. These are updated regularly as new material is published. It is also important to take note of seminal works in the area, particularly those that offer an overview of the approaches to an extant literature upon a particular topic. For example, Easterby-Smith (1997) has published a review of organizational learning from the perspective of six different disciplines. A systematic review of knowledge in small and medium enterprises (SMEs) can be seen in Thorpe et al. (2005). Both could be used as starting points for researchers investigating these particular areas. Another way of getting started is to begin with the relevant studies written on the topic over the years. A quick search in Google Scholar should identify these texts and often they will in turn provide interesting references. The main drawback of this is that it quickly widens the field of research and this can work against the need for research focus. Some journals give a systematic précis of the articles published in editions of that year. For example, the *Journal of Marketing* offers such a précis: over several pages it covers all types of significant articles and publications in all aspects of marketing (e.g. distribution, publicity, sales or strategy) for that volume.

It is also an excellent strategy to join subject-specific research communities. This can be a very fruitful way of getting to know like-minded colleagues who are working in a similar field or on a similar topic, not just in a researcher's own country, but all over the world. An example of such a network is the British Academy of Management (www.bam.ac.uk/groups). It has special interest groups that currently cover 14 different fields in management and related activities. Many useful leads and references can come from participating in e-mail discussion groups. Contacts for such groups are often found at conferences or similar academic associations. For doctoral candidates this kind of networking is perhaps even more important than for those simply engaged on an individual research topic, as it will bring them in touch with other researchers who are or have been undergoing the same experience and share similar research interests. Doctoral streams and colloquia are organized by most of the big international conferences such as the British Academy of Management (BAM), European Group of Organizational Studies (EGOS), the American and European Academies of Management (AoM and EURAM), the European Doctoral Network (EDEN) and the European Institute for Advanced Studies in Management (EIASM). All these groups enable researchers to submit their current research for discussion and debate with fellow doctoral candidates and senior academics. In addition, there are conferences organized by disciplines within management and these again often have their own doctoral provision, for example the British Academy of Marketing and the Institute for Small Business and Entrepreneurship.

The British and American Academies of Management both also have special interest groups, which cover a range of disciplines and cross-disciplinary topics; they hold regular seminars and workshops and are very welcoming to new researchers. This is an excellent opportunity for researchers to read-test their work in front of experienced academics who are well known within the field and can provide essential feedback. Perhaps it is also worth noting here that researchers often publish their most recent work as working papers, published through their own universities or through symposia. In addition to the opportunities that have been mentioned, it is a good idea to conduct a systematic search; this will be explained later on in this chapter.

Focus

As has been discussed in Chapter 2, focusing the research often is a challenge. Especially during the stage of the literature review, it is essential to maintain focus, otherwise too much information can be paralysing and research can move in a fruitless direction. The literature

TABLE 5.1 Overview of sources

Source	Strengths	Weaknesses
Library	A lot of information available in hardcopy, special literature can be ordered.	Time consuming, often basic knowledge and not the latest research in the field.
Google Scholar	Quick and easily accessible, easy to get an overview of a topic.	Broadens the field, loses the focus, soft copy, does not always show the relevant articles.
Special Interest Groups	The latest research, share ideas and get feedback.	Accessible through average Universities.
Web of Science	Focused search on author/journal/keywords.	Often require membership.

review, and the way that it is presented in a report or theses, presents another challenge. A literature review often starts off from a broad strategy to become more focused with a narrow research scope. Conceptualizing a broad field can be difficult; bringing together a broad cross-section of papers and articles can be a gargantuan task. Mind-mapping to identify linkages to other research is a useful way to establish some order to this complexity. The mind-map in Figure 5.1 illustrates an example of a systematic review of the roles played by creativity and innovation in science and engineering throughout industry and academia.

ELEMENTS OF LITERATURE REVIEW

There are a number of stages and different types of literature review, each with different criteria. The elements include: (1) an overview of the research topic under investigation; (2) critical judgement; (3) a supportive assessment of the literature; and (4) an attempt at an objective process of review (Huff, 2009). All these need to be included in a literature review, especially in a doctoral dissertation. The overview becomes useful in the early stages of the research. The critical review should be done when the key articles/areas have been identified. A supportive search often comes towards the end of the research, to make sure no new important research has been published that is of significance to your work. The systematic review takes more time in order to map the field in tables, but gives a good overview of the field and what articles you have consulted to make it fit in the existing research.

Overview of the research topic

When starting a new research project it is important to get an overview of the topic that is being investigated. This will contribute to the understanding of how it has developed over

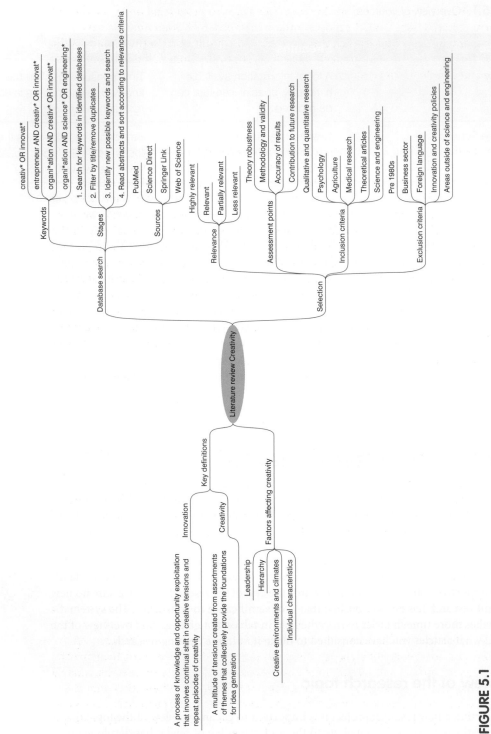

FIGURE 5.1

Mind-map of a literature review using the Freemind software

time, key concepts, strengths and weaknesses. This will also provide an understanding of the current research trends and the most common methods used. Sometimes, to get a view of the economy or a specific market, it is necessary to consult other sources, such as the *Financial Times* or the *World Investments Reports* (WIR) by the United Nations Conference on Trade and Development (UNCTAD).

Critical review

Once you have established an overview of the research area, you need to assess the research with a critical mind-set. A critical review is defined as 'a critical evaluation of the literature according to argument, logic and/or epistemological or ontological traditions of the review subject' (Petticrew and Roberts, 2006: 19). What are the weaknesses of previous studies? Have they missed any important aspects? Are they using the right methodology? By identifying key journals for your research, you need to discuss them in a critical way in the literature review. What are the main arguments, contributions and methods? It is important to keep in mind that your aim in the literature review can change as a result of critically reviewing more literature, which is a part of the flexible research design. The critical reflection of the literature should start as early as possible, when the researcher feels confident with the overview picture. This will help to identify weaknesses in published research and to identify research gaps. The critical mind-set of questioning the literature instead of accepting it continues throughout the research. At some point there has to be an end so you will not be overloaded with information.

Supportive search

Because a research project can take years, new research will emerge during the project. Therefore a literature review is not something you do once and complete it. Instead it is a continuous process throughout the research project. Sometimes it is necessary to consult and review additional literature after the fieldwork, if a new aspect has emerged from the data. Because new research constantly develops it is necessary to consult new literature that has emerged, or was not in your original review. This needs to be done until the very end of the project, to make sure no important study has emerged that is omitted.

Systematic review

Before researchers begin objectively to examine the topic under study, it is necessary to consider how the review will develop and benefit their studies and understanding. It may unintentionally lead to researchers being too objective at the expense of using their creativity, for example, combining different aspects, concepts or methods. However, there may be other reasons for such an approach. It might be for personal development reasons, where a researcher has little or no familiarity with the field, or because the systematic, comprehensive aspect within the frame of reference of the literature is part of the purpose of the review. In essence, a systematic review involves two processes. First, defining review protocols and mapping the field by accessing, retrieving and judging the quality and relevance of studies in your research area. Second, reporting the findings to identify where gaps in the current research exist and so indicate where your research might make a useful contribution, very much in the way we have already discussed.

Typically, literature reviews that go under the name of systematic reviews are restricted to published peer-reviewed academic articles that exist within management and organization studies fields, because it is through peer-reviewed publications that the quality of the research and its relevance can be judged and maintained. A systematic review is defined as 'a review that strives to comprehensively identify, appraise and synthesize all relevant studies on a given topic' (Petticrew and Roberts, 2006: 19). It is recognized that there are a limited number of searchable databases for book chapters and reports, though currently there are a number of national and university libraries working to increase the number of books available online. The choice of bibliographic databases will depend upon what access is available, although as we have discussed, universities often subscribe to a number of them. The articles can often be accessed through several search paths, and sometimes not all the sources will publish the full text of the article. Therefore, one might need to consult different databases or access the journal through the university library; after all, serious students need to be in touch with the literature in which they wish to be taken seriously.

The objective is to identify a number of key articles; exactly how many will depend on your focus and their centrality to your interests, without excluding important key studies. To further assist in limiting the search, exclusion criteria can be used, which have been discussed earlier in this chapter. The point behind systematic reviews (i.e. why they are systematic rather than simply personal choice) is that each filtering decision is noted down and is transparent for others to see what you have done and so judge the relevance and substantive nature of your review. Articles that are returned are not seen to have been selected on the basis of personal preference. Each database will yield a list of potentially useful studies using search strings alone. The review being systematic means the criteria for judging which study goes into which list have also to be identified and justified. So again a degree of self-reflection might also be useful here, covering, for example, concerns such as: data quality, access, theory development and ambition, links to research question, and so forth. With some studies there may be wholly inadequate abstracts and this may mean that the introduction and/or conclusions of the article need to be examined – what is sometimes referred to as 'examining in detail'.

The chosen studies in the literature review need to be discussed and contrasted to justify the use of each one of them. The categories chosen will be yours and they will reflect the sense that you make of what has gone on already in your research, which areas have been covered and in what depth so you can more confidently see the relevance and contribution your work makes to the whole. It may be useful to revisit the example of studies and look at knowledge used in professional firms. The analysis of the studies may look to group those studies by types of methodology used, by titles of journals in which they are published, by types of firm studied, and by the conclusions reached; each of these being further classified where common themes can be discovered. To assist in this process (especially if a large number of studies are to be read), coding software such as NVivo can be used to support the analysis (further discussed in Chapter 8). The resultant categorization then forms the basis of the structure for writing up your literature review; the conclusion of which will be a discussion of where your own work will relate, complement and/or challenge existing studies as we show in Chapter 11.

One of the problems with systematic reviews is that they often encourage the reading of abstracts. Some academics have made cutting remarks about researchers who are happy to quote material that they have not actually read (but instead have assimilated concepts and ideas from other articles). One must be clear and point out if the material is a quotation from a secondary source. An author cited by another author is the only way in which the reference can be cited when a reference is made that stretches beyond what we physically possess or know, to what we have not read. It is advisable to avoid quoting this kind of material as it can lead to difficulties concerning comprehension and interpretation, dangerous even if the citing or quotation is not entirely improper.

TABLE 5.2 Pros and cons of systematic reviews

Pros	Cons
• Collection from a broad range of sources	• Could limit creativity and intuition
• Aids interdisciplinarity as it highlights cross disciplinary themes	• Could overlook important 'grey literature' e.g. reports
• Increases transparity of the review	• Restricted to the accessibility of sources
• Increases replicability of the review	• Keyword search strings need to be identifiable
• Being 'systematic' offers a sense of rigour	• Older 'scanned' texts can't be reached
• Aids the process of synthesis through the increased scope possible	• Relies on databases that support 'keyword' search
	• Relies on the quality of the abstract (often limited to 100 words)

SOURCE: THORPE ET AL. 2005

There is value in presenting a concrete example where systematic review was used in a study. One such review is illustrated here in Example 5.1, which is the work of Thorpe et al. (2005) who conducted a systematic review of how SMEs create and use knowledge.

EXAMPLE
5.1

The study by Thorpe et al. (2005) had a number of key stages.

Background preparation

A review panel was first formed consisting of the study's authors. The panel considered prospective sources of information, deciding on using peer-reviewed journals – both practitioner and academic. Books, reports and book chapters were excluded on the grounds that they did provide the opportunity for searchable bibliographical databases. The team then used terms relevant to the study as keywords to determine the most appropriate databases given the peculiarities of the research. Thus, words such as know* and learn* were employed. The asterisk (*) helps retrieve variations and related words to the ones entered in the search. For example, searching for the

(Continued)

(Continued)

word know* encapsulates knowledge and its derivatives, including 'knowing'. The returns were analysed and used as guides in narrowing down the type of databases. In this case the databases with the highest number of returns were chosen, which were ABI ProQuest, Business Source Premier and Ingenta (incorporating Science Direct). Up to this point the process involved identifying relevant databases. The next step was to do detailed keyword searches.

Keyword search

Since the topic was knowledge and learning within SMEs, the team's principal keywords and search strings included know*, learn*, SME or small firms, and entrepreneur*. When keywords were deemed to complement one another the word AND was used to enable the retrieval of a comprehensive result (for example know* AND learn*). Where they were seen to be substitutes OR was used instead (an example here is SMEs OR small firms). Of course know* and learn* may also be viewed as substitutes, and this was reflected in searches, with keyword searches alternating between the formats know* AND learn*, and learn* OR know*.

Exporting results

The results were downloaded into the ProCite software program. This gave each paper's keywords and abstracts. In the first instance, the team sifted through the abstracts determining each article's relevance to the subject of study. Those articles considered irrelevant were excluded as were those from other fields such as education and engineering. The key guiding idea at this stage was relevance and not the depth of the articles.

Further exclusions

With the articles put together, the next step was to interrogate them based on a number of criteria: theory robustness, implications for practice, coherence between data and arguments put forward, theory, relevance to SME knowledge (on account of findings, methods and theories) and contributions made. The result of this exercise was the identification of papers that dealt with SME knowledge while meeting the set criteria.

Themes and conceptualizations

The study portrayed a landscape of studies into SME knowledge and produced broad themes as well as sub-themes about the subject. These findings were eventually published as an academic paper.

Remember that at this stage it is only abstracts that are being examined so a great deal depends upon the coverage and clarity of the abstracts concerned and journal style does vary enormously.

The pros and cons of searching systematically

EXERCISE
5.1

In pairs, discuss the advantages and disadvantages of using systematic searches compared to a more personally directed approach to the identification of appropriate sources.

ALIGNMENT WITH STUDY CONTEXT AND APPROACH

A review of the literature may be in a single disciplinary area or in several areas, depending on the nature of the research and its subject area. Regardless of the setting and the issue being investigated, it is paramount that there is some kind of alignment between the research methodology to be adopted, its context and the approach used. Studies concentrating on a narrow subject domain will require a critique of the literature in that specific area. However, multidisciplinary and practice-based studies might require a review that spans different literatures and synthesizes them.

Whether the nature of the study focuses on one discipline or takes a more multidisciplinary approach, the literature review will need to be consistent with the study as a whole. This means that the study's epistemology, strategy, literature review, design, methods and empirical sections should all be linked and demonstrates an internal coherence (see Chapters 2 and 3). At the same time, as we have indicated, a simple description of previous research is not sufficient. Rather, the review needs to incorporate interpretation and analysis as well as being critical so as to underpin the research questions identified. Patriotta (2003) offers an example of the way he has conducted his literature review (see Example 5.2 below).

Literature review by Patriotta

EXAMPLE
5.2

In his book entitled *Organizational Knowledge in the Making*, Patriotta (2003) reviews the literature on knowledge within firms and identifies different perspectives, including the cognitive, knowledge-based, 'situated' and techno-science approaches. He offers a critical interpretation of different perspectives, acknowledging their respective strengths while also identifying areas that require clarifying. He concludes by arguing for an integrated and multi-faceted approach to the subject. What becomes apparent to him is that the pluralistic approach adopted has led to his ability to propose that there are in fact three methodological lenses, which transcend the narrow epistemological boundaries of current perspectives on organizational knowledge. These three lenses are suggested as being breakdown, time and narrative.

A subject-search then demands as a pre-condition the *identification of keywords* of one's subject area. A researcher should not think, though, that he or she has to find an exact match with those words used in the library to name a subject. Any classification system provides for alternative 'labels' to identify a category, and the researcher's part is to be aware of the most likely alternatives. It might be helpful to write a list of the different ways that a subject area might be described. An alternative term might be as straightforward as changing the word slightly, for example when using 'organizational knowledge' as keywords; it would also be useful to try typing in 'knowing'. Most databases allow the researcher to use a 'wildcard' when a term can have several endings, for example 'know*' would search for 'knowledge' and 'knowing' in some databases. Check the individual databases for the different forms these wildcard symbols take.

There are two main ways of tackling a literature search; either the researcher has and needs a wide overall review of the literature in a specific field or they know exactly the articles that they want and simply need to collect these. Selvin and Stuart (1966) refer to these as 'trawling' (when it involves a wide sweep to see what can be brought in) and 'fishing' (which involves a more targeted search). Trawling and fishing should not be seen as opposites, more as different starting points, independent of the extent of the researcher's prior knowledge and focus.

Before setting out on a trawl, that is, sweeping up whatever information exists on a topic, time can be saved by a researcher in deciding and being selective in what he or she is after. Before preparing for a search researchers should identify the types of information that they require. They can then prepare searches for the different resources, i.e. searches within a catalogue will be more general than those on a database and so on. Try to think a little bit about what you are attempting to look for so you limit what you get from the search and can be more confident that what you do retrieve relates to what you want to know more about. More specifically, a researcher needs to think about the keywords that can be used to identify a field of study. Using keywords, operators such as AND, OR and NOT can be combined to create search statements and refine searches. Most articles carry keywords beneath the abstract that identify themes addressed in the study. These can be invaluable filters when looking to focus one's literature review. It is useful to remember, however, that being too broad in terms of the keywords used will lead to too many references (often thousands) to handle, whereas being too focused may produce limited and orthodox returns.

Three of the pitfalls that might be encountered in conducting a literature search are:

1 The concept and label of the subject you are investigating might develop during the research process. For example, returning to our search under organizational knowledge, the wrong keywords can give some way-out titles, e.g. 'The organization of bees: knowledge of cellular structures'. Keywords clearly work better in some fields than others, but even these outlying titles can sometimes help to refine your objectives. If your search reveals many works on apiaries then you may be prompted into using hives and worker bees as at least appropriate metaphors for organizational knowledge; your conception of what is included in your subject expands. If no matches can be found, then different keywords, sometimes broader, will need to be used. If on the other hand the research is too wide, more specific keywords will need to be used.

2 Your own analysis will not be substituted by an existing detailed analysis of research literature. Researching, as we have discussed before, is not exclusively about refining what has been said by others, it is also in part an act of synthesis and in part

about evaluation. A detailed analysis of the subject will provide the keywords to commence the search but will not do it all for you.

3   One single document will not answer the essential points you are searching for. For example, a complex group of keywords such as: consumer, culture, scale, measure, psychometric, will not automatically lead to specialized articles in the marketing literature dealing with problems of cross-cultural equivalence of the scales of measures used in commercial consumer marketing research. It is even less likely to lead to a specific book on the subject. Consequently, when entering a library be willing and ready to consult a selection of materials.

A keyword search using ABI (ProQuest)

EXAMPLE
5.3

An example of too broad a keyword might be 'management' or 'innovation'. There will literally be hundreds of thousands of articles using this term, in many different disciplines, with different meanings and linked to different concepts. It may refer to different aspects of management or innovation. Too narrow a keyword might be crucial. The noun is a very specific form of knowledge asset, and while used internationally in no way captures the entire range of activity associated with new product development and exploitation. The point that we make here is that terminology is very important. In order to find out what one wants from the mass of information in the library, a researcher needs to identify his or her interests clearly. In the example below we illustrate how the use of different keywords and combinations of them give different results. The title of this search example is, 'How is management of innovation and new technology dealt with in the corporate social responsibility literature', the searches are limited between the years 1995 to 2010 in the database ABI (ProQuest). The numbers of hits returned are shown below.

Search string	Number of hits
Manage* AND innovat* AND tech*	71269
(Corporate responsibility OR environment) AND innovate*	41904
(Corporate responsibility OR environment) AND innovate* AND tech*	23051
Corporate responsibility AND tech*	691
Corporate responsibility AND innovate*	374
Corporate responsibility AND environment AND innovate*	140

Investigating different software

EXERCISE
5.2

In groups, decide one common research question/topic and let each member use different software to collect the literature. Compare and analyse the outcome. If the outcome differs, discuss why it differs and how you used different search terms.

SOURCES OF INFORMATION

As we have discussed in the examples of the literature used, management comprises a wide range of subjects and is continually expanding as a discipline and body of knowledge. Fortunately there are a number of bibliographical publications and document services that can assist in searches. General literature and bibliographical publications which are the key to information searching fall roughly into seven broad groupings:

1 World Wide Web (Internet)

2 Books

3 Journal articles

4 Conference and working papers of research in progress

5 Theses (PhD, MBA, MSc)

6 Government publications, official statistics, annual reports and company specific information

7 Reference works, guides to the literature (general/particular subject areas)

Each of these will be dealt with in detail separately but a good strategy for a researcher is to begin by exploiting what can be obtained physically or electronically through databases and licences from your own library. Out of the different sources of information mentioned above, conference papers and some books often demonstrate the 'latest' research in the field and therefore any research should make use of these sources in a complementing way. If necessary the research can be extended through borrowing books from other libraries through the inter-library loan system (bear in mind that this can take several weeks). Electronic resources have now extended to include books and many journals have a service that includes much if not all of their archive as well as articles approved for publication in future editions, which is invariably referred to as 'online early'. This offers advanced sight of articles accepted for publication in future editions. These electronic versions of the article are identical to those that will eventually be published (apart from the fact they have no date) in the journal and cannot be altered or changed.

Websites: the Internet as an enabler and an adjunct

One method of undertaking research that has become much more of an everyday action of both doing business and conducting management research is the Internet. From its beginnings in the late 1960s as a means of networking the US Defence Agency, through the introduction of the World Wide Web, to the current Internet information structure, the Internet has had a high input on the ways in which information flows and where information resides. Its impact is also felt in the way research is conducted.

Raymond Lee (2000) has outlined the potential uses of the Internet as an 'unobtrusive' way of gathering data for social research. He argues that the wide availability of personal computers now affect the researcher in a new way to acquire, store and manage data. The advantages are fourfold: first, access to 'unusual' groups has become easier, due to their increased visibility and the lessening of time and space constraints. Second, it is possible to trace patterns of social interaction and social trends through a record of Internet usage and perhaps through the tracing of Internet trends. Third, researching through the Internet may well provide a very reliable means of guaranteeing anonymity both to respondents and the researcher during research projects, which could be useful in researching sensitive topics. Fourth, the Internet may enable social researchers to trace social processes more easily than through face-to-face interaction.

One of the themes that we have touched on in Chapter 1 of this book is the importance of creativity. The Internet could encourage both respondents and researchers to be more playful in research projects. There are also the issues of ease and relative low cost (both in terms of time and resources), which research via the Internet provides. Surveys could be distributed more easily than through the post; email may provide a way both of making initial contact and conducting *ad hoc* interviews; and the Internet itself provides an enormous documentary resource for the researcher to exploit.

However, these advantages should perhaps be balanced with a number of obvious problems. First, the relativity of the data (as with any data) must always be considered; bluntly, is the source to be trusted? Data made available through governmental websites, for example, may be much more reliable than data posted by someone from a lobby group. (This of course, does not imply that state-sponsored websites are somehow value-free or neutral and should not be considered critically!) Second, the use of the Internet to conduct empirical data collection must also be considered in the light of the huge increase in electronic traffic over the last few years. Just as a survey may end up in the bin of a manager who receives it in the post, so might the email and attachment (perhaps even more so with the increase in viruses and the care with which people are reminded to open attachments). Response rates, therefore, may be at least as low as for postal surveys. Third, the lack of physical contact needs to be considered (what Lee (2000) calls the 'disembodied' nature of Internet interaction) and may lessen the richness of the data collected. Fourth, and relatedly, the impact of the 'asynchronous' nature of the majority of Internet interaction. This relates to the relatively small opportunity to communicate with respondents in 'real time' and may be something to consider when assessing data collection electronically.

The enormous information resource that is potentially available is both, as Lee suggests, a blessing and a curse. The sheer volume of information makes finding what you are looking for both more likely and more difficult. This is where **search engines** play their part. Lee (2000) has some suggestions when deciding which search engines to use, particularly the choice between the active and the passive. Active engines search (or 'crawl') through the Internet pages themselves, cataloguing by vocabulary used or by sites visited. Passive engines on the other hand, depend on the page 'owner' forwarding a description to the search engine administrator. Each has inherent advantages and disadvantages: active searching may generate more contemporary links, and a larger number; passive engines may however, be more relevant in the 'hits' presented to you.

Of course as with any data collection, the best way of moving forward is to try out different approaches. In this way experience will help the user decide between alternatives. The now ubiquitous Google does have a very useful offshoot called Google Scholar, which if used in the advanced search mode provides the most relevant links, is easy to use, is often the quickest and has no advertising. There are also social networking sites and a growing interest in web 2.0. Other search engines with similar offerings include:

- Webcrawler: www.webcrawler.com
- InfoSeek: www.infoseek.com
- Yahoo: www.yahoo.com
- Lycos: www.lycos.com
- Altavista   www.altavista.com

These search engines can offer different results from the same search, therefore it might be worthwhile not to depend only on one source or search engine, but to search for the information through different sources. Social network websites such as LinkedIn, Facebook and Twitter offer a new means to share research ideas and literature review tips in real time. People who are reading an interesting article or book can 'update their social network status' to share this article or to have an online discussion about the content or concepts of an article. Wikis can also be useful sources of information. They are online databases that allow users to add and edit content – the most well-known of these is Wikipedia. As a range of users can change the content of the database, researchers should use their common sense and verify anything they are taking from a Wiki source. Therefore if approached with caution, a Wiki can be a useful way of gathering preliminary information.

Finally, a caveat. Lee (2000) notes that an increasing amount of the information and data available through the Internet will be charged for. The initial ethos of the Internet, based on sharing information and ideas in a safe academic forum, has become commercialized through both online trading and the sale of data. As a rule of thumb, it may be best to work with the idea that the Internet will not provide 'something for nothing' in terms of data. Often your library will subscribe to journals allowing you direct access to articles, but equally often you will be asked to pay a fee to get access. It is worth checking alternative sites to determine whether what costs through one is free through another. The Internet is undoubtedly of great use in identifying and honing research questions and issues, and in facilitating communication and it will continue to grow in importance.

In connection with getting hold of specific material of relevance, it is important to know something about a bibliographical aid known as 'citation indexing'. Briefly, a citation index brings together all the other papers that have subsequently made reference to a given paper, and is the only indexing method that enables a researcher to search forward in the literature. This type of indexing is based on the concept that an author's references to previous articles identify much of the earlier work that is relevant to his present paper, and are themselves the best indicators of its subject. The Science Citation Index has been available to researchers in the sciences and technologies since 1963. In 1973, the **Social Sciences Citation Index** was launched, with coverage of 1,000 journals. This was a major development in literature searching for social scientists, as its value increases as the database grows in size with the passage of time. To begin searching for articles on a particular subject in the Social Sciences Citation Index, a researcher only needs to know the name of one author who has written something on or related to the chosen topic; he can then find all the articles up to the present that have cited the earlier article.

Books

Most libraries classify books in subject themes according to one of the major published classification schemes (for example, the Dewey Decimal System), often with some modification to suit local requirements. Browsing among books can be a useful way of providing an overview but it is always likely to be a partial one. If all aspects of literature were grouped in a single place, literature searching would be a simple undertaking. Often, however, the subjects are scattered around and range, for example, from economics to industrial sociology to psychology. The logic of this stems from the general structure of knowledge that is far from being immediately obvious. Sometimes it can be difficult to know where to classify a book, for example, the consequences to business after UK entry into the single European market. The online catalogue is, therefore, the best place to start a search for books. If the subject is a fairly specific one, it could be the case that there are no books on the topic and there may be a need to look under a wider heading in the subject or keyword index. Here you are likely to find several references and if there is a bibliography, it will refer to other works such as books and papers in journals. This should point the way to other potentially useful material.

The subject index and catalogue can also point to bibliographies that exist in the library's stock. If it is obvious at this stage that there are other published bibliographies that are relevant to the research then the next step is to consult one of the guides that list bibliographies. The Bibliographic Index Plus (www.hwwilson.com/Databases/biblio.htm) is a list of both separately published bibliographies and those occurring in books and articles. By examining this, it should be possible to find references to promising bibliographies including books that are in stock in the library.

The output of published material has become so great that it is unlikely that any library, however large, will be able to meet all of a researcher's needs from its own resources. So, once the stock of books available in one's university library has been reviewed, you may want to take things further and see what else has been written. To do this, the appropriate national bibliographies need to be consulted listing the book output of individual countries. Copac provides free access to the merged online catalogues of 19 of the largest university research libraries in the UK and Ireland (www.copac.ac.uk). The British Library Public Catalogue (BLPC) offers free online access to over 10 million records of items in the British Library Collection, and includes a document ordering link (http://opac97.bl.uk). Similarly the Bulletin Board for Libraries (BUBL) provides access to online public access catalogues by region (http://link.bubl.ac.uk:80/libraryopacs). The British Library offers a social sciences web portal: www.bl.uk/reshelp/bldept/socsci/about/socialsciences.html.

A comprehensive list of links to world libraries is usually available on most university websites. To undertake an effective search you will need to know the foreign equivalents of the subject keywords being searched and access to a translator or interpreter may also be necessary. For the non-linguist, there are information sources that refer to works that have been translated, such as the Index Translationium and the British Lending Library's BLL Announcement Bulletin.

Before concluding this section about books, it is worth mentioning the existence of catalogues from other libraries that can be a very useful source. These printed or online catalogues are, of course, restricted to the holdings of the library concerned, but are not limited to the output of any particular country. Very large libraries such as the British Library or the Library of Congress (USA) contain almost all publications in the English-language and a large percentage (although on the decline) of foreign-language publications. In addition, there are such online national/international catalogues as Copac, Bibliothèque Nationale (Paris), Deutsche Bibliothek (Germany) and Biblioteca Nacional (Spain). Specimens of more specific catalogues can be supplied by such institutes as: the Institute of Chartered Accountants, which goes under the name of Current Accounting Literature and also by the

Baker Library from the Harvard Business School, entitled Core Collection – An Author and Subject Guide (www.library.hbs.edu).

Journal articles

For research, perhaps the most important area is the access you can get to journals. These hold the key to the most up-to-date research and are the sources that researchers need to make sure they cite on proposals; they also represent the means by which the most recent research is placed in the public domain, and because of the screening employed (through the refereeing process adopted by the highest ranked journals) they represent quality. There are a number of ways in which articles on relevant topics are to be found. For example, the researcher could simply leaf through some of the best-known business journals in order to spot how journals deal with particular topics or themes by using their annual indices, which usually produce a subject and author guide, but usually a student would register with **Zetoc**. Zetoc provides access to the British Library's electronic table of contents of around 20,000 journals and 16,000 conference proceedings annually. The service is free to all those in higher education institutions. What you get is not full text but instead tables of contents; however, once an issue has been identified of interest, links enable you to access the full text. Complete Exercise 5.3 below to register with Zetoc (http://zetoc.mimas.ac.uk).

EXERCISE
5.3

Set up a ZETOC alert

Log into the homepage of Zetoc at http://zetoc.mimas.ac.uk. You should then enter your username and password, which you should be able to get from your central library. Your institution may use Athens logins or individual institutional logins but your librarian should be able to give you this information. Once logged in follow the instructions on the site. More detailed information about setting up a Zetoc Alert may be found at http://zetoc.mimas.ac.uk/alertguide.html.

Some libraries keep up-to-date summary catalogues to be consulted on the spot, i.e. content pages of everything new in a particular month. And, it is often also possible to sign up with publishers to be informed of new issues. However, a far more effective way of locating articles is to use the appropriate abstracting and indexing services, since by doing this a researcher can scan as many as several hundred journals at one time; where articles appear useful the expectation now is for them to be able to offer a full text service. As you are able to view the abstracts first it will help you decide whether an article is worth downloading or not. Using this approach, it is possible to discover references that a researcher would not normally come across. The abstracts give the precise reference for an article and offer a summary, while the 'index' is limited to simply the bibliographic details. Some of these abstracting and indexing databases also offer access to the full text article directly from the database, though where this isn't the case use the library catalogue of your home institution to see if the library subscribes to this journal either in print or electronically.

Most Business Schools' libraries as well as several universities offer a wide range of abstracts and indices covering a range of management themes, the majority of which are now in electronic format. Perhaps the two most useful general services are ABI Inform and Business Source Premier. Emerald is also a full text database of journals although it only covers Emerald's own journals.

In addition to the general 'abstracts and indices' there are several others that focus on specialized fields, such as, for example, International Abstracts of Human Resources, International Abstracts in Operations Research, Marketing Information Guide, Packaging Abstracts, Psychological Abstracts, Training Abstracts and many more. Others such as Public Affairs Information Service Bulletin (PAIBS) are very useful for retrieving information on affairs connected with the international public environment, while the current Technology Index, although being on the boundary of management studies can also be very useful.

Keeping yourself abreast of what is coming out is essential. The majority of journal publishers offer an alerting service whereby researchers can be informed of new articles published in their areas of interest and some libraries have their own systems on offer. An easy way to keep yourself regularly updated is to log onto Zetoc Alert. This is an Internet based awareness service, which sends out emails to alert of new publications in the field that is specified (http://zetoc.mimas.ac.uk).

Theses, dissertations and research in progress

For those undertaking higher degree research as well as those who are undertaking research generally, it is often important to know what theses have already been completed, if only to identify the individuals to make contact with. There are several ways of knowing just what research is being conducted. In Britain theses are available through the Index to Theses with Abstracts accepted for Higher Degrees by the Universities of Great Britain and Ireland (published by Aslib). Dissertation Abstracts International provides electronic access to international dissertation abstracts by library subscription, or free on the Internet for two years (http://proquest.umi.com). In France, there is a national register of current theses managed by the University de Paris-X Nanterre. There is also DOGE, an abstract of the underground literature on management in France, mainly research papers and theses.

In the US, Dissertation Abstracts International offers one of the largest and up-to-date lists. It is divided into several parts: Humanities and Social Sciences (Section A); Physical Sciences and Engineering (Section B) and the European Abstracts (Section C). Dissertation Abstracts covers most theses produced in North America, copies of which can be borrowed within a few weeks at a very reasonable price from the British Library Document Supply Centre at Boston Spa. Management is contained in Volume 8 of the index. A check needs to be made under the keyword. If there are no titles of interest listed, then the individual volumes will need to be checked. If no theses are found, it should not be considered a waste of time since it is helping to ensure that there is no duplication of research. As the cost (in time) of duplication of research is high, searches of this kind can be a very worthwhile exercise. There is currently an initiative under way through Je-S to make this process all electronic. The European countries have similar systems to the American Dissertation Abstracts. For example, in Germany, the Jahresverzeichnis der Deutchen Hochshulschriften and in Britain, the Aslib Index to Theses, as mentioned above.

Information on research actually in progress is not easy to come by and it is here that experienced researchers, who tend to build up contacts over the years, have a considerable advantage. Being members of a British Academy of Management Special Interest Group or one of the American Academy of Management Divisions can give access to a vibrant network. The Economic and Social Science Research Council's newsletter *The Edge* brings the latest and most topical social science research to key opinion formers in business, government and the voluntary sector. Other possible sources of information include the registers of current research published by several leading Business Schools. In France there are newsletters such as *Courier du CNRS*.

Government publications, official statistics

On a case-by-case basis, libraries choose to classify official publications either separately or include them within the general catalogue. In Britain, researchers should refer to the Annual List of Government Publications or, if necessary, to the monthly or daily lists. This involves first looking at the index at the back of each list for headings that appear to be of interest or 'fit' the keyword describing the subject. There are many published introductions to government publications and official statistics and many libraries produce their own guides to their stocks. For more comprehensive information on what official statistics are available, the Central Statistical Office's Guide to Official Statistics is an invaluable source (www.statistics.gov.uk). An online resource of the British Publications Current Awareness Scheme is available online (www.bopcas.com/). Another useful free electronic resource is the National Statistics website (www.statistics.gov.uk).

Some international organizations also offer important statistical information. The Organization for Economic Co-operation and Development (OECD), for example, provides information on the economic indicator statistics on international trade and statistics on products (see OECD online at www.oecd.org/statistics). The FMI sums up the main economic and financial data for all EU member states. The ONU statistical directory and the Communantes European (Official Statistics Bulletin for the EU members) are both useful sources. An online catalogue for The Stationery Office (formally the HMSO) can be found at www.thestationeryoffice.co.uk.

Reference books, general and specialized bibliographic guides

The final group of publications that a researcher needs to know about are a group of publications which are general guides to the literature or subject areas. New researchers can use reference works, for example to become aware of any organizations relevant to their interests and these can indeed be fertile sources of information.

In the UK, consult publications such as A.J. Watford's *Watson's Guide to Reference Material* (1980–87), *Current British Directories* or its European counterpart, the *Current European Directory*. Directories such as *Kompass* and *Who Owns Whom* (the FT500 is now only available through the FT website) also constitute useful sources of business information. In France, researchers could use, for example, *Sources d'Informations Statistiques*, published by Editions Ytem or the *Bottin Administratif*. For those who need detailed financial information on a company, services such as FAME (Bureau van Dijk, www.bvdep.com) or Global Business Browser (OneSource, www.onesource.com/index.htm) supply financial data on most sizable businesses as well as the main European companies, as the DAFSA does in France (www.ihsglobalinsight.fr/produits/). Data is also held for unit trusts. Other sources are the *International Stock Exchange Yearbook* and a specialized journal published by the Financial Times Business Service, *Mergers and Acquisitions*, which includes relevant information on mergers and acquisitions. Services such as Datastream and Exstat give direct access to financial data. In France, Diane supplies electronic data on French businesses. Share prices can be consulted on Datastream, and on similar products such as Perfect Analysis and Hemscott, or on the financial pages of the *Financial Times* or the *Wall Street Journal* depending on the financial market being analysed. For up-to-date press comment on individual companies, the most useful are Lexis-Nexis or Factiva.

Conference papers and working papers series (WPS)

Conference papers and WPS are a good way to access 'new' research. Papers accepted in both working papers series and conference proceedings have been through a review process and can be considered as pre-publication versions of journal articles and books. As a result, it can be work in progress, not finalized work, under submission or forthcoming in a journal. Conference papers are published papers in the context of an academic conference, while working papers series often are published within a university. The main advantage of this source of information is that it is 'fresh research' and can be used in a literature review.

Organizing your material

To avoid being flooded with references whose contents and quotations are difficult to control, mechanisms for organizing become essential. We therefore recommend devising a system of storing your results, either an electronic database or something much simpler. There are both low-tech and high-tech options here. The low-tech option is to use standard handwritten record cards in subject and alphabetical order: don't dismiss these just because we live in an electronic age! Having things permanently visible can be an advantage as we will see in Chapter 8 when we examine the various merits of different methods of data analysis. The high-tech option involves using computer software such as Endnote or ProCite to which the references can be exported. The advantages of using reference software are twofold. First, if the lists are still too large they permit filtering using features such as keyword and journal searches. They also allow the researcher to collate the different lists from the different databases, and so remove duplicate studies. Second, once the relevant studies have been reduced to a manageable size, they allow the researcher to organize them according to relevance of their own research topic. It is at this stage that the studies can be divided into: relevant, partially relevant and less relevant. Universities and colleges often subscribe to a specific package such as EndNote or ProCite, which are packages specifically designed to help students keep track of their references, and it can be worth trying the software before deciding which one to buy. They can be set up in such a way that the reference can be linked through to your institution's electronic library and so in effect an electronic copy of all your references can be held at the touch of a button. Remember that this usually only works from the university's main site and off-site use of this link can be difficult. Figure 5.2 illustrates references in the EndNote reference system from a PhD student in Management.

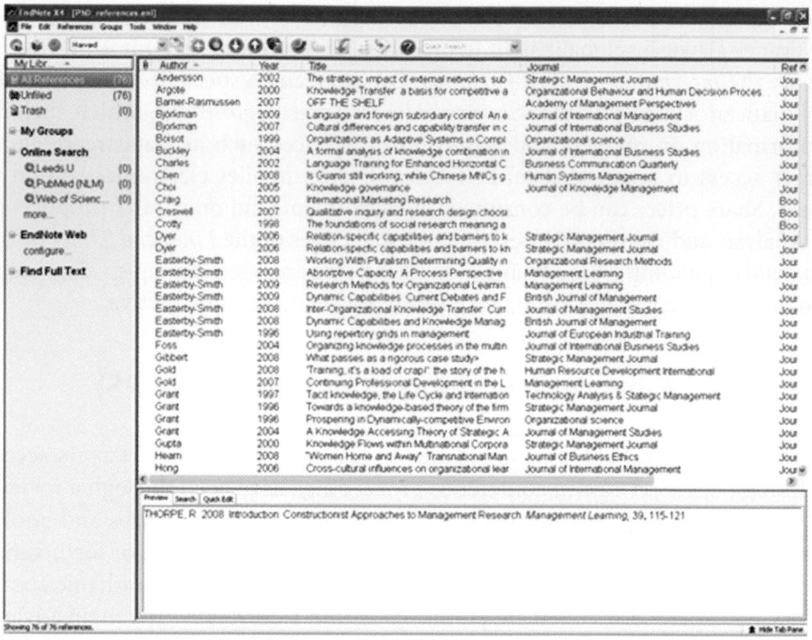

FIGURE 5.2

Endnote
reference list

These packages do not have to be used in conjunction with bibliographic databases, and can be used as an electronic catalogue of those studies you have deliberately and personally chosen. The advantages of these packages are that in addition to being widely available and often accessible simply through registering as a student, they are also compatible with the growing number of bibliographic databases. The process of installing EndNote produces an additional tool bar in Microsoft word. This can help speed up the addition of references to the review and bibliography through enabling the 'cite while you write' option. The use of EndNote can aid the search process to better integrate emerging review themes. For example, by using the search functionality within the program the literature collected can be interrogated in more detail.

It might appear an obvious point to make, but one tip is to make sure all references are recorded. No one will believe it but once books have been read and returned to the library shelves or radio programmes have finished and the day they were broadcast forgotten, it is extremely difficult and very time-consuming to find references unless the researcher has developed some kind of systematic cataloguing system. If the researcher has a personal style that precludes systematically writing on cards or typing them into a database as the literature is being read, then at the very least go for a low-tech option of using a cardboard box or a shopkeeper's spike for references. This way they are in one place and can be retrieved later! Using a software package goes a long way to alleviating this problem. Once stored and backed up they can be used again and again. As time goes on, you can build up your own library of references, with associated abstracts and keywords. This software also enables you quickly and accurately to create your own bibliographies when writing and to do so according to the dictates of all manner of citation styles (typically these will be Harvard or Chicago styles).

Whatever system you use there is a need to build bibliographies from the start of a research project. The bibliography must not be written at the end of the research work. One can simply use a text organizer such as Word, which allows material to be sorted alphabetically. What follows is how you might approach a review of a particular area or field. First, you need to consider the type of review that is to be undertaken. Remember, the aim you are trying to achieve is how the findings and concepts of what has gone before help the argument that you are trying to develop. The review is seeking to identify themes, patterns and contradictions that help you to take a position and locate your own work.

Experience of doing a literature review

Select two journal articles relevant to your topic. The first should have been published within the last two years, the second should have been published before 1990. You should identify the following themes in each paper:

1 What was the research question?

2 What theoretical approach underpins each paper?

3 What methodology was adopted for the collection of data?

4 How were the data analysed?

5 What were the nature and the size of the sample?

6 What were the key findings?

7 How many times has the article been cited?

CONCLUSION

In this chapter we have aimed to provide insights into where to find relevant literature and other sources for a research project, and what aspects are important when actually writing a literature review. The key points of this chapter, therefore, are:

 The literature review is a continuous process, requiring writing and re-focusing throughout the research project.

 The review should be used as a tool to strengthen your personal argument, rather than blindly repeating what has been said before.

 As with research in general, the review is about crafting.

Which literature researchers use for their literature review is, of course, influenced by the questions they want to answer in their research project. The questions that researchers ask in their research projects are in turn affected by the philosophical assumptions that underlie the way they see the world. Which different philosophical assumptions there are, and in what way these may direct a research project, will be discussed in the next chapter.

FURTHER READING

Gash, S. (2000) *Effective Literature Searching for Research*, Aldershot: Gower.

Huff, A. (2009) *Designing Research for Publications*. London: Sage.

Petticrew, M. and Roberts, H. (2006) *Systematic Reviews in the Social Sciences: A Practical Guide*. Malden, MA: Blackwell.

Tranfield, D., Denyer, D. and Smart, P. (2003) 'Towards a methodology for developing evidence-informed management knowledge by means of systematic review', *British Journal of Management*, 14 (3): 207–22.

CREATING QUALITATIVE DATA

6

LEARNING OBJECTIVES

 To understand a range of different methods of data collection that belong to the qualitative research tradition.

 To understand how these approaches of data collection offer different perspectives according to the focus of the research.

 To appreciate the advantages and disadvantages to the various qualitative data collection methods.

METHODS FOR QUALITATIVE DATA COLLECTION

In this chapter we examine a number of approaches and tools for collecting qualitative data; these are called modalities. Many of them are quite loosely specified, which offers the researcher considerable opportunity to use their creative abilities. We have attempted to move away from presenting a simple list of methods and instead we have grouped them into headings that depict to us the basic approaches that are available.

First, we discuss approaches that set out to collect information (data) from organizational members whether they are managers or employees, which we call natural *language data*. This approach aims to use language data to gain insights into social and organizational realities. This takes place through discovering the views, perceptions and opinions of both individuals and groups through the language they use; the main method to achieve this is the **in-depth interview**. Valuable information can also be gained, however, from diaries and the examination of a range of textual data such as company reports or video recordings. Our second grouping is through *observation*, such as ethnographic approaches. Here the kind of data that is collected is rather different from that in the first group and includes the examination and understanding of symbols, settings and observations in a context. There are various methods that fall into this category, including participant observation, non-participant observation and, increasingly, visual methods. Third, we examine how understandings might be gained through *interaction*. Examples of interactive methods are photographs or other **visual metaphors**. Often this approach involves research through close and direct interaction and co-operation of the researcher with individuals or groups. We also address approaches to the co-production of knowledge using action-research-type methods and we discuss the practicalities of Mode 2 methods of knowledge production. Fourth, this chapter contains a section that looks at some general issues that surround qualitative methods of data collection, which will include a brief discussion of the use of case studies, and a reminder of ethical issues involved and the necessity of reflexivity of the researcher's own involvement.

Access is an issue that relates to all modalities mentioned above. It affects the modalities through language (e.g. interviews), observation (e.g. ethnography) and interaction (e.g. action research). *Securing access* may have an effect on the research. Once a gatekeeper has shown some interest then preliminary contacts are best followed up by letter, email or telephone call. This can fulfil three distinct purposes. The first is credibility, especially if the approach can be made using the headed notepaper of an independent body – a university, institute or college. Second, it may assist co-operation in the future; and third, it provides the opportunity to send further details about the research. This latter is the researcher's opportunity to set out in detail what is required. The phenomenal growth in business and management courses over the last two decades has had both negative and positive effects on the likelihood of gaining access. On the one hand there are now a lot of other students and institutions competing for access to a limited number of organizations; on the other hand, there are now large numbers of managers who have taken management degrees themselves (and some may still be studying on part-time schemes), and they are likely both to understand and to be sympathetic towards the researcher's objectives.

COLLECTING DATA THROUGH LANGUAGE

Interview preparations

Before adopting any method of data collection, it always helps to be clear about the overall objectives of the research. This applies to the choice of the in-depth interview as a method, as well as to the wide range of ways in which interviews may be conducted. Jones (1985) highlights a number of issues that researchers need to consider in order for interviews to be successful. The first is the problem that all researchers must resolve – how much structure to put into the interview. Jones argues that no research exists without presupposition, by which she means all researchers have some level of understanding prior to the interview of the research surrounding the interview topic. She further outlines that researchers often enter the interview situation with some key questions; however, these are likely to change as new and interesting areas are uncovered and researchers may want to tailor their questions depending on the participant's position or response.

Interviews can be highly formalized and structured, for example, as in market research, or they can be quite unstructured, akin to free-ranging conversations (see Table 6.1). Although interviewing is often claimed to be 'the best' method of gathering information, its complexity can sometimes be underestimated. It is time-consuming to undertake interviews properly, and they are sometimes used when other methods might be more appropriate. If researchers wish to obtain answers to a number of fairly simple questions then a questionnaire might well be more appropriate. Highly structured interviews are based on carefully prepared sets of questions piloted and refined until the researcher is convinced of their 'validity'. The assumption is made that the interviewer will ask each interviewee the same question in the same tone of voice. The simplest form of such interviews is where there are short answers to questions and the interviewer simply ticks boxes and no deep thought is required by either party. These are the type of interviews that take place in the shopping areas of towns and cities every Saturday morning and their primary aim is to gain a quantitative result from a carefully targeted sample (see Chapter 9). Within certain limits of accuracy (dependent on such things as the choice of location and the time of day that respondents are asked) we can then infer that, for example, 20 per cent of a population thinks one thing, and 10 per cent thinks another. Large numbers (hundreds or thousands) will be required in order to have confidence that the responses obtained can be generalized to the population at large and this, for example, is very much the territory of the professional political pollster.

Particularly in the case of using less-structured interviews, we would encourage researchers as they collect their data to make choices as to which line of questioning they should explore further, and which lines of inquiry to discard. Certainly, researchers need frameworks from which to plot out the developing themes, but as Jones reminds us, although they are to some extent tied to their frameworks, researchers should not be 'tied up by them'. One way in which this can be achieved is to prepare a checklist, sometimes referred to as a **topic guide**, which can be used as a loose structure for the questions. Although there may be some deviation from the sequence in order to follow interesting lines of inquiry and to facilitate an unbroken discussion, the interviewer should attempt to cover all the issues mentioned.

TABLE 6.1 Types of interview

Level of Structure	Type of Interview
Highly structured	Market research interview
Semi-structured	Guided open interview
Unstructured	Ethnography

Finally, on the subject of structure, the researcher should be warned against assuming that a 'non-directive' interview, where the interviewee talks freely without interruption or intervention, is the way to achieve a clear picture of the interviewee's perspective. This is far from true. It is more likely to produce no clear picture in the mind of the interviewee of what questions or issues the interviewer is interested in, and in the mind of the interviewer, of what questions the interviewee is answering! Too many assumptions of this kind lead to poor data, which is difficult to interpret. Researchers are therefore likely to be more successful if they are clear at the outset about the exact areas of their interest. In the section on avoiding bias this issue is dealt with in more detail.

It is important to be aware of the advantages and disadvantages of the different ways of conducting interviews. Whereas structured interviews allow for a high degree of standardization of questions and answers, more open (or semi-structured and unstructured) interview questions often give a higher degree of confidentiality as the replies of the interviewees tend to be more personal in nature. In addition, the interviewer does have the opportunity to identify non-verbal clues that are present, for example, in the inflection of the voice, facial expressions or the clothes that the interviewee is wearing; these can be used to develop secondary questions. Sometimes these verbal clues may offer important reasons for misinformation (Sims, 1993).

This chapter deals primarily with in-depth interviews where the main purpose is to understand the meanings that interviewees attach to issues and situations in contexts that are not structured in advance by the researcher. For a more detailed use and application of highly structured questionnaires, readers should refer to Chapters 9 and 10.

Skills required

Understanding issues from an interviewee's point of view can be extremely difficult, especially when the respondent may not have a clearly articulated view of the answers to the questions posed, or may not wish to divulge sensitive information. It is here that the skills of the interviewer come to the fore.

McClelland (1965) conducted careful studies about common sense notions of 'motivation'. He concluded that people cannot be trusted to say exactly what their motives are, as they often get ideas about their own motives from commonly accepted half-truths. For example, a person may say that he is interested in achievement because he has made money.

But a careful check using different probing methods may reveal quite a different picture. Often people simply are not aware of their own motives. Mangham (1986) in his studies of managerial competence met this problem. From his survey work conducted quantitatively, he found that many managers sought subordinates who could better motivate staff and act in leadership roles within their organizations. In follow-up interviews he was able to ask managers exactly what they meant by leadership. Some gave ambiguous answers and became confused, offering examples of leadership that ranged from highly autocratic styles to highly democratic forms.

From a positivistic standpoint, the fact that there is ambiguity about the meaning of 'leadership' invalidates the research, but for the in-depth interviewer who probes, questions and checks, this is important data. The fact that people are confused and cannot agree on what they mean by leadership or the way they construct particular situations is the essence of the research. The skills of an interviewer then, centre on the ability to recognize what is relevant and remember it, or tape it, so that afterwards detailed notes can be made. This requires one to be perceptive and sensitive to events, so that lines of inquiry can be changed and adapted as one progresses. Above all, interviewers need to be able to listen, and to refrain from projecting their own opinions or feelings into the situation. This is more difficult than it sounds, since one of the ways of obtaining trust is to empathize with the respondent. The interviewer needs to listen to what the person wants to say, and what she does not want to say, without helping (Mayo, 1949). In recognizing these situations, non-verbal data might be crucial in providing clues, for example the loss of eye contact, or a changed facial expression. From time to time during the interview, as patterns or uncertainties arise from the interview, it is useful to check one understands by summarizing what has been said. This should be presented as a way of seeking clarification. The process of 'testing out' is a way of safeguarding against assuming too quickly that understanding has been achieved.

Laddering

As questions are asked, the researcher might like to think about how to get more from one question. Employing the technique of *laddering* will help the respondent move from statements of fact or descriptive accounts about the questions posed upwards in such a way that they gradually begin to reveal the individual's value base. The way to achieve this is to ask 'why' type questions. An example of this process can be seen in Example 6.1, and the hierarchical value map to which it relates is shown in Figure 7.30. The technique is very valuable for qualitative researchers; however, sensitivity and common sense do need to be applied as a persistent use of wide questions can spoil an interview as the respondent will eventually run out of things to say. Varying the way in which the question 'why' is asked, as Susan Baker does in Example 6.1, will make the exchange more varied and interesting.

Laddering down is where the researcher seeks to obtain illustrations and examples or occurrences of events. For example, the researcher might say, 'Could you give me an example of that?' Or, 'When was the last time that happened to you?' Through such a process, it is possible to explore a person's understanding of a particular construct. A laddering up-and-down using five or six questions (the number of themes contained in a topic guide) will quite easily fill out the whole of an interview, while in the process gaining significant insights into the topic under investigation.

Laddering

Question: Anything else about the design?

Answer: I think the weight of the shoe is important. The shoes shouldn't be too heavy.

Question: Why is this?

Answer: Because a lighter shoe is more comfortable.

Question: Why is this important to you?

Answer: It means I can move around quickly at tennis …

Question: Tennis is important to you?

Answer: Yes … I like it … It means I can get some fresh air … It's good for the heart, the nerves and your cholesterol … It makes me feel better. I feel good when I play tennis.

Source: Baker and Knox, 1995: 85

Experiment in laddering

In pairs, ask one another a simple question that relates to a personal view or preference the person might have. Then try to ladder up from this question to see if you can learn something about the person's values (normally this can be done by asking 'why' type questions). Then ladder down to see if you can learn something about the detail that surrounds these preferences (this is normally done by asking about specific instances).

Avoiding becoming biased

Readers will see in Chapter 9, on quantitative research methods, that **interview bias** – where the process of conducting an interview might influence the responses given – is regarded as crucial. With in-depth interviewing the issue is a slightly different one. Since the aim of in-depth interviews is to uncover the meanings and interpretations that people attach to events, it follows that there is no one 'objective' view to be discovered which the process of interviewing may bias. However, there is a very real concern about interviewers imposing their own reference frame on the interviewees, both when the questions are asked and when the answers are interpreted. The researcher is in something of a dilemma for, as has been suggested in an earlier section, open questions may avoid bias, but they are not always the best way of obtaining the information one may wish to know; nor are they always the best way of putting an interviewee at ease. But the issue of bias gives a pull in the other direction.

In order to avoid bias, there is often the tendency for researchers to leave questions open. There will be some occasions when researchers will want to focus on discovering responses to specific alternatives, and in this case **probes** can be useful as an intervention technique to improve, or sharpen up, the interviewee's response. A number of probes are listed in Example 6.2 below.

Probes in data collection

EXAMPLE
6.2

- The basic probe simply involves repeating the initial question and is useful when the interviewee seems to be wandering off the point.

- Explanatory probes involve building onto incomplete or vague statements made by the respondent. Ask questions such as: 'What did you mean by that?', 'What makes you say that?'

- Focused probes are used to obtain specific information. Typically one would ask the respondent, 'What sort of ...?'

- The silent probe is one of the most effective techniques to use when the respondent is either reluctant or very slow to answer the question posed. Simply pause and let him or her break the silence.

- The technique of drawing out can be used when the interviewee has halted, or dried up. Repeat the last few words he or she said, and then look at the interviewee expectantly or say, 'Tell me more about that' or 'What happened then?'

- Giving ideas or suggestions involves offering the interviewee an idea to think about – 'Have you thought about ...?', 'Have you tried ...?', 'Did you know that ...?', 'Perhaps you should ask Y ...'

- Mirroring or reflecting involves expressing in your own words what the respondent has just said. This is very effective because it may force the respondent to rethink his or her answer and reconstruct another reply, which will amplify the previous answer – 'What you seem to be saying/feeling is ...' To avoid bias, probes should never lead. An example of a leading probe might be: 'So you would say that you were really satisfied?' Instead of which the interviewer should say: 'Can you explain a little more?' or 'How do you mean?'

Approaches to data collection

In-depth interviews The importance of in-depth interviews is summarized by Burgess (1982: 107): '[the interview] is ... the opportunity for the researcher to probe deeply to uncover new clues, open up new dimensions of a problem and to secure vivid, accurate inclusive accounts that are based on personal experience'. Most interviews are conducted on a one-to-one basis, between the interviewer and the interviewee. The label 'qualitative

interview' has been used to describe a broad range of types of interview, from those that are supposedly totally non-directive, or open, to those where the interviewer has prepared a list of questions, which he or she is determined to ask, come what may. While, as Jones (1985) outlines, there are a range of practices and therefore theory between these two extremes of interviewing technique, the main aim of qualitative interviewing is generally seen as attempting to gain an understanding from the respondent's perspective, which includes not only what their viewpoint is but also why they have this particular viewpoint (King, 2004). As Kvale (1996) notes, the aim of qualitative interviews should be to collect information that captures the meaning and interpretation of phenomenon in relation to the interviewee's worldview (see Chapter 8 on phenomenographic analysis). Researchers must therefore be able to conduct interviews so that the opportunity is present for these insights to be gained. Failure to achieve this might well result in a superficial exchange of information, which might well have been better achieved via a semi-structured questionnaire.

In order to be able to achieve these insights, the researcher will need to be sensitive enough and skilled enough to ensure that he or she not only understands the other person's views, but also, at times, assists individuals to explore their own beliefs. Later in this chapter, we will discuss a number of techniques that might help the researcher do this to advantage. Interviews, both semi-structured and unstructured, are therefore appropriate methods when:

1 It is necessary to understand the constructs that the respondent uses as a basis for his or her opinions and beliefs about a particular matter or situation.

2 The aim of the interview is to develop an understanding of the respondent's 'world' so that the researcher might influence it, either independently or collaboratively as in the case with action research.

3 The step-by-step logic of a situation is not clear; the subject matter is highly confidential or commercially sensitive; and there are issues about which the interviewee may be reluctant to be truthful other than confidentially in a one-to-one situation.

It is important to note that managers can sometimes prefer telephone interviews. They are easily rescheduled and as such offer more flexibility, and managers feel less committed, because they do not have an obligation to host the researcher at the setting. However, exactly because of these reasons, telephone interviews are not always of a benefit for a qualitative researcher and, therefore, it is very important *when* telephone interviews are used. They may, for example, prove very effective in the context of real-time and process-based research. In such research projects, researchers are interested in understanding the detail of a situation and an exact 'real-time' chronology of events. In order to establish chronologies, it is perfectly reasonable for the researcher to have frequent telephone conversations centred around current activities and decisions rather than retrospective developments. These kinds of telephone interviews are even more effective, as in such situations both the interviewer and interviewee have most likely already had face-to-face interviews and the additional telephone interviews simply increase the thickness of the data collected. Researchers though would be well advised to avoid telephone interviews if they have never met the interviewee before, but if they have already established a good relationship of trust then even fairly unstructured interviews over the phone can be successful.

Group and focus interviews   Interviews need not necessarily take place on a one-to-one basis, and for some types of investigation, group interviews can be very useful. These take the form of loosely structured 'steered conversations'. They are used extensively in market research and increasingly in politics.

In any interview, the skill of the interviewer both as initiator and facilitator is of vital importance. In focus group interviews this role is called a moderator, and the added complexity of the situation means that the skills of initiating and facilitating are of particular relevance in a group interview. As Walker (1985) outlines, a group interviewer should not attempt to conduct numerous interviews simultaneously but rather to create a situation where all participants feel comfortable expressing their views and responding to the ideas of those around them. Although the focus interview is loosely structured, it should never be entirely without structure (Stokes and Bergin, 2006). The format of the interview should be organized by using what is called a 'topic guide'. This is a résumé of the main areas of interest that are to be explored. It is designed so that while still covering the general areas of interest it also allows unforeseen areas to emerge. In addition, the discussion venue needs to be chosen with care. Ideally, in common with in-depth interviews, it should take place in surroundings within which the participants feel relaxed and unthreatened. This can often be on their home ground, for example in a meeting or conference room close to the office. Alternatively it might be in neutral territory such as a business school, a club or a hotel.

However, the problems of group interviews can sometimes outweigh the advantages. Social pressures can condition the responses gained, and it may well be that people are not willing to air their views publicly. Our own view is that criticisms such as this illustrate the mistake of applying the wrong criteria for assessing the technique. Focus group interviews can be extremely useful in applied market research studies and are used to great effect as an exploratory tool in other types of qualitative research. Curran and Downing (1989), for example, used the technique to good effect as a means of validating the questionnaire responses made by owner-managers in a largely quantitative study that sought to understand the utility of the UK government's consultation strategies with small- and medium-sized firms. Further reading is given at the end of the chapter for those who wish to study this method in more detail.

Diary methods   There is quite a long history of using diaries as a basis for social research in the UK, one of the most interesting examples being the Mass Observation studies during the Second World War. Here a substantial number of ordinary people were recruited to keep diaries of everything they did for one day each month, and they were also asked to report on specific days, such as bank holidays. Analysis of these diaries was intended to show how the British population in general was reacting to different aspects of the war (Calder and Sheridan, 1984). Diaries can be either quantitative or qualitative depending on the kind of information that is recorded. They can be useful in management and organizational research on a number of levels. At one level, diary keeping by organizational members can be a simple journal or record of events. A quantitative analysis might take the form of activity sampling from which patterns may be identified statistically. This approach is sometimes used by management services practitioners who wish to measure the frequency of certain activities so that they can reorganize or 'improve' the work, whereas at other times it is used by managers to reflect on aspects of their own work, like in time management analysis (see, for example, Stewart, 1967, 1982). At another level, diaries might take the form of a personal journal of the research process and include emergent ideas and results, reflections on personal learning, and an examination of personal attitudes and values, which may be important at the data analysis and writing up stages. At yet another level they can provide a rich qualitative picture of motives and perspectives, which allows the researcher to gain considerable insight into situations being examined. It is this latter use of a diary that we wish to explore in a little more detail here.

There are a number of advantages to using diaries. First, they provide a useful method for collecting data from the perspective of the employee. Whereas in participant observation the researcher cannot help imposing to some extent his or her own reference frame as the data is collected, in the diary study the data is collected and presented largely within the reference frame of the diary writer. Second, a diary approach allows the perspectives of several different writers to be compared and contrasted simultaneously, and it allows the researcher greater freedom to move from one situation or organization to another. Some detachment also prevents the researcher becoming too personally involved.

Third, they allow the researcher to collect other relevant data while the study is in progress and enable him or her to carry out much more analysis than the participant observer would be able to carry out in the course of their fieldwork. This is the opportunity to collect information not only from the perspectives of different individuals, but also through using different data sources. Finally, although diary studies do not allow for the same interaction and questioning, they can sometimes be an alternative to participant observation when, for example, it is impractical for a researcher to invest the time in an extended longitudinal study as observer.

A number of important lessons were learnt from a multiple diary study conducted by Bowey and Thorpe (1986) in an English coal mine during a national study into incentive schemes. These lessons are described in Example 6.3 below.

EXAMPLE 6.3

Diary study of incentive schemes

First, it was found to be important to select participants who were able to express themselves well in writing. In cases where there was doubt and a group of associates had been asked to keep a diary, a judgement had to be made as to the likely consequences of the individual taking offence if he was excluded. Second, some structure was found necessary to give the diarist focus. To assist this, a list of general headings developed from earlier pilot studies was provided.

Please write about the following:

1   Your relationships with other people, including your supervisor, your workmates, anyone you supervise and other people you come into contact with.

2   Any particular difficulties you encountered during the day with machinery, raw materials or other people.

(Continued)

(Continued)

3   If the incentive bonus scheme affected you at work, and if so in what way.

4   Anything you were especially pleased about or made you feel angry.

5   Anything else you feel is important, especially if it is anything to do with the incentive bonus scheme.

A third lesson highlighted was the need for continued encouragement and reassurance during the study. An earlier pilot study had left diarists very much to their own devices, and they had continued to write for only four to six weeks. In the main study, where regular contact was maintained and feedback given in the form of additional questions or classification, almost two-thirds of the sample kept writing into the third month, and more than a quarter completed the full three-month period. An improvement we might have made would have been to supplement the diaries with interviews. This would have enhanced the effect of maintaining interest as well as providing the opportunity to probe areas of interest further.

Fourth, the importance of the need for confidentiality was confirmed. In a pilot study, jotters had been issued to record instances that occurred during the day and this had led to problems. One particularly uncomplimentary entry in a respondent's jotter had been left in an accessible place and was read by the person described. This caused the relationships between the two people to be soured even though thoughts entered 'in the heat of the moment' did not generally reflect the opinions of the individual. It was therefore decided that even at the cost of a loss of spontaneity it was preferable for diaries to be written up away from the workplace.

Finally, the study confirmed individuals' willingness and enthusiasm for co-operating at every level. There was no evidence to justify the view that individuals might be nervous of participating in this kind of research. The experience showed that there was more nervousness among the researchers themselves who felt that they 'dare not ask' or that asking people to maintain a diary for up to three months would be unacceptable to those under study.

Source: Bowey and Thorpe (1986)

All diarists in the study described above (including those who stopped writing before the end of the three-month period) maintained that they had welcomed the opportunity to express their feelings, observations and opinions about their life and work to somebody who was interested. All maintained that they enjoyed writing them, and some confided that they were flattered that outsiders were taking an interest in them as individuals. No payment or other inducements were made, although pens and folders were regularly provided. This was sufficient reward for many and it reinforces the point, made in the section on interviewing, about how important it is to find out what individuals wish to gain from participating in the research. As with participant observation, the setting up of a research study such as this involves considerable time and effort. There were numerous meetings required to gain access and our purpose had to be explained to management and union officials separately. The practicalities of undertaking diary research are fully discussed in Bowey and Thorpe (1986).

Keeping a research diary

It is a good idea to keep a research diary in which you record the current stage of your research, your ideas about what is emerging that might represent findings and your contribution, as well as how you feel about the research at the time of writing. If there are difficult issues in relation to the research process, these should also be recorded.

In pairs, discuss whether you think keeping a research diary could help you, particularly in relation to your research approach.

Postcards   'Postcards as a method of data-gathering in organizations provide one means of overcoming some of the recognized difficulties of research' (Thorpe and Holt, 2009: 157). Postcards by post and email (e-postcards) can be used to overcome the problem of access in, for example, interviews, interpretation of events in an ethnography and hermeneutics within organizations. While interviews, diaries and ethnographies are some of the more traditional methods of obtaining an understanding of a complex social phenomenon, postcards are argued to offer a new perspective to overcome some of the barriers to the previous methods. Furthermore, it is an easy way to collect information, especially electronically. A postcard is designed as the traditional postcard from the nineteenth century, with a picture, addressee and sender details, and a few questions with space to answer these. The picture is often a metaphor of the research, or of something that can be associated and related to the research topic. The postcard design attracts immediate attention and has an easy structure. It is simple and quick for the respondent to answer a few questions and send the card back to the researcher. The response time is shorter with e-postcards than with postcards by post. The use of e-postcards can also save money if they are sent to a large sample. One further advantage of this method is that the data arrives 'transcribed', in written form, ready for the researcher to start the analysis. Figure 6.1 below illustrates how a postcard can take form.

General interview concerns

Using in-depth interview as your main method of obtaining qualitative data in a successful way, however, does not only depend on researchers' personal interview skills, their capacity to organize and structure their interviews and their ability to avoid bias. There are six important practical issues involved in conducting interviews that may affect the outcome of an interview and of which the researcher should be aware. These six issues are: obtaining trust, being aware of social interaction, using the appropriate language, getting access, choosing the location for the interviews and recording interviews.

Obtaining trust is an important element in ensuring that interviews will provide the researcher with the information he is looking for. Obtaining trust can be a difficult issue, especially in one-off interviews where the people involved have not met before. Failure to develop trust may well result in interviewees simply resorting to telling the researcher what they think he or she wants to know. But an open and trusting relationship may not be possible or sufficient when dealing with particular elites or individuals in positions of

Images of Britain: Stonehenge – Just a bunch of old stones or a pinnacle of human achievement in astronomy, engineering and spiritual insight?

Please answer the four questions below by clicking on and typing in the spaces and return as an email attachment to Professor Richard Thorpe at rt@lubs.leeds.ac.uk. **Many thanks**

What do you regard as your ultimate goal in business?	To be well known as excellent in ability to challenge thinking and develop the true potential of others, in a variety of ways, while enhancing my own life situation.
Why is this your goal?	Because I have realized that this is what I have always wanted to do from being a small child, and because it gives me great 'job' satisfaction.
Who/what helps or hinders you in reaching your goal?	Who/what helps? Having time allocated separately from family life helps me to focus on what needs doing My new found ability to strike up relationships and make opportunities by just ringing people up Persistence and determination Listening to what others say and then if necessary ignoring it Belief that I am doing the right thing for me at this time Finding a network of like-minded people Who/what hinders? Organising house and family Working alone
If you could picture your goal – what image or object would best symbolize it?	It would be a purple shiny runner bean seed – which embodies the development and growth which I support in every area of my life, from my garden to my business to my family and in my art-work.

SOURCE: GOLD, IN THORPE AND HOLT (2010)

FIGURE 6.1
Postcards

power, as we have discussed in Chapter 4. One way to obtain trust is to make sure that one is well clued up about the company. A scan through the company's website will give a quick impression of the issues that are currently considered significant. Another way to obtain the trust of the company one wishes to research is to present the research in a professional and enthusiastic way so that the company sees a benefit, as managers will be weighing up the likely costs (and benefits) of the potential intrusion.

Social interaction between the interviewer and the interviewee is another important factor that may influence the interview process. Jones (1985) suggests people will attribute meaning and significance to the particular research situations they are in. The questions an interviewer may ask and the answers an interviewee gives will often depend on the way in which their situations are defined. Similarly, Jones (1985) points out that interviewees will 'suss out' what researchers are like, and make judgements from their first impressions about whether they can be trusted and be told everything or whether they might be damaged in some way by data that could be so used. Such suspicions do not necessarily mean that interviewees will refuse to be interviewed, but it might mean, as Jones indicates, that they just 'seek to get the interview over as quickly as possible, with enough detail and enough feigned interest to satisfy the researcher that he or she is getting something of value but without saying anything that touches the core of what is actually believed and cared about in the research' (1985: 50). It is furthermore important to be able to recognize when an interviewer is being misinformed (Sims, 1993). Individuals will often select answers between complex truths, rather than providing the 'whole truth', simply because it would take too long to give all the nuances.

Using the appropriate language is another practical issue that should be kept in mind when preparing for and conducting one's research. It is not a good strategy to baffle a potential gatekeeper by using too many theoretical concepts, but clarity also needs to be ascertained with respect to the interviewee's use of language as what is said may not always be what is meant and the sky might indeed be blue like an orange. In Table 6.2 we provide a few examples of the way words may be interpreted.

The location of the interview and the setting in which the interview takes place is a fifth element that can be important. Using a manager's office, for example, might not be perceived as a neutral space by other employees, as was experienced first-hand in a study by Thorpe (Bowey and Thorpe, 1986). One strategy used by a PhD student, Neil, was to conduct interviews well away from the workplace. When researching into aspects of management development, he undertook this fieldwork by sitting in the first-class compartments of

TABLE 6.2　Use of words and the different impressions they can give

Words	Impression Given
Student	Implies an unskilled 'amateurish' inquiry, which may be a waste of time, although unthreatening.
Researcher	Implies a more professional relationship, although questions of access might need to be managed more carefully.
Interview	Implies a formal structured interrogation, which is under the control of the researcher.
Discussion	May make managers feel more relaxed and less threatened, with the potential for genuine exchange.

trains. He would sit next to executive-looking individuals armed only with a folder marked 'Management Development' in the hope that managers would talk to him. This they usually did, and without prompts he was able to elicit their views on a range of management development issues. What struck Neil was the extent to which the views and opinions expressed by managers, off-guard and to a person they were unlikely ever to meet again, contradicted the 'reality' contained in much contemporary management literature. Had the interview taken place in the manager's office, the results might well have been quite different. This example not only illustrates how a researcher managed to obtain data that the manager may have found hard to articulate in his office; it also shows how a method can be undertaken in a 'natural setting' where each views the other as having equal status. This kind of research would normally be extremely costly, yet it does illustrate the lengths that might be required to obtain data.

Recording interviews is a sixth aspect that may affect the outcome of an interview. The decision of whether or not to use a tape recorder depends on an interviewee's anxiety about confidentiality and the use to which any information divulged can be put. Anxiety can be minimized, for example, by handing over the responsibility for switching the tape on and off to the interviewee, so that when he or she does not wish certain parts to be recorded, they can just switch off the machine. The main reasons in favour of using a tape recorder are that it aids the listening process and gives the opportunity of an unbiased record of the conversation. Good audio recordings are essential for accurate transcripts and also enable the researcher to re-listen to the interview, so he or she may well hear things that were missed at the time. A PhD student was even able to gain the trust of three managers of medium-sized companies, and these were examined in depth to such an extent that she was allowed to video them over a three-month period. This included during company meetings and also with clients (see Clarke, 2007). If interviewees oppose the use of recording interviews, researchers should depend on their own ability to take accurate notes and write down everything they are able to remember as soon as possible after the interview has ended.

Interviewing

The qualitative researcher needs to have good personal engagement to gain trust so that 'good' data can be obtained. Think about a time when you have been interviewed, either as a research respondent or at a recruitment interview. Did the interviewer appear to do anything to gain or lose your trust?

EXERCISE
6.3

Critical incident technique

One method of teasing out information, which is often used alongside interviews, is the **critical incident technique**. Proposed by Flanagan (1954), the technique offers an opportunity to go straight to the heart of an issue and collect information about what is really being investigated, rather than collecting large quantities of data that may or may not be directly relevant to this. Flanagan saw the approach as a 'a set of procedures for collecting direct observations of human behaviour in such a way as to facilitate their potential usefulness in solving practical problems and developing broad psychological principles'. By 'incident', Flanagan meant any observable human activity that is sufficiently complete in itself to permit inference or prediction to be made about the person performing the act. To be 'critical', the incident must occur in a situation where the purpose or intent of the act seems fairly clear to the observer and where its consequences are sufficiently definite to leave little doubt concerning its effect.

The technique has been used by qualitative researchers to great effect, particularly in conjunction with in-depth interviews as we have indicated above. Respondents might, for example, be asked to track back to particular instances in their work lives and to explain their actions and motives with specific regard to those instances. In his PhD research, Thorpe used the technique to ask owner-managers of small companies what had been their particular barriers to growth. At a given point in the interview he would ask if there had been any particular problems in the development of the company. He would then encourage the manager to explain that problem in some detail and illustrate how the problem was eventually surmounted. From this example he would begin to develop ideas about how individuals managed particular problems and about the information they used in doing this. It is important to use material that can be substantiated since there are criticisms of the technique relating to recall, and the natural tendency of individuals to use hindsight in rationalizing the past.

Secondary sources

Secondary data sources can consist of company or government reports, archival data, advertisements, newspaper articles and books. Secondary data sources are sometimes used as a complement to primary data sources (such as interviews), and sometimes data consists only of secondary sources. Secondary sources are often easily available in business research and can include information related to a specific company, market, customer, product and supplier. Search engines on the Internet can facilitate the search for secondary sources for websites and data banks.

The advantages of secondary data are, first, a saving of time and effort for the researcher. Second, the data sources are often of high quality especially if published by companies or governments. It does not mean that one should not be critical; one should always evaluate the source of the information. Third, a historical perspective can be achieved from secondary sources, which might not be feasible to get through primary data. The main difference between secondary data and primary data is that primary data is collected by the researcher and thus can frame the data collection after the research questions. The main advantage of secondary sources is that the data does not necessarily fit into the research we want to investigate. Therefore, it is essential to let the research questions guide and frame the data (Ghauri and Grønhaug, 2010).

COLLECTING DATA THROUGH OBSERVATION

Observations are the second modality presented in this chapter. Watson (1994) understands an ethnographic approach as implying some kind of close involvement in an organization. The object is to gain an insider perspective so that detailed understandings can be gained of other people's realities. Observations are often used in ethnographic approaches, but not always!

Bryman and Bell (2007) also reflect on the differences between ethnography and participant observation and conclude that they may not be entirely synonymous in people's minds, as many see ethnographic approaches as being more than simply observation alone and involving perhaps the collection of information in a variety of different ways. One of the interesting developments in recent times has been the way, through the growth of digital media, that researchers can get access to contemporary records made by individuals, so blurring the distinction between the researcher and the researched. Les Back, for example, has been illustrating how mobile phone cameras can be used by researchers to better understand every event. His work has been characterized as 'reinventing the observer' (2006); Figure 6.2 illustrates passengers walking down one of the London Underground tunnels following the bombings in 2005.

FIGURE 6.2
Tube passengers walking along the tracks following the London bombings

In our view, participant observation offers a broad framework for understanding ethnographic approaches. There is a very extensive literature on participant observation and ethnography, particularly in sociology and anthropology. Since organizations can easily be viewed as 'tribes' with their own strange customs and practices, it is by no means surprising that observation has also been used in organizational and management research. The purpose of participant observations is to 'uncover accounts which may not have been accessed by more formal methods like interviews' (Anderson, 2008: 151). The main challenge of participant observation is to maintain the balance between respecting the participants and their context.

The term can be divided into four different types of participant observations introduced in Table 6.3 below.

TABLE 6.3 Four types of participant observations

Complete participant conceals the intention to study and observes the setting the researcher is in.
Participant-as-observer does not conceal the intention of observation and instead builds relationships and participates in the context. This is the most common type of participant observation in management and business studies.
Observer as participant focuses on superficial relationships and does not have the same level of interaction as participant-as-observer. Here the researcher occasionally asks questions to gain an understanding.
Complete observer maintains distance to the object and context under study to mainly observe the surroundings.

SOURCE: ANDERSON, 2008

Donald Roy (1952) used the method to great effect when working as a company employee in the machine shop of a large company. He was able both to show how workers manipulated the piecework incentive scheme, and to understand the motives behind this. For anyone wishing to learn about the craft of participant observation and how the method might be written up, they could do no better than to read one or two of the original articles Roy produced from his research, 'Quota restriction and goldbricking in a machine shop' (1952) or 'Efficiency and "the fix"' (1954).

EXAMPLE 6.4

A social constructionist perspective conducting a rural ethnography

Experiencing tea plantation in Sri Lanka as the research site

In this research conducted by a PhD student, the aim of the research was to understand how different communities construct, maintain and change their self-identities. The research took place within the particular context of workers on a tea plantation in Sri Lanka. During the fieldwork phase, the student became far more aware of her own identity as a researcher than had hitherto been the case, and she was able to see and understand her identity both as an academic and as a Sri Lankan national. The latter enabled her to understand the social and cultural values and her Buddhist background enabled her to live with the community and adapt to the prevailing social norms. At times she saw herself as an outsider while at others she became an insider within the research site. Living both outside and inside different tea plantations, developing close relationships with local people, she was able to make sense of the practices and rituals she was able to observe. At times some of the elders became protective and supportive of her as a female young researcher. When inside the plantation, she seized the opportunity to spend as much time as possible with those on the plantation, talking and observing. Due to the size of the plantation, when 'on site' she was often accompanied by a representative from management, which, although meant to be helpful, made it difficult for her to get close and establish the kind of trusting relationship she would have liked. She later learnt that part of the difficulty

(Continued)

(Continued)

experienced was due to the fact that workers had even been warned by the police not to talk to strangers inside the plantation. This made them hesitant to approach her although as she got to know them she developed sufficient trust to win their confidence. The PhD student summarizes her experiences of an ethnographic approach as being a complex process. The process is not a logical step-by-step approach, and skills of sensitivity are required as well as a flexibility and willingness to change the plan and to be open to where the research might lead.

FIGURE 6A
Tea leaf picking

FIGURE 6B
Communal activity

The role of the participant observer is by no means simple. There are many different ways of handling it. In the previous edition we proposed a different scheme, based more explicitly on the possibilities available in management or organizational research. These were: researcher as employee; research as explicit role; interrupted involvement; and observation alone. These we still feel are useful to researchers; however we now propose a fifth, which Collinson (1992) refers to as 'semi-concealed research'.

Researcher as employee

One role a researcher can take is that of employee. Here he or she works within the organization, alongside others, to all intents and purposes as one of them. The role of researcher may or may not be explicit and this will have implications for the extent to which he or she will be able to move around and gather information and perspectives from other sources.

This role is appropriate when the researcher needs to become totally immersed and experience the work or situation at first hand. Sometimes it is the only way to gain the kind of insights sought. For example, in a study conducted by Thorpe (1980), which used this approach, the researcher was able to gain an understanding of how management's failure to address the motivational needs of the workforce led to disillusionment and apathy (see Example 6.5).

EXAMPLE
6.5

Researcher as employee

Poor planning of work meant that men were often bored: by experiencing this boredom himself, Thorpe was better able to understand its causes and the ways in which the employees attempted to alleviate it. His team developed a pattern of activity where they worked for the first hour or so, and then they took a break, had a wash and a walk outside. On certain days they changed their overalls in the laundry, which involved a walk of about 600 yards and a break of about half an hour. After mid-morning the pace became much slower, and after lunchtime very little work was done at all.

On one occasion (a Wednesday afternoon) the researcher saw that the conveyor belt was beginning to back up for no apparent reason. On questioning his colleagues about it, he learnt that they saw this as a good strategy to put pressure on management and guarantee themselves overtime at the weekend at time and a half. Since overtime working had to be notified to the employees three days in advance it was important to slow things down on Wednesday. By Friday the backlog had all but been cleared but the promise of the overtime remained, making for a fairly easy Saturday morning's work!

Naturally, in the above example, Thorpe's questioning did not stop at just what was observed, for it then became of interest to know *why* the extra pay was required, *why* this strategy was used in preference to others, and so on.

In the above-mentioned example, not all individuals involved were aware of the research taking place. However, the company chairman and the works convener had agreed to the research being conducted as they saw the merits of the research. It is important to remember that it is perfectly possible to negotiate access without the consent of everyone at the location where the study is to take place as long as no harm comes to any of the respondents. In a recent example, a PhD student was able to gain access to conduct a three-company case comparison of the effect of performance-related pay on the behaviour of school teachers by taking a job as a 'dinner lady' in one school, a playground supervisor in another and a classroom assistant in another. Although the 'dinner lady' role was not ideal, it served its purpose in getting close and helped the early formulation of ideas. In such studies, gaining access can be extremely difficult and we cannot pretend that getting agreement is a simple matter; the point is that it should not deter. Of course those who study part-time have access to this kind of study, although 'insider research' raises its own problems. But for students who require part-time work to undertake their studies to make ends meet, they can be sitting on very rich research material without realizing it. As we have indicated in Chapter 4, participant observation invariably raises *ethical* dilemmas, particularly when conducted in a covert way. These dilemmas need to be considered carefully by researchers, preferably before they embark on fieldwork. People may be resentful when they learn of the presence of a covert researcher, but as more and more people study for management qualifications on a part-time basis, there is a growing acceptance that employees may be researchers. The final section of this chapter will briefly return to the question of ethics.

This latter point raises another issue related to complete participation: the problem of a crisis of identity. Getting to know people quite well, even being invited into their homes, and then reporting on them in a covert way is, for most researchers, regardless of ethics, a difficult task. The researcher in the above example remembers his own experience vividly. He was some 300 miles from his academic base and unable to obtain help or support from colleagues and found it difficult not to experience a confusion of roles. Complete participation is not just a matter of being an employee for three months or so, keeping a diary and analysing the results at a distance at a later date. It involves observing, participating, talking, checking, and understanding and making interpretations, all of which are required if complete participant observers are to share and understand the employee's experience.

Linked to this is the time period over which this kind of activity has to be sustained. It is not unusual for studies to take several months with results taking a long time to produce. It must also be noted that the method is one of high risk. As we have discussed, studies are often extremely difficult to set up, anonymity is a problem, and considerable resources may be consumed in their execution with no guarantees that the method will yield the insights sought. Finally, and this also applies somewhat to other qualitative methodologies, the complete observer role can be both a physical as well as an intellectual challenge. In the case of Thorpe's research, for example, it required the researcher to complete a day of manual work and then in the evening continue the process of interpretation so that new lines of enquiry could be continued the following day.

Research as the explicit role

A second way of managing the role is for the researcher to be present every day over a period of time; but this time entry is negotiated in advance with management and preferably with employees as well. In this case, the individual is quite clearly in the role of a researcher who can move around, observe, interview and participate in the work as appropriate.

This type of observer role is the most frequently favoured, as it provides many of the insights that the complete observer would gain, while offering much greater flexibility and avoiding the ethical problems that deception entails. Roy (1970: 217) describes the advantages of the approach: 'The participant as observer not only makes no secret of his investigation: he makes it known that research is his overriding interest. He is there to observe. The participant observer is not tied down; he is free to run around as research interest beckons'. Eileen Fairhurst (1983) used this type of approach in a study of employees' attitudes to organizational rules. She chose for her research a geriatric nursing ward, and this is where she met her first problem. It took a considerable amount of time to obtain agreement to conduct her research in a particular unit, for two reasons, which illustrate a number of problems involved in this type of research. The first was that different consultants in the hospital viewed 'research' in two distinct ways. Some saw it as something in which they must become personally involved and 'vet'; others saw it as a self-indulgent activity of which they wanted no part.

Even after she had gained agreement for the location of the research, there were additional problems associated with the sensitive focus of the study. Old people are especially vulnerable, and there was real concern that researching them might be viewed as a form of exploitation. To experience delay in the setting up of this kind of study is not in any way unusual. Thorpe's researcher-as-employee study, and the diary study that will be discussed later, took a number of months.

Researchers, as we have discussed with interviewing, must find strategies that will allay people's fears, and offer the organization or the managers and employees who control access either reassurance or something in return. This might involve many meetings and even presentations to the employees about the aims and potential value of the research. Once accepted, Fairhurst explained how a principal task was to move from a position of stranger to that of friend – someone who could be trusted. When she had achieved this, she found individuals were very willing to tell her about the organization, whether they were nurses, cleaners or ward clerks. While on the wards, she felt it appropriate to help make beds and assist generally, for example, with the distribution of food and drink at meal times, and to collect bed linen or clothes for patients. At such times she was not only participating but strengthening relationships. She also recalls that there were times when she simply had to observe, for example when patients were spending time with occupational therapists or physiotherapists, or on the occasions when she did not possess the technical qualifications to take any role in the work. People understood this and accepted it.

The key skill is to be sensitive enough to know just what role is required in each situation. This is influenced almost entirely by the circumstances at that particular time. For example, Fairhurst explains that it would have been conspicuous if she had stood or sat apart, rather than offering help when the wards were short-staffed. On the other hand, night staff were always short of work, and as a consequence she spent much of the time during this period observing, listening and talking with nurses.

Interrupted involvement

A third kind of role involves the observer being present sporadically over a period of time, moving, for example, in and out of the organization to deal with other work or to conduct interviews with, or observations of, different people across a number of different organizations.

The essential characteristic of the researcher taking this role is that the process is not one of continuous longitudinal involvement as we have described in the previous examples.

In addition, the role is unlikely to contain much actual participation in work. Instead, it provides a model for what is often seen as the participant observation method: spending a period of time in a particular setting and combining observation with interviews.

Observation alone

In many ways, the role of complete observer is hardly a 'qualitative' method, since the researcher avoids sustained interaction with those under study. This type of observation is used in the field of management services where, for job design and specification purposes, requests are made for 'objective' accounts of the content of work; it can also be used in conjunction with other methods when lists of managerial competencies are being developed.

As a technique, it is of very little use to those interested in a social constructionist view. Even when used in the discipline of management services, practitioners often fail to obtain people for accounts of their own actions because of the requirement for detachment. The observer role is often disliked by employees since it seems like snooping, and it prevents the degree of trust and friendship forming between researchers and respondents which, as we have noted, is an important component of the other methods. However, for trained practitioners, such techniques do give extremely accurate pictures of what takes place and how long they take, even if they fall short of giving a full account of why things are happening.

Semi-concealed research

This kind of research is not entirely the same as the categories we have discussed above. Rather, it relates to an increasingly popular **critical management studies** tradition and involves researchers negotiating access into organizations with research agendas that they do not always want to reveal to all of the respondents they meet, for fear of being presented with an image of the company from a particular perspective. **Semi-concealed research** is not the same as covert research, in that the researchers are open about their rationale for studying in the company. The aspect of concealment relates to the way the focus of the research is defined and the view the researcher takes on the practices under observation. An example of this would be the research of Collinson (1992), who conducted his research into the recruitment and selection practices in large companies. His particular focus was on how the mainly white, male, middle-aged managers controlled entry into the companies in ways that had the effect of excluding women.

Finally, it could be argued that much management research conducted for postgraduate qualifications is a form of **auto-ethnography** (Hayano, 1979) or self-ethnography (Alvesson, 1998). With research defined in this way, it is possible for a student to study their own work context or observe their own colleagues using the opportunity as an insider. According to Hayano (1979), for this kind of process to be completely self-ethnographic, the researcher needs to be able to identify completely with the group under study and to be accepted as a full cultural member of the group that they seek to study. This approach to the research does have its drawbacks as although it appears to avoid many of the practical difficulties associated with participant observation (distance, time and so on associated with conducting research in someone else's organization), it does enable an outsider to see differences and ask difficult questions. To study those 'not like us' is one of the main features of traditional ethnography; as telling someone else's story, it is argued, comes better from an outsider, and in doing so we come to know ourselves better. Conducting auto-ethnography also raises complex questions as to the role of the researcher at both the data collection stage and the writing stage. These issues we touch on in more detail later in the chapter.

Video recording

Despite the pervasive nature of the 'visual' in our everyday lives, management research has continued to privilege verbal forms of communication over visual forms. Historically, visual methods of data collection have been viewed as being highly subjective, difficult to interpret and prone to researcher bias. Consequently, most qualitative management research has been limited to textual data-gathering techniques. Yet, as Secrist et al. (2002) note, despite all the eloquent verbal descriptions of their research experiences that writers provide, it is often suggested that words alone cannot communicate the complex and intricate situations they encounter. Consequently, there has been an increasing interest in what visual methods can offer management researchers. Yet there remain very few examples in the field of management where visual methods of data collection have been applied.

One attempt at applying a visually based methodology is Cunliffe's (2001) postmodern perspective on management practice, where she video-taped interviews she conducted with a number of managers. She subsequently played these video-taped interviews back to the managers to explore with them how they had co-created meaning through the course of the interview. In this way, the meaning of the interviews was discussed and deciphered in collaboration with the participant, as a form of co-inquiry. In another vein, a body of research known collectively as 'workplace studies' (Luff, Hindmarsh and Heath, 2000; Heath and Hindmarsh, 2002) has made use of video-tape to examine the effects of the material environment on action and interaction. Such studies focus on interaction and technology in a variety of organizational settings. While interesting, neither of these approaches aims to understand what the visual means in relation to wider understandings but rather focuses on in-depth, context-reliant and micro-level understandings.

Example 6.6 illustrates the utility of visual methods, based on a recent work by Clarke (2011), who employs a visual ethnographic approach to explore entrepreneurs' use of visual symbols in the creation of legitimacy for their ventures. Although visual ethnographic approaches, which involve video-taping individuals in contexts of natural interactions, have a long-standing tradition in the fields of visual sociology and anthropology, this is the first attempt to employ such an approach in the management domain.

EXAMPLE
6.6

Using visual tools in a research study

Clarke (2011) incorporated visual tools into her research in order to explore how entrepreneurs use visual symbols to create legitimacy for their ventures. This study is based on material collected during visual ethnographies of three entrepreneurs where she

(Continued)

(Continued)

captured videos of entrepreneurs in a range of different interactions with investors, employees and customers over a three-month period. She was aware of the influence that the video-camera could have on the unfolding interactions and attempted as much as possible to reduce the 'reactivity' of participants. Over time, participants became accustomed to the use of the camera and reacted less to its presence. The camera used was also small, compact and portable, making it as unobtrusive as possible. Approximately 60 hours of raw video-taped interactions were digitized and captured for audio and video analysis. She found that entrepreneurs use a range of visual symbols during performances to stakeholders, namely: settings, props, dress and expressiveness. Entrepreneurs used these visual symbols in order to present an appropriate scene to stakeholders, to create professional identity and emphasize control, and to regulate emotions. When used systematically, visual symbols help entrepreneurs access much-needed resources through addressing low levels of legitimacy that typically exist when novel ventures are launched. More experienced or serial entrepreneurs are likely to be more effective at employing a wider range of visual symbols systematically during interactions with stakeholders. By studying in detail how entrepreneurs use their visual surroundings during performances with stakeholders, this study shows that language is only one of the symbolic tools used by entrepreneurs. This study illustrates not only the rich information garnered about entrepreneurial processes using a visual approach but also the potential future utility of visual ethnographies and other visual methodologies in the field of management.

Images, however, do not need to be the main focus of attention or topic in order to warrant a researcher using visual data in their research. Indeed, as Pink (2001) highlights, the relation of images to other sensory, material and linguistic details of the study will result in the images being of interest to most researchers. Pink goes on to argue this is not a suggestion that video and other visual data collection strategies should replace text-based approaches in research, but rather they should be used as a complementary and additional source of data.

Birgit Schyns et al. (2011) have used this approach to great effect in their studies of how leaders are perceived by followers in different cultures. In her and her colleagues' research, different nationality groups were asked to draw a picture of a leader and, from these, understandings were gained into the dimensions and perspectives of very different national groups in relation to leadership. Figure 6.3 below shows one of the outputs from this study, illustrating the wider societal purpose of leadership in relationship to followers as seen by students from East Asia. In this example it can be seen how effective leaders are expected to take responsibility for employees' and their families' well-being.

Choice of role

Clearly, the choice the researcher makes as to which role he or she will assume in the project is important. Some factors that may be kept in consideration when making this choice are addressed in this section.

FIGURE 6.3
Drawing depicting an effective East Asian leader

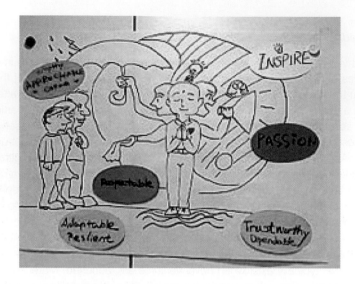

SOURCE: SCHYNS ET AL., 2011: 403

- *The purpose of the research* may provide a researcher with an indication of which role is most appropriate. Does the research require continued longitudinal involvement, or will in-depth interviews conducted over time give the kind of insights required?

- *The cost of the research* is another factor that needs to be kept in mind. To what extent can the researcher afford to be committed for extended periods of time, and are there any additional costs involved such as training or housing costs?

- *The extent to which access can be gained* may seem a simple issue, but is also important to be aware of when choosing a researcher's role. Gaining access where the role of the researcher is either explicit or covert can be difficult and may take time.

- *The extent to which the researcher is comfortable in the role* is of course vital to the choice. If the researcher intends to keep his or her identity concealed, will they also feel able to develop the kind of trusting relationships that are important?

- *The amount of time available* can also be influential. Some methods involve a considerable commitment of time.

Whichever method is chosen, each provides the means to obtain a detailed understanding of values, motives and practices. As Fairhurst (1983: 321) comments, 'The crucial personal skill is to be seen as someone who can be trusted no matter what role is adopted – this will enable much to become possible'.

Advice for those going 'into the field' is not hard to come by. Legend has it that Evans-Pritchard, a very eminent anthropologist, would advise all his research assistants before they set off to distant lands to go and get themselves a decent hamper from Fortnum and Masons, and to keep away from the native women (Barley, 1986: 17)! Evans-Pritchard also advised students to 'get a large notebook and start in the middle, because you never know which way things will develop'.

UNDERSTANDING DATA THROUGH INTERACTION

In this section, our aim is to illustrate the ways in which researchers can work with respondents to make joint sense of what is taking place. Collecting data through interaction is the third of the modalities presented in this chapter. Many of these methods also illustrate a distinction between the use of the method as a way of collecting 'data' or information, and the way that tools can be used to stimulate respondents into reflecting on their practice (as well as their views and ideas) with the distinct purpose of bringing about change. Used in this way, they become 'tools for thinking' that can be extremely helpful for both individuals and for groups.

Tools that stimulate discussion and debate, although varying in their richness, act also to simplify and reduce the uncertainties and ambiguities that so often surround many management situations. So, for example, we suggest here that if there are likely to be differences between the researcher and the researched, which stand in the way of arriving at common understandings, then 'richer media' such as face-to-face interviews and visual tools (as opposed to questionnaires or reports) should be introduced.

To develop this notion, we point to Daft and Lengel's (1986) study, which suggested that most organizational situations are characterized by uncertainty and that this uncertainty is very often caused by an absence of information or ambiguity, caused by equivocality. What researchers need to do therefore is find ways of reducing the uncertainty and the equivocality, both in obtaining data and in the way that the information is exchanged. In this section but also in Chapter 7, we illustrate some of the tools and approaches that can be used to do this; many will be seen to employ some kind of visual media component (e.g. cognitive, mapping, visual metaphors, photographs and repertory grids). Of course an additional feature of this approach is that both parties learn and as a consequence the approach can lead to development for those being researched. The following section offers some suggestions as to the approaches that might be considered.

Mapping techniques: a way of creating and making sense of qualitative data

There are various tools and mapping techniques that help the researcher create data, reflect upon it and analyse it. Two common techniques are the repertory grid technique and cognitive mapping (see Chapter 7).

Photographs and visual metaphors

The use of photographs and visual metaphors can be a useful way of gathering information when there is only a small amount of data on an issue to begin with, getting information is proving difficult, or the matter under discussion is seen as contentious or problematic. The general public and employees of an organization can contribute to research through the use of photographs. In the same way as newspapers often request updated pictures from the public, researchers can do the same. Researchers can also ask employees and participants to take pictures of specific events that the researcher is interested in. This can serve as a complement to, say, interviews, diaries and postcards.

Assessing the role that photography has played in organizational research, Buchanan (1999) found that while it has enjoyed a rich tradition in disciplines such as sociology and anthropology (Collier and Collier, 1986; Harper, 1994; Banks, 1995), it has been used far less within the field of management. As a consequence, he deliberately planned his research so as to use photographs to stimulate discussion and debate between members of staff at a hospital as part of a programme to re-engineer the patient's experience. He argued that if something of relevance can be seen, it can be discussed and possibly altered. Buchanan's purpose was to collect photographs in order to record complex scenes and processes that could provide 'non-reactive' records and observations. He found that the photographs really helped the study. The use of photographs clearly triggered informants to talk much more about the ideas they had around the images and this helped to develop a more complex understanding of the chains of activity that occurred. Photographs of the process also contributed to a more accurate sequencing of this as well as to a more detailed written analysis of the process. Once accomplished, the sequence was shown to a number of groups within the hospital and again additional complex details were added in the discussions and debates that they engendered. Drawing on the notion of social poetics, it can be suggested that the pictures offered the opportunity for a situation to be held captive (Wittgenstein, 1953) such that it allowed the possibility for new connections and relationships to emerge that would otherwise remain hidden from view, and that, once recognized, the new connections could help set a course for managerial action.

In the post-industrial age, this is perhaps not so conceptually different from the way work study engineers used photographs including cyclographs and chrono-cyclographs to determine the paths of movements. But, unlike the industrial engineers from the past, there isn't the same belief that all members of the organization will interpret this information in a similar way from the common standpoint of shared interests and values. The use of images, it appears, does enable great complexity to be represented and better understood.

Using visual metaphors is another approach that aims to elicit the views of individuals or groups. Individuals, for example, might be asked to represent the issues that concern them in the form of pictures or drawings. This use of pictures, this time created by the individuals or groups themselves, can be a powerful way of developing understanding and for groups to move forward with a vision for the future. An example of a group of managers being asked to draw a picture of the organization as if it were a person is shown in Example 6.7 below.

EXAMPLE 6.7

A visual metaphor

In research conducted in a large multinational, the approach was used to explore how the senior staff viewed their organization (Simpson, 1995). The research was conducted using a series of focus group interviews. At each session, the groups were asked the following questions:

(Continued)

(Continued)

1   If the organization was a parent, how do you think it would relate to its children?

2   If you were asked to write an honest character reference for the organization, what would it say? Some guidance here included how well it performed in its most recent job, its most recent job, its achievements, anything else that individuals thought was important.

3   Try to imagine the company as an old friend whom you have not seen over the last ten years. How would you judge whether their personality had changed?

4   Finally, individuals were asked to draw a picture of the company as the 'person' is today.

The questions produced very rich data indeed, which was taped and analysed, but perhaps the most interesting aspect of this metaphor approach was the drawings the individuals produced and their interpretation. An example is shown below.

The way the group discussed the drawings was as follows:

Jean: He's a man again, is he?

Mirjam: Yes.

David: Yes, I think he is a man.

Mohamed: It's impossible to get away from that, I think.

Jean: Tell us about your picture; what does your picture show for us?

Mohamed: Shall I defend this? Since I drew it I got the short straw! Well, I was thinking of the bumbling uncle type person, perhaps not the sharpest person in the world, but at least you might get your

(Continued)

(Continued)

	pocket money off him. Next time you meet him he's got 30 years young; he'd got a flat top, a nice suit and a BMW. What was I trying to show [indicating hand on the drawing]? I'm not much of an artist as you can see, was basically just 'No!' It looks like 'on yer bike', which is just as appropriate.
Lisa:	What's this in his other hand?
Mohamed:	It's a mobile phone; it's trying to show he's a yuppie, flat-top hair, double-breasted suit, trendy glasses, small chin.
Lisa:	It's interesting about the other hand because we thought there would be a lot of gesticulation rather than the sort of verbal interaction; it's sort of hi and over there …
Liam:	We were going to put him with a bag of money in one hand …
Lisa:	But the portable phone gets that across.
Jean:	So he's gone from being a friendly uncle to a yuppie?
Mohamed:	Yes.
Clare:	And younger instead of older?
Mohamed:	Yes, yes.
Jean:	Perhaps we should all find out what he is on then!
Lisa:	Didn't that also happen to the bloke who sold his soul to the devil?
Jean:	I don't know.
Mohamed:	What's the film called, it's a baseball film, basically about an old guy who sold his soul to the devil, it's the Faust legend – and became a young baseball player – I don't know what happened to Faust, whether he got younger.

The above interpretations of the changes that had occurred revolved around the symbolism of a more business-like future, the more conservative style of dress – double-breasted suit and a more frantic (even harassed) appearance – and symbolized the increasing pace of organizational change and activity. An overall theme of the pictures from all the groups was the recognition of the change there had been from a friendly, caring, calm demeanour to an aggressive impersonal characterization of the organization. This example illustrates how, by making comparisons, in this case with something invented, a metaphor picture can help people to articulate their hopes and fears in a relatively non-threatening, non-confrontational and even humorous manner. Drawing pictures and drawing metaphors in

groups may also enable employees to work to create a shared landscape, to which they all have contributed and to which they all can see their contribution and role.

Action research

As we have discussed in Chapter 3, action research is a particular method that is about change and intervention and within which researchers and practitioners work with practitioners on matters of concern (Eden and Huxham, 1995; Saunders et al., 2003). Eden and Huxham (1996) suggest that as the interventions will naturally be 'one offs', they can be criticized for their lack of repeatability and lay themselves open to a claim of lack of rigour. Those contemplating their use do need to be clear on their endeavour, which is through a process of change and improvement, bringing theory and practice together. Action research transcends descriptive and explanatory accounts of organizations. According to Gummesson ([1988] 1991), a researcher comes with a theoretical trajectory or a 'pre-understanding' of a research topic and setting. While it is common for other research approaches to be explicit about researcher biases at the outset of a research project, it is important for action research to resist making assumptions before the project, because alternative interpretations are likely to emerge if pre-understanding is suppressed (Eden and Huxham, 1995). Although they recognize that this might be difficult to achieve in practice, at least it should be pushed into the background as far as possible. As a result, the analysis of the research may be enriched, which in turn may facilitate finding new insights and concepts.

Researchers who want to use the action research method should be aware that the skills that are required to conduct action research are not entirely the same as the skills needed for other research methods. Eden and Huxham (2007: 539) identify 15 characteristics of action research, which they recognize might be hard to achieve but nevertheless need, in their view, to be considered. These 15 characteristics are revealed in Table 6.4 below.

TABLE 6.4 Characteristics of action research

Fifteen characteristics of action research

1 Action research demands an integral involvement by the researcher with an intent to change the organization. This intent may not succeed – no change may take place as a result of the intervention – and the change may not be as intended.

2 Action research must have some implications beyond those required for action or generation of knowledge in the domain of the project. It must be possible to envisage talking about theories developed in relation to other situations. Thus it must be clear that the results could inform other contexts, at least in the sense of suggesting areas for consideration.

3 As well as being usable in everyday life, action research demands valuing theory, with theory elaboration and development as an explicit concern of the research process.

(Continued)

TABLE 6.4   (Continued)

4   If the generality drawn out of the action research is to be expressed through the design tools, techniques, models and methods then this, alone, is not enough. The basis for their design must be explicit and shown to be related to the theories that inform the design and which, in turn, are supported or developed through action research.

5   Action research will be concerned with a system of emergent theory, in which the theory develops from a synthesis of that which emerges from the data and that which emerges from the use in practice of the body of theory that informed the intervention and research intent.

6   Theory building, as a result of action research, will be incremental, moving through a cycle of developing theory, to action, to reflection, to developing theory, from the particular to the general in small steps.

7   What is important for action research is not a (false) dichotomy between prescription and description, but a recognition that description will be prescription, even if implicitly so. Thus presenters of action research should be clear about what they expect the consumer to take from it and present it with a form and style appropriate to this aim.

8   For high quality action research a high degree of systematic method and orderliness is required in reflecting about, and holding on to, the research data and the emergent theoretical outcomes of each episode or cycle of involvement in the organization.

9   For action research, the process of exploration of the data – rather than collection of the data – in the detecting of emergent theories and development of existing theories must be either replicable or, at least, capable of being explained to others.

10   The full process of action research involves a series of interconnected cycles, where writing about research outcomes at the latter stages of an action research project is an important aspect of theory exploration and development, combining the process of explicating pre-understanding and methodical reflection to explore and develop theory formally.

11   Adhering to characteristics 1 to 10 is a necessary but not sufficient condition for the validity of action research.

12   It is difficult to justify the use of action research when the same aims can be satisfied using approaches (such as controlled experimentation or surveys) that can demonstrate the link between data and outcomes more transparently. Thus in action research, the reflection and data collection process – and hence the emergent theories – are most valuably focused on the aspects that cannot be captured by other approaches.

13   In action research, the opportunities for triangulation that do not offer themselves with other methods should be exploited fully and reported. They should be used as a dialectical device, which powerfully facilitates the incremental development of theory.

14   The history and context for the intervention must be taken as critical to the interpretation of the likely range of validity and applicability of the results of action research.

15   Action research requires that the theory development, which is of general value, is disseminated in such a way as to be of interest to an audience wider than those integrally involved with the action and/or with the research.

Of course, the researcher needs to be skilled in techniques for probing and eliciting information from respondents. But the researcher is also required to have good facilitation skills, and the ability and flexibility to alternate between the roles of co-interventionist with practitioners and academic researcher who steps back and derives abstractions about the immediate experience. Example 6.8 offers an understanding of what action research may entail. For a more detailed literature on the use of action research, see the Further Reading list at the end of the chapter.

EXAMPLE
6.8

Action research

Huxham (2003) relates a retrospective account of how a particular research team set about analysing data on leadership in a health promotion partnership with which the research team worked. In the first instance, each of the researchers individually studied the data and identified what occurred over the course of the interventions, either through verbatim quotations or general and interpretive descriptions. Then, the team convened meetings and started negotiating on meanings of those interpretations and why these were considered of relevance to leadership within the particular setting. The researchers proceeded to form categories of related issues and interpretations. Huxham explains:

> Gradually clusters of data and interpretations began to emerge. We also added in concepts deriving from the literature. On this occasion we used the mapping software, Decision Explorer. [...] Decision Explorer is a convenient tool because it allows large volumes of data to be handled flexibly. (2003: 244)

In the example given, Decision Explorer was not the only means of data analysis; Post-it' notes were also employed at times. A third stage involved sifting through and dissecting the contents of each cluster with a view to identifying linkages from which a conceptual framework was created. Here, again, the researchers first attempted to identify the linkages individually and then came together to discuss and agree how the various clusters might be linked. The outcome was a combination of the acceptance of some of the clusters and an abandonment of others for lack of adequate data. At the end of this third step a core number of clusters were formulated all linked with leadership.

The subsequent step incorporated reflection on what had been achieved up to that point, but it also encompassed testing the emerging framework in contexts other than the setting in which it was generated.

The fifth and final stage focused on refining the different clusters into a framework, enriching with theoretical justifications and disseminating in academic circles through conferences while at the same time ensuring there was a practice link by engaging with other practitioners.

GENERAL CONCERNS RELATED TO THE COLLECTION OF QUALITATIVE METHODS

A major issue to be kept in mind while doing qualitative research is the relevance that the research has to the respondents. If respondents do not see any benefit or value in the study, they might produce fake or exaggerated information. As such, the issue of relevance to the respondents can be linked in with the above issues of obtaining trust and balancing the right social interaction. However, many individuals find benefit in talking to an independent outsider about themselves or learning something about future changes in the organization as in action research. In any event, researchers should be able to recognize and capitalize on these situations and offer them as benefits or advantages to interviewees in exchange for participation. This is the strategy that underlies much work in the tradition of participative action research (Reason and Bradbury, 2001). The more they are willing to be open, the more both parties are likely to gain. In addition, interest and commitment shown by the interviewer often produce far better results than clinical detachment.

Another important issue to be aware of at all times when conducting research, whether it be qualitative or quantitative in nature, is ethics. Although Chapter 4 has reviewed some of the main ethical issues that may be encountered in any form of management research, we feel it is necessary to repeat the pertinence of the issue. The most important thing to keep in mind is that under no circumstances should the researcher bring harm to the people he or she researches. This refers to issues such as being sensitive to difficult issues and handling them in a discreet fashion, but also to not disclosing confidential information. It also includes issues of being honest with the people the researcher works with, for example in the case of semi-concealed participation. What is important is that researchers understand the ethical issues involved when dealing with qualitative methods. By understanding the implications of the choices they make, they will be better placed to recognize any effect they may have on the nature of the relationship formed, and therefore on the data that is collected.

Lastly, some attention needs to be given to the issue of reflexivity. When collecting data, researchers need to think about their roles and the way they affect the research process. The reflective journal is a way of being reflective and using a critical mind-set about the research in progress. As discussed earlier on in this chapter, qualitative research attempts to capture subjective understandings of the external world from the perspective of participants and abandons the task of representing an 'objective' unchanging external reality. Auto-ethnography is the subjective experience of the researcher, which is different from ethnography. While ethnography is a method of collecting data through observation of others, auto-ethnography is the researcher's own experience, not that of others. The use of auto-ethnography is increasing in business, management and communication studies.

Rather, qualitative research aims to develop knowledge on how participants' understandings are created through patterns of social interaction. In this way, communication is seen as a 'formative' process in which individuals' worldviews are created through interaction with the social world around them. In relation to this, qualitative researchers suggest that meanings are continuously negotiated and renegotiated. However, failing to take account of the place of the researcher in the construction of these understandings enables researchers to remove themselves from the processes that are occurring and allows them to make pronouncements on the role of others. This unfortunately brings a static understanding to meanings that are inherently fluid in nature (Alvesson and Sköldberg, 2000).

For this reason, the notion of reflexivity has become central to any discussion of the collection and representation of qualitative data. While reflexivity may be seen to involve the questioning of 'the threads of philosophical and methodological certainty implicit in the goal of mainstream social science to provide an absolute view of the world' (Cunliffe, 2003: 984), it is difficult to find a commonly agreed definition of reflexivity. In effect, a range of diverse definitions from all corners of the social sciences have been put forward. However, what they all share is a deep underlying scepticism for the truth claims forwarded in any form of social science research. One definition commonly used, which may be helpful to students in attempting to understand what is meant by reflexivity, is that outlined by Alvesson and Sköldberg (2000: 5), who define reflexivity as continuous awareness and attention to 'the way different kinds of linguistic, social, political and theoretical elements are woven together in the process of knowledge development, during which empirical material is constructed, interpreted and written'.

Aiming to incorporate reflexivity into their research practice, many qualitative researchers aim to be aware throughout the research process of how the various elements of their identities become significant during the research process and write this into the research presentations (e.g. Brewer, 2000; Pink, 2001). This often involves paying tribute to social categories such as race, gender and class, and writing these attributes into the research process. This strategy, it is proposed, allows the researcher to understand how their personal characteristics may have in some way influenced the research process and affected their understanding of the results. However, there has been increasing criticism of such approaches to reflexivity. As Cunliffe outlines (2003: 990), 'critics of reflexivity argue it has little to offer … questioning what is real, what is knowledge, and who (or what) is self, leads only to intellectual chaos, self-indulgent navel-gazing aporia … and politically motivated subjectivism'. Therefore some qualitative researchers argue that reflexivity involves too much introspection on the part of the researcher, which may both problematize the research process and paralyse the researcher. While reflexivity has been discussed in this chapter, these issues are no less relevant in the representation of this data; therefore, students should keep these ideas in mind when reading the chapter on qualitative data analysis.

CONCLUSION

In this chapter we have aimed to provide an overview of some of the main methods for collecting qualitative data: through the modalities of language, observation and interaction. The key points of this chapter that we would like to emphasize are:

 Qualitative research is a creative process, which aims to understand the sense that respondents make of their world.

 There are many techniques for doing this and although we can give guidelines, each piece of research is unique and the decision must be taken as to which of these alternative and often competing approaches is most appropriate.

 As the research process is close and emergent, the relationship of the researcher to the researched must be taken into account.

Chapter 6 has focused on the collection of qualitative data, and has discussed issues that may be of importance while collecting data. The analysis of qualitative data, however, is a whole different story, with different issues that need careful consideration. Chapter 7, therefore, will elaborate further on this.

FURTHER READING

Alvesson, M. (2003) 'Beyond neopositivists, romantics, and localists: a reflexive approach to interviews in organisation research', *Academy of Management Review*, 23 (1): 13–33.

Ghauri, P. and Grønhaug, K. (2010) *Research Methods in Business Studies*. Essex: Prentice Hall.

Lupton, T. (1963) *On the Shop Floor: Two Studies of Workshop Organization and Output*. New York: Macmillan.

Reason, P. and Bradbury, H. (2001) *Handbook of Action Research: Participative Inquiry and Practice*. London: Sage.

Thorpe, R. and Holt, R. (2009) *The Sage Dictionary of Qualitative Management Research*. London: Sage.

FRAMING QUALITATIVE DATA

7

LEARNING OBJECTIVES

 To understand the different approaches to the analysis of qualitative data and what this means for the practice of data analysis.

 To understand how different software packages can support the analysis of qualitative data.

 To understand the use of a range of co-production techniques.

INTRODUCTION

In this chapter we use the term *framing* to refer to a range of ways in which information or data can be made sense of. The analogy is akin to a window. The shape of the window and the perspective taken will determine exactly what is observed. There are many ways in which data can be analysed. What researchers need to bear in mind is that most methods of analysis can be used for a wide variety of data. It is important, however, that the researcher chooses methods of analysis that are consistent with the philosophical and methodological assumptions made in the research designs that underpin the study, as we have discussed in Chapters 2 and 3.

One of the most common issues that qualitative researchers face is how to condense highly complex and context-bound information into a format which tells a story in a way that is fully convincing to others. In the case of management research, this goes beyond the requirements of 'good journalism' where sources are well referenced and interpretations are 'balanced'. It requires both a clear explanation of how the analysis was undertaken and how the conclusions were reached, as well as a demonstration of how the raw data was transformed into meaningful conclusions. Chapter 6 has given the reader some ideas of how qualitative data might be collected and Chapter 11 discusses how findings might be written up in the project or thesis. This chapter, then, indicates a number of ways in which we might make sense of qualitative data and how systems can be developed that will make the links between the data collected, the analysis undertaken and the inferences drawn explicit. Most of the time this does not mean that all the data collected has to be displayed, but at least a sample of the data is needed for illustration so that the same logic path can be followed and an independent view drawn.

In many ways the issues about the analysis of qualitative data are closely linked to the different research philosophies discussed in Chapter 2. If the researcher is working from a social constructionist perspective, then he or she will attempt as much as possible not to draw a distinction between the collection of data and its analysis and interpretation. Researchers who prefer a more positivist approach will see a sharper distinction between data and the process of analysis, to the extent that the data collection and analysis may well be performed by different people. They will also be more concerned with examining frequencies within qualitative data, which will enable them to turn it into numeric form, although as we will see later in this chapter this is not always the case. We present, for instance, a number of hybrid examples that have become more popular and appealing with the advent of computer data analysis software. After all, numbers are both seductive and persuasive, and for many managers, or funders, the political need for numbers wins through against attempts to provide rich descriptions.

ANALYSING NATURAL LANGUAGE DATA

The next sections will examine the different ways in which a researcher can analyse natural language data. As Chapter 6 has demonstrated, there is more than one way to collect natural language data, such as in-depth interviews, diary studies or video records. Similarly, there is more than one way in which the collected language data can be analysed, and the following section will cover six different methods that allow for an analysis of natural language data: content analysis, grounded analysis, social network analysis, discourse analysis, narrative analysis, conversation analysis and argument analysis. As with collecting qualitative data, the choice that the researcher makes for a particular method of analysis depends largely on what the researcher wants to find out.

CONTENT ANALYSIS AND GROUNDED ANALYSIS

Building on the differences in research approach and thus analysis, the first two methods of natural language analysis will be discussed together: **content analysis** and **grounded analysis**. In the first approach, content analysis, the researcher interrogates the data for constructs and ideas that have been decided in advance. In the second, grounded analysis, researchers tend to let the data speak for itself and although they are still employing a process, they allow for more intuition to guide them in the development of their understandings of the data. This latter approach is more holistic than content analysis and often takes on a cultural and historical dimension, which may even suggest the need for a longitudinal approach. With grounded analysis, the researcher stays closer to the data and any observations made need to be carefully placed in context. As with any research it is important that the data that form the basis of the research conclusions remain available for scrutiny, which practically might extend to taking transcripts in a separate folder or ring binder in with you to the oral defence.

Although we characterize these two positions as competing alternatives, between them lies a raft of practice and in many ways the choices that researchers face lie on a continuum (see Table 7.1) between content analysis where, as King (1998: 118) suggests, codes are all predetermined and where their distribution is analysed statistically (e.g. WordSmith), and grounded analysis, where there are no *a priori* definitional codes (e.g. NVivo and ATLAS.ti).

TABLE 7.1 Qualitative data analysis: content versus grounded methods

Content analysis ⟵⟶	Grounded analysis
Searching for content (prior hypotheses)	Understanding of context and time
Causally linked variables	Holistic associations
Objective subjective	Faithful to views of respondents
More deductive	More inductive
Aims for clarity and unity	Preserves ambiguity and contradiction

Content analysis

Content analysis methods have been used successfully in the examination of historical artefacts. In one such study, analysis was made of Caesar's accounts of his wars in Gaul. Researchers identified certain key phrases or words, which they counted and the frequencies were then analysed. The selection of these would depend on the hypothesis the researcher wished to prove or disprove. In the case of Caesar's accounts of his campaigns, the hypothesis that was tested related to the forms of money that were used. A similar kind of content analysis has been used to try to determine the authorship of anonymous plays by analysing the use of words and the recurrent patterns of certain words or phrases, and even more recently to determine whether criminals' statements have been added to, or amended, by others at some later date!

EXAMPLE 7.1

Research into payment systems: content analysis

In the study of payment systems (see Chapter 6 in Bowey and Thorpe, 1986) content analysis was used to analyse data. A number of problems immediately became apparent: control over the data collection process had been poor due to the number of people who had been involved – not all the core questions had been asked of each respondent and, in addition, due to a shortage of tape recorders, field notes had been taken but transcripts were not available for all the interviews, which made comparability difficult. This was far from satisfactory! However, to solve this difficulty, all the material was read by each member of the research team.

Subsequently, three substantial interviews were chosen and read in detail and coded by three researchers. Issues that appeared to require further elaboration in further interviews were identified. Then, the coding frame that had been developed was discussed with all the researchers and modified in the light of inconsistencies. At the same time definitions were agreed in relation to the three pilot interviews and detailed notes were made of how answers might be interpreted. Finally, all the interviews were distributed to all the researchers and the same analysis framework used to interpret them.

Regular checks were made to reduce the number of inconsistencies between coders. Once all interviews had been coded they were transferred into SPSS to sit alongside data derived from a large-scale survey of over 1,000 employees.

In this example all the information had derived from interviews although many of the themes identified had been identified as relevant in advance. However, new unexpected themes could be accommodated and added into the framework. At a later date, using this method, it was possible to compare answers derived from interviews with those derived from questionnaires; moreover it was possible to separate these into definite responses and probable responses.

We have seen in the above example that more than one hypothesis was tested and multiple interviewers and coders were used. Moreover, the separation between the collection and the analysis stages is clear. There are also issues raised about how common understandings were arrived at between those involved. The study offers an example of the way in which qualitative data was coded and then imported into a quantitative dataset and analysed together. One of the most influential sourcebooks on content analysis is by Miles and Huberman (1994). They offer a range of ways whereby information might be analysed in order to capture the complexity of all sorts of qualitative data in a variety of circumstances. At the heart of the process is a matrix format, which captures the constructs (extant or emergent) usually on one axis and the respondents or occurrences on the other. Although this method of data analysis is quite definitely still qualitative, it is possible to introduce some element of quantification into the process.

Template analysis (King, 1998) is a method of analysis where the researchers look for themes among their data. Conceptually similar to the kind of frames that are often used in science, the template once designed is laid over the data in order to reveal patterns in the data. The list of codes (e.g. the template) is often decided before the analysis but can be updated and adapted throughout the analysis. Because of this, it is argued that template analysis is located at the interface between content analysis (predetermined codes) and grounded theory (where codes emerge during the analysis). As a consequence template analysis is a flexible tool and because it can be managed manually it is often widely used. Some even suggest that it is preferable to those types of grounded analysis approaches that follow rigid conventions and very specific procedures for both collecting data and the analysis of data. In template analysis a code is a descriptive heading or label for certain text. Some headings can be more interpretative, for example 'relationships at work'. Codes are usually organized hierarchically in order to provide a general overview with more details in the sub-codes. In addition to this, template analysis supports parallel coding (mainly from a positivistic perspective), where the same text belongs to different codes on the same hierarchical level.

Miles and Huberman (1994) provide an expanded sourcebook on qualitative data analysis. It entails examples of many different methods of analysis. It is important to highlight that there are different ways of analysing the same data for different purposes. A checklist matrix 'is a format for analysing field data on a major variable or domain of interest' (Miles and Huberman, 1994: 105). The aim of the research shown in Table 7.2 was to answer the questions: (1) What were the components of the original plan for implementation? and (2) Were the requisite conditions for implementation assured before it began? (Miles and Huberman, 1994: 105). The first column is condition, the second users and the third administrators.

Checklist matrices are useful when a new area is explored. The matrix can develop during the analysis, so one starts with a few easily identifiable components. The checklist can also facilitate the data collection and make it more systematic and encourage comparison. It is important to justify for the selection of quotes and how rankings are made.

Of course, this is only one type of matrix design that is constructed for one particular purpose and what we want to draw attention to is the degree of flexibility that is possible. As such, matrix designs can range from simply counting the occurrence of various phenomena, to matrices that order variables against the dimension of time (for an example of this, see Miles and Huberman, 1994: 201), to those that simply display qualitative data.

TABLE 7.2 Checklist matrix: conditions for supporting preparedness at Smithson School

Condition	For Users	For Administrators
Commitment	*Strong* 'wanted to make it work'.	*Weak* at building level. Prime movers in central office committed; others not.
Understanding	*Basic* for teacher ('felt I could do it, but I just wasn't sure how'). *Absent* for aide ('didn't understand how we were going to get all this').	*Absent* at building level and among staff. *Basic* for two prime movers ('got all the help we needed from developer'). *Absent* for other central office staff.
Materials	*Inadequate*: ordered late, puzzling ('different from anything I ever used'), discharged.	Not applicable.
Front-end training	*Sketchy* for teacher ('it all happened so quickly'); no demo class. *None* for aide: ('totally unprepared. I had to learn along with the children').	Prime movers in central office had training at developer site; none for others.
Skills	*Weak-adequate* for teacher. *None* for aide.	One prime mover (Robeson) skilled in substance; others unskilled.

SOURCE: ADAPTED FROM MILES AND HUBERMAN, 1994: 107

Grounded analysis

Grounded analysis offers the more 'open' approach to data analysis and is closely linked to the concept of **grounded theory**. Again, the source of data can be texts produced from empirical research (for example, interview data) or extant texts, which might take the form of company reports or diaries. At this end of the qualitative data analysis spectrum the structure is derived from the data rather than imposed on the data externally, as often is the case with the positivist approach. This means that the data is systematically analysed so as to tease out themes, patterns and categories that will be declared in the findings. As we pointed out in Chapter 5, we are in difficult territory here as there is no one clear agreed approach, and even the methodology that was proposed by Glaser and Strauss (1967) originally to give some structure to the process has undergone many changes and developments and has been the subject of acrimonious debate. Locke (2001: 33) reminds us that the original methodological monograph was written 'as a polemic against hypothetical-deductive; speculative theory-building and its associated research practices that characterized the sociological context of the time'. Glaser and Strauss's work not only encouraged researchers to be more courageous in using their imagination and creativity when developing theory but their work also showed researchers a rigorous method by which this could be done.

Below we suggest a practical approach to sifting through volumes of non-standard data. In order to make the procedure more understandable we explain it in the way both ourselves and our colleagues have used it. We introduce some coding terminology into the process so links can be made to texts on grounded analysis. The method assumes that one is working with transcripts of in-depth interviews – one of the more intractable analysis problems. We consider that there are seven main stages to such analysis:

1   *Familiarization* – First re-read the data transcripts. When reading, draw on unrecorded information as well as recorded. This is where any additional field notes and your personal research diary can be important to the process of analysis. Glaser (1978) suggests that at this initial stage researchers should remind themselves just what the focus of the study is, what the data suggests and whose point of view is being expressed. The relationship between the research and the people interviewed should also be accounted for.

2   *Reflection* – At this stage desperation may begin to set in. There is usually so much rich data that trying to make sense of it seems an impossible task. Evaluation and critique become more evident as the data is evaluated in the light of previous research, academic texts and common sense explanations. The kind of questions researchers might ask themselves are:

   ● Does it support existing knowledge?

   ● Does it challenge it?

   ● Does it answer previously unanswered questions?

   ● What is different?

   ● Is it different?

3   *Conceptualization* – At this stage there is usually a set of concepts that seem to be important for understanding what is going on. For example, in an examination of performance these might include: management style, technology, absence rates, demographic qualities of the labour force, locus of power and so on. These concepts that respondents mentioned are now articulated as explanatory variables, and need to be coded. Charmaz (2006) suggests codes should be simple and precise and actions preserved with the process remaining open and the researcher staying close to the data.

4   *Cataloguing concepts* – Having established that these concepts do seem to occur in people's explanations, they then can be transferred into a database. **Focused codes** are more directed and more conceptual and analytical and **axial codes** specify categories or sub-categories and specify the dimensions of a category. There is an issue of labelling that needs to be resolved which relates to whether the language used is that of the people concerned or you use your own terms. Our view is that it is probably helpful at this stage to use your own terms providing a trace is kept of how they were derived. Although there may be pressure to use computer packages for your analysis there is a debate about the

way the software structures the data and where there are modest amounts of data it may still be worth considering manual methods.

5   *Re-coding* – Whether computers are used or not the process is usually highly iterative and there will need to be an element of going back to check against the original data and comparing incidents in order to identify particular properties. It may well be individuals in the same organization were interpreting what appears to be similar concepts in very different ways. In these cases re-coding will be necessary.

6   *Linking* – At this stage the analytical framework and explanations should be becoming clearer with patterns emerging between concepts. This is the stage of developing **theoretical codes**. This is achieved by conceptualizing 'how substantive codes may relate to each other as hypotheses to be integrated into a theory' (Charmaz, 2006: 121–49). One can now begin to link the key variables into a more holistic theory. At this stage it is often worth producing a first draft, which can be tried out on others, both colleagues and respondents, so that the argument and supporting data can be exposed to wider scrutiny and some degree of verification.

7   *Re-evaluation* – In the light of the comments of others, the researcher may feel that more work is needed in some areas. For example, the analysis may have omitted some factors or have over-emphasized others. This stage takes some period of time, and as with the other stages it may have to be undertaken more than once.

The researcher may well feel that for much of the time the analysis of qualitative data is chaotic and extremely messy.

Since the early development of grounded theory there has been considerable development of the method, not least by Glaser (1978, 1992, 1998), by Strauss (1987), and by students of both authors, notably Corbin (Strauss and Corbin, 1990, 1998). What is more, over the years their published views have diverged considerably. Glaser has persistently advocated a more open, flexible approach in which the theory emerges from the data, almost without human intervention. He is hostile to the elaboration of analysis procedures and wrote a critical book where he claimed that the fractured, technical approach being adopted by Strauss's approach was tantamount to a 'whole new method' which forced data into categories. This made the process too rigid and uncompromising (Glaser, 1992). Strauss and Corbin (1990, 1998) on the other hand moved in the direction of increased prescription and elaboration. Their strategy for sampling data operates at three levels – open, axial and selective – which are defined in Table 7.3.

The following example (Example 7.2) is taken from a research project conducted by Thorpe and Danielli on the use of a local park. It follows some, but not all, of the advice from the protagonists discussed above. First, the researchers used a predetermined sample framework (and hence did not use theoretical sampling). Second, they did not use the system of open, axial and selective coding in a systematic way; and third, they focused on identifying a clear storyline using information from outside their own study (which goes against the advice of Glaser).

TABLE 7.3 Data sampling process recommended by Strauss and Corbin (1998)

Coding Practice	Theoretical Sampling Strategy
Open	Open sampling – relatively indiscriminate sampling of people, places and situations that will provide the best opportunities for collecting relevant data.
Axial	Variational and relational sampling – focused sampling of people, places and situations that will provide opportunities to gather data about the properties and dimensions of the categories as well as how the categories are related to each other. Data gathering in terms of coding paradigm is also clearly implicated here.
Selective	Discriminate sampling – very focused and deliberate sampling of people, places and situations that will fill in and refine the storyline of the core categories and the proposed relationships between categories.

A study of a northern park

EXAMPLE
7.2

Thorpe and Danielli's study was into the use of a local park, and information was collected from ten different groups of park users. These included: a women and toddler group, representatives from two schools who used the park as a consequence of changes in the requirements of the national curriculum, an Asian women's group (the area was predominantly built up with a high ethnic population), a disabled group (who used the uncongested pathways to exercise and use their wheel chairs), a young Asian youth team (who used the bowling green to play football!) as well as others. Interviews were transcribed and analysed using the grounded theory approach described. What was striking as a category from the data collected from each group was the way fear emerged as one of the main constructs for each.

This is what Strauss and Corbin would describe as an axial code. But further sampling of the data in the transcripts showed the manifestation of fear was quite different in each group. For the women and toddler groups, it was fear of large groups of Asian boys playing football on the bowling green. For the Asian boys, it was fear of being intimidated by white youths if they went to the sports hall in the town centre. For the Asian women's groups, it was a fear of spirits, which they thought inhabited parts of the park, particularly those parts that were poorly lit where the trees hung over the walkways.

Through further discriminant sampling it was possible to connect this category to other categories such as absence. Over the years for a variety of reasons there had

(Continued)

(Continued)

been a gradual withdrawal of park staff, the community charge had put pressure on the level of service the council was able to provide, which curtailed the time park staff could spend in the park, and into this space left in the park, anti-social elements and behaviour had begun to develop. Understanding the context and inter-relationships between variables in this way is extremely important for qualitative researchers and hence the researchers decided to go beyond the specific case under examination to show the context within which it was located. So, for example, when explaining and presenting the results of the above park study and the experiences of individuals in relation to the park, Thorpe and Danielli placed the concept of a northern town park in the context of its role in civic society in late nineteenth- and early twentieth-century Britain.

The story is one of a six-day working week for many manual workers, when religion still played a significant part in people's lives and when going to church on Sunday was a time when the family could be together and when 'Sunday best' clothes were worn. One of the places where individuals could promenade was in the park. Cars were few and far between and other forms of transport limited and expensive, so parks were local places where people could meet and enjoy themselves and congregate. The increase in affluence and the decline of religion, the changing hours of work and now Sunday shopping have all been contextual factors to the traditional uses of town parks and a reason for their decline and the problem needs to be understood in this context.

One final lesson from this particular study is perhaps apocryphal and relates to what happened when the findings were presented to the council. The leader of the council sub-committee thanked Richard Thorpe for his presentation but questioned him as to the validity of the study as there were no large samples or statistics. Later during coffee, park warden staff approached him to say that the report revealed something very close to their experiences on a day-to-day basis.

Whatever approach is adopted, the content analysis of qualitative data is time-consuming, often costly and requires either good (written-up) field notes or verbatim transcripts to be available. Often in applied research where the focus of the investigation is relatively clear and a large number of interviews may have been conducted by different people, some standardization of the process may well be necessary. However tackled, the method should allow the researcher to draw key features out of the data, while at the same time allowing the richness of some of the material to remain so it can be used to evidence the conclusions drawn and help to 'let the data speak' for itself.

EXERCISE
7.1

Piloting your approach to analysis

In pairs, discuss the focus of any pilot study that you intend to carry out before your main study. Discuss how extensive this should be and how it can be carried out to best effect, including how much analysis will be carried out and the method(s) that will be used.

COMPUTER AIDED ANALYSIS

Computer Aided Qualitative Data Analysis Software (CAQDAS) is the general term describing the software packages that can be used to aid the analysis of qualitative data, such as text, audio, video and graphics. There are many **CAQDAS** packages available, such as ATLAS.ti; HyperRESEARCH; MAXqda; QDA miner; NVivo; Qualrus and WordSmith. All CAQDAS packages have a general array of tools that make structuring and managing large volumes of data easier and, further, can increase the accessibility of data. Of course, each package is also in some way purpose-built, that is each package will have tools that are particularly suitable for a certain analytical approach, among other factors. The use of CAQDAS packages, particularly for their data management and functionality and capacity to increase accessibility, can help the researcher to get 'closer' to the data while also increasing the accuracy, transparency and overall rigour of the data analysis process and outcomes. Moreover, as research becomes more collaborative, CAQDAS packages represent a more efficient way of sharing data and knowledge among peers and co-investigators; this is especially so because of the capacity in many of them to generate all kinds of outputs such as reports and models. Table 7.4 outlines some of the analysis tasks that CAQDAS packages are often used for.

TABLE 7.4 Core tasks of CAQDAS packages

Task	Rationale
Project management	Plan and manage your project using memos, a project diary and other features.
Data management	Support for a wide range of document types and large volumes of data helps to create an 'audit trail'. Additionally, detailed and customizable workspaces, along with the capability to document developing ideas in memos and annotations, aids in 'tagging' and helps to organize and structure data and developing ideas.
Searching and mapping data	All CAQDAS packages have an array of search capabilities from simple word searches through to complicated multiple attribute searches that can interrogate data sets and retrieve coded data. Additionally, most packages include tools to visually map data, for example, through the use of creating models, charts and relationship diagrams.
Analysis	Coding functions facilitate the thematic analysis of data and enables the researcher to make sense of and conceptualize the data. Further, the capability to re-code data and link themes to developing ideas in memos aids continuity and can increase the overall transparency of the analysis process.
Sharing and outputs	Most CAQDAS packages have the ability to generate outputs such as reports, models and charts, which can help to visualize data that is being conceptualized and relationships that are being made. Further, this enables data and analysis to be easily shared among the research team.

Choosing the right package

Setting aside the tools that most of the packages have in common, such as basic search capabilities, how might you choose between the many packages available? Which one might be most suited to your project? These questions are almost impossible to answer directly, but there are some considerations that you might factor into your decision that can help to significantly reduce the difficulty of the decision and narrow your choice down to just a few packages. Three of the main considerations that can help you to identify the right package for your project are:

1   What are you looking for from your data? Create patterns and gain quantitative insight OR develop concepts and identify themes.

2   What will you need to do most? To search for OR to code data.

3   What is the state of the data? Is it naturalized OR denaturalized?

To exemplify how a choice might be made taking some of these considerations into account, imagine for a moment that you have just conducted a case study, and you have generated data using semi-structured interviews and observation. You decided early on that you are particularly interested in gaining a deeper understanding of the substantive area, and therefore you have opted for a grounded theory method of analysis. Now you are faced with the first consideration, what are you looking for from your data? There is little empirical evidence in your substantive area from which to structure search queries or inform rigorous, in-depth searching of the data; therefore you are more interested in what will *emerge* from the data. Thus in this scenario, you are more concerned with conceptualization and thematic analysis of the data. The answer to the first consideration then brings you to the second consideration: will you be primarily searching or coding the data? Coding relates to the practice of assigning 'codes', which are essentially descriptions, to selections of data; this is usually conducted in an iterative fashion and results in the conceptualization of data. Consequently, for this consideration you necessarily decide you are looking for emergent concepts from the data. Lastly, you arrive at the data preparation stage. In this scenario, data preparation means that interviews will need to be transcribed and field notes and observations will need to be similarly typed up or 'digitized'. The consideration here is whether data is prepared in a naturalistic or *de*naturalistic fashion. For example, will your interviews be transcribed to include every utterence and slightest detail such as involuntary vocalizations (naturalized transcription) or will you produce denaturalized transcripts that omit these specifics? As your final choice, you decide that although you will transcribe the interviews faithfully, you are more interested in the meanings and perceptions of the interviewee and so there is no requirement for naturalized transcription. In answering these considerations, the choice of which software package becomes somewhat clearer; your aims, data and analytical approach are more suited to a 'code-based' package such as **NVivo** or **ATLAS.ti**.

To demonstrate the other extreme, briefly consider this alternative scenario. You have conducted the same study, using the same methods. However, this time there is a substantial empirical foundation to the substantive area and your study is particularly concerned with analysing discourse. Prior to undertaking the study you have conducted a literature review and have a generated a list of keywords that you would like to search for during the discourse analysis; in other words, you are looking for patterns and word frequencies (quantitative insight). Consequently, you decide that you will primarily be needing to *search* during your analysis. Lastly, your overall analytical approach (discourse analysis) necessitates naturalistic description because every small detail may be of importance. With this different set of answers, you conclude that you will need to use a software package that is purpose built for the deeper level of textual analysis that you require; such packages are known as 'text-based' packages. Table 7.5 provides an overview of the discussed considerations.

In Table 7.5 you will notice that there is a column named 'both' that suggests there are CAQDAS packages which cater for all needs. While this is the case, it is only the case to a certain extent; code-based packages such as NVivo and ATLAS.ti also have some of the functionality found in text-based packages such as keyword search and the capacity to search for strings of words. However, an important point that should be borne in mind here is that while such packages can be considered as 'hybrids' they are not *purpose built* for handling both text- and code-based work. For example, the use of a package such as WordSmith would facilitate more in-depth, broad work on a textual level, whereas the use of NVivo to achieve the same aim where the specific tools are not present would likely mean that the same level of analytical depth may not be achieved. In reality, your aims, methodology and analytical approach should enable you to distinguish between the need for either a text- or code-based package; the decision beyond this of *which* package within

TABLE 7.5 Type of CAQDAS package

Type of CAQDAS Package				
Considerations	**Project Factors**	**Text-based**	**Code-based**	**Both**
What are you looking for?	Patterns and quantitative insight	X		X
	Concepts and themes		X	X
What do you need to do with the data?	Search	X		X
	Code		X	X
What is the state of the data?	Naturalized	X		X
	Denaturalized		X	X

either of these categories may be a little more difficult. To help with this decision it might be useful to factor in some secondary considerations such as:

- Can your data be easily converted for use in a CAQDAS package if it is not already in a supported format?
- To what extent will you require the automated functionality that some packages offer?
- Although it is a qualitative research project, will your study include both qualitative and quantitative data?
- Is your methodological/analytical framework compatible with the use of computer software?
- Do you need to share your data and analyses electronically, perhaps even across multiple investigators?
- Have you any existing experience with CAQDAS packages and will you need extra training for the package you have identified? Do you have sufficient time and funds for this training?
- What is the availability of packages at your institution? If they don't support the one you need, can you acquire a copy easily and will your computer be able to run it?

The final consideration, that of availability, is one that leads us into the next section; we have taken into consideration the packages that are most commonly available in the market today and thus those which are likely to be supported by your institution in order to show how CAQDAS packages have been used in real projects. The data used throughout the following section are from two recent PhD projects that used NVivo 8 and WordSmith in combination with different methodological and analytical approaches. WordSmith is a commonly used text-based package which has functionality and capabilities that are representative of the range of text-based packages you might encounter. However, there are two packages that dominate the code-based package market, NVivo and ATLAS.ti. The differences between these packages can appear subtle, which makes it hard for researchers to choose one over the other; therefore here we use the same data to walk through the same example in both packages.

Here it is important to pause for a moment before moving on to the examples in order to consider four points we feel it is important to emphasize in regards to the use of computers for analysing qualitative data. First, the success and the strength of the analysis always depend on the judgement of the researcher, and computers cannot substitute for this. Second, packages and programmes need to be chosen for, and be appropriate to, the tasks required. Third, it may sometimes be easier to analyse qualitative data by hand; and fourth, beware of the possibility that the availability of computer analysis may lead to an emphasis on counting the frequency of categories, at the expense of understanding the *quality* of ideas and experiences.

Working with NVivo: creativity in multidisciplinary scientific laboratory groups

Before undertaking work in any CAQDAS package it is important to undertake sufficient training and allow for a period of familiarization with the software you will be using. In combination with the software developer's guides and any training courses they may offer, another excellent source of reference is *Using Software in Qualitative Research* (Lewins and Silver, 2007), which offers a step-by-step guide to using computer software in qualitative research, including detailed sections on NVivo and ATLAS.ti.

The following examples provide an overview of the use of NVivo in a study that used an ethnography methodology in order to investigate creativity in three different multidisciplinary scientific laboratory research groups. The study was conducted by a PhD student at Leeds University and involved two years of observational work and over 120 interviews; the aim was to elucidate factors that might influence creativity in multidisciplinary scientific research groups. While some studies might use an analytical or theoretical framework to guide coding efforts in NVivo, this study took a grounded theory approach and, as such, themes were allowed to emerge from the data without the use of a framework.

Familiarization and data preparation   Before beginning work in NVivo it is important to understand two key aspects; imported data within your project, such as a transcript, is known as a *source* and your developing ideas or concepts are known as **nodes**. The *workspace* in NVivo is the area through which menus, other types of views and many different options can be accessed; it can also, to an extent, be customized for your particular style of working. NVivo 8 does have built-in transcription software, although this package is not built specifically for transcription and therefore when transcribing large volumes it may be more beneficial to use a purpose-built transcription package to make use of the specialist tools they have.

The first stage of working in NVivo is preparing your data for use in NVivo. The first task here is to check what kinds of file types are supported; NVivo 8 supports many different file types including PDF and Microsoft Word documents. If your file type is not supported and cannot be converted to one that is supported then it can still be used in your NVivo project through making it an *external source* (an external source in NVivo acts as proxy to the actual source whereas an *internal source* is included within the project). When you are ready to import your source(s) you will need to plan how your project will be organized, for example, whether you will have a casebook and what type of folder and file hierarchy you will use and how your sources will be labelled. It is important to plan this *before* you begin importing and coding data, as retrospectively altering file names, hierarchy and other attributes and options can make your project more complicated to work with.

Conceptualizing and developing your data and ideas   Once imported and organized the next stage is to begin analysing your source(s). In NVivo the method of analysis is through the application of 'codes' to selections of data; this is usually an iterative process, which can be performed while data is still being collected. Essentially, codes can be thought of as the definition or description you assign to a particular selection or multiple selections of data. In NVivo, these codes are shown as 'nodes', for which there are two basic types: free nodes and tree nodes. When data is coded initially, *free nodes* are created, this type of node is non-hierarchical and can easily be modified and re-coded whereas *tree nodes* can be hierarchical and used to structure developing concepts. This coding process can either be 'emergent' or guided by a theoretical or analytical framework; in the former data is coded into themes and develops into independent concepts whereas in the latter data would be coded into pre-existing, user-defined codes. To exemplify the process of coding (without a guiding framework), refer to the text below (and Figure 7.1) taken from the transcript of an interview conducted in the PhD study into creativity and observe how the text is then assigned codes.

> *Interviewer*: 'From day to day, what factors, if any, would influence your decision to seek help on a problem or idea you have?'

> *Group member*: 'Well, around here you know who's who. You have to be careful about who you approach for help and if I have an idea I don't just talk to anyone in the lab. People like me, at this level, we try to avoid looking stupid in front of more senior lab members who have much more authority and knowledge'.

There are a number of ways this transcript could be interpreted and coded. If this interview was being coded after several others then these factors might be coded under existing codes. Here we will assume we are identifying codes in the first round of coding and thus the following codes have been generated: 'Approach Anxiety' and 'Perception of Authority'. Figure 7.1 shows the coding process and Figure 7.2 shows the end result of this coding. It is important to note that, such as in Figure 7.1, there are a number of words coded around the key phrase '...be careful who you approach...'; this can be useful when interrogating the data at a later stage and helps to remind you of the context or whole story when viewing many different excerpts from multiple sources, such as when reading all instances coded under a single node. Furthermore, once coded, it is good practice to then annotate the coded data or write in a memo any thoughts you have as to why you have coded data in a particular way; this is especially important in the early stages of the coding process when your view of the data might be less sophisticated than after several rounds of coding on many sources.

FIGURE 7.1

Coding in NVivo

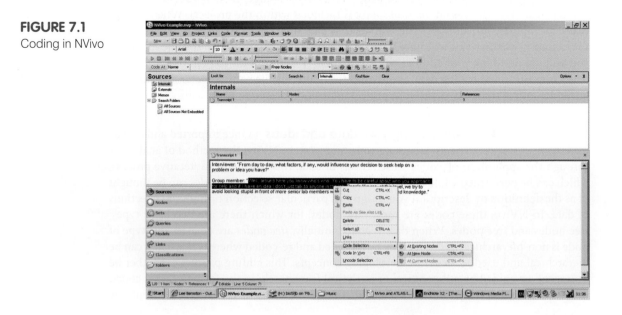

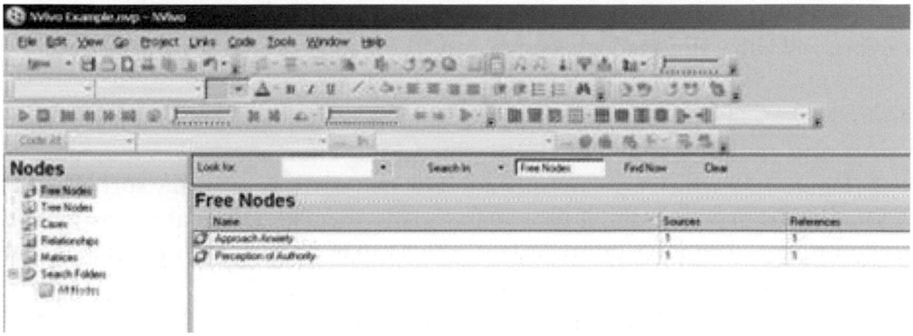

FIGURE 7.2
After coding in
NVivo

After several rounds of coding many more codes have been developed, some of which are very similar and may therefore be merged into a single node. In NVivo this is achieved by right-clicking to *cut* a node and then right-clicking on the desired node and selecting *merge into node*. This process transfers all coded instances into the node you now consider to be the most suitable for conceptualizing the combined nodes; in addition data can also be un-coded, coded under multiple nodes or any number of other operations can be performed. In facilitating such a high degree of interaction with data through coding and free nodes, NVivo enabled the refinement of codes as knowledge and ideas developed throughout the interview analyses. Figure 7.3 gives an overview of the codes that were generated at this stage of the analysis; the Sources and References columns are particularly noteworthy. The Sources column shows how many sources the data in a particular free node belongs to whereas the References column shows the number of coding instances within a free node. Taken together, these columns can be used to gauge what concepts might be more important than others, which ones need to be developed, and so on. However, use caution when quantifying coding efforts in this way as a free node with the highest number of sources

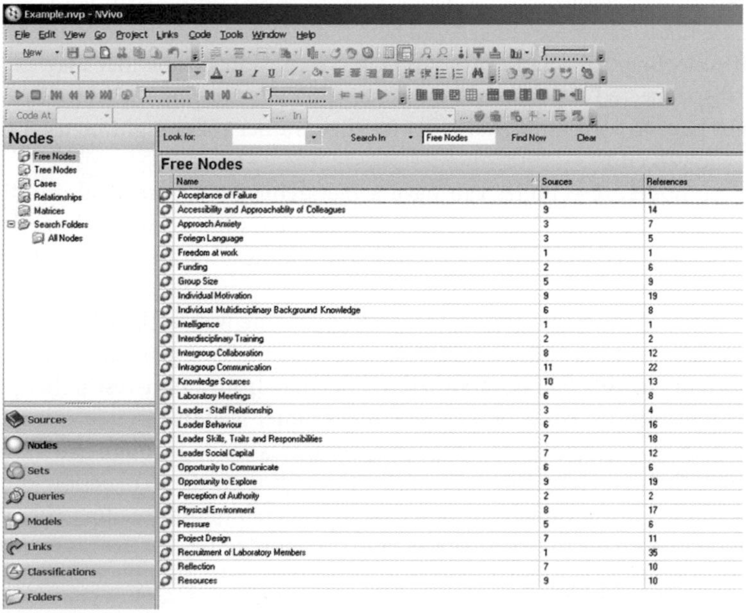

FIGURE 7.3
Overview of codes

and references may not necessarily be the most important influencing factor; only you as the researcher will know this through your observations and experiences while collecting the data.

Structuring and making sense of data   The coding effort resulted in a number of free nodes (Figure 7.3), which are currently not linked in any way or in any sort of order. In this example, the primary aim of data analysis is to thematically analyse the data in order to allow themes to emerge from the data, which can be subsequently developed into concepts through an iterative process of coding and interacting with the data. Ultimately, these concepts may then provide the foundation for theory-building, any theory developed in this way would thus be 'ground' in the data, hence the grounded theory approach to data analysis used in this example. In order to achieve this, the codes (free nodes) first need to be given structure and meaning; NVivo facilitates this process through an array of features and functions that help to interrogate and make sense of the data. For example, one can: search for and retrieve coded data; use the query function to retrieve data that is attached to specific attributes such as all female responses to a question; or conduct word searches that retrieve all coded data with the specified word plus five words either side. This is particularly advantageous in, for example, reminding yourself of the context in which the coded data was collected (e.g. where was the scientist when they yelled '*eureka!*', or, how were they feeling?) Aside from advanced search functionality, there are other ways in which you can begin to bring structure and therefore meaning to data in NVivo, such as through linking nodes to memos and other non-text date such as audio and pictures.

The following two examples show how this might be done using *tree nodes* and *sets*. Before using tree nodes and sets to structure your free nodes, it is important to first have a good overview of the data. In the example used in this chapter some of the free nodes in Figure 7.3 are quite obviously connected as they are based on very similar concepts; however, some are not so obviously linked and here the researcher will need to use their experiences from collecting the data in order to help create connections that may exist between apparently disconnected concepts. A noteworthy point here is that the use of tree nodes and sets does not have to wait until analysis is finished, rather they might be used throughout the overall analysis effort.

Unlike free nodes, tree nodes can have a hierarchical structure and are displayed in NVivo as a *parent node* with any number of *child nodes* linked beneath it. Further, free nodes can also be added to child nodes, and so on, adding additional layers of hierarchy. In the above example, which uses codes generated in a study of creativity in scientific research groups, a number of the codes (free nodes) relate in some way to the leaders of the groups studied. In this way, these codes might be categorized under a general heading of 'leadership' as shown in Figure 7.4. It is important to note that, from a non-researcher perspective, it is difficult to categorize some of the child nodes under leadership; one example of this is the 'Freedom at Work' child node. This connection was made through the more in-depth understanding that the researcher had gained through their data collection efforts. While freedom at work is not uniquely just a factor in leadership, the freedom that the laboratory group members have to explore ideas (and therefore to be creative) is to a large extent

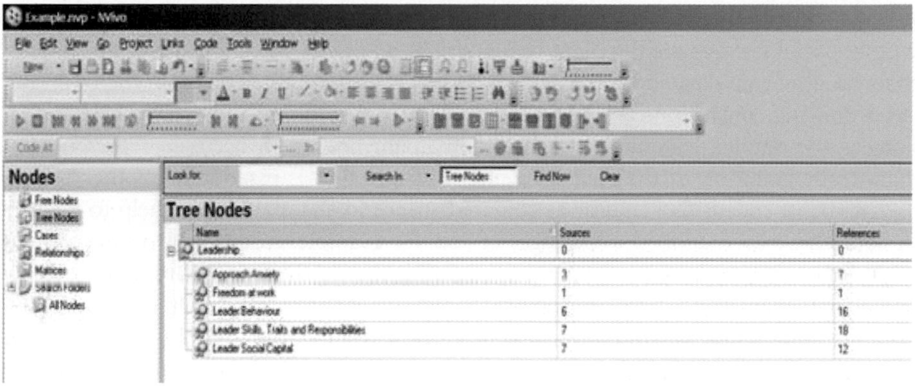

FIGURE 7.4
Tree nodes in NVivo

dictated by whether this kind of activity is supported by the group leader. Subsequently, it can be organized under the developing concept of leadership.

Rather than assigning a hierarchy to developing concepts (free nodes) it might be more useful to simply group similar free nodes into collections, which can then be given an overarching title. In NVivo such groups are known as a *set*. They are useful throughout the data collection and analytical processes as they do not alter your data; they are simply collections of *shortcuts* to the actual data, nodes or so forth and thus deleting or editing them does not make critical changes to your developing project in NVivo. Sets represent a useful way in which to 'act out' your thinking before making significant and sometimes irreversible changes to your coding and data. In using selected free nodes from the PhD study example (shown in Figure 7.3), Figure 7.5 illustrates how factors associated with the creativity of individual laboratory group members are initially grouped together using the sets feature in NVivo. At this stage of the coding process for the PhD study example given, it is unclear whether the *individual factors* set will develop into an independent concept or whether the themes within this set can be broken down further; this will require further coding and data interrogation to find out.

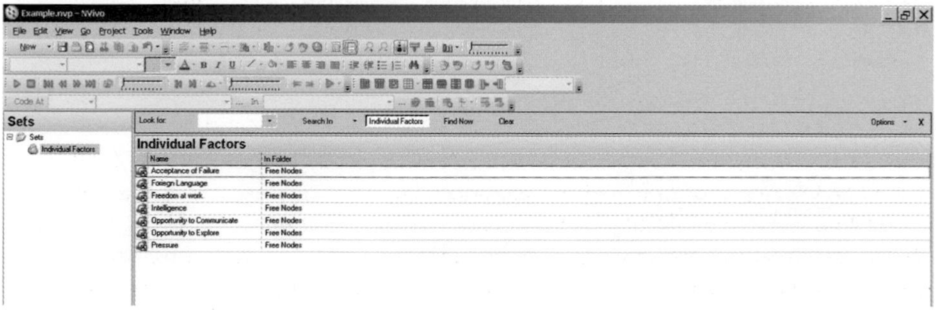

FIGURE 7.5
Individual factors in NVivo

Visualizing data   Aside from the features highlighted in the previous worked examples, some other useful features are the *chart, coding stripe* and *model tool*; these are useful ways in which to visualize your data and coding efforts. However, caution must be used when working with and drawing conclusions and focus from quantifying tools such as charts and coding densities as the outputs generated by these tools might not be an accurate representation of what's really going on in the data. The coding stripes tool is essentially another way to view what you've coded; they appear as coloured stripes in the margin and help to identify which codes have been applied to passages of text, for example. Additional to the coloured stripes, there is a greyscale stripe that shows the coding density, this can be useful for quickly identifying how many codes have been applied to a particular area of data. On the other hand, *models* are a more visual way to represent your ideas or results from analysis work; they can be used to show relationships between nodes and other project items and can be printed or exported as a picture. Taken again from the previous example study into creativity, the basic model presented in Figure 7.6 shows the two previously identified developing concepts of *leadership* (tree node) and *individual factors* (set) in a model. It is particularly important to note what type of connection two or more nodes or data points have, either: associative, one-way or symmetrical. In the model, the leadership child nodes are shown as having a one-way relationship to the parent node, *leadership*. However, in relation to the nodes contained within the set 'individual factors', these are displayed in the opposite manner, i.e. the overarching node 'individual factors' is associated with multiple nodes. Fundamentally, the model in Figure 7.6 is showing that there are some associations (not necessarily *relationships* at this stage) between factors in the leadership concept and the developing individual factors concept. These associations are shown by the connecting lines *without* arrows and highlight how data in the codes – opportunity to explore, freedom at work, acceptance of failure and intelligence – have some associations with data coded under the 'freedom at work' node in the leadership concept. Additionally, the model suggests that an individual's 'opportunity to communicate' is in some

FIGURE 7.6

Associations in NVivo

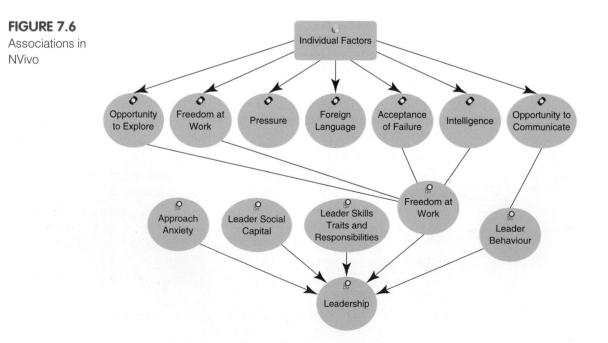

way associated or influenced by a leader's behaviour. In this way, models are a good way to share thoughts on how concepts and analyses in general are progressing and can be somewhat easier than using node report printouts to explain the same relationships.

Working with ATLAS.ti: creativity in multidisciplinary scientific laboratory groups

ATLAS.ti is another CAQDAS package that can be used to help the researcher manage and analyse data. The functionality and features of ATLAS.ti can be grouped into three areas: those which aid analysis on a textual level; those which facilitate conceptual level analysis; and those which help play a role in project management. ATLAS.ti has a slightly different architecture to NVivo in that the project database can only be external; that is, the data used in a project is stored elsewhere on the computer and ATLAS.ti simply links to these files. This has implications for where files are stored and how they are moved around on the computer; it is advisable to store all project files within the same folder. However, once linked to, ATLAS.ti provides the same fundamental functionality as NVivo; essentially the project files can be viewed and worked with via the ATLAS.ti user interface (workspace). In order to provide a clear comparison of these two programmes, the same data will be used for examples here as was used in the NVivo 8 section.

Familiarization and data preparation ATLAS.ti uses slightly different terminology to NVivo and it is essential to be familiar with this before you start a new project. Table 7.6 provides an overview of some of the key terms you will need to be familiar with. ATLAS.ti

TABLE 7.6 A list of key terms used in ATLAS.ti 6.2

Technical Term	Meaning
Hermeneutic unit (HU)	This is the all-encompassing project file. Once opened, all files that are contained within a project also become available.
Primary documents	Primary documents (PDs) are documents that you wish to include in your project as a source for analysis. They need to be *assigned* to your project and can be text, audio, video or graphical. These files are held external to the project file.
Assign	This is a term used to describe the process of linking your PDs to your HU (project).
Quotation	This is a specific selection of a PD that the researcher considers important; quotations are not limited to text PDs.
Codes, supercodes and coding	A code is typically an overarching term that is used to classify quotations; note that a quotation can belong to more than one code. Supercodes are groups of codes. Coding is the process of classifying quotations, and potentially other codes, in an iterative process of conceptualization.
Memo	This is essentially a diary-like tool, where you can write thoughts relating to different aspects of a project.
Objects	These are objects within the project such as quotations, codes and memos.

TABLE 7.7 An overview of the key tools available in ATLAS.ti 6.2

Tool	Use
HU Editor	Main workspace that is primarily used to view and manage PDs.
Object Managers	Essentially, these are 'floating' windows that enable access to, and management of, project objects.
Family Manager	A 'floating' window that enables the researcher to access and manage 'families' of codes, PDs and memos.
Query and Text Search	These are two different tools that collectively facilitate both basic and complex query and text searches.
Object Crawler	This is used to search across an entire project including: codes, memos, PDs, families, etc. However, it is restricted to text-only parts of the project.
Network Editor	Facilitates the construction of semantic networks, which can help to visualize connections and relationships between project objects.
Auto Coding	This tool has the capability to search PDs and automatically apply user-defined codes to specific text.

supports a wide range of file types, including those supported in NVivo, along with some added support for Google Earth files; however, it is important to check the manufacturer's list of supported file types as this can change over the course of software revisions. Once you have assigned one or more primary documents to your project file, there are myriad tools available for use, which help facilitate the analysis of the data within your primary documents; some of the key tools are summarized in Table 7.7.

Building your project   Once all of the PDs you wish to use in your project have been created, edited and are ready to be *assigned* then the first step is to open ATLAS.ti and save your new project. It is a good idea to save the project file (HU) to the same folder as your PDs; further, ensure that you do not need to edit any of the PDs *after* they have been assigned to your project, as this can cause problems with file recognition. Next, assign any desired PDs by going to Documents > Assign > Assign. In the example shown in Figure 7.7, an interview transcript from a PhD study into creativity in multidisciplinary scientific research groups has been assigned.

Now that the PD has been assigned to the project, any number of actions can be performed, the actions covered in the following sections show how data within the assigned transcript (Figure 7.7) can be coded and conceptualized using the basic features of ATLAS.ti 6.2. For a more in-depth overview of ATLAS.ti and information on more advanced features, interested readers are directed to the Further Reading list at the end of this chapter.

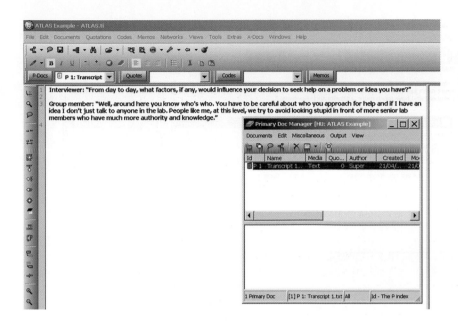

FIGURE 7.7
The ATLAS.ti workspace showing an assigned primary document (transcript) and document manager

Identifying and coding data   In principal, coding in ATLAS.ti follows the same logic as coding in NVivo; data is classified using a code or multiple codes and then codes are conceptualized through being grouped and managed in different ways; additionally, visual models can also be used to visually map relationships and associations between codes. In practice, however, the coding process in ATLAS.ti is a little different. Perhaps the most important difference is that in ATLAS.ti, selections of data (quotations) are classified as independent project objects; they do not have to be coded to be retrieved. This also means the same functionality, such as the creation of relationships, that can be applied to other objects like codes and memos can also be applied to quotations. This arguably enables a greater degree of 'closeness' between the researcher and the data as it allows yet another level of analysis underneath the level of codes. In this example, the first stage is now to create 'free quotations' from the desired data within the assigned transcript; this is achieved by simply selecting the text, right-clicking and selecting 'create free quotation'. Once created, free quotations can be viewed and managed in the Quotation Manager and from the interactive margin area. The managers for quotations, codes, memos and PDs can be accessed through their respective buttons next to the main toolbar drop-down menus; these buttons and the results of the free quotation stage are shown in Figure 7.8. At this point it is worth noting that, as in NVivo, quotations, codes and other project objects in ATLAS.ti initially appear as non-hierarchical.

The next stage in the coding process is to create codes in order to classify the quotations. Codes can be created by accessing the Code Manager, selecting 'Codes' and then selecting 'Create Free Code'. As in the NVivo example, two codes have been created: 'Approach Anxiety' and 'Perception of Authority'. In order to now 'code' the free quotations, it is simply a case of selecting the appropriate quotation (this can be done easily via the interactive margin) and 'dragging and dropping' it into the relevant code in the Code Manager; the coded free quotations are shown in Figure 7.9, note how the associated code name is now

FIGURE 7.8

Overview of two free quotations created from an interview transcript

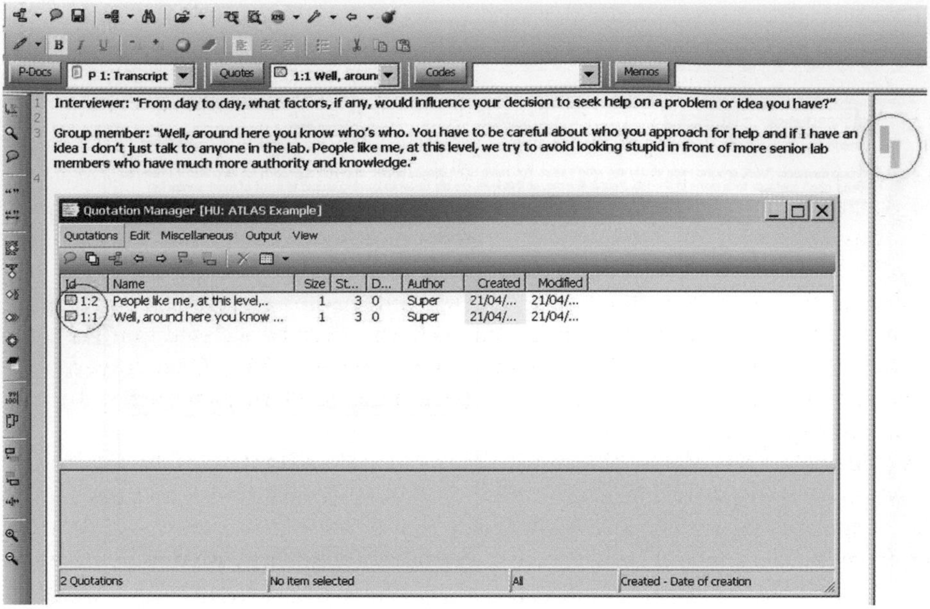

NOTE: ALSO VISIBLE ARE THE QUOTATION INDICATORS IN THE 'MARGIN AREA' (CIRCLED IN GREEN) AND THE QUOTATIONS IN THE QUOTATION MANAGER. WITHIN THE QUOTATION MANAGER NOTE THE IDENTIFICATION OF THE QUOTATIONS (CIRCLED RED); THE FIRST NUMBER RELATES TO THE PD OF THE QUOTATION AND THE SECOND NUMBER RELATES TO THE QUOTATION NUMBER. IN THIS EXAMPLE THERE ARE TWO QUOTATIONS FROM PD1.

FIGURE 7.9

Free quotations are now coded under the codes *Approach Anxiety* and *Perception of Authority*

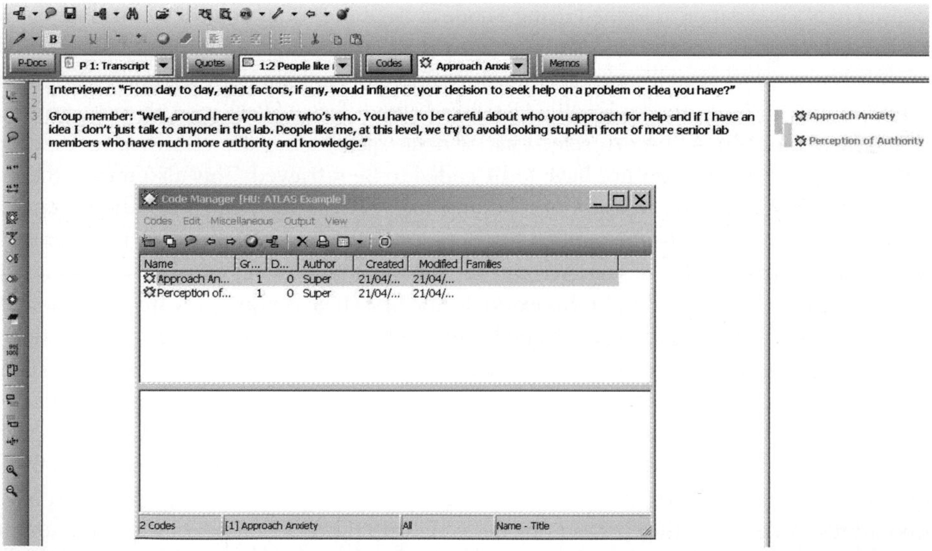

also displayed next to the quotation in the margin area when viewing the PD. In a similar fashion, new free quotations can also be created by dragging and dropping selections of data into the Quotation Manager. It should also be borne in mind that there are numerous other ways in which you can work with the PD, such as annotating and linking text, audio or graphics to memo notes.

As you develop a larger and larger selection of codes, you will need to begin to sort these in order to make sense of what the data is telling you. Just as in NVivo, there are a number of tools in ATLAS.ti that can aid you in this task; for example, the use of 'families'. Families are essentially a collection of project objects: PDs, quotations, memos or codes that have been grouped because they are thought to relate to a similar theme. However, a family can only consist of one type of object. In order to provide a comparison to the NVivo example, Figure 7.10 shows a group of codes that all relate to creativity in research group leadership, therefore, they have been organized into a code family named 'Leadership'. Families can be created and managed using the Family Manager, which can be accessed from the Code Manager (the yellow circular button to do this is shown in Figure 7.11). Once created, families can be used in a number of ways, for example as a way of filtering and sorting data and as variables in queries.

As a side note, users of ATLAS.ti might also want to take advantage of the auto-coding tool, which is a little more advanced that in NVivo 8. This tool applies user pre-defined codes to specific text automatically, which can be useful for large amounts of data and when there is a clear and reliable concept to be coded. However, caution must always be used with automated features of CAQDAS packages as context cannot be analysed and in some way the automatic process removes the intuition and logic of the researcher from the coding process.

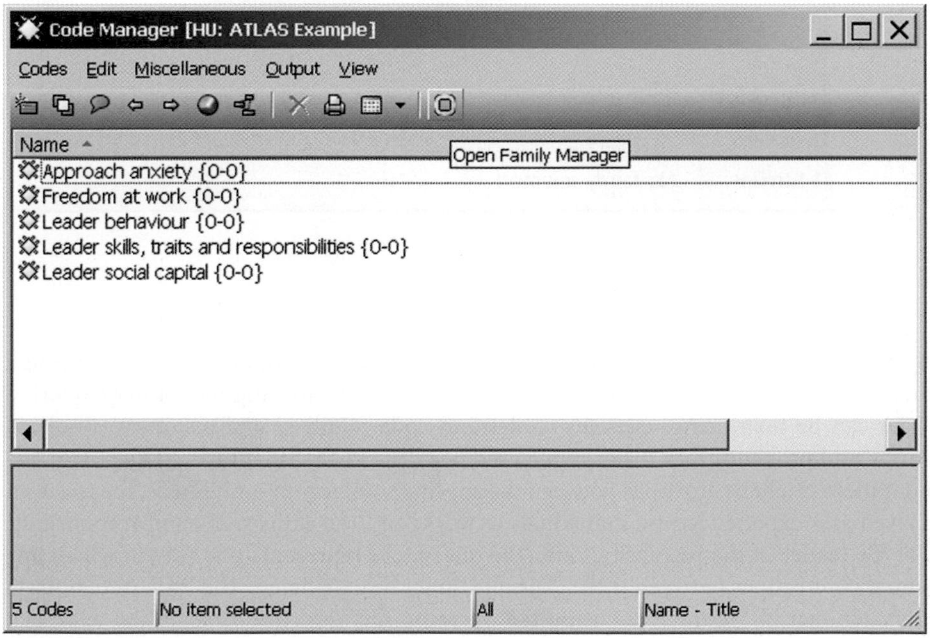

FIGURE 7.10
Displayed in the Code Manager are five codes that are all related to creative leadership

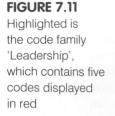

FIGURE 7.11
Highlighted is
the code family
'Leadership',
which contains five
codes displayed
in red

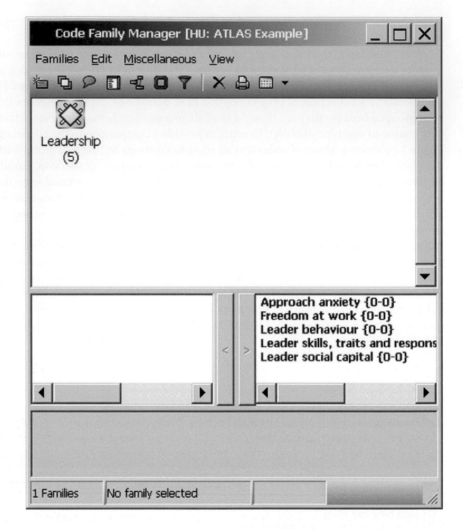

Retrieving and interrogating data In ATLAS.ti data is primarily retrieved through the use of the query tool, which enables the use of basic and highly complex queries. Queries can be built using *operands* (codes and code families) and *operators* (Boolean, semantic and proximity). In the example used here, the PhD student would like to understand if there might be any links between the approach anxiety of individuals, the freedom perceived and experienced by individuals at work, and the skills traits and responsibilities of the leader of the research group. The query tool represents one way in which any potential connections between these concepts might be elucidated. The PhD student built a query (shown in Figure 7.12) using the operator 'OR' and the three codes: approach anxiety; freedom at work; and leader skills, traits and responsibilities. This query returns

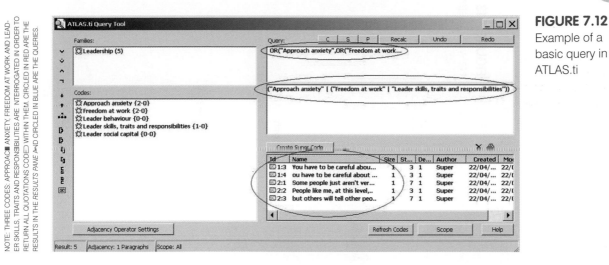

FIGURE 7.12
Example of a basic query in ATLAS.ti

all the quotations that are contained within these three codes, which now enables the PhD student to explore the quotations and create any necessary relationships and associations. It is also worth noting that as well as the query tool, there is a text search tool that can handle a variety of text searches within PDs such as matching patterns of text along with other more standard text searches. Alongside the text search and query tools, there are a number of other notable tools such as the word cruncher, object crawler, object explorer and redundant coding analyser.

Visualizing and modelling   Similarly to NVivo, ATLAS.ti has a modelling tool that offers the researcher the capability of creating graphical 'networks'; a network in this sense can be defined as a set of nodes and links. A node represents a project object, almost all project objects can be presented as nodes in a network. Building a network is useful for visualization of, for example, the progress of a project or how a theory or concept is developing. On the other hand, networks can be used for tasks other than visualization, such as in the retrieval of quotations (in this instance networks are known as 'Semantic Operators'), which can be useful for generating thematic quotation lists, e.g. all the quotes that belong to codes that have been conceptualized using a network. However, the following examples will show how networks might be used to conceptualize coding efforts in the previous examples and not the more advanced functions of the network tool; see the Further Reading list for more information on advanced network functions.

When constructing a network, the Network View Manager window provides all the functionality required, such as creating a new network; it also lists all existing networks. The two basic stages of network creation are: first, import the desired nodes and second, create links between them. One particularly useful element of the networking tool in ATLAS.ti is the capability to visually show *relation*; in other words, what the nature of the link is. This is very useful in understanding how concepts (codes) relate to one another across the project and, subsequently, for building theory. Additionally, users can define their own 'relations', which adds another level of descriptive and conceptualization capability. Figure 7.13 exemplifies

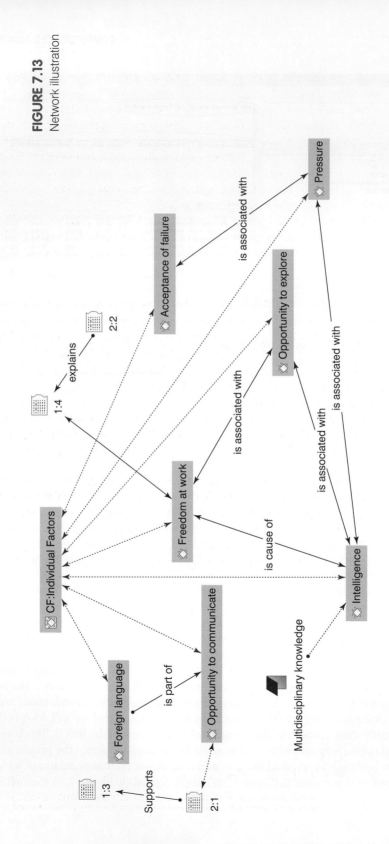

FIGURE 7.13
Network illustration

how, through the use of nodes and links, the inner relations and structure of developing concepts can be visualized.

This network shows a developing concept (factors of individual creativity) in the previously used PhD project example. At the top level, note how the code family (CF: Individual Factors) has automatically linked nodes; these are the codes that have been grouped within this code family. Further, note the descriptive links, which give an indication of the nature of the relation between two (or more) nodes. Of further interest is the variety of project objects that can be used as nodes, for example a memo on 'multidisciplinary knowledge' helps to explain how intelligence is related to individual creativity.

Yet another level of complexity that can be added to network diagrams is the addition of other networks as nodes. This is important because it allows you to create a higher level of classification; entire networks can be networked to give a detailed 'big picture' view of the project.

Other useful tools Besides networks, there are other ways to visualize, map and interconnect data; the use of hypertext is one such way to achieve these. Essentially hypertext enables a more in-depth level of coding because it provides a way to link text to text. This is very useful for developing richer 'relations' between passages of text. For example, a passage of text that supports what is being discussed in another passage of text can be linked to the other passage of text with the relation 'support' being shown too. Furthermore, such hyperlinks can then be used to retrieve passages of text, for example one might search for all text supporting passage X. Additionally, they can also be seen readily in the margin area, which provides a useful reminder of other available evidence when coding or re-visiting documents. Figures 7.14 and 7.15 show a hypertext map and margin area view respectively.

Finally, aside from textual and conceptual level tools, there are functions in ATLAS.ti that aid project management and the sharing of projects. First, in terms of sharing and archiving, there are many different output options such as the generation and reports along with the ability to print images of networks and many other project elements. Additionally there are some specialist output options such as the ability to export certain parts of project data to SPSS for statistical work. Collectively, the various output options in ATLAS.ti enable

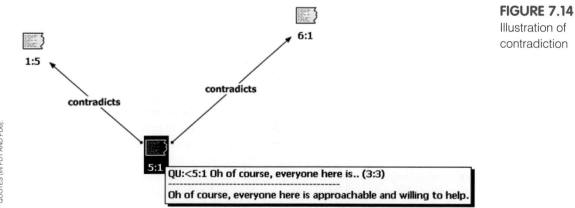

NOTE: THIS IS A GRAPHICAL REPRESENTATION OF HOW THE FIRST QUOTE IN PD5 APPEARS TO CONTRADICT TWO OTHER QUOTES (IN PD1 AND PD6).

FIGURE 7.14

Illustration of contradiction

FIGURE 7.15

Atlas.ti map illustration

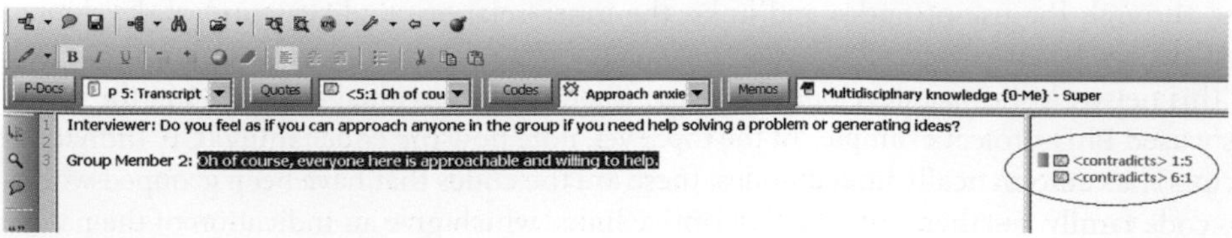

NOTE: THE MAP SHOWN IN FIGURE 7.14 IS AS IT IS SEEN FROM THE STANDARD WORKSPACE. THE INFORMATION RELATING TO THE HYPERTEXT LINKS CAN BE SEEN IN THE MARGIN AREA (CIRCLED RED) IN FIGURE 7.15.

the researcher to keep a detailed paper trail, which is potentially helpful for maintaining the transparency of the coding process, an important factor for increasing the objectivity of grounded approaches to analyses.

In regards to collaborative work in ATLAS.ti, there are several features that can help. First, users are able to 'pack' projects into a 'bundle' that is more easily transported, e.g. to another machine. Additionally, projects can be split and merged, which might be particularly useful when multiple researchers are responsible for analysing different documents of a joint project. There is, however, one fundamental consideration when making use of the collaborative tools in ATLAS.ti and that is the external database architecture. Users need to be very careful when transporting project files such as HU files and PDs; further, altering the folder structure where these files are stored can create problems. Full guidance is offered on these functions in the open manual available with ATLAS.ti.

A grounded approach: NVivo 8 or ATLAS.ti 6.2?

The question of which of these two CAQDAS packages is best for the job is one that many researchers often ask, but it is one that cannot be wholly answered. The best answer is that both packages offer tools that facilitate the fundamental process of *coding*. Further, relative to other packages such as WordSmith, one might consider these two packages similar in the sense that they are likely more suited to a grounded approach. However, NVivo and ATLAS.ti differ in several ways: the architecture of the software; how they function and how the user interacts with the software; and in the range and type of tools that are offered to support the coding process.

NVivo offers a familiar user interface akin to some Microsoft Office environments while ATLAS.ti can, at first, appear overwhelmingly complicated. However, the floating manager windows and other features of the ATLAS.ti interface enable more than one type of project 'object', such as codes, to be viewed simultaneously. Dissimilarly, although simpler, this is not possible through NVivo's user interface. Another important distinction is the external database system of ATLAS.ti versus the internal (or external) system of NVivo. The external system of ATLAS.ti means that the user should be a lot more careful about moving the project file, folders and documents whereas this is less of an issue in NVivo. Another difference is in how each programme handles PDF files; the new version of ATLAS.ti covered here has much improved PDF functionality, which is arguably much better than the PDF-handling capabilities of NVivo 8. This is important because almost all scholarly articles are now electronically published in PDF format, and further, using PDF format can make sharing documents easier. On another note, both tools have advanced functionality for interrogating data, although ATLAS.ti can take this one level deeper through the 'hypertext' functionality. Lastly, both packages have a good range of output options and ways in which data can be modelled and visualized.

Ultimately, these packages only aid the analysis process, it remains the job of the researcher to provide the intellectual input and make sense of what is being observed. To this end, a researcher taking a grounded approach should think carefully about what features they will most likely need from a package. For example, if surveys are going to be the primary method of data generation and combined with an analytical framework then the auto-coding features might appeal. On the other hand, if no theoretical or analytical framework is being used then strong data management and deeper interrogation capabilities might be more favourable. Conclusively, there is no definitive answer to the question 'which package is right for me?' Researchers should consider, among other factors, the types of data they will generate, what they need to do with this data and if they need to transport the data regularly.

WordSmith

WordSmith is a corpus linguistic analysis software developed by Mike Scott in 1996, predominantly for use by teachers and students in linguistics. However, the software is so versatile that it lends itself to a variety of studies and is particularly useful in analysing large amounts of text. Previously distributed by Oxford University Press, WordSmith is currently distributed by Lexical Analysis Software Ltd and can be bought online and downloaded fairly easily. In addition, the software runs on most PCs although it can be memory intensive, requiring a large amount of hard disk space. It is therefore worth checking the computer memory requirements before installing it.

The approach taken by WordSmith is one of combining several tools as opposed to a one-size-fits-all approach. It begins with the creation of a *corpus* (plural *corpora*), which may be defined as 'a collection of written or spoken material in machine-readable form, assembled for the purpose of linguistic research' (Oxford Dictionaries Online). This main corpus is then analysed against a reference corpus, which allows for the generation of a list of keywords using the KeyWord function. The software also has a WordList tool that computes the total number of words in the corpus and presents them alphabetically or in order of their frequency. Finally, the Concord tool allows for the analysis of words and phrases in their linguistic context.

To illustrate the use of WordSmith outside linguistics, below is a part of a PhD study employing discourse analysis in which WordSmith was used to analyse the talk about corruption in the Kenyan press from 1993 to 2007 in the wake of what are arguably two of the largest corruption cases in the history of the country. In this instance, the study began by analysing the texts (newspaper articles in this case) in their linguistic context as a means of identifying emerging and competing discourses, which are then analysed in the wider social, political and economic context of their production and consumption.

To begin the study newspaper articles were selected, numbered and saved in date order to allow for chronological analysis, which was an important aspect of this study. For example, an article appearing in the *Daily Nation* on 13 March 1998 was saved as: 'ARTICLE_14_MARCH_13_1998_THE NATION'. This was repeated for all articles, and saved to folders according to their year of publication. The articles (by folder) were then combined to form one document in order of publication date.

The next step was to convert the texts from Microsoft Word format into a plain text format and upload them onto WordSmith for textual analysis. A step-by-step explanation of the subsequent analysis is given below.

Step one: keywords   The first step was to identify keywords in the corpora. These are words that occur 'with unusual frequency in a given text' (Scott, 1997: 236). In order to compile a keyword list, WordSmith begins by compiling a word list from the corpus, through its WordList function. The most frequently occurring words from this process were articles, conjunctions and prepositions, the majority of which were not seen as relevant to the study.

Step two: comparison   The second step involved comparing the word list from the main corpus to that from a reference corpus in order to generate the keyword list and from this process a total of 127 keywords were finally selected based on ubiquity (the sense of being everywhere in the text) as well as the extent to which the researcher judged them to be interesting, unusual and/or relevant to the study. For example, the word would have to appear a significant number of times in the corpus, and be deemed intriguing enough for inclusion. By illustration, the word 'plunder' appears 59 times in 7 out of the 15 years covered by the press corpus. This was considered to be significant enough for inclusion to the keyword list.

Where variations of the same word appeared several times, the root word was taken (where appropriate) and the subsequent search within the corpora conducted with the addition of an asterisk at the end of the word. 'Scandal', for example, appears 5,806 times as a keyword and 'scandals' appears 1,673 times. In this example, 'scandal' was taken as part of the final word list and applied as 'scandal*' in order to capture its full range of extensions appearing in the corpora. However, 'Britain', for example, was taken as a separate word from the word 'British', as WordSmith could not capture both in a search for 'Britain*' in the corpora.

This process of sifting through the initial keyword list, removing 'noise' as well as words that may not be relevant to the study, facilitated the formulation of the final keyword list. The creation of this list formed the initial stage in mapping the emergence and development of various discourses over time. It was recognized that the language in use would evolve over time and vary around events and perhaps also be experienced and perceived slightly differently by the participants.

Step three: concordance   Having established the keywords, the next step involved searching for each keyword in the corpus. This was done by use of the Concord function in WordSmith, which makes a concordance by searching for a specified keyword in all chosen texts and presents a concordance display. This display shows the keyword in a different colour from the surrounding text (blue in this case) and gives, at a glance, a basic idea of the context in which the word is used.

To illustrate, consider a search for 'corrupt' in the press corpus. This word (and all its variations) occurred a total of 13,173 times and is present in the entire dataset ranging from 1993 to 2007, as presented in Figure 7.16.

In addition to information on the number of times a keyword appears in the text, the concordance view also presents details for each entry, for example, the entry number, the concordance line, word-position and so on. In addition, each result-row is extendable, which allows for more text to be displayed around the node-word (see Figure 7.17).

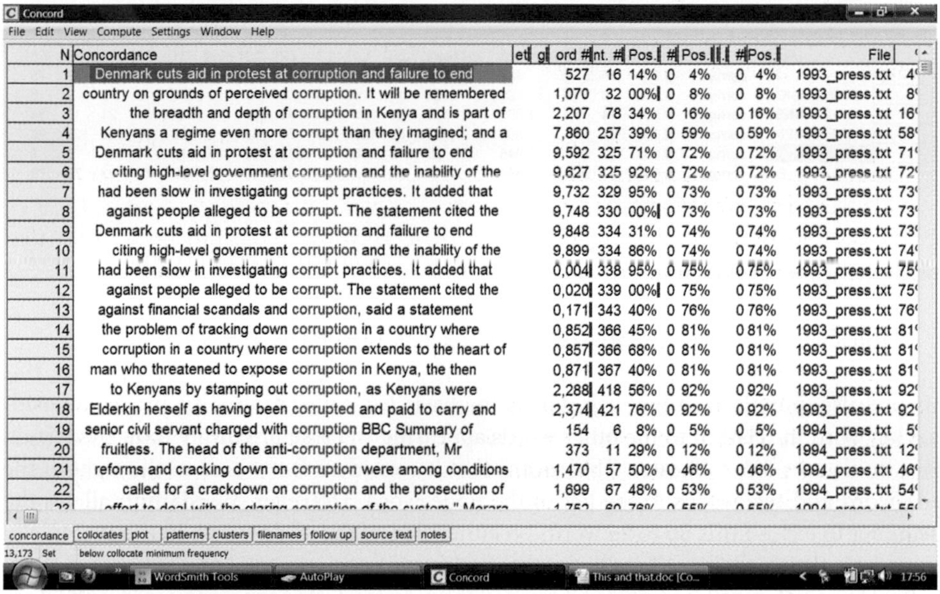

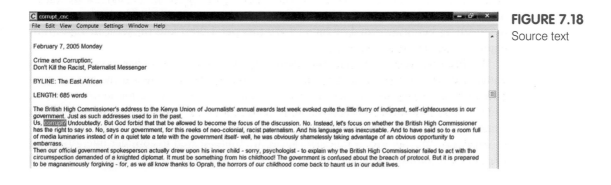

FIGURE 7.16
'Corruption' concordance from press corpus

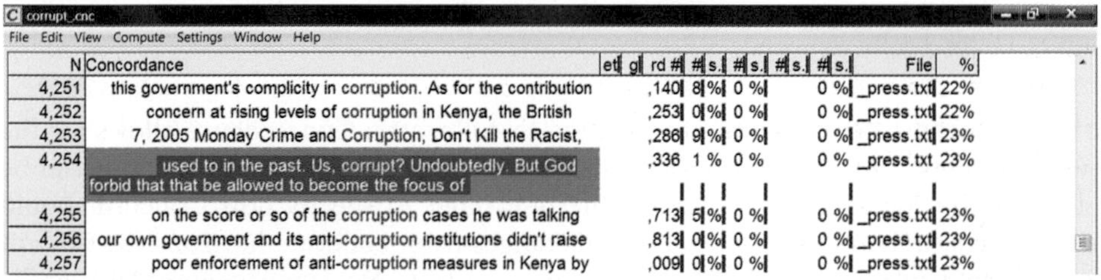

FIGURE 7.17
Extended concordance row (see highlighted selection)

It is also possible to click through each entry in order to view the corresponding source text, in order to get more specific information regarding the context in which the word has been used. For example, the source text for entry 4,254 in Figure 7.18 below is an opinion piece appearing in *The East African* on Monday 7 February 2005.

FIGURE 7.18
Source text

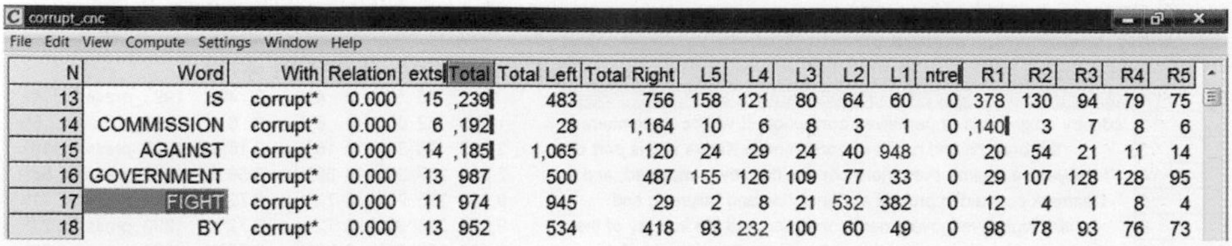

FIGURE 7.19

Collocates of
'corruption*' in
press corpus

N	Word	With	Relation	exts	Total	Total Left	Total Right	L5	L4	L3	L2	L1	ntre	R1	R2	R3	R4	R5
13	IS	corrupt*	0.000	15	,239	483	756	158	121	80	64	60	0	378	130	94	79	75
14	COMMISSION	corrupt*	0.000	6	,192	28	1,164	10	6	8	3	1	0	,140	3	7	8	6
15	AGAINST	corrupt*	0.000	14	,185	1,065	120	24	29	24	40	948	0	20	54	21	11	14
16	GOVERNMENT	corrupt*	0.000	13	987	500	487	155	126	109	77	33	0	29	107	128	128	95
17	FIGHT	corrupt*	0.000	11	974	945	29	2	8	21	532	382	0	12	4	1	8	4
18	BY	corrupt*	0.000	13	952	534	418	93	232	100	60	49	0	98	78	93	76	73

Understanding collocates

'You shall know a word by the company it keeps' (J.R. Firth, 1957: 11).

This premise, popularized by Firth, forms the basis for collocation. This process considers a keyword in relation to the other words appearing in close proximity to it. By default, WordSmith uses 5/5 collocates. This means that it considers five words to the right of the node-word and five words to the left of the node-word. However, WordSmith allows the researcher to extend this up to 25 words on either side of the node-word. In the example in Figure 7.19, the word 'Fight' (see highlighted selection) occurs a total of 974 times as a collocate of the node-word 'corrupt*'. Of these, 945 are to the left of the node-word, and 29 are to the right. Immediately to the left (L1), there are 382 occurrences, hence the phrase 'fight corruption', which may give an insight to the perception of 'corruption' as something that needs to be forcefully removed.

Plots, patterns and clusters   In addition to collocates, Concordance allows for the viewing of plots, patterns, clusters and filenames. Ultimately, all these functions can be customized by coding notes that allow the researcher to specify how Concord should conduct the search and display results. This ranges from collocate horizons (number of collocates to display on either side of the node-word), to the language used and can be accessed via the buttons at the bottom of the Concord window (see circled section in Figure 7.20).

Figure 7.20 also shows a plot-view of the occurrence of the node-word 'corrupt' in the press corpus. In this view, the results have been arranged chronologically starting from texts produced in the year 1993 at the top, to the year 2007 at the bottom. This shows the first appearance of the word in the texts, how often it occurs within each text and the dispersion within that text. In the example in Figure 7.20, a basic observation might be that the word is used less before the year 1999, with the highest number of occurrences being recorded in 2006 (5,670 hits per 1,000) and the least in 1996 (only eight hits per 1,000).

Delving even deeper into the data, WordSmith allows the researcher to view emerging patterns based on how all the variations of the node-word are used in the text, as illustrated in Figure 7.21. In this view, all the variations of the node-word found in the text are displayed in the centre, and words that are most common relative to the node-word are displayed on either side in order of their occurrence.

Alongside the patterns, it was also valuable in this research to consider interesting and relevant word-clusters that frequently occurred in the text. In this regard, WordSmith

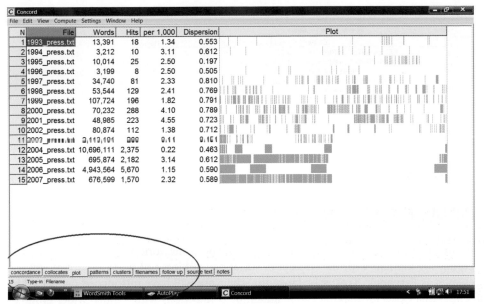

FIGURE 7.20
Plot of 'corruption' in press corpus

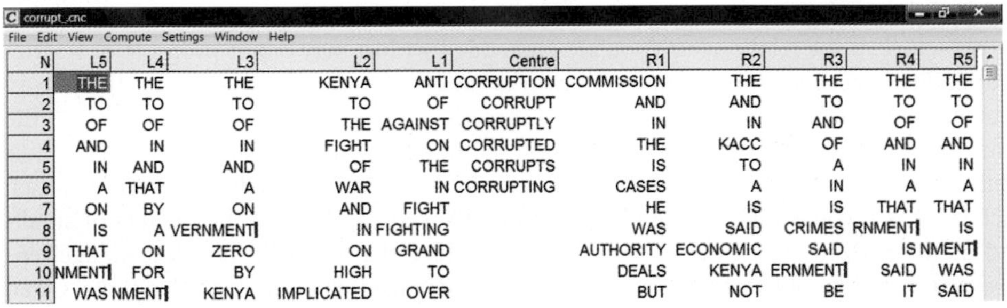

FIGURE 7.21
Patterns for the node-word 'corrupt*' in the press corpus

presents word-clusters as shown in Figure 7.22. In this example, the three-word cluster 'the fight against' appears 446 times in the text. It is also possible to view clusters based on how closely related they are, by clicking the 'Related' button. For instance, the clusters 'corruption investigations in', 'corruption investigations the' and 'corruption investigations into' are considered to be closely related and are hence displayed together, one immediately after the other, in the related-view.

Finally, WordSmith comes with a user guide embedded in the software, which enables the user to explore the tools as they use them. These guides are very detailed and are supported by an online step-by-step guide, which means that most people do not need formal training in order to use the software. The illustration given above demonstrates one approach to using WordSmith tools and is in no way exhaustive. Indeed, there are numerous ways in which these tools may be combined and this is what makes this software so adaptable.

FIGURE 7.22

Clusters for the node-word 'corrupt*' in the press corpus

N	Cluster	Freq.	Length	Related
1	KENYA ANTI CORRUPTION	1,228	3	
2	ANTI CORRUPTION COMMISSION	1,145	3	
3	THE KENYA ANTI	1,021	3	
4	FIGHT AGAINST CORRUPTION	520	3	
5	THE ANTI CORRUPTION	491	3	
6	THE FIGHT AGAINST	446	3	
7	TO FIGHT CORRUPTION	326	3	
8	CORRUPTION COMMISSION KACC	314	3	
9	CORRUPTION IN THE	219	3	
10	WAR ON CORRUPTION	209	3	
11	WAR AGAINST CORRUPTION	205	3	

SOCIAL NETWORK ANALYSIS

The third method of natural language analysis is social network analysis. Most researchers today are familiar with the concept of social networking and many no doubt will use sites such as Facebook, Twitter or LinkedIn. Their use will have introduced people to the potential that exists for making and maintaining connections with a much wider group of people than was ever possible before. What this phenomenon has done is to highlight what we have known for years, that everyone is embedded in a rich pattern of social relationships and that these relations are important (see Eden, Jones and Sims, 1983,) to the extent that the structure of the relationships you are embedded within may either promote or restrict your ability to get access to resources. Networks have the potential to affect everything from your mental health to your success in your career. So, for example, two individuals in the same organization with exactly the same skill set may differ in their success based on their ability to network and connect. In the evolution of business knowledge research in which Richard was involved, it was the networking and social capital that the owners of small- and medium-sized businesses engaged in that enabled them to gain new knowledge represented by measurable interactions in which they engaged when making decisions. Often this knowledge passed tacitly between individuals and the learning derived occurred 'naturally' as part of work-related events (see Davies and Easterby-Smith, 1984). This feature of thriving or otherwise is related to a variety of very differing influences and resources being available via networks. Network research then seeks to examine networks through issues of similarity (membership, location, gender), forms of relationships, e.g. kinship relationships, likes and dislikes, conversations with others or exchanges of information (Borgatti et al., 2009: 894).

The historical basis for social network study is wide and emerged through the disciplines of anthropology, sociology and mathematics (see Borgatti et al., 2009, for a full explanation of network analysis in the social sciences). Moreno (1934) was one of the first researchers to explicitly 'map' the social connections of people. Examining the relations of young children he was able to provide an explanation as to why some children would be more likely to run away from home based on the connectivity with, and influence of, other children. In work-based studies, Granovetter's (1973) work on studying how people locate job opportunities was highly influential. Essentially he concluded that people rely heavily on information from those people with whom they are loosely or remotely connected (strength of weak ties). This is partly because those people close to you often know and exchange the same (redundant) information; we get more novel information from remote connections or those people less connected to the others in your closer group. Coleman (1988) on the other hand developed the theory that the ability to build trust, through development of norms, is stronger and more likely in more 'closed' cohesive groups. This tension can be examined in a very simple network below (see Figures 7.23a and 7.23b). Company A is connected to a range of other firms and the structure has a high number of structural holes (companies not connected to others). This structure may provide company A with a host of novel information, which it can use in its other relations to 'play off' against the other firms in the network. In company B, all the companies are connected or 'bounded' meaning any knowledge is more likely to be known by all companies in the network to the point where company B no longer has the competitive advantage and is constrained. However, in a situation where a high degree of trust is required then the cohesion of company B would be preferable as closed or cohesive groups are more likely to develop the norms and behaviours related to trust behaviour.

In organizational studies today the range of research and theory is large and growing (see Brass et al., 2004; Kilduff and Brass, 2010, for a full review of network research in organizations). A snapshot of the research from organizational studies shows social networks in or between firms will be affected by gender (Ibarra, 1992) and minority status of employees (Mehra, Kilduff and Brass, 1998), and will differ depending on the formal organizational

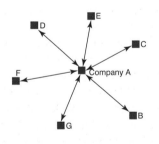

FIGURE 7.23a
Company A

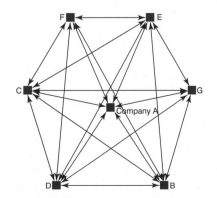

FIGURE 7.23b
Company B

FIGURE 7.24
Complex network
visualization

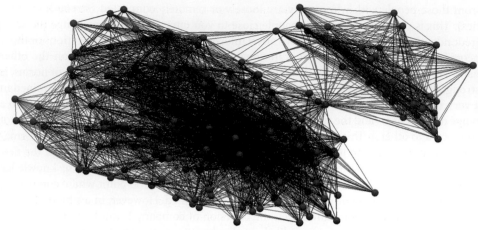

SOURCE: CREATED IN KEYPLAYER (BORGATTI, 2006) BY RICH DEJORDY BASED ON DATA PROVIDED BY EUROPOL

structure (Shrader, Lincoln, and Hoffman, 1989). Network relations may affect personal attitudes (Burkhardt, 1994), organizational innovation ability (Tsai and Ghoshal, 1998; Ahuja, 2000; Obstfeld, 2005), and ability to share differing levels of complex information (Hansen, 1999). Strong ties can affect firm failure rates (Uzzi, 1997) and knowledge sharing networks are affected by the nature of competitive relations (Bouty, 2000).

Interest in understanding the nature of social networks in or between organizations has grown outside of academia as well. Organizations are increasingly interested in analysing their own social networks as this gives them a mechanism to understand how certain properties affect organizational activity. Imagine two new companies being merged; they are unlikely to immediately form strong, well inter-connected working groups and may well rely on existing, pre-merger ties. An understanding of the links can provide ideas about making interventions to improve communication or related outcomes, dependent on the issue at hand.

Today a combination of matrix algebra and graph theory has combined through increasingly complex software to undertake statistical analysis and to create graphical representations of complex social groups. Software packages such as UCINET, Pajek, Siena and EgoNet provide a range of approaches dependent upon research objectives. Some are more suitable for longitudinal data or analysing vast networks like those in Figure 7.24. Here structures can reveal a multitude of theoretical possibilities.

DISCOURSE ANALYSIS

A third approach to the analysis of natural language data is **discourse analysis**. This particular approach takes into account the broader social context in which the conversation takes place, and therefore is less concerned with simply a detailed analysis of transcripts. Ann Cunliffe (2008) defines discourse analysis as a term that covers more than one single approach to analyse language; talk, written text, social practice and physical/symbolic artefacts. It also does not restrict itself to conversations alone, but may for example use other textual sources such as newspaper articles, computer conferences or advertisements as the basis for analysis. In addition, discourse analysis might consider data such as signed language (body movements, hand signals and so on) to make a point about meanings where there is a response. There are three main ways of viewing discourse: as structure, rhetoric or as process (Gergen, 1999). Gergen suggests that to view discourse as a structure is to see it as a set of recurring conventions such as metaphors or narratives that are woven throughout both our speech and ways of living. The second perspective, that of discourse as rhetoric, suggests that there is a hierarchical aspect to consider in any research. Here the concept is not seen simply as about the art of persuasion but also about power. Recognition will therefore need to be made about, for example, why some groups within organizations are favoured over others and how this is manifest in rhetoric. Yet a third perspective is to analyse how lives are influenced and 'constituted' through the ongoing process of conversation. As a summary, we might conclude that language and linguistic systems and practices are formative in shaping social and organizational realities.

Cunliffe (2008) suggests that within organizational and business studies the analysis of discourse has essentially been divided into two main streams, discourse analysis and **critical discourse analysis**. Discourse analysis she argues takes a social constructionist perspective, while critical discourse takes a postmodern and poststructuralist point of view and examines discourse from the perspective of rhetoric. Critical discourse analysis in addition also places an emphasis on aspects of where power lies within relationships (Chouliaraki and Fairclough, 2010) as well as 'ideologies that are created by and represented in language' (Fairclough and Hardy, 1997; Cunliffe, 2008). For Cunliffe it is the emphasis that is placed on context that distinguishes critical discourse analysis from traditional linguistics. The context she argues is influenced by factors such as space, time, practice, change and frame (Chouliaraki and Fairclough, 2010; Leitch and Palmer, 2010). It has been the case that critical discourse analysis has offered a useful critical analysis tool both for social scientists in general and for business, organizational and management studies scholars in particular, which enables an examination of aspects of power and persuasion within organizations to be considered in the context of a research study. For a further overview of the key dimensions and the variety of discourse positions that are possible, see Alvesson and Kärreman (2011).

Marshall (2000) suggests that using discourse analysis offers an alternative to perspectives that examine organizations and individuals through the lens of psychology. This indicates that the way the approaches to discourse have developed has emanated from various theoretical positions, all strong fields in their own right, for example, literary theory, linguistics and activity theoretical perspectives. In terms of interpretation, Potter and Wetherell (1988) identify three interconnected concepts, namely function, variation and construction, which are explained below.

- *Function* refers to the practical ways discourse might be used, for example, to explain, justify or excuse, as well as to legitimize the power of particular management groups.
- *Variability* refers to the fact that the same event, the same social group or the same personality may be used to describe the same thing in many different ways as *function* changes.

- *Construction* relates to the notion that discourses are manufactured out of pre-existing linguistic resources and in this manufacturing process an active selection process takes place whereby some formulations will be chosen and others will not (Potter and Wetherell, 1987: 171).

In summary, two important issues need to be noted. One relates to the concept of contradictions, dilemmas and arguments that exist within discourse (Billig, 1988, 1991). A second relates to the notion of identity. Shotter (1993) and Wertsch (1991) both build on different theoretical traditions that highlight the dialogic nature of human thought and action, a concept that sees language as a mediator of social means, whereby its active use serves to unify the internal and external world, the subject with the object, thought with action. One shortcoming of discourse analysis is that it is mainly inductive and studies the use of language; as a result there is more than what can be articulated. A more detailed overview can be found in Cunliffe, 2008. Later on in this chapter we will discuss how argumentation is used to help managers understand their beliefs and ideas.

NARRATIVE ANALYSIS

Narrative analysis, a fourth approach to analysing natural language data, is based on collecting people's accounts of events, real or imagined, and then analysing them through a narrative methodology. Narratives include ways of talking about experience and stories told by organizational members. As a research tool this approach has become increasingly useful in organizational studies, where much research involves the interpretation of experience in some form or another. The method is useful in the analysis of interview data but can also be used with other text-based media. Tsoukas and Hatch (1997) suggest that stories give us 'access to and appreciation for context', which is a vital requirement for the making of meaning and our understanding if a constructionist analysis is to be adopted. Stories:

- are concerned with the temporal ordering of ideas;
- usually tend to focus on the sequential patterning of events and the role of various actors within them;
- enable a researcher to build a complex picture of social situations in order to examine the actions of the various actors in a story, and explore their own values, ideas and beliefs.

Narrative analysis, then, can be applied to data in the form of interviews, corporate texts, videos, websites and autobiographical accounts. Narrative researchers may study organizational narratives, for example, founding myths about how a company came to embody certain values (see Boje, 1991, 1995), individual narratives of organizational life and identity (e.g. Sims, 2003), or narratives of change and resistance (e.g. Humphreys and Brown, 2002). In doing so they will identify plots, characters, tropes, and different types of narratives that offer insights into such issues as organizational culture, strategy, change, identity and the nature of management.

Storytelling is a common way of communicating within organizations. Managers, entrepreneurs and employees tell stories as a way to describe and accomplish their everyday work, presenting vision statements or sending messages of heroic events that have taken place in the past. Compared to many of the approaches illustrated in this book a focus on the analysis of storytelling is a relatively recent activity. Notwithstanding, there is no single definition, although a story is generally thought to describe an experience(s) with emotions, which has a start, a middle and an end (Boje, 2008). Storytelling invites researchers to recognize the producers of the story, and how they are shared, co-produced and co-organized. Managers work in an environment where they are used to telling stories and researchers often have a great deal of opportunity to find examples of them. Managers are taught and socialized to evaluate stories often in complex and ambiguous circumstances. Stories can be a way of expressing visions and goals, exchanging information (and knowledge), for instructing others how to act and even a way to evaluate the past. Storytelling can also occur among individuals or collectively. The 'storytelling organizations' explore the stages in which storytelling is performed, and how storytellers are controlled and constructed. It is the 'collective storytelling system in which the performance of stories is a key part of members' sense-making' (Boje, 2003: 43).

Boje suggests there are four main streams of storytelling in organization and business studies: bureaucratic, quest, chaos and postmodern. In the first, bureaucratic storytelling, stories are linear, rationalized and attempt to make the control of the employees and the organization more predictable. The quest is the second form of storytelling, where the mission is to have the most compelling story. This often begins with a call, journey and return; often it is the voice of the CEO of the company that gets the most attention here. The third type of storytelling is chaos, where the stories are lived and not told. Therefore it is anti-narrative, without coherence and it is inherently non-linear – here, no one is in control. The fourth type of storytelling has been referred to as postmodern, which like the former lacks coherence but unlike chaos the storyteller works in a conscious self-reflexive manner (Boje, 2003: 43).

Within these streams there are a number trends that can be discerned. The first is one where stories are investigated out of context, i.e. interview text. A second is one where stories are produced within a particular context, for example from a functionalist standpoint (in organizational cultural work). Yet a third trend is where a managerialist perspective is taken. Here storytelling is used as a tool; these stories are usually positive with a happy ending. One might suggest, for example, how a complex organizational change might turn out to be ignoring all the possible problems that might result. The fourth and final trend is a story that takes a functionalist/managerialist perspective and includes research within critical theory, postmodernism and poststructuralist. The main focus of this approach is for the researcher to highlight the multiple approaches to interpretation of the story and to attempt to uncover hidden stories and perspectives (in contrast to reporting only the storyline of one spokesperson). Here pluralism is celebrated so that there might be perspectives that pick up themes in relation to gender or race. Boje (2008) argues that the critical issue is how knowledge becomes transferred from an individual(s) to the organization. Managerialist and functionalist researchers set about transferring 'knowledge' and ideas, whereas critical theorists see their role as liberating individuals from exploitation in the knowledge transfer process through the plurality of the perspectives set out, while those undertaking storytelling from a postmodern perspective examine a variety of storytelling forms. The main message here is that the researcher's approach to the story will differ depending on its purpose and focus (Boje, 2008: 214).

CONVERSATION ANALYSIS

A fifth method of analysis for natural language data is **conversation analysis**. The analysis of conversations stems from an ethno-methodological tradition (see Cunliffe, 2008). It deals with the conversation that is built on underlying rules, expressions and practices. It can be used when the data is in the form of transcripts of naturally occurring conversations between two or more people (i.e. meeting observations, interviews). Conversation analysis has been used extensively by Silverman (1993, 2000) to examine, for example, the way judgements are formed in selection interviews and how teachers converse with classes of schoolchildren. There are three fundamental assumptions to conversation analysis: (1) that all conversations exhibit stable, organized patterns irrespective of who is talking; (2) that conversations are organized sequentially, and that it is only possible to make sense of a statement in relation to an ongoing sequence of comments; and (3) that analysis should be grounded in a detailed empirical examination of the data. There are a few things the analyst looks for in conversation analysis, these are, for example: where words are placed; the order of who is speaking; how statements are challenged or confirmed; where pauses, gaps, questions are used; and the choice of words. This emphasis on detailed empirical analysis has resulted in very precise conventions for transcribing tapes. We give some examples in Table 7.8 below.

TABLE 7.8   Simplified transcription symbols

Symbol	Example	Explanation
[	A: for quite a [while B: [yes, but	Left bracket indicates the point at which the current speaker's talk is overlapped by another's talk.
=	A: that I'm aware of = B: = Yes. Would you confirm that?	Equal signs, one at the end of a line and one at the beginning, indicate no gap between the two lines.
.hhhh	I feel that .hh	A row of h's prefixed by a dot indicates an in-breath; without a dot, an out-breath. The number indicates the length of breath.
( )	future risks and ( ) and life ( )	Empty parentheses indicate an undecipherable word.
_____	What's up? _____	Underscoring indicates some stress through pitch of amplitude.

SOURCE: SILVERMAN, 1993: 118

Comparison and choice rational for different approaches to the analysis of linguistic perspectives

Table 7.9 illustrates a comparison of linguistic approaches (natural language data) such as discourse analysis, analysis of figures of speech, narrative analysis and frame analysis. Discourse analysis explains the relationship between discourse and social reality while figures of speech devices shape thoughts such as metaphor, metonymy, synecdoche and irony. Unlike discourse analysis, analysis of figures of speech focuses on rhetorical devices and thus uses the individual level to understand how individual actors make sense of local interactions.

TABLE 7.9   Comparing linguistic perspectives on embedded agency

	Discourse Analysis	Analysis of Figures of Speech	Narrative Analysis	Frame Analysis
Unit of language	Collection of texts	Rhetorical devices	Stories, biographies, speeches	Frames
Level of analysis	Discourse in relation to macro sociological forces	Micro cognitive sense-making and macro worldview	Micro interactional and macro myth	Micro language use in relation to social action
Key constructs	Structure, content, genre	Analogy, metaphor, metonymy, synecdoche and irony	Identity/ character, temporality, chains of events	Frame alignment, extension, amplification, transformation
Linguistic mechanisms	Contextual, intertextual, interdiscursive	Comparison and interaction of the source and target concepts	Coherence and fidelity of the story	The alignment (congruency and complementarity) of frames between actors and environment
Theoretical approach on language	Emphasis on how words use us	Emphasis on how words use us	Emphasis on how we use words	Emphasis on how we use words
Position on action/motion map	Transformation of action to motion	Transformation of action to motion	Transformation of motion to action	Transformation of motion to action

SOURCE: ADAPTED FROM GREEN AND LI (2011)

ARGUMENT ANALYSIS

Yet another way in which discourse can be used and analysed is through **argument analysis**. Some researchers (Gold, Holman and Thorpe, 2002; Gold, Thorpe and Holt, 2007) have also used argument analysis explicitly as part of a management development intervention (see Example 7.3). Arguments in this context are used both to interpret an individual's view of their role or their understanding of the management process as well as in a developmental way. An example would be to get managers to write stories of events at work and then asking them to critically reflect on what they have produced so that they can reflect on their written accounts and can become more conscious of the ideas they have, how they were formed and how they might be changed. Such a process, it has been found, can lead to a change in their behaviour. This section explains argument analysis and also illustrates how knowledge can be gained by researchers through close interaction with respondents. Two approaches are illustrated, the first employs the ideas of Toulmin (2001), the second is based on the work of the philosopher Gadamer (1989); both aim to develop critical thinking in managers and as a consequence improve their effectiveness as managers.

Perhaps the prominent exponent of argument analysis is Toulmin (2001). His approach identified three components within an argument: claims made by individuals, data (the information the individual draws on to make the claims) and warrants. Warrants are the justifying means used by individuals for the arguments posed. When this framework is used in a management development context the text of the story is seen as the 'data' and from it the claims and the warrants can be deduced. Example 7.3 below illustrates how this might take place.

EXAMPLE
7.3

Helping managers become more reflective – based on the work of Toulmin

In their study of Barclays Bank managers, Gold, Holman and Thorpe (2002) asked managers to write accounts to help to reflect and change. The aim was to develop the quality of critical thinking, defined as the ability to reflect on actions taken or views held in a group of the bank's middle managers.

The research process was part of their programme for development, and a number of managers (eight in total) were asked to reflect on their practice with a view to develop their skills of critical reflection and through the process to strengthen their practice.

There were many stages:

1   Develop a 'story log' and write about significant incidents (note the use of critical incidents here as discussed in Chapter 6). Where possible the managers were encouraged to choose stories that involved themselves and others.

2   State why they cared about the particular issues described and what they believed was the explanation for events as they emerged in the story – this part of the task was completed in small groups.

(Continued)

(Continued)

3 Identify the claims that they had made in the stories and provide an explanation for these claims.

4 Go back into their organizations and substantiate the data on which these claims were based, i.e. search out the data that supported the claims made.

What became apparent immediately, and is important to note, was that some managers quickly became aware that they lacked sufficient evidence to support the claims they made, while others found that the evidence that they had offered was at best spurious, at worst wrong. For example, one manager had misread someone else's opinion as a fact.

For many, the process described above was profound. Not only because they had gained an insight into how to understand and analyse arguments, a skill that is considered useful, but also because many took so much for granted without checking. Accordingly, the insights that they had gained offered a new approach to a key managerial task.

A second example also uses the critical examination of a narrative approach by a manager. This example, however, is based on the work of Gadamer (1989) and in particular his principle of work truth and method. In this text Gadamer advances a theory of philosophical hermeneutics that places importance in the 'practice of understanding'. When using this as part of a management development process the aim was to develop managers' critical faculties and surface perspectives that are important in problem solving that would otherwise remain hidden (Gold, Thorpe and Holt, 2007). The approach and the process, from the Leeds researchers, was one that sees thinking and doing as being part of the same process and not separate to managers immersed in the flux of everyday life. In terms of the research method that was adopted, managers were asked to keep accounts of problematic situations they faced at work in the form of a diary and then were asked to reflect on what they had written using a structured process. In this example managers were asked to represent three aspects diagrammatically (see Figure 7.25). First, managers were asked to write about situations so as to better understand them in one segment; second, in another segment they were asked to interpret what they had written by reading reflexively, and third, in the remaining segment they were encouraged to 'reason authoritatively' with respect to the interpretations they had drawn, to consider possibilities that might lead to some solutions and to make a persuasive articulation for the solution they saw as having the most potential.

In the exercise each manager agreed to keep a record of the use of the three Rs over a period of ten weeks in the form of a small log or memo book. A review took place after a four week period and again after ten weeks when the findings were discussed.

All the managers who conducted the exercise, facilitated by a member of the research team, demonstrated a considerable willingness to embrace the approach without falling back on generalized models of behaviour with which to frame their responses. As they worked through the process it was clear that they acquired new understandings and gained in experience by engaging critically with their own ideas and assumptions and the researchers gained valuable insights into the perspectives of the management team.

FIGURE 7.25

From the three 'Rs': reading, writing and reason

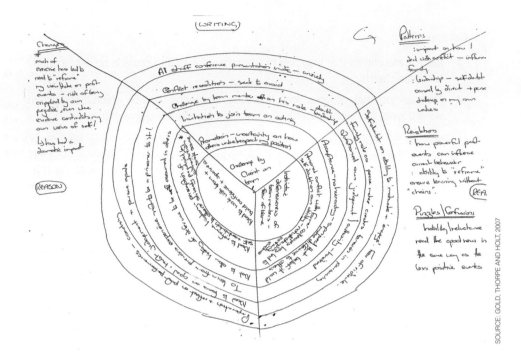

In his book *Why?*, Charles Tilly (2006) describes four varieties of *reasons*. The categories of *reason* he assigns are: conventions, stories, codes and technical accounts. The first *reason*, that of convention, is characterized by distinction and deviation, for example, 'my train was late' or 'she's a lucky girl'. Stories are defined as 'explanatory narratives incorporating cause-effect accounts of unfamiliar phenomenon or exceptional events' (Tilly, 2006: 15). This might be, for example, events such as the 9/11 catastrophe or perhaps winning a prize. Codes he defines as actions such as religious penance or a legal judgement. The fourth *reason* is technical accounts, for example, how an expert (i.e. surgeon or engineer) explains various phenomena. Each way of offering *reason* he argues contains distinctive properties but the *reasons* can also be overlapping. The reasons are illustrated in the Table 7.10 below.

TABLE 7.10 Tilly's four varieties of reason

	Popular	Specialized
Formulas	Conventions	Codes
Cause-effect accounts	Stories	Technical Accounts

Observation

As we have seen, social action can be studied through language, and visual methods (i.e. pictures, video recordings and metaphors) can be used to gain a deeper knowledge and understanding and to discuss and describe problems. Visual tools therefore become important in the problem setting process and problem solving can benefit from the 'interpolation between linguistic and visual tools' (Thorpe and Cornelissen, 2003: 65). Images and visual media can convey a message to a wider audience, and can be used to facilitate sense-making and interpretability. One framework to illustrate how the use of different kinds of media that might affect the quality of communication between individuals and departments within an organization is shown in Table 7.11. There are two dimensions, the degree of difference between individuals and departments and extent of dependence that exists between the individuals and departments.

What Table 7.11 illustrates is that when the degree of difference between individuals or departments is high and when there is a high degree of interdependence, the richer will be the media that is required to communicate between individuals.

TABLE 7.11 Visual media

		Interdependence between individuals or departments	
		High	Low
Dependence between individuals or departments	High	**High Difference, High Interdependence** Structure: Rich media to solve differences and large amount of information to handle interdependence Examples: full time integrators, task forces, matrix structure, repertory grids, cognitive mapping.	**High Difference, Low Interdependence** Structure: Rich media to resolve differences and small amount of information. Examples: occasional face-to-face or telephone meetings, personal memos, planning, self-contained units, photographs, visual metaphors.
	Low	**Low Difference, High Interdependence** Structure: Media of lower richness and large amount of information to handle interdependence. Examples: plans, reports, budgets, diagrams, photographs.	**Low Difference, Low Interdependence** Structure: Media of lower richness and small amount of information. Examples: rules, standard operating procedures, reports and budgets.

SOURCE: ADAPTED FROM DAFT AND LENGEN (1986: 565)

GAINING KNOWLEDGE THROUGH INTERACTION

Analysing interaction behind the obvious – repertory grids

Repertory grids and cognitive maps are tools for uncovering individuals' or a group's view of the world and enable the simple and relatively immediate presentation of complex information.

Based on personal construct theory (Kelly, 1955), a repertory grid is a representation of a manager's perception of their world. The technique is useful for investigating areas that the respondent might not have thought much about, or which they find hard to articulate. It has been used extensively in areas such as career guidance and for the development of job descriptions. In the case of Example 7.4 below, a housing manager within a large metropolitan council used the approach to assist in the identification of what householders valued in terms of bathroom and kitchen design.

EXAMPLE
7.4

Repertory grid

Mackinlay (1986) used the repertory grid technique to elicit the values and perceptions that householders in a particular housing district had of different types of bathroom and kitchen colour schemes and layouts, as elements to be compared and contrasted, one against the other. He showed these to householders, and asked them to compare and contrast the different photographs and in so doing elicited the 'constructs' they used to differentiate between the photographs and to reveal their likes and dislikes. The method proved extremely useful, with the photographs helping to resolve differences and deal with the complex issues involved in the notion of what people valued and preferred. This demonstrates that grids can elucidate what might not be immediately observable, so that new insights or perspectives can be gained.

Repertory grids help individuals to look, not just at the words people use, but also at the wider constructs they use when making decisions and taking action. Often these may not even be known to the individuals themselves, so representation in the visual form of a grid can be the beginning of a process whereby individuals learn more about the ideas they have, how they might have been formed and how they might be changed.

Grids can also be used in group situations as a basis for discussion about how different people view the world and they enable complex relationships to be represented with the objective of building up shared understandings (Easterby-Smith, Thorpe and

Holman, 2010). The technique is used to understand an individual's perceptions and the constructs they use to understand and manage their world. A repertory grid is a mathematical representation of how an individual differentiates between objects or experiences in his or her world. Repertory grids can also be used with people who have low verbal ability, making them particularly useful for children and people with language difficulties.

The standard procedure for generating a repertory grid is as follows:

1 Decide on the *focus* of the grid. This should be quite specific and the interviewee should be reminded of this focus at regular intervals. These might be qualities required of a manager in a particular function, the particular work content of a given job, or the features of products currently competing with one's own.

2 Select with the interviewee a group of *elements* (between 5 and 10) which are relevant to the chosen focus, and which are also likely to provide a good range. If, for example, the focus of the grid was on the skills required of a manager it would be appropriate to choose individuals who were familiar to the interviewee, some of whom he or she regarded as particularly able, some of average ability and some of below average ability.

3 *Constructs* are elicited, usually by asking the respondent to compare and contrast elements in groups of three, known as triads. Each element is written onto a card and then three cards are selected at random. The interviewee is asked to decide which pair of cards is similar in a way that also makes them distinct from the third. They are asked to provide a word or phrase that describes the pair, and a contrasting word or phrase to describe the remaining card. For example, in the case of a grid with the focus on the competencies required of a manager, someone might choose two cards of named people as similar because they see them both as *dynamic*, and the third as *staid*. In this case the construct elicited is a continuum on which *dynamic* is at one end and *staid* is at the other. This process is repeated with different triads of elements until a reasonable number of constructs (perhaps 6 to 10) have been produced.

4 Each of the elements needs to be *linked* to, or rated against, each of the constructs. This can be done in several different ways: by deciding which of the two 'poles' of the construct provides the best description of the element; by determining the position of the element on a rating scale (often 7 points) constructed between the poles of each construct; or by rank-ordering each of the elements along the dimension indicated by each of the constructs. The results of these ratings or rankings are recorded as ticks and crosses, or as numbers in a matrix.

Small grids can be analysed manually, or by eye, by looking for patterns of relationships and differences between constructs and elements. This can form the basis of an interesting col-

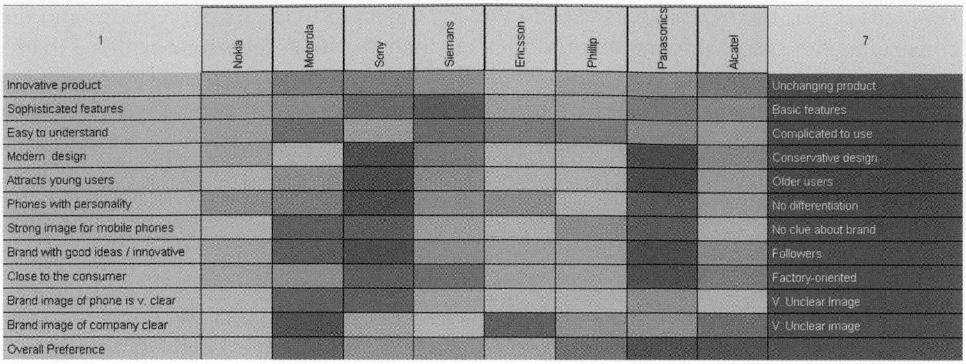

FIGURE 7.27
Repertory grids in the mobile market

1	Nokia	Motorola	Sony	Siemens	Ericsson	Philip	Panasonics	Alcatel	7
Innovative product									Unchanging product
Sophisticated features									Basic features
Easy to understand									Complicated to use
Modern design									Conservative design
Attracts young users									Older users
Phones with personality									No differentiation
Strong image for mobile phones									No clue about brand
Brand with good ideas / innovative									Followers
Close to the consumer									Factory-oriented
Brand image of phone is v. clear									V. Unclear Image
Brand image of company clear									V. Unclear image
Overall Preference									

laborative discussion between interviewer and interviewee. With larger grids (say, 5 × 5, or upwards) it is more common to use computer analysis packages. Figure 7.27 shows a marketing example analysed using GridSuite, where a PhD student was interested in aspects of brand preference. The study recognized the very different approaches being adopted (even by the same company) and aimed to identify how consumers were influenced by brands.

The completed grid shows how the respondent questioned has made comparisons between a range of mobile phones. In the example, phones by Siemens have been compared with phones from Nokia, Motorola, Sony, Ericson, Philips, Panasonic and Alcatel. Their comparisons range from answers that mention the 'personality' of the phones to practical dimensions such as ease of use. The example shows that respondents have been asked to rate the constructs elicited on a scale (one to seven) and the computer has colour coded the results (the darker the shading the higher the score given by the respondent for a given construct). The colour coding offers a visual impression of which phones score highly or less highly on the constructs elicited.

In terms of analysis there are two very different kinds of output in terms of visual representation. One produces a map that plots the elements within dimensions, and axes, defined by the constructs. What this map shows in Figure 7.28 is that there are two main components in this grid that together explain nearly 70 per cent of the variance. These are labelled component 1 (54.8 per cent) and component 2 (16.1 per cent). A name is usually assigned to these components, which describes the aggregated components. In this example component 1 might indicate characteristics in the phones that inspire users as opposed (at the other end of the dimension) to characteristics that are less inspiring. Component 2 (which explains less of the variance) might be named Uninspiring. From this grid the computer can place the mobile phones under investigation onto the two axes, which indicates the extent to which they possess the constructs elicited from the grid.

Another way of representing the analysis of a grid (Figure 7.29) takes the form of a dendrogram. Dendrograms show how close the constructs are to one another in terms of how they have been scored. Where the 'tree' branches are close the indication is that the two

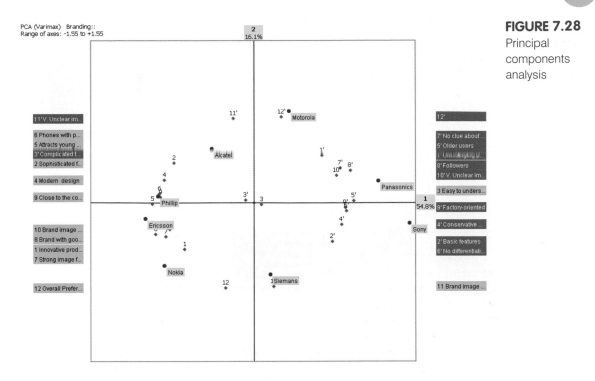

PCA (Varimax) Branding::
Range of axes: -1.55 to +1.55

FIGURE 7.28

Principal
components
analysis

constructs have something in common and therefore might be connected. The grid below shows a dendrogram using the same data as used in Figure 7.28.

In Figure 7.29, instead of a researcher dealing with 12 constructs the dendrogram suggests that it may be possible to collapse the constructs into only four main categories. This process is analogous to the process researchers undertake when conducting grounded approaches to data analysis. In this case researchers would look for similarities in the suggested links and assign a name to the higher level construct.

Grids have both advantages and disadvantages as shown in Table 7.12, which indicates the main advantages and disadvantages of using repertory grids, identified by Stewart, Stewart and Fonda (1981).

Our view is that grids offer not simply assistance in seeing patterns and associations and as a consequence new insights but they also provide a medium of communication that can spur new understandings and new acts of sense-making (Easterby-Smith, Thorpe and Holman, 2010). So they are not simply a graphical representation of an individual manager's concerns and beliefs, but operate in a reflexive manner (see Harper, 1989) helping managers respond to the map or picture that is produced.

For those interested in learning more about the repertory grid technique further reading is provided at the end of this chapter and Easterby-Smith, Thorpe and Holman (2010) illustrate a number of applications in the field of management.

FIGURE 7.29

Branding of mobile phones

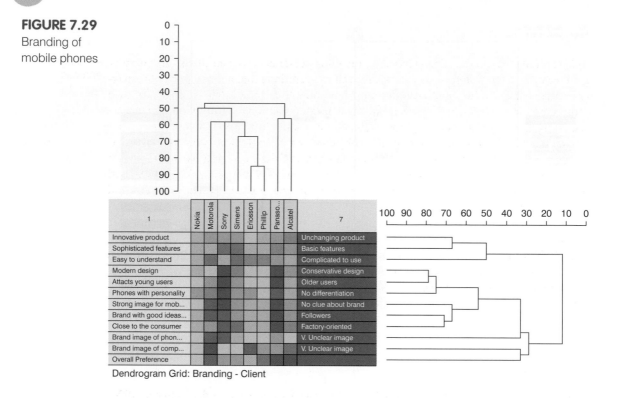

Dendrogram Grid: Branding - Client

TABLE 7.12 Pros and cons of using repertory grids

Advantages	Disadvantages
It involves verbalizing constructs that otherwise would remain hidden.	Grids are hard work to complete and can take considerable periods of time: a 20 x 10 matrix can take up to one and a half hours.
It is based on the individual's own framework, not that of the expert.	They require a high degree of skill from the interviewer if the interviewee's construct framework is to be fully explored.
It provides insights for both the researcher and the researched.	They can be difficult to analyse and interpret, and there is some danger that individuals will rely on the structure of the technique to produce packaged, rather than meaningful, results.
	The technique has become 'popular' and as a consequence is sometimes used mechanistically, forgetting the underlying theory of personal constructs.

Cognitive mapping

This method of data collection is based on the same personal construct theory as repertory grid technique. **Cognitive mapping** is a modelling technique that aims to portray managers' ideas, beliefs, values and attitudes and show how they inter-relate. A cognitive map represents the relationships between the constructs of a number of individual managers regarding a managerial issue or problem (Eden, Jones and Sims, 1983). A cognitive map is not supposed to be a scientific model of an objective reality in the way some influence diagrams are, but instead should be a presentation of part of the world as a particular person sees it – it can never be shown to be right or wrong, in an 'objective' sense (Eden, Jones and Sims, 1983: 44). Cognitive maps therefore capture managers' professed theories-in-use, and their conceptual and symbolic uses of language.

Cognitive maps can work at either an individual level or the level of the group and can be used *statically* as a method of simply data collection (instead of field notes) or dynamically with groups of managers. As with repertory grids, various *tools* have been produced that help mediate the intervention, many are computer-based that offer added promise to enhance strategic thinking. We begin with examining individual approaches before giving some examples of the collective uses of cognitive mapping.

Individual cognitive maps

Figure 7.30 shows a typical individual map produced by a PhD student (Baker, 1996) undertaking a comparative study of consumer perceptions. In this example we provide a map about running shoes.

The map is produced through questioning and laddering. The lines running between the numbers (content codes) represent the linkages. Readers will notice that there are fewer values at the top of a map than attributes (at the bottom of the map), consequences tend towards the middle. This map might be interpreted in the following way. The dominant element in the map (primary value 26) is *well-being*. Below this there are three further elements each of which has a large number of elements that lead into them; these are: 2 *design*, 3 *weight/shape* and 14 *enhanced performance*. Baker and Knox's (1995) interpretation is that it is the design of the shoes that enhances the performance, well-being chain and this is illustrated by the high number of relations among its respective elements, which implies that the product was purchased for the perceived benefits it might deliver in terms of performance.

In order to gain understanding and in order to interpret it, the interviewer needs to again go through a process of laddering discussed earlier in the book, in order to explore the person's understanding in more depth. As constructs are thought to have a hierarchical relationship, the process of laddering employed in the interviews helps to gain a better understanding of a person's construct system. *Laddering down* (also called pyramiding) is where the interviewer explores a person's understanding of a particular construct, *laddering up* is where the interviewer explores why a particular construct is important to them and helps to explore a person's value system.

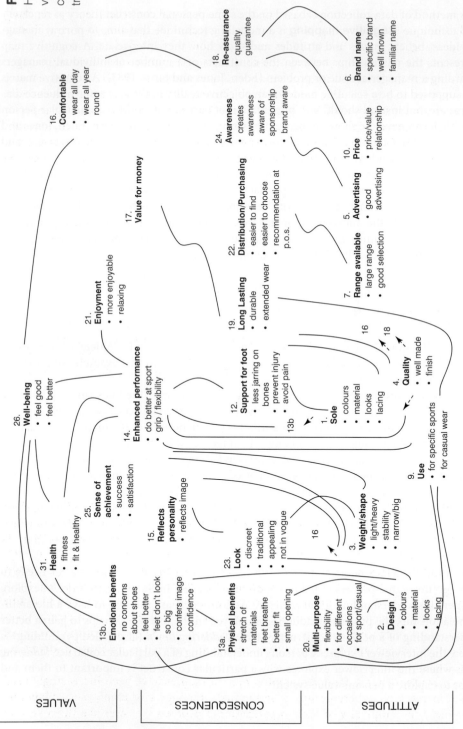

FIGURE 7.30
Hierarchical value map: combined trainers

VALUES

CONSEQUENCES

ATTITUDES

26. **Well-being**
• feel good
• feel better

31. **Health**
• fitness
• fit & healthy

25. **Sense of achievement**
• success
• satisfaction

16. **Comfortable**
• wear all day
• wear all year round

17. **Value for money**

21. **Enjoyment**
• more enjoyable
• relaxing

24. **Awareness**
• creates awareness
• aware of sponsorship
• brand aware

18. **Re-assurance**
• quality guarantee

6. **Brand name**
• specific brand
• well known
• familiar name

10. **Price**
• price/value relationship

5. **Advertising**
• good advertising

22. **Distribution/Purchasing**
• easier to find
• easier to choose
• recommendation at p.o.s.

19. **Long Lasting**
• durable
• extended wear

7. **Range available**
• large range
• good selection

14. **Enhanced performance**
• do better at sport
• grip / flexibility

12. **Support for foot**
• less jarring on bones
• prevent injury
• avoid pain

4. **Quality**
• well made
• finish

1. **Sole**
• colours
• material
• looks
• lacing

16

18

13b

15. **Reflects personality**
• reflects image

23. **Look**
• discreet
• traditional
• appealing
• not in vogue

3. **Weight/shape**
• light/heavy
• stability
• narrow/big

9. **Use**
• for specific sports
• for casual wear

13b. **Emotional benefits**
• no concerns about shoes
• feel better
• feet don't look so big
• confers image
• confidence

13a. **Physical benefits**
• stretch of materials
• feet breathe
• better fit
• small opening

20. **Multi-purpose**
• flexibility
• for different occasions
• for sport/casual

2. **Design**
• colours
• material
• looks
• lacing

16

Dominoes

A less systematic way of developing constructs and one that might be preferred, particularly where there are issues of power and control present (for example, when working with senior managers), is to use a process called dominoes. This method allows the manager more control over the process and can save considerable time. The process involves the researcher simply identifying elements (whether these are people or objects) and placing them in front of the manager all at the same time. The managers are then asked to group the elements into patterns and to explain aloud as they do this the rationale for the groupings and patterns that are chosen. Their comments are then recorded by the researcher and questions can be asked to obtain clarification as necessary. Using this approach the exercise can often be 'fun' to complete and differences between elements that produce the constructs can be drawn out.

Dominoes

Ask a colleague to identify five people in their life. These should be a mixture of people they both like and dislike. Get them to write them down on cards and place them on the desk in front of you. Now ask them to find a feature that differentiates some of these individuals from the others and ask them to place the names of those with similar features adjacent to each other. Now ask them to supply a word or phrase that best describes the common attributes held – this is one construct. Now repeat the process and see how many different constructs can be found.

EXERCISE
7.2

Group maps

Cognitive maps are now being used by researchers in a whole variety of contexts, from helping managers clarify and design strategy to providing tools of mediation. Used interactively they can help groups think around issues as well as formulate plans. Such approaches have spawned an industry known as strategic support, and the improvement on computers and software has enabled a large number of software products to be designed, which can sit within a group of managers or employees to help them map out their perspectives on problems or issues within an organization and from this collective set of views clarify next steps. Used in this way the research clearly takes on an action research flavour, where change is most decidedly part of the process of data collection, making the approach an attractive proposition for those undertaking consultancy.

As a consequence, cognitive mapping methodologies have been increasingly used in action research, where groups of individuals, managers or employees collaborate to model the complexity of their organizational problems as *they* see them so that they can be subsequently analysed and solved. Here the focus is not just on collecting and presenting large amounts of data but in stimulating new learning that will lead to change – hence its use in strategy development. Originally a manual system, the computer packages now available (for example, **Decision Explorer**, an example of its use is given under action research in Chapter 6) provide powerful support both to assist the analysis process as well as the exploration of an organization's strategic options (Eden, 1990).

Eden is critical of the traditional view that the formulation of strategy can be conducted quite independently from its implementation. One of the advantages of cognitive mapping is that the process enables those taking part to challenge the views and perspectives of others and it is often the realization of differences between individual managers and the following discussion which proves most useful by giving prominence to distinctions and making connections that might otherwise be overlooked (Eden and Ackermann, 1998). A final beneficial outcome of the cognitive mapping process is that it helps managers reach a collective judgement about issues that are ambiguous, complex and often of a contested nature. In the words of Thomas and Thomas (1928: 47), 'If men define situations as real, they are real in their consequences'.

In practice, members of an organization are brought together in a room facing a blank wall or large projector screen. The focus of the session or problem on which they are to work is presented to them by a researcher or facilitator. In comfortable surroundings and with a permanent supply of coffee the individuals then begin to consider aspects of the situation. Each contribution made is either written down on Post-it˚ notes (called Ovals) or stored by computer, and the unfolding cognitive map, which represents the individual's view of the issue, is projected on the screen or posted on the wall for them to alter and refine.

The approach not only allows individual managers to offer their perceptions of a problem, but gives those responsible for strategy formulation the opportunity to understand the perspectives of others. In this context interaction among participants and collaboration between researcher and researched is most decidedly a good thing. An example of using a cognitive mapping approach is indicated below and represented in Figure 7.31.

This example involved the use of a cognitive mapping approach in the strategy development process when working to surface issues and produce an agenda for change in a hospital merger. Both hospitals were 'hot' sites and as such had the prestige of dealing with accident and emergency patients. As a consequence both hospitals had maternity wings (for which accident and emergency on site was a necessity), both had different members of parliament representing their local catchments and historically both had been part of different regional health authorities and as a consequence had very different culture systems, organization structures and even uniforms. Following pressure from both the government (for reasons of efficiency) and the Royal Colleges (for reasons of improved clinical practice) to merge, researchers undertook an action learning approach to change. At one stage in the process of change they introduced the concept of cognitive mapping as a tool to surface the views of the senior management team and to engender debate. Working with the management team from both hospitals (all managers and all the clinical directors), maps were created to depict both collective and individual perspectives of the issues faced by the hospital in the context of the impending merger. By first interviewing managers and clinicians individually a number of maps were created, which were then discussed and debated within a larger group. The trigger questions for discussion were:

1 What was their vision for what needed to be done for the merger to be a success?

2 What actions needed to be taken for this to be realized?

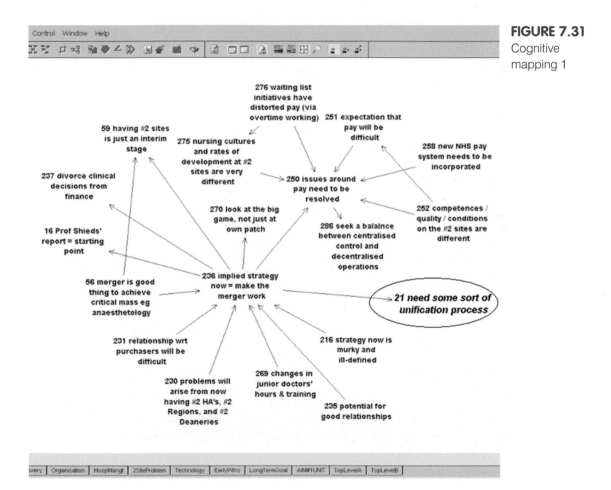

FIGURE 7.31

Cognitive mapping 1

FIGURE 7.32

Cognitive
mapping 2

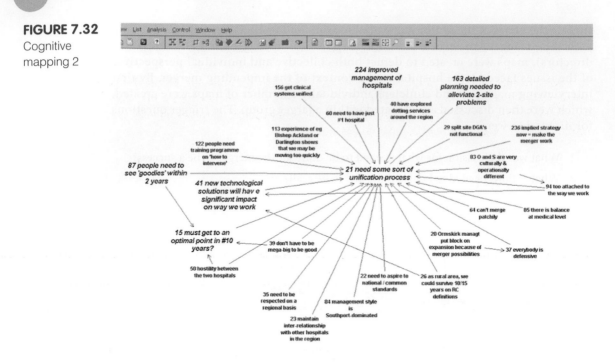

The maps were then modified with the views expressed captured and grouped and structured into a causal map offering a synthesis of each participant's view upon the two
questions. Simultaneously, managers were asked to discuss the suggested clustering of
concepts and the content and priorities of the strategic issues. One of the early observations was the speed at which it helped the group surface the strategic issues facing the
hospital.

An initial review of the map, a part of which is shown in Figure 7.32, indicated the
complexity of the problem. There were a multiplicity and diversity of social, economic
and governmental issues facing the hospital as well as conflicting views about the current
state of the organization and the likely challenges it faced. Despite these differences we
observed that during the cognitive mapping process we faced few difficulties achieving
interaction between team members as they negotiated their way through the dynamics of reaching consensus on the key strategic issues presented, which can be seen to
indicate a collective form of organizational learning (Churchill, 1990). The main issues
broken down by cluster were political, performance related, staff development, communications and reputational. What we found using this technique was that it enabled all
those involved to experience the difficulties of other departments and with this insight
begin to understand how the hospital functioned as a whole. The map produced reduced
the messiness and ambiguity that characterized the situation and provided the different
groups with the ability to:

1 Manage the resultant complexity by identifying emergent themes.

2 Prioritize these themes so that they could be subsequently developed.

As a consequence, discussion of the cognitive map as a group not only enabled the transmission of information and the implications that the issues raised might have for the management of the local authority, but it also helped to overcome disagreement about goals, the interpretation of issues, or subsequent courses of action.

CONCLUSION

In this chapter we have attempted to provide an overview of some of the main ways of capturing qualitative data and making sense of it. The main points raised are that:

 A commitment to qualitative research is likely to derive from the researcher's view about which features of the world are significant and relevant to his or her enterprise.

 A key question will be whether the quality of experience is more important than the frequency of opinions and events.

 The best method for the analysis of the data and whether computers can be employed to aid the analysis process and the presentation of the results.

Along the road of qualitative research there are also many dilemmas. There is the problem of gaining public access to private experiences, and the difficulty of deciding how and when to impose any interpretive frameworks on this. There is the question of how accurate one's information is, and how accurate it needs to be, or can be. And there is the continual tension underneath the research process between creating meanings and counting frequencies. It is in the next chapter that we consider some of the methods and issues associated with the latter problem.

FURTHER READING

Ackermann, F. and Eden, C. (2011) *Making Strategy: Mapping out strategic success*, 2nd edn. London: Sage.
Offers a hands-on practical guide to the strategy making process which includes the use of mapping techniques.
Boje, D. (2001) *Narrative Methods for Organisational and Communication Research*. London: Sage.
Offers a guide for researchers to examine alternative discourse analysis strategies. The book sets out eight options for use in organization and communication research.
Locke, K. (2001) *Grounded Theory in Management Research*. London: Sage.
Offers a comprehensive overview of the debates and possibilities available to researchers when considering grounded approaches to data collection and analysis.

CREATING QUANTITATIVE DATA

8

LEARNING OBJECTIVES

 To be able to select an appropriate form of sampling design for the objectives of the research.

To be able to select among alternative sources of quantitative data according to the purpose of the research, taking into account the benefits and drawbacks of each.

To be able to design structured questionnaires using well-defined questions and appropriate forms of measurement scale.

INTRODUCTION

This chapter is divided into three main parts. The first section examines the importance of sampling design, starting with an analysis of why sampling matters and an introduction to different forms of sampling design. The second part covers three sources of quantitative data: collecting data through surveys, collecting data through observation and using secondary data sources. Each has benefits and drawbacks, and we consider how to make choices between them. The last section looks at the process of measurement in two parts: how to design structured questions for surveys and interviews, and alternative forms of measurement scale for recording responses.

SAMPLING DESIGN

When decisions are made that can have significant consequences for people it is important that those decisions are based on evidence. The trustworthiness of the evidence base for decisions depends on many factors, and in this chapter we focus on how to collect evidence in the form of quantitative data. We begin with the difference between a **population** and a **sample** drawn from that population. The term population refers to the whole set of entities that decisions relate to; while the term sample refers to a subset of those entities from which evidence is gathered. The **inference** task then is to use evidence from a sample to draw conclusions about the population.

Samples are very commonly used, both for research and for policy-making. Companies estimate morale among employees from surveys of samples of employees (either by deliberately picking names from the payroll, or by letting employees choose whether or not to respond). For example, companies such as Gallup and Towers Watson are leaders in carrying out such opinion surveys, and one of the benefits that they claim is that they can compare the profile of a company (and sub-units within it) with that of other companies where the same survey questions have been used. This gives a method of benchmarking, which senior management often find very informative and powerful in shaping their strategy. Many companies also use small-scale surveys repeated frequently (perhaps once a month) as a kind of barometer of how employees or customers are feeling. This can be very valuable during the course of a period of major change. During the UK general election in 2010 opinion polls appeared every day monitoring the state of the electorate and their response to the offerings of the political parties. The UK government uses sample surveys of companies on their annual pay negotiations in order to get an estimate of wage inflation in the economy. In most countries, estimates of activity in the labour market (whether people are unemployed, self-employed, economically inactive and so on) are derived from samples and not from complete counts.

Principles in judging the quality of a sample design

Sometimes, a research project involves collecting data from every member of an organization, but more often this is not the case and the researcher needs to decide on a sampling strategy. A sample might be: a proportion of employees in an organization, a selection of companies operating in a specific market, a number of specific periods of time for assessing the quality of customer responses in a call centre, or a selection of transactions for audit purposes. For each of these examples, the researcher has to make a decision about what the sampling unit is (the person, the company, the transaction and so on), how many sampling units to take, and on what basis sampling is to be undertaken.

Generally speaking, the purpose of collecting data from a sample is to enable the researcher to make statements about the population that the sample is drawn from. Many people say that they only want to talk about their sample data, but we almost never believe them. Even if there is no formal generalization beyond the sample, both the writer and the reader are interested in what this study's findings tell us that would be useful when thinking about other settings. This places a responsibility on researchers, whether we like it or not, to say where our findings might be relevant.

The claims that can legitimately be made from sample data depend absolutely on the relationship between the sample and the population. Get the sampling wrong, and accuracy in calculating the results is of no consequence. The opposite is also true: get the sampling right, and even rough-and-ready calculations or 'eyeballing' of the data can be immensely valuable. There are two basic principles that underlie decisions about sampling design: **representativeness** and **precision**.

Representativeness in sampling   The accuracy of conclusions drawn from a sample depends on whether it has the same characteristics as the population from which it is drawn. If the sample is systematically different in some way, then the sample is biased. A simple definition of bias in sampling is that it occurs when some members of the population have a higher chance of being included in the sample than others. There are two steps involved in defining a sampling design. The first step is to draw up a **sampling frame**, a list of all who are eligible to be included in the study. The second step is to achieve a valid response from all those included in the sampling frame. **Bias** can be introduced into a sampling strategy in many ways, through choices made in the design of the study itself and also through features of the process of collecting data:

1 *Exclude groups of people*: leave out home-workers, casual staff, new recruits, part-timers.

2 *Distribution method*: send out your survey using an out-of-date list of mailing addresses to exclude those who have recently moved; distribute by email to exclude those without a PC on their desks.

3 *Language used*: use English to exclude those who don't speak English, and introduce biasing factors for those who do because of differences in how well people can use the language.

One of the key ways of judging the representativeness of a sample is to compare the characteristics of the sample to those of the population; and this kind of information is commonly reported in published papers that are based on surveys. Even if the sampling frame accurately represents the population, non-response is a major source of problems in getting outsiders to believe the results. In itself though, non-response is not a problem, as long as those who do respond have the same characteristics as those who do not. Of course, there is usually a big problem in assessing whether this is true, because (obviously) non-respondents did not respond. It is sometimes possible to get some idea about potential bias due to systematic non-response by comparing those who respond quickly with slow responders on demographic variables and also on the central variables in the research. The idea is that the slow responders will be more similar to non-responders than are those who reply quickly. If the slow responders have similar characteristics to rapid responders, then the researcher can have greater confidence that non-responders would also have been similar; and this helps to build credibility in a survey.

Improving response rates in surveys A high response rate in a survey is clearly important: it gives a larger body of data, which the researcher can use to address research questions, and it makes it much more likely that the sample is representative of the population of interest. We list below a number of steps that the researcher can take to increase response rates:

- Make the task easy and short.
- Explain the purpose clearly, so that respondents can see its value – there is always a cost in responding to a survey, so explain the benefit that makes up for that cost.
- Give incentives to take part.
- Give assurances of confidentiality and anonymity.
- Send out reminders.

Underlying these steps is a simple principle: because providing data is a cost to each respondent then the principle is to reduce the effort involved as much as possible and increase the perceived benefit as much as possible.

The shorter the questionnaire, and the simpler the questions, the more likely it is that people will reply; so thinking carefully through the objectives of the study and making sure that every question contributes to those objectives will have a payoff. The researcher should also try to convince people that the effort they put into replying will be of benefit, either to the respondents themselves or to something that the respondents will find worthwhile. Incentives to participate can sometimes make a difference, though this can be expensive if respondents are paid. Rewarding those who reply may also be difficult if the survey is anonymous (since the researcher will not be able to identify individual respondents). Offering guarantees of confidentiality and anonymity is important for ethical reasons (see Chapter 4), but will help to build trust and therefore response rates. Finally, most people lead busy lives and the researcher's survey may not arrive at a convenient time. Sending out reminders is an important factor in increasing the likelihood of response.

Precision in sampling – sampling proportion and sample size Precision is about how credible a sample is. For example, opinion polls conducted before elections in the UK, as well as in many other countries, use samples that are very much smaller than the population of registered voters. How confident is it possible to be about predicting election outcomes from opinion poll samples? Does the precision of the estimate depend on how big the sample is? It seems plausible that it should. Does it also depend on what proportion of the population the pollsters talk to? If the number of electors is 10,000 then a sample of 1,000 (i.e. 10 per cent) might be OK. However, many people would be less happy with a sample of 1,000 if the number of electors was one million instead (0.1 per cent). Intuitively, this proportion seems too small. However, the first intuition is correct, but the second is not.

Nguyen (2005) provides a clear and graphic example of cooking chicken soup to show why the size of a sample matters but how big a proportion the sample is of the population (the **sampling proportion**) does not. Consider three scenarios: cooking at home for four people using a small pot, cooking for a dinner party with 12 guests using a medium-size pot, and cooking a banquet for 200 wedding guests using a huge cooking pot. Regardless of the number of guests, the only way to tell if there is enough salt in the soup is to taste it. The way to find this out is: first, stir the soup so it is well mixed and is the same all the way through, and second, use a tablespoon to draw off some soup. A tablespoon will do because there is no point taking more than that. Taste it all and there is no soup left for the guests; taste more spoonfuls and each will taste just the same, so nothing is learned. It is not necessary to use a large ladle to sample from the large pot simply because the pot is bigger, or a tiny spoon to sample from the small pot because the pot is smaller. There is no need, because the same sized tablespoon is enough to judge the adequacy of the seasoning regardless of how big the batch of soup is, as long as the pot is stirred first.

The soup in the pot is the *population*; the spoonful to taste is the *sample*. The size of the spoon is the **sample size**, and that is what matters. The cook needs enough soup to be able to make a judgement about the pot as a whole. Now apply these principles to the task of making judgements about attitudes in a society towards an issue of concern. Consider the question of whether organizations should aim to maximize their profit or should consider their social responsibilities. The precision of the answer to this question has nothing to do with the size of the population but rather depends on the size of the sample. Small samples will always be less precise than large samples.

Combining precision and representativeness to achieve a credible sample   We have looked at the two design principles of bias and precision, and clearly both are important in achieving a credible sampling design for a quantitative research project. Low bias means that conclusions from a sample can safely be applied to the population, and high precision means that the margin of error in the claims that are made will be low – the researcher can expect to be precisely right (see Table 8.1). However, high precision is no way of saving a study where the sample is biased (precisely wrong). Giving very precise answers to the wrong question will not endear a researcher to his or her supervisor, just as it does not help in getting high marks in an examination! Most projects carried out by students (at whatever level) are a compromise in some way, simply because resources are limited. As a result, there will always be trade-offs when it comes to decisions about design. Is it better to have a large sample (giving higher precision) if the cost of achieving it is to introduce bias into the sample achieved? Put more simply, which is better: to be imprecisely right or to be precisely wrong? In our opinion, the answer is straightforward. Imprecisely right is better: it is preferable to have a sample that properly represents the population even if the precision is lower because of a small sample.

TABLE 8.1 Principles in designing a sample

		Bias	
		High	**Low**
Precision	High	Precisely wrong	Precisely right
	Low	Imprecisely wrong	Imprecisely right

Probability sampling designs

This section describes forms of sampling design where the probability of each entity being part of the sample is known. Some sampling methods have the same probability for every entity in the sample, while others have the same probability within segments of the design but differing probabilities across segments.

Simple random sampling   Every sample entity (company, employee, customer, etc.) has an equal chance of being part of the sample. In the past, this was done using printed random number tables. Now computers are used for this, and it is easy to draw up a list of random numbers as a basis for selecting a sample.

Stratified random sampling   One drawback of **simple random sampling** is that it can mean that small but important parts of the population are missed altogether or sampled so little that the researcher cannot make confident statements about them. For instance, customer surveys of a healthcare facility would be badly served by a simple random sample. Most users of a healthcare facility have relatively minor ailments and perhaps visit only once or twice in a year. There will, however, be a small number of patients with major health problems whose treatment is perhaps extensive. It is quite reasonable to expect that a sample should be informative about the very ill minority as well as the mildly ill majority. The way to achieve this is to divide the population up into homogeneous groups called *strata*, and then take a simple random sample within each stratum. **Proportional stratified random sampling** has the same sampling proportion within all strata; but this has the disadvantage that rare groups within the population would be badly represented. The way to deal with this problem is to take a larger proportion of sample units in small strata, and a smaller proportion in the larger strata. This is called **non-proportional stratified random sampling**.

Systematic random sampling   **Systematic random sampling** relies on there being a list in some form or other of the units in the population that the researcher is interested in. This might be a customer database, or a list of employees of a company or students registered in a university. Suppose that a researcher wants to achieve a sample of 500 students in order to assess their satisfaction with the virtual learning environment (VLE) system that a university has just introduced. If there are 20,000 students then 500 represents a sample of 2.5 per cent, corresponding to selecting 1 in 40 students from the population. This proportion could be achieved by choosing a number at random between 1 and 40. If that number were 27, then the researcher would go down the list taking every 27th student in order to derive a sample list of 500 names. What this process relies on is that the population list is essentially organized randomly, so that picking in this systematic way does not introduce bias. There could be a problem if the list is ordered alphabetically by individuals' last name, since all those students with the same name will be listed together and individuals with the same name will have less chance of being selected than if the list were randomly ordered.

Cluster sampling   Any method that involves random sampling will lead to practical problems where the population units are spread very widely, such that the cost of approaching them is very high. **Cluster sampling** deals with this by first dividing up the population into what are called clusters, and then by sampling all the units within the selected clusters. A study of company success in emerging economies might first identify all the countries where the company operates, select randomly a number of those countries to study in detail, and then approach all the relevant contacts in those countries. This would allow the study to use local research staff who are familiar with the language and culture of each country.

Multi-stage sampling   **Multi-stage sampling** combines together the methods described above in order to achieve higher operational and technical efficiency. For example, **stratified random sampling** divides the population into strata and then samples from within all of them. Instead, a study might use a sampling approach at each level, and this is very common in large-scale social research. Suppose there was a national change in the organization of schools to give greater management autonomy to head teachers, and researchers wanted to know whether this change had any effect on the performance of students in schools. It would be very inefficient to select students at random, even if the research team actually had a national database of all school students. It makes more sense to divide the country up into regions, select some regions for detailed attention, identify all the schools in the targeted regions, and then select a sample of schools. Having defined a sample of schools within selected regions, the same process could be used to sample classes within the selected schools, or perhaps take a sample of students from all of the classes in a selected school. In this example, the criterion of randomness applies at each of several stages in the design of the study; hence the name multi-stage sampling. The aim is to balance the need for representativeness of the sample with the highest possible cost effectiveness.

Why are probability sampling designs valuable?   It is only with probability sampling that it is possible to be precise about the relationship between a sample and the population from which the sample is drawn. Knowing what this relationship is allows the researcher to make a firm judgement about the relationship between characteristics of a sample and characteristics of the population from which the sample was drawn. All forms of **probability sampling design** have this feature in common – it is always possible to state the probability of each individual respondent being selected for inclusion in the research study. The statistical theory behind the inference process (often called significance testing – we discuss this in the next two chapters) relies fundamentally on sampling based on probabilities. There is always uncertainty about any claim made from data; but using probability sampling designs can allow the researcher to quantify that uncertainty. Thus, sample data can tell us whether the risk associated with using a mobile phone while driving is higher, but only a properly constructed sample design can allow us to decide how worried we should be about that extra risk.

Non-probability sampling designs

Non-probability sampling methods all share the same characteristic: that it is not possible to state the probability of any member of the population being sampled. As a result, they can never give the researcher the same level of confidence as probability-based sampling does when drawing inferences about the population of interest from a specific sample.

Convenience sampling   This method of sampling involves selecting sample units on the basis of how easily accessible they are, hence the term **convenience sampling**. A student who uses an MSN Messenger contact list for their dissertation is taking a convenience sample. Such a sample may well be representative of the individual's own social network, but is clearly not representative of students as a whole or of the population of the UK. Convenience samples are very common in research, because they are – well – convenient! They clearly are not proper probability samples, and it is impossible to guarantee that any sample achieved in this way represents a specific population that may be of interest. However, they can have a value. It rather depends on what the purpose is for collecting data. For a very long time, people thought that all swans were white because no one had ever seen one of any other colour. As explained in Chapter 3, it only takes an Australian researcher with a convenience sample of one black swan to prove the old generalization to be wrong.

Quota sampling   **Quota sampling** divides the relevant population up into categories (perhaps male/female, or country of origin for students) and then selection continues until a sample of a specific size is achieved within each category. The aim is to make sure that each of the categories is represented according to the quota proportions. For example, in doctoral research on whether the Internet empowers consumers, quota sampling enabled the researcher to ensure he or she had users of a variety of ages; while a convenience sample would be more likely to result in a preponderance of people similar to the researcher and his or her friends.

Purposive sampling   In **purposive sampling**, the researcher has a clear idea of what sample units are needed, and then approaches potential sample members to check whether they meet eligibility criteria. Those that do are used, while those that do not are rejected. Market researchers (the people in shopping centres with clipboards) often use this approach, when they target, for example, women in a particular age range who are also mobile phone users. The first questions would establish the respondent's age and mobile phone use – presumably it is not necessary to ask the person's gender!

Snowball sampling　**Snowball sampling** starts with someone who meets the criteria for inclusion in a study who is then asked to name others who would also be eligible. This method works well for samples where individuals are very rare and it is hard to identify who belongs to the population. Dissertation students often do this by starting out with people they or their supervisor know personally, and then ask those people to pass them on to others who would also be suitable. It works well too for individuals, groups or companies that are part of networks whose membership is confidential.

Why are non-probability sampling designs valuable?　The sampling approaches described in this section are answers to a variety of practical problems that researchers have encountered in carrying out their work. But how do these sampling methods stack up against the key quality criteria of bias and precision that we started this section with? *Precision* is most straightforward, since its main focus is the size of the sample achieved. A convenience sample can meet the first requirement of a big-enough sample most easily; quota sampling and purposive sampling both aim to ensure that every sector in a sampling design is filled; while snowball sampling addresses the problem of ensuring an adequate sample of hard-to-find people. However, the principle of *bias* is where non-probability sampling methods can most easily fall down, especially for convenience sampling. Many management researchers have been seduced by the lure of large samples (perhaps feeling themselves under pressure from journal editors to report large samples) and achieved them simply through collecting respondents by any means (MBA classes, lists of Facebook friends and so on). There is no guarantee that the findings reported are credible, since the credibility of findings relies in large measure on the character of the sample. It is not surprising then, that reviews of research often highlight contradictions in findings between different studies, given that researchers often take little care in defining their sampling design.

SOURCES OF QUANTITATIVE DATA

In thinking about where to get data that could be analysed using quantitative methods, there are broadly two ways of going about it: researchers can collect their own primary data or they can use secondary data already collected and stored within archival databases. Each approach has advantages and disadvantages. Broadly, collecting one's own research data gives control over both the structure of the sample and the data obtained from each respondent. This gives greater confidence that the data will match the study objectives. On the other hand, that benefit comes at a price since it can be much more expensive (in time and effort) to collect one's own data, compared with using secondary data from an existing archive. The downside of using secondary data sources is that the quality of the data may be more uncertain, and the researcher does not have control over either the sample or the specific data collected.

Collecting data through surveys

Surveys can be good ways of collecting data about the opinions and behaviour of large numbers of people, as long as they are done well. The choice between them will depend on many factors, so that there is no single best way. Survey data can be collected either through self-completion questionnaires where respondents record their own answers, or can be administered by interviewers face-to-face or over the telephone. While these two methods still have an important place, advances in communications technology have brought a variety of new options within the scope of the researcher in business and management. The new methods offer many advantages, and bring challenges, which are also opportunities of course.

Self-completion questionnaires **Postal questionnaire surveys** have the advantage that the cost per respondent is low for large samples compared with any method that requires face-to-face contact with individuals, especially when the sample members are widely dispersed. On the other hand, response rates can be very low (for many researchers, a 20 per cent response rate would be regarded as good) because there is no personal contact with the respondent that can encourage co-operation. Financial or other inducements are sometimes effective, but the normal guarantee of anonymity makes it difficult to reward people for responding because the researcher has no way of knowing who has replied and who has not. The researcher has little control over whether the person targeted is the one who answers the questions (CEOs are reputed to hand survey questionnaires over to their PAs to fill in on their behalf), and also over how they answer them. As a result checking the quality of data from postal surveys, both completeness and accuracy, is particularly important.

Another application of modern communications technology is the **web-based survey**. As the Internet becomes a taken-for-granted part of business and domestic life, carrying out web-based surveys (Gunn, 2002) is rapidly becoming commonplace. Instead of mailing a questionnaire to each potential respondent and asking them to mail it back, the questionnaire is located on a website, and each respondent is sent the web address in order to access it. The survey is then completed online, and responses are stored directly in an online database for statistical processing later. Tools such as Qualtrics (www.qualtrics.com), Surveymonkey (www.surveymonkey.com), VoVici (www.vovici.com) and Zoomerang (www.zoomerang.com) have dramatically reduced the cost of web surveys by making each step in the process easy for those without technical training. The internet offers a number of attractions for web surveys. Internet-based surveys can be customized for individual respondents much more easily than can postal surveys. Moreover, the interactivity of web technologies gives a number of advantages: pop-up instructions and drop-down boxes can explain parts of the web survey that are more difficult to understand; questions at different points in a survey can be personalized using responses to earlier questions; and through skip-logic and conditional branching it is easy to skip over topics that are not relevant based on answers to earlier questions. It is also possible to build in dynamic error-checking of answers to ensure that people respond consistently throughout. Finally, data can be downloaded directly into analysis programs such as Excel or SPSS, avoiding the cost of data entry and transcription errors. Berghman, Matthyssens and Vandenbempt (2006) provide a good example of a web survey.

Interviewer-administered questionnaires   **Structured interview surveys** are much more expensive per head because an interviewer has to be present while each respondent's answers are recorded. The cost of interviews includes the time of the interviewer, which has to cover initial training, time spent in setting up each interview, travel to where respondents are located, and an allowance for broken appointments. They are most often used when accurate data are the main priority, and where there are complicated instructions for how to answer survey questions or where different questions need to be asked depending on individual circumstances. It is almost always better to have a smaller dataset of accurate answers than a larger dataset riddled with errors. Many people are understandably reluctant to divulge confidential or personal sensitive information in a postal questionnaire, and a skilled interviewer can build a relationship of trust with respondents that can reassure them about why the data are needed and how they will be kept secure. An interview method may be the most effective way to collect survey data for groups such as customers in a shop or a service facility, where postal addresses or other contact details are not available.

     Telephone interview surveys are now commonplace in many research projects, since they combine the low cost of the postal survey with the interactivity of the face-to-face interview. So much of day-to-day business is conducted now by phone that most people are very familiar with the technology. Collecting data by telephone is of most value where the design of the research project requires contact with respondents who are widely dispersed (so that travelling to them would be time-consuming and expensive) or where the researcher is located in a different part of the world (for example, many Asian students studying in the UK want to conduct their research in their own country, but cannot afford to travel there to collect data). This task has been made much cheaper in the last few years by the rapid development of voice-over-IP (VOIP) technologies such as Skype (www.skype.com), which use the Internet to transmit voice, so that the cost of a call does not depend on distance.

Advantages and disadvantages of alternative survey strategies

EXERCISE
8.1

Below are three different research projects where survey methodology might be appropriate. Taking into account the topic, the resources available to you and the target group draw up the advantages and disadvantages of the four methods of administering your survey. Which method will you use and why?

(Continued)

(Continued)

	Postal survey	Web survey	Face-to-face interview survey	Telephone interview survey
A small project on the site where I work to assess views on introducing charges for car parking				
Advantages				
Disadvantages				
A worldwide survey in a multinational company of staff attitudes to HRM practices				
Advantages				
Disadvantages				
An investigation to understand the nature of bullying within the Social Services Department of a local authority				
Advantages				
Disadvantages				

Collecting data through observational methods

Observational methods are used in order to code and analyse behaviour, which may include visual data as well as behavioural data (Banks, 2008). Behaviour may either be coded live or be recorded (for example using audio or video or by capturing key presses and screen displays on a PC) for later coding. The most common way in which observational methods are used is with the observer as a non-participant, although participant observation can also be used, as was discussed in Chapter 6.

Types of observational data   There is no single way of classifying observational data, because behaviour is very complicated and the purposes of studies vary enormously. The most obvious distinction is between verbal and non-verbal aspects of behaviour. The researcher may be interested in *verbal* behaviour – the words that people use to express meanings through the content of messages, complexity of syntax, formal vs informal language – in order to explore different ways of explaining how to perform a task. *Non-verbal* behaviour is divided into vocal aspects to do with tone of voice (angry, apologetic, loving, calm and so on), pitch (high or low) and the pacing of speech (talking quickly or slowly), and also visual aspects to do with facial expressions, gestures, body posture and so on. A detailed analysis of the success or failure of a negotiation exercise would need to include an analysis of these aspects of non-verbal behaviour since they carry a substantial proportion of information. For example,

Mehrabian's (1981) experimental studies of communications of feelings and attitudes led him to the following formula:

$$\text{Total Liking} = 7\% \text{ Verbal Liking} + 38\% \text{ Vocal Liking} + 55\% \text{ Facial Liking.}$$

In other words, most of the information about whether one person likes who they are talking to comes not from what is said (only 7 per cent) but on how it is said and on their facial expressions (93 per cent). We can conclude that relying for data only on a written transcript of what was said during a conversation or a meeting will miss much of the most important information about what is going on, particularly regarding relationships between people.

Factors affecting observational data   There are a number of things that need to be kept in mind when designing studies that will use observational data. First, **observer effects** are common, which refers to the fact that most of us behave differently when we know (or think) that we are being observed. Often, initiatives within local communities rely on exactly these effects to influence the behaviour of members of the public: those boxes on poles at the side of the road often do not contain speed cameras (but they might, so we slow down). From the perspective of research, observer effects are bad news since they alter the very thing that the researcher is interested in learning about. Consider how difficult it is for many people to pose naturally for a photograph: it is easy to tell the difference between a natural smile and a posed smile since the muscle groups used are different. In practice though, people whose behaviour is being recorded quickly get used to being observed and forget about the cameras. One way to avoid observer effects is to act covertly so that no one knows that they are being watched, but this violates one of the basic principles of ethical research, that research participants give their informed consent to take part in a study (see Chapter 4). Indeed, recording of telephone calls without consent is illegal in the UK, and that is why calls to companies often start with a message saying that calls may be recorded or monitored for security and quality control purposes.

The second factor to bear in mind in using observational data relates to how decisions are made about *what behaviour is sampled*. Some kind of selectivity is inevitable, simply because human behaviour is so rich and complex. One approach is to try to obtain a complete record, and then sample from within it later. A popular TV programme in many countries is *Big Brother* (first developed in the Netherlands), where individuals live in the 'Big Brother House' and a large number of cameras record what they do. Each person also wears a microphone at all times so that what they say is recorded. Even if the output from every camera and every microphone is available for analysis, some kind of selectivity is essential. The programme editors broadcast a tiny proportion of all that material; and their editing judgements can be a source of complaint and comment. For example, inmates of the house often complain that the programme did not show the 'real me' when features of their behaviour that show them in particular way are selected and others neglected. A second approach is to record only a sample of behaviour: either by *time* sampling (for example, take a photo every two seconds, or record for five minutes every hour through the day) or by *activity* sampling (for example, record every phone call that is a customer complaint, or select company orders for a specific range of products).

Coding observational data One of the most widely used systems for coding behaviour in small groups is *Interaction Process Analysis* (IPA) originally developed by Bales (1950, 1970) and later modified. The original system grouped behaviour into 12 categories according to a focus either on social-emotional aspects of the relationship (for example, liking vs disliking) or on aspects of the task (for example, giving answers vs asking questions). The categories form six pairs: for example, seems friendly vs unfriendly; gives vs asks for information. Using the IPA requires substantial training for observers to break behaviour down into discrete units and then classify each unit into one of the categories. A more detailed elaboration of the IPA is the System of Multiple Level Observation of Groups (SYMLOG) (Bales, Cohen and Williamson, 1979; Bales, 1988). The two forms of the system code either values or behaviour into 26 categories, which can then be combined to give a position in a three-dimensional interpersonal space: dominance, friendliness and task-orientation.

EXAMPLE
8.1

Using observational data

A Masters student sat in as an observer on selection interviews for engineering apprentices and coded some aspects of the verbal and non-verbal behaviour of each candidate during the interview. Interviews were classified according to the outcome (accept or reject) and were then examined for differences in the behaviour of the candidates. All the candidates treated the interview as a formal situation and were nervous: they sat upright in the chair with their legs together in front of them and their hands together on their knees. The candidates who were *accepted* showed that they were interested in the interviewer by lots of eye contact, and smiling. They reinforced their replies to the interviewer's questions by moving their head – nodding or shaking. By contrast, the *rejected* candidates avoided eye contact with the interviewer, and showed their apparent lack of interest by wandering eyes when the interviewer was talking, and they were much less expressive in their non-verbal behaviour.

EXERCISE
8.2

Types of questions that observational data can answer

In groups, consider the research questions in the box below. Each group selects one of the research questions. The task is in two parts:

1 Draw up a coding scheme for the types of behaviour that the group is interested in.

2 Design a sampling strategy for collecting the data.

Then bring the groups together to present their coding schemes, and compare them. What factors influence the content of the coding scheme and the choice of sampling strategy?

(Continued)

(Continued)

Research question	What data to collect	How to sample
Do people buy more cold drinks in hot weather?		
Does background music in a store alter customers' buying behaviour?		
Do employees interact differently with a female boss?		
How do people use online help sources?		
When do people who work in different places (virtual teams) switch between media (instant messaging, email, video-conferencing, phone) in order to manage a project?		
How does the style of the call handler influence the effectiveness of telephone helplines?		
In negotiations, how do same-sex and mixed-sex groups differ?		

Using secondary data – databases

The final method of getting quantitative data that we consider in this chapter is using archival sources of secondary data. Most research areas in business and management have data collected by other people. Organizations and individuals keep many different kinds of data for a variety of reasons: regulatory reasons (for example, personal tax records), for monitoring past and present performance, and as a protection in the event of requests for information about the basis for past decisions. Although much of this data is confidential, a research study may gain access to data provided they meet confidentiality conditions. It is also the case that data of many kinds have to be deposited in archives, which can then be accessed for research purposes. Some of that data is in the public domain, though access to other material may depend on licence agreements of some kind, which the researcher's host institution may have negotiated.

Examples of **financial databases** include the following:

- Compustat (www.compustat.com) provides annual and quarterly income statements, balance sheets, cash flow and supplemental data items for North American companies.

- Datastream (www.datastream.com) is one the largest financial statistical databases, and holds current/historical financial data for international companies/indices and bond data.

- SDC Platinum (http://thomsonreuters.com/products_services/financial/financial_products/a-z/sdc/) is an international mergers and acquisitions database.

- The Wharton Research Data Service (WRDS, www.whartonwrds.com) provides access to databases in the fields of finance, accounting, banking, economics, management, marketing and public policy.
- The Center for Research in Security Prices (CRSP, www.crsp.com) holds a variety of databases including: monthly/annual security prices, returns, and volume data for the NYSE, AMEX and NASDAQ stock markets.

It can be very valuable to work with data collected for another purpose, but it is most unwise to plunge straight into a data archive without thinking carefully. The most important factor affecting the quality of what can be done with secondary data is the design of the database. Generally speaking, archival data will have been collected according to a specific design, which means that the researcher's first task in assessing the value of secondary sources is how close the study objectives are to those that influenced the original collection of the data. For example, someone who is interested in how small- and medium-sized enterprises (SMEs) are using the Internet to internationalize their businesses is unlikely to find an archive of publicly quoted companies of much use, since SMEs are much smaller than a typical publicly quoted company.

EXAMPLE
8.2

Using databases

A doctoral student in her PhD work looked at cross-border mergers involving a British company taken over by a non-UK company. She started her search using the Thomson Financial M&A database to identify mergers that met her criteria. Here is her story:

> In my thesis, I needed to draw up a list of acquisitions with particular characteristics, which I would later contact. I needed only majority acquisitions, and it allowed me to search for above 50 per cent acquisitions. I also needed only UK companies that were bought by foreign companies – the database allowed me to 'include' or 'exclude' acquirers and targets from particular countries from my search. For example, by 'excluding' UK acquirers I was able to search only for foreign acquisitions. It also allowed me to search for deals of a certain age, completed as opposed to only announced deals, deals of a certain value, deals in a specific industry, etc. The database also contained very small as well as very large M&As. Overall, I found it an incredibly versatile tool. I was able to get the list of M&As with the precise specifications that I wanted in a matter of minutes. Thomson Financial, however, did not provide me with addresses or websites of the companies, so I had to search for these myself.

Many archives contain company records for each year (things like profits figures and so on). Databases differ in their coverage of companies – some are more comprehensive for US companies, others for European companies, while yet other databases only contain data for companies above a minimum size. A researcher interested in other regions, for example the growth of Latin American companies, may find it difficult to locate sources of data. Another problem is that of linking data over time for organizations in a world where companies are formed, they grow, they merge with others and they die. Thus profits data for a company will only be available for those periods where it is independent, so that a takeover will mean that it becomes part of a larger organization, while re-structuring may leave the name intact but changes the sub-units that make it up. It may thus prove impossible to compare like for like over a lengthy period of time. The practical consequences of dealing with such changes are outlined in Example 8.3.

Designing a study to assess the impact of the Sarbanes-Oxley Act, 2002

EXAMPLE 8.3

Consider the research question of assessing the impact on companies of the Sarbanes-Oxley Act of 2002, which changed the governance regulation and reporting obligations of US public companies after the Enron scandal (see Chapter 3, p. 37). The obvious way to assess its impact is to use data for companies before and after the Act came into force. The first task is to decide on a sampling frame (whether to select companies within specific sectors, or companies of a specific size) and the second is to decide what time points to look at (e.g. three years before and after the Act came into force). The research could end up with four kinds of sample, and there are issues with all of the sampling strategies.

The first approach is to select only companies with complete data throughout the study period. This makes the most sense on the face of it, since it gives a complete picture for the whole of the study period. It gives good answers to the question of how key variables change for companies whose ownership structure stays the same throughout. However, it misses out the following: companies that went out of business at any time on the study period, start-ups during the study period and companies that were involved in merger and acquisition (M&A) activity.

The second approach is to select all relevant companies at the start of the sampling period regardless of whether they still exist. This strategy would ensure that the researcher has a sound sample at the start of the study period, but then the study design suffers from the same problem of incomplete data for companies that went out of existence or changed their structure through M&A activity. This would make it impossible to compare data before and after; but it could still be possible to assess a slightly different question: the likelihood of a company surviving intact until the end of the study period (this is called 'survival analysis' in statistics).

The third approach is to select all relevant companies at the end of the sampling period regardless of when they came into existence. This ensures a sound sample at the end of the study period, but suffers from incomplete data at the start for companies that are newly formed or re-formed from M&A activity.

The final approach is to select a representative sample of companies at each sampling point, with varying amounts of data for each. This would give a representative

(Continued)

(Continued)

picture of companies at each point, but the analysis of change over time would be greatly complicated by different patterns of incomplete data.

Given that there is no ideal solution, a researcher will need to weigh up the relative merits of each alternative and the risks involved. Much will depend on how much change there has been in organizational structures during the study period, and the precise nature of the research questions under consideration.

Where companies are required by regulation to report particular kinds of information, then that is what they will do. When regulations change, there will be an associated change in what is recorded. As a result, great care needs to be taken by the researcher to make sure that the data have a consistent meaning throughout the study period. For example, Wall, Jackson, and Davids (1992) were interested in whether empowering shop-floor workers by allowing them to manage machine breakdowns had an effect on productivity. Each machine had a tachograph (similar to those used in vehicles to record driving performance), which automatically logged when the machine was working and when it was not. Production managers also kept their own records of production within each of the departments for which they were responsible. However, the research team had to design their own productivity measures, once they found that company managers had made several changes during the study period to how they recorded productivity. Line managers had designed productivity indices that helped them to achieve the objectives set for them by the company's senior management; but there were frequent changes to corporate priorities during the study period and managers responded to shifting priorities by adjusting what they measured and how they measured it.

The task of the researcher is to interpret the data recorded in a secondary data archive in terms of particular study objectives. This might mean forming *derived* measures by aggregating variables together to form an index, or by creating rates rather than absolute amounts. For example, comparing absolute change rarely makes sense, while percentage change relative to a starting point is generally more informative. Other examples are: measures of earnings per share, which take into account differences in company capitalization; productivity indicators (such as those used in the study in the previous paragraph), which relate outputs to the resources needed to deliver them; sickness rates for companies, which adjust number of days of recorded sickness absence according to the number of employees.

QUESTIONNAIRE DESIGN

In the last section of this chapter, we look at structured forms of asking questions and recording the answers that people give to them. Research on how politicians respond to questions asked by probing journalists showed that there are apparently 46 ways of avoiding answering a straight question. If that really is true, then how much more difficult is it to interpret answers when the questions themselves are not well-structured?

Principles in designing structured questions for surveys and interviews

There are five principles of good design when thinking about how to word questions. The first principle is that *each item should express only one idea*. If a question asks more than one thing at the same time, then how is it possible to know which one people are thinking of when they give an answer? The second principle is to *avoid jargon and colloquialisms*. Jargon is insider knowledge in the form of expressions that some people (but not others) know. So, using it only makes sense where it is possible to be confident that respondents are all 'in the know'. Colloquialisms are informal expressions in a language that may not be familiar to people who are not native to that country, or do not belong to a specific group. Mobile phone text-speak is becoming that, where 'cu l8r' is simple for some ('see you later') but impenetrable to others. The message is clear: play safe and use plain language. The third principle is to *use simple expressions*. Using the active rather than the passive tense is generally better ('I did it' is better than 'It was done by me'). Dividing up complicated arguments into a series of simple steps is better than expressing it all in one long sentence.

The fourth principle is to *avoid the use of negatives*. In English, this is often done by adding 'no' or 'not' to a verb in order to give the opposite meaning; but two problems can arise. The first is that a quick read of a sentence may miss the negative, so that the respondent answers a question the wrong way around. There is research by Schmitt and Stults (1985) which suggests that around 10 per cent of respondents in large-scale studies may make this kind of mistake; and it obviously disturbs the clarity of data analysis. The second problem is that scales such as the **Likert scale** are bipolar – they go from negative (*disagree*) through neutral (*not sure*) to positive (*agree*). People who feel good about something would have to show it by disagreeing with a statement worded negatively. This means it can get tricky to work out how to report what they feel.

The final principle is to *avoid leading questions*. The concept of a **leading question** comes from legal settings, where the way that a question is phrased gives a strong lead on what answer is expected. All research has an element of 'leadingness' about it – the researcher chooses what to ask about, and this focuses attention on some areas and not on others. However, leading questions do more than this: they make it easier for the respondent to give the answer that the researcher wants, instead of the answer that the respondent thinks is right.

Examples of poor question wording

For each question below:

1 What is the problem?

2 Which of the five principles is violated?

3 Re-write the question, and explain why your version works better than the original. (Clue – this might involve replacing it with more than one question.)

(Continued)

EXERCISE
8.3

(Continued)

How strongly do you agree that smoking is harmful to health?

☐ Not at all ☐ Slightly ☐ Quite strongly ☐ Very strongly

How good is your voting record in local elections?

☐ Not at all ☐ Quite good ☐ Very good ☐ Excellent

If you wanted to express your opinion about genetically modified foods would you consider taking part in a boycott of your local supermarket?

☐ Not at all ☐ Probably not ☐ Not sure ☐ Probably ☐ Definitely

How much do you agree or disagree with the following: Politicians never keep the promises they make before an election, once they are in office.

☐ Strongly disagree ☐ Disagree ☐ Not sure ☐ Agree ☐ Strongly agree

How much do you agree with the following: My supervisor is dynamic and well organized.

☐ Strongly disagree ☐ Disagree ☐ Not sure ☐ Agree ☐ Strongly agree

How much do you agree with the following: I am not satisfied with the progress of my research.

☐ Strongly disagree ☐ Disagree ☐ Not sure ☐ Agree ☐ Strongly agree

How much do you agree with the following: The presence of humorous literary allusions is conducive to an accessible presentation mode in academic pedagogy.

☐ Strongly disagree ☐ Disagree ☐ Not sure ☐ Agree ☐ Strongly agree

Exercise 8.3 gives some examples of poorly worded questions that might be asked in a questionnaire survey or an interview. Some have been taken from real research, while others have been invented to make a point. The exercise invites the reader to think through the design principles, work out what is wrong with each example question and then devise a better form of words. Like many things in life, asking clear questions seems remarkably easy until we set out to do it ourselves.

Measurement scales for recording responses

There are two kinds of measurement scales that researchers commonly use, and they differ according to the number of distinctions between alternative points on the measurement scale. **Category scales** consist of few distinctions, while **continuous scales** consist of many distinctions.

Category scales   These may be either unordered (these are called nominal scales) or ordered (these are called ordinal scales). The difference between nominal and ordinal category scales lies in whether shuffling the assignment of numbers to categories makes any difference to the meaning of the variable. **Nominal scales** have no natural ordering. A study by Goldacre, Davidson and Lambert (2004) considered the ethnic origin of UK medical consultants, recorded as White, Black, Asian, Chinese and Other. It makes no sense to treat a concept such as ethnic origin as anything other than a nominal scale since the five ethnic groups could equally well be written in any order. Similarly, studies of branded consumer products coding countries of origin could list them in any order. By contrast, **ordinal scales** have a natural ordering. An example of an ordinal scale is socio-economic status, such as the classification scheme used by the UK government (the Registrar General's classification: I professional, II Intermediate, IIIa Skilled non-manual, IIIb Skilled manual, IV Semi-skilled, V Unskilled), which is based on such criteria as educational qualifications and occupation. Similarly, honours degrees awarded to UK undergraduates are graded as first class, upper second class (2:1), lower second class (2:2) and third class. The higher the aggregate mark in assessed work, the higher the degree classification.

Sometimes, however, the status of a variable in a research study is less clear. For the purpose of recording trade flows, country of origin would be recorded on a nominal scale. However, a project on boycotts within Arab countries of consumer products might well rank countries according to how closely they are associated with the USA, thus giving an ordinal scale. This illustrates an important point: that concepts or variables do not carry around with them a measurement scale that is intrinsic to them. Rather, the properties of scales are just that, properties which apply when we measure something.

The measurement of attitudes and opinions   Psychologists are not alone in being interested in what people think about things: the effect of the Lisbon Treaty on political relationships within Europe, the reputation of the company that supplies their electricity, and so on. Everyone has opinions, and there is a lot of money to be made out of knowing what those opinions are. It is no surprise then that a lot of attention has gone into understanding effective ways of measuring attitudes and opinions.

Alternative attitude response scales

EXAMPLE
8.4

My organization is a friendly place to work. How much do you agree or disagree with this statement?

☐ Agree   ☐ Disagree   (agree/disagree scale)

☐ Strongly   ☐ Disagree   ☐ Not sure   ☐ Agree   ☐ Strongly   (Likert scale)
disagree   agree

Consider the statement 'My organization is a friendly place to work' (see Example 8.4). The simple-minded approach would be to ask people whether or not they agreed with the statement. However, this approach misses out on a lot of useful information because strength of opinion varies. There is a world of difference between someone who likes to listen to rock music from time to time and the fanatic who has every Guns N' Roses CD plus bootleg copies of their live concerts. To capture some of this subtlety, Rensis Likert developed a five-point response scale that still bears his name, the **Likert scale**. The scale has a neutral mid-point to allow for the possibility that an individual may have no opinion on an issue. Then, on each side of the mid-point there are two alternative response options to record moderate and extreme views for or against. Both types of attitude response scale are ordinal scales in that *agreeing* reflects a more positive attitude towards the issue raised than does *disagreeing*.

Continuous scales   Continuous scales are types of ordered scale so that it is possible to speak about more or less whatever is being measured according to the value on the scale. The difference between the two types of continuous scale, interval and ratio, lies in whether there is a true zero point. If there is a true zero point on a scale, then that gives a **ratio scale**; and it is possible to speak meaningfully of a data point of 20 being twice as high as another data point with a value of 10 (for example). Height is measured on a true ratio scale, and we can meaningfully speak of an adult being twice as tall as a child. Time is also measured on a ratio scale, for example how long it takes for MBA graduates to get a job after their programme finishes. A graduate's income compared to what it was before joining the MBA programme is also measured on a ratio scale.

If there is no true zero point (as, for example, temperature where we have Celsius and Fahrenheit scales), then we have an **interval scale** at best. On an interval scale, differences between alternative values can be described meaningfully, but ratios cannot. Suppose we have four data points with values of 1, 2, 9 and 10 measured on an interval scale. We may say that the difference between the first two data points is the same as the difference between the last two; but not that the last data point is ten times bigger than the first. Travelling from England with a temperature of 15° to Hong Kong with a temperature of 30° is a doubling of temperature when we measure in degrees Celsius but not in degrees Fahrenheit (15° Celsius is 59° Fahrenheit, while 30° Celsius is 86° Fahrenheit). Many continuous measurement scales in social science are truly interval scales rather than ratio scales. The difference is captured succinctly by asking the question: is the data still meaningful if a fixed value (say 50) were subtracted from each score? For much data on attitudes or preferences, scales are arbitrary and such an adjustment would not matter.

CONCLUSION

The assumption that underlies the methods described in this chapter is that the researcher uses quantitative data derived from a sample in order to draw conclusions about a defined population. The material we have covered in this chapter is:

(Continued)

(Continued)

 Types of sampling design and the criteria that the research can use to select a form of design that is appropriate for a specific purpose.

 Sources of both primary and secondary data, emphasizing the issues involved in using each source which can affect the quality of data that are available for analysis.

 The process of measurement.

At each stage of the data collection process, decisions made by the researcher can influence the quality of data that can be obtained and the inferences that can be made from that data about the character of the population of interest. The next two chapters describe methods for analysing quantitative data. In Chapter 9, we first consider ways of summarizing key features of data and then examine the principles and practice of hypothesis testing which allow the researcher to make inferences about populations based on evidence from samples. Chapter 9 considers univariate tests, taking one variable at a time; and Chapter 10 extends this treatment to cover the multivariate case where many variables are dealt with simultaneously.

FURTHER READING

Bales, R.F. (1988) 'A new overview of the SYMLOG system: measuring and changing behavior in groups', in R.B. Polley, A.P. Hare and P.J. Stone (eds), *The SYMLOG Practitioner*. New York: Praeger, pp. 319–44.
Bales, R.F., Cohen, S.P. and Williamson, S.A. (1979) *SYMLOG: A System for the Multiple Level Observation of Groups*. New York: The Free Press.
These two texts describe the System of Multiple Level Observation of Groups (SYMLOG), which is a more detailed elaboration of the IPA.
Couper, M.P. (2008) *Designing Effective Web Surveys*. Cambridge: Cambridge University Press.
This is a useful source for web-based surveys.
Sapsford, R. (2006) *Survey Research*, 2nd edn. London: Sage.
This offers a comprehensive introduction to different kinds of sampling design for social science research and the principles that inform how a researcher might choose between them.

SUMMARIZING AND MAKING INFERENCES FROM QUANTITATIVE DATA

9

LEARNING OBJECTIVES

 To be able to choose effective ways of summarizing key features of data.

 To know which summary measures to use for location and spread of data.

To understand which statistical tests to use when comparing groups and testing association between variables.

INTRODUCTION

Business and management is maturing as a discipline, and this maturity is shown in many ways. Its conceptual thinking is becoming more sophisticated, and there is increasing evidence that scholars are not just developing clever ways of thinking about the business of business but are also putting their ideas to the test. How to gather quantitative data has been dealt with in the previous chapter. Here, we will look at the tools that management scholars use when their empirical evidence is in the form of numbers – quantitative data.

The most obvious feature of quantitative data – evidence expressed in the form of numbers – is their sheer quantity. It is generally expensive in time and money to accumulate good quality data, and so researchers make the most of each study participant by collecting as much data as possible from each person, and quantitative research designs also often involve large samples. The big challenge then is seeing the wood for the trees – identifying patterns in numerical data and making sense of those patterns. In this chapter, we address this in two parts. First, we consider the key features of numerical data and the common indices that are used to assess those features. The second part of the chapter introduces the logic of statistical inference as a tool for 'going beyond the data' and introduces a variety of statistical tests for looking at data one variable at a time.

Quantitative methods are an important part of the research process in business and management, something which, as we discussed in Chapter 4, is especially true of American journals. Table 9.1 gives some examples from two of the leading journals in strategy and marketing of research questions that have been addressed using quantitative data. Behind the most sophisticated research question and the most complex datasets, however, is a simple basic principle. All quantitative researchers do the same two things: they identify what features tell the best story about the data (we call this **summarizing** the data) and then they look for patterns in the data that can be used to draw conclusions about the study's research questions (we call this making **inferences** about populations based on sample data).

The idea behind summarizing and making inferences is a simple one, which can be illustrated quite easily. The year 2010 was a bad one for BP, following the explosion on the Deepwater Horizon drilling rig, which killed 11 people and led to a massive leak of oil into the Gulf of Mexico. The company's share price showed a high of 655 and a low of 302 for the year; reflecting the impact of the explosion on the investment community's view of BP's reputation and its future viability. Behind the bald figures of share price movements is also an inference process – one might say a kind of guesswork or betting – that predicts what the future profits of BP will be, based on its past performance. The judgements of investment analysts are based on an inference process (not formal statistical inference, but rather informed guesswork) about future data on the performance of BP. Management researchers follow the same kinds of inference processes when they make judgements about the world based on their data.

Example datasets for the chapter

This chapter uses datasets from a variety of sources. Table 9.2 shows the midday temperature for selected world locations on Thursday 2 December 2010. The lowest temperature recorded in the table is a distinctly cold -15°C in Moscow; while the highest temperature is

TABLE 9.1 Examples of studies using quantitative methods from *Strategic Management Journal* and the *Journal of Marketing*

State-owned enterprises (SOEs) in China (Ralston et al., 2006). They compared the organizational cultures of state-owned enterprises with private-owned enterprises and foreign-owned businesses in order to decide whether SOEs are dinosaurs or dynamos for China's economic future.

Should multinational enterprises (MNEs) adapt their marketing strategy to each market or standardize across markets? (Katsikeas, Samiee and Theodosiou, 2006). They looked at the international marketing strategies of US, Japanese and German MNEs operating in the UK. They found that standardization only makes sense when there is a good fit to the market environment.

Knowledge transfer in business-to-business relationships (Dyer and Hatch, 2006). They found that Toyota were much better than US car companies (GM, Ford and Chrysler) in getting better quality out of their suppliers. They concluded that there can be specific capabilities within relationships between customers and suppliers that are not easily transferable to other relationships.

How to influence a company on environmental issues (Eesley and Lenox, 2006). They used a database of secondary stakeholder actions to check out what it takes to get positive responses out of companies.

Home or away? – where to put your HQ (Birkinshaw et al., 2006). They found that MNEs put their business unit headquarters overseas when it made sense for *internal* reasons; while the location of their corporate HQ was influenced most strongly by the demands of *external* stakeholders – global financial markets and shareholders.

Is corporate social responsibility (CSR) smart as well as good? (Luo and Bhattacharya, 2006). They used secondary data archives to test the link between CSR activities such as cash donations and employee volunteerism, customer satisfaction and the market value of the firm. They found that CSR can be smart – good for the company – but there is a dark side too.

What do website visitors value on a manufacturer's site? (Steenkamp and Geyskens, 2006). The authors found that the answer depends on the country where the consumers live. They looked at over 8,000 consumers from 23 countries, visiting the sites of 16 consumer packaged goods companies.

a very pleasant (but perhaps rather humid) 33°C in Bangkok. The table itself is presented in alphabetical order according to the name of the location, and so it is not easy to gain much of an impression of what this body of data looks like. Figure 9.1 uses a stem and leaf plot to organize the data in a rather more helpful way.

Stem and leaf plot   This form of display groups the data into a number of categories (called stems), and then shows the number of data points within each category (each data point is called a leaf). The stems are labelled according to the second digit of each data value. At the bottom of the plot, the temperatures of 30° and higher are grouped under the stem labelled as '3', the temperatures of 20–29° are grouped under the stem labelled '2', and so on. The lowest temperatures of -10° and below are grouped together at the top of the plot under the stem labelled '-1'. In this plot, there are six stems, and the column to the

TABLE 9.2   Maximum midday temperatures for 94 world locations, Thursday 2 December 2010

Alicante	13	Madeira	18
Amsterdam	–6	Madrid	5
Athens	23	Majorca	14
Auckland	19	Malaga	15
Bahrain	24	Malta	20
Bangkok	33	Melbourne	23
Barbados	29	Mexico City	15
Barcelona	9	Miami	28
Beijing	4	Milan	1
Beirut	25	Mombasa	31
Belgrade	8	Moscow	–15
Berlin	–8	Mumbai	32
Bermuda	20	Munich	–4
Bordeaux	2	Nairobi	25
Brussels	–5	Naples	15
Bucharest	0	New Orleans	12
Budapest	1	New York	15
Buenos Aires	30	Nice	10
Cairo	22	Nicosia	24
Calcutta	26	Oslo	–14
Canberra	24	Paris	–2
Cape Town	26	Perth	24
Chicago	–4	Prague	–10
Copenhagen	–2	Reykjavik	–2

(Continued)

TABLE 9.2 (Continued)

Corfu	20	Riga	–8
Delhi	22	Rio de Janeiro	29
Dubai	28	Riyadh	22
Dublin	–1	Rome	14
Faro	14	San Francisco	9
Florence	12	Santiago	21
Frankfurt	–7	Sao Paulo	26
Geneva	–1	Seoul	12
Gibraltar	13	Seychelles	25
Harare	18	Singapore	31
Helsinki	–3	St Petersburg	–9
Hong Kong	23	Stockholm	–12
Honolulu	28	Sydney	25
Istanbul	21	Tel Aviv	28
Jerusalem	28	Tenerife	21
Johannesburg	26	Tokyo	21
Kuala Lumpur	30	Toronto	16
Lanzarote	20	Vancouver	7
Las Palmas	21	Venice	4
Lima	21	Vienna	0
Lisbon	11	Warsaw	–8
Los Angeles	19	Washington	6
Luxor	27	Zurich	–3

SOURCE: THE TIMES, 3 DECEMBER 2010

left shows how many leaves there are attached to each stem. There are four locations in the coldest category (stem value '–1'), and the leaf shows the second digit of the temperature

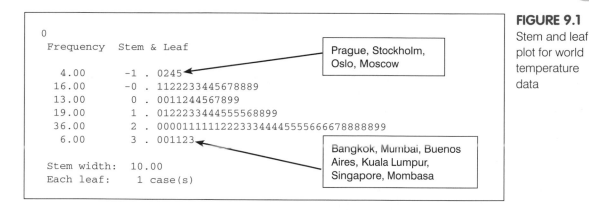

FIGURE 9.1
Stem and leaf plot for world temperature data

for each one: Prague (–10°), Stockholm (–12°), Oslo (–14°) and Moscow (–15°). The next stem is labelled '–0' and holds the leaves showing locations with temperatures between –1° and –9°. The frequency column shows that there are 16 of these locations and, with the exception of Chicago and Reykjavik, they are all in Europe. As many readers will remember well, December 2010 was a period of record low temperatures. At the other end of the distribution, the plot shows six locations with temperatures of 30° or more: Bangkok, Mumbai, Buenos Aires, Kuala Lumpur, Singapore and Mombasa.

Having introduced the dataset, we now turn to describe different ways of summarizing key features of the data.

SUMMARIZING AND DESCRIBING DATA

There are three sections to this part of the chapter. The first looks at ways of showing the shape of data distributions, and it capitalizes on the highly developed capabilities that humans have for seeing visual patterns. The second section considers a variety of measures that summarize data in terms of different attributes. The third section draws out two formal characteristics of summary measures that we can use to help us understand why alternative measures work the way that they do. These formal characteristics give the criteria for making smart choices about which summary measures to use in practical situations.

Showing the shape of data distributions

Although Table 9.2 reports the temperature scores, the general shape of this set of data is really hard to visualize from a table of numbers. Many of the characteristics of data distributions that have important consequences for analysis and interpretation can be seen very easily provided that data can be displayed informatively. Two obvious forms of data display are provided by most statistical packages: bar charts and histograms. A **bar chart** summarizes the distribution of a category variable: bars are drawn to represent each category and

FIGURE 9.2

Bar chart for the temperature data from Table 9.2

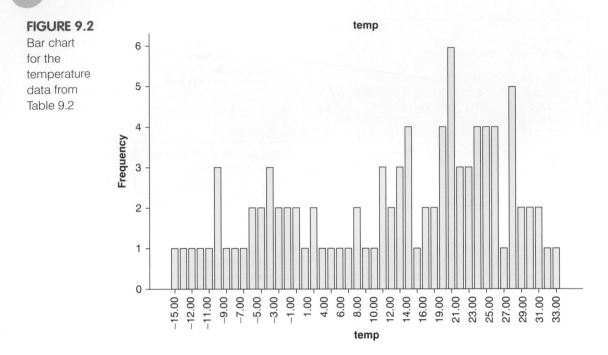

the length of the bar reflects the number of cases in the category – the more people, the longer the bar. If variables are measured on an ordinal scale, then it would be strange to do other than order the bars in the chart accordingly. For variables on a nominal scale, where the categories are not ordered, it makes sense to apply some thought to how to order the bars on the chart. A **histogram** is a bar chart drawn for a continuous variable, after grouping adjacent scale points together.

Bar charts   Figure 9.2 shows a bar chart for the temperature data from Table 9.2. Along the bottom of the chart is the measurement scale for the variable, the temperature in °C, and runs from -15°, the lowest value recorded in this dataset through to +33°, the highest value recorded for these data. Essentially, the bar chart is a visual representation of the frequency table. Each figure in the **frequency distribution** is translated into the height of a bar in Figure 9.2. The height of each bar is marked by the vertical axis of the figure, labelled frequency; and this shows how many respondents gave each alternative response. The higher the bar, the more respondents recorded this answer.

Histograms   A histogram is a special form of bar chart, with the points on the scale grouped into a smaller and more manageable number of categories. The histogram in Figure 9.3 shows the temperature data with the 94 different scores grouped together into 15 categories instead of 45. The labels on the horizontal axis are the mid-points of the categories shown by each bar. Histograms have immediate visual appeal, and show gross features of data very easily. The peak in the data around 20° is more obvious, and the 'holes' in the data have been hidden by combining categories together. The shape is thus smoother to the

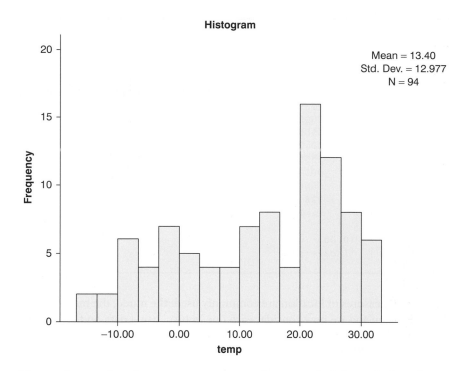

Histogram

Mean = 13.40
Std. Dev. = 12.977
N = 94

FIGURE 9.3
Histogram
for
temperature
data from
Table 9.2

eye. We can also see that there are more values at the top end of the scale than there are at the bottom. These data thus are not completely symmetrical.

This chapter started with a table showing 94 temperature values; but it is obviously impossible to carry all that information around in one's head (some values stick in the memory: the lowest and highest values, temperatures in one's favourite holiday locations and so on). Instead, it is much more efficient to capture some key features of the data in convenient summary form. This section covers three features of data that are most informative and most useful: **location**, **spread** and **symmetry**. We will describe summary measures of some of these key features of data, and following that we will examine a number of formal properties of summary measures that will make it easier to make choices between alternatives.

Summary measures of location

The obvious starting point for summarizing a large set of data is with an index that locates the data as a whole on its measurement scale: in general *high*, *middling* or *low*. For example, if there is a risk to consumers due to contamination of a batch of chocolate during manufacture (as in the case of Cadbury's chocolate early in 2006), then how big is the risk? Is it so minute that any impact on community health would be hard to detect, as the company argued when challenged by the UK Health and Safety Executive? As a second example, how big will the market be for live TV on mobile phones? Will it catch on, or will it go the way of the tiny market for us sending our pictures to others with our mobiles? Whatever the researcher is interested in measuring, and however large or small the dataset, most people would be interested in where on its measurement scale the data as a whole are located.

FIGURE 9.4

Stem and leaf display for CEO compensation data

```
$million Stem and Leaf

Frequency   Stem and Leaf

  63.00          0 . 6666777777777777777777777777888888888888889999
                     999999999999999
  49.00          1 . 0000000000000011111111111111122222222222333333444
  28.00          1 . 5555555566666777888888889999
  12.00          2 . 001223333444
  13.00          2 . 5555666788899
   9.00          3 . 000123334
   8.00          3 . 56668899
   3.00          4 . 224
  15.00 Extremes    (>=48)

 Stem width:     10.00
 Each leaf:      1 case(s)
```

Four summary measures of location are commonly used: the mode, the median, the mean and the mid-mean; and we now consider each one in turn, using data on the pay for Chief Executives of US companies. Overall compensation data for the 200 highest paid CEOs in the United States in 2009 are reported in www.Forbes.com, and summarized in Figure 9.4. The lowest total compensation is $6.86 million, and the highest compensation is a scarcely believable $556.98 million.

Mode   The **mode** is a simple form of summary measure of location: it is the commonest value among a set of scores. For some purposes, the mode as a measure of location can be informative (for instance, the music charts focus on who sells the most copies of their work), but on the other hand, the mode has some quite severe drawbacks. The original CEO compensation data are reported in $million rounded to two decimal places; and almost all values are unique – there is no single modal value. However, the stem and leaf plot (Figure 9.4) shows the scores as whole numbers, and the modal compensation value is $7m. Grouping the scores together in different ways would create a different modal value depending on how the grouping is done. Thus, a problem with the mode as a summary of location for data on a continuous scale is that it depends upon how scores are grouped. A second problem is that it ignores the rest of the data and conveys nothing at all about what other values there might be in the data. Finally, there may be more than one mode so that this measure of location need not have a unique value. All in all then, the mode is rarely a serious tool for summarizing location of data in management research.

Median   The **median** is the middle value once scores have been placed in rank order, either from largest to smallest or from smallest to largest. It is the value that divides a set of data in half. Where there is an even number of data points, the median is halfway between the middle two, in this case $12.86m. For an odd number of data points, the median is simply the middle one, counting in from either end. The median has some important properties, which are easy to grasp intuitively:

1 Every observation in the data contributes something to determining the value of the median, unlike the mode. That makes the median more meaningful as a summary measure of location because it uses more of the information in the data in estimating location.

2 Most of the data points do not contribute much – it is the rank position of a data point that matters rather than its precise value. That makes the median less efficient than it might be (it throws away the values of each observation and replaces them with rank-order information) but it has the great advantage that the median is insensitive to odd things happening to extreme scores. Adding a million to the largest data point (perhaps by forgetting to put in the decimal point when entering the data) does nothing to the median because it does not change the fact that this is still the largest data point. It also makes the median useful where the measurement scale is not particularly precise, and the researcher cannot be certain of the accuracy of the numbers.

3 The median works better for data where the category at the top of a grouped continuous scale is open-ended. Examples include the following:

   a Sometimes we judge ability by how quickly people complete a task, but some people may not finish in the time allocated. For those people, we over-estimate their ability because all we know is that they would take *at least* as long as the maximum time allowed.

   b Family size may be judged on the basis of the number of children, and it often happens that the largest category is recorded as more than three (or four or five) children. These data will under-estimate the actual number of children in a sample of families.

   c Data on survival rates following exposure to toxic hazards in the workplace will typically be over-estimates if they include people who were exposed to the hazard but are still alive at the time that data are collected.

   This kind of grouping of data at one end of the scale is called *censoring*. It gives no trouble at all for calculating the median, whether the censoring is at the bottom of the scale (left censoring) or at the top of the scale (right censoring).

Mean   The **mean** is the average value formed by adding all the scores and dividing by how many data points there are. The formula for the mean is:

$$M = \Sigma(X) / n$$

where M stands for the mean, X represents each data value, n indicates how many data points there are, and the Σ symbol is a summation sign. The mean CEO compensation level for top US CEOs is \$23.4m. Just like the median, every score contributes to forming the mean; but the mean differs because it takes into account how big each score is. This can be both a benefit and a disadvantage. By using the mean as a summary measure of location, the researcher can be confident of making the most of the information in the data about where the data are centred. On the other hand, using the mean assumes that each data point is accurately recorded.

Mid- mean The **mid-mean** is an average formed by first removing scores equally from both extremes of a dataset and then working out the mean of the remainder. It is part of a family of summary measures called **trimmed means**, which differ in how much is trimmed from each end of the distribution of data points. The mean is a zero per cent trimmed mean (with nothing trimmed); while the median is a 50 per cent trimmed mean. The mid-mean is a 25 per cent trimmed mean, the mean of the middle half of the data. It uses rank order information (like the median) to select data points to ignore; but then uses the data values themselves (like the mean) to calculate the summary index.

Comparing summary measures of location The different summary measures of location for the CEO compensation data in Figure 9.4 are as follows:

> Mode – $7m (data rounded to nearest whole number of millions)
> Median – $12.86m
> 5% trimmed mean – $17.37m
> Mean – $23.44m

There are substantial differences between these estimates of where the centre of the data lies. The modal (or commonest) value is around $7m; while the median shows that half of the top 200 CEOs earn $12.86m or more (of course the other half of the sample earn less than $12.86m). The mean gives the highest value of all, $23.44m, which is more than three times as much as the modal value.

Why do the summary measures of location differ so much? A clue is given in Figure 9.5, which shows that the data for the top CEOs are highly skewed. Three quarters of the top 200 CEOs earn less than $30m, while those at the very top of the ranking list earn substantially more than that; with Lawrence Ellison, CEO of Oracle, alone earning $556.98m (the same total compensation package as the bottom 65 CEOs in the sample combined). The median is based on the ranks of the scores; while the mean takes the size of each data point into account. Thus Ellison's salary influences the mean but not the median.

Which of these summary measures is most useful? The answer is that all of them are useful but for different purposes, while none of them is universally useful. Each summary measure captures different aspects of the data, which contain information about the feature of locatedness. When researchers calculate one of these summary measures to report where a dataset as a whole is located on its measurement scale, they are implicitly making a judgement about what matters in the data. If they want to emphasize what is typical (in the sense of commonest), they might prefer the mode. However, attention on inequalities in income in an organization, for instance, might lead someone to choose

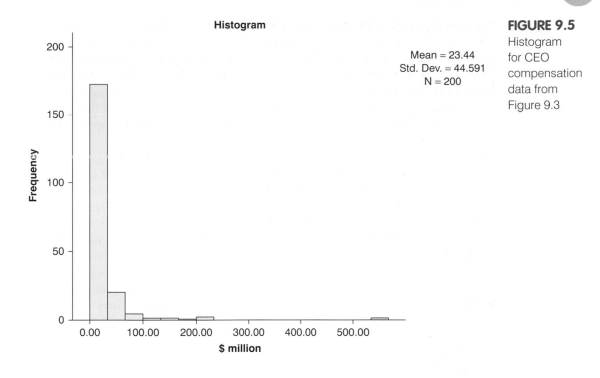

FIGURE 9.5
Histogram for CEO compensation data from Figure 9.3

the median, which will show that half of the organization earns less than £x, while another group might prefer the mean because it takes into account the much higher pay of the most senior officials in the organization, which makes the pay levels look generally higher.

The most widely used summaries of location are the mean and the median. Less common, but useful, are the mid-mean and other forms of the trimmed mean. An important point to note is that even something so simple as working out an average is a choice. The consequences of making different choices about summary measures of location depend very much on the characteristics of a specific dataset, and which features of the data the researcher wishes to emphasize.

Supermarkets engage in strenuous price comparison campaigns in order to persuade people to shop with them. Consider the following:

1   Waitrose offering to match Tesco on 1000 'everyday' branded items.

2   In-store tickets reporting the equivalent price of an item in another supermarket.

3   A guaranteed cheapest price on a 'shopping basket' of items.

What are the implications of each of these for the total cost of a family's weekly shop?

EXERCISE
9.1

Summary measures of spread

Of course, most samples of data will contain variability around a central value with some people scoring higher than others. How much spread there is around a measure of location is a valuable way of capturing something extra about a dataset as a whole. Three common measures of spread are the range, the mid-range and the standard deviation. Like the measures of location considered in the previous section, each one captures different aspects of data.

Range   The **range** is the distance between the largest and the smallest scores. For the temperature data in Table 9.2, the lowest recorded midday temperature was -15° and the highest was 33°, so the range is 33 – -15 = 48°. On a single day then, the spread of temperatures across a sample of locations in the world was enormous. The range of CEO compensation scores in Figure 9.4 is also large ($556.98m – $6.86m = $550.12m). While the range is easy to calculate, it is also potentially very misleading. Most people have seen the banner headlines in shop windows – up to 50 per cent off? This means that at least one item is discounted by this much, but says nothing about how many other items are treated in the same way. The same goes for the advertisements for cheap seats on airlines, where there is no mention of how many of the seats on a given flight are actually available at that price. Any summary index based on an extreme statistic (either largest or smallest) can be dangerously misleading.

Mid-range (interquartile range)   The **mid-range** is the range of the middle half of the data, calculated by dividing the data into quarters (the boundaries between them are called quartiles). The values in the data that mark the boundaries between four equal sized segments are called quartiles, and the mid-range is the difference between the first quartile and the third quartile. It is often given the name **interquartile range**. The second quartile is the median, with two quarters below and two quarters above. Calculating the mid-range starts in the same way as calculating the mid-mean: trim off the top and bottom quarter of the data values. Then, the mid-range is the difference between the largest and the smallest values in the middle half of the data: for the CEO compensation data in Figure 9.4, the mid-range is $14.98m. The mid-range gives a better indication of how diverse the data are, especially where the data are skewed by a few extreme scores at either end. Note that the compensation package for the highest paid CEO has a dramatic effect on the range, but none at all on the mid-range.

Standard deviation (SD)   The **standard deviation** measures the average spread around the mean; it is the most typical distance (or deviation) of scores from the mean. The formula for the standard deviation is:

$$SD = \sqrt{(\Sigma(X-M)^2 / n\text{-}1)}$$

where SD stands for the standard deviation, $\sqrt{}$ is the square root symbol and the other symbols are the same as in the formula for the mean.

The SD is calculated by working out the average squared deviation around the mean (this is called the **variance**) and then taking the square root. For each data point in turn, first work out how far it is above or below the mean (these are called deviations). The mean of the scores in Figure 9.4 is 23.44, so the deviations around the mean are calculated like this:

$$556.98 - 23.44 = 533.54$$

$$222.64 - 23.44 = 199.20$$

....

$$6.87 - 23.44 = -16.57$$

$$6.86 - 23.44 = -16.58.$$

Next, each of the deviations is squared to remove the ± sign, and the average squared deviation is calculated by dividing by the number of items minus one. This gives the variance. The reasoning behind subtracting one before calculating the mean deviation is technical – dividing by n-1 rather than n makes the sample SD an unbiased estimate of the population SD. Finally, take the square root of the variance to give the standard deviation. For these data, the variance (based on $200 - 1 = 199$ as the sample size) is 1988.38, and the standard deviation is 44.59.

Comparing summary measures of spread

Just as we argued for summary measures of location, there is no single answer to the question of which measure of spread is most useful. The range is a measure of how much of the measurement scale is covered by sample data, from largest to smallest. This is sometimes useful to know, but is heavily influenced by a few extreme scores; while the mid-range is more informative especially for data that are distributed symmetrically and follow roughly a bell-shaped curve.

The most widely used summaries of spread are the standard deviation and the mid-range; and measures of location and spread tend to be paired together. Thus, the mean and the standard deviation are the basis for many parametric significance tests, while the median and the mid-range are the basis for many non-parametric significance tests. Both types of test are described in the next section of this chapter.

The importance of symmetry

A third characteristic of the shape of a set of data is the extent to which scores are distributed evenly around a central value: that is, whether the data are symmetrical. *Positively* skewed data have many small values concentrated together and few large values strung out to the right; and the long tail of the data is to the right. The CEO compensation data in Figure 9.4 are positively skewed. Most of the data are located at the low end of the distribution; while 15 CEOs out of 200 receive extremely high pay packages. By contrast, *negatively* skewed data have many large values concentrated together at the top of the distribution and few small ones strung out at the bottom; the long tail of the data is to the left.

Why pay attention to symmetry in data? This feature is important for two reasons. Extreme values at either end of a distribution (but most likely at the high end of the range) may indicate gross errors, for which reason they should be sought out (perhaps by looking to a completed questionnaire in order to correct transcription errors, or by returning to the source of derived data) and correct values inserted instead. Data that are strongly asymmetrical are less naturally described in terms of summary measures of location. When data are symmetrical the mean and median will tend to coincide, while a symmetrical and unimodal distribution will tend to have the modal value (the most frequently occurring one) at the same point as the mean and median. When data are skewed, the different summary measures will not coincide. The mean will be influenced by the relatively small number of extreme scores, while the median will not be because it simply records the value below which 50 per cent of the scores lie.

Formal features of summary measures

This section looks at two characteristics of summary measures, robustness and efficiency, which give a stronger conceptual basis for the choices that a researcher makes between alternative summary measures of location or spread.

Robustness   The extent to which a summary measure is sensitive to disturbances in data quality is known as **robustness**. There has been a lot of work by statisticians examining the consequences of robustness (or the lack of it) for commonly used summary indices and analyses which are based on them (see Jackson, 1986). Disturbances in data quality can arise either from small changes to many data values (for example, by grouping of values on a measurement scale into a few categories) or by large errors in a few data values (for example, by transcription errors). A summary measure is robust if disturbances like these do not greatly alter its value; while summary measures that are very sensitive to such disturbances are not robust.

We now examine three of the summary measures of location: the mean, the median and the mid-mean. Since the *mean* is the total of all the data points divided by the sample size, changing even a single data point through a transcription error would alter the mean. The more extreme the value introduced in error, the bigger would be the influence on the value of the mean. Similarly, small changes to all of the data values through, for example, grouping adjacent scores together on the measurement scale, would also alter the mean. It is obvious, therefore, that the mean is not very robust.

Since the *median* is based on the ranked scores, the effect of a single transcription error would be small, and if the error were made with either the largest or the smallest data value the median would not change at all. Changes such as coarse grouping of adjacent scores on the measurement scale would also have little effect on the value of the median. The *mid-mean* uses rank-order information to define the middle half of the data, and so extreme scores introduced in error will not have a major impact on its value, and in this respect it is robust like the median. Both the mid-mean and the median are thus more robust than the mean, and using either in preference to the mean would protect the researcher against disturbances in measurement quality.

Efficiency Think of getting the juice out of a lemon. First you have to cut the lemon in half. After that there are options. However, the way that Jamie Oliver (a UK celebrity chef) uses is to squeeze each half in his hand; this has high screen appeal but does not give all the juice that is there – its efficiency is quite low. Another way is to use a juicer to macerate the flesh of the lemon and then filter out the juice. The juicer does not look so appealing on the TV, but it is more efficient because it yields more juice. Applying this principle to statistical analysis, **efficiency** refers to how much a summary measure captures all the information within the data that is relevant to what is summarized. For summary measures of location, the mean is the most efficient index we know because it uses everything about the data that is relevant to summarizing where the data are located on their measurement scale. Of course, that is the very reason why we sometimes do not use it, because some scores are suspiciously large or because we do not trust the fine detail. The median is much less efficient than the mean, since it replaces scores with their ranks, while the mid-mean (as well as other varieties of trimmed mean) is almost as efficient as the mean.

Summary of formal features of summary measures The two characteristics of summary measures tend to work in opposite directions: the mean is generally preferable to the median because it is more efficient, but on the other hand the median is more robust. A lot then depends on the quality of data that the researcher has available and on how well variables are measured. Researchers who have confidence in the quality of their data will tend to prefer using summary measures, which are high in efficiency, such as the mean for location and the standard deviation for spread. These will work particularly well for data that are broadly symmetrical and do not have rogue values which are more extreme than the bulk of the data. On the other hand, where data are more rough and ready, and the researcher may be less confident about measurement quality, summary measures based on ranks (the median for location and the mid-range for spread) may be used with more confidence.

GOING BEYOND A SAMPLE

Relationships versus differences

Most introductory statistical texts organize their presentation of significance tests into two categories, according to whether the focus of attention is on differences between groups or on relationships between variables. This book is no different; and so we explain the basic idea behind each of them, and then explain why the difference is actually an artificial one.

The idea of *group differences* is a simple one. It addresses questions such as:

1　Are small start-up businesses more innovative than large bureaucratic ones?

2　Are there more men than women on the boards of companies?

Each of these can be translated into a question about whether groups differ on a summary measure of a dependent variable (for question 1 the dependent variable is the level of innovation; while for question 2 the dependent variable is the percentage of women at board level). Tests have been developed to deal with variations in the number of groups and also in the kind of dependent variable (see later in this chapter).

The idea of *relationships between variables* is also quite a simple one. It addresses questions such as:

1　Is there a link between sunny weather and how people feel at work?

2　Does greater company use of social media (such as Facebook and Twitter) increase their reputation with customers?

Each of these questions is concerned with a pattern of association between two variables: are high levels of one variable (for example, the number of hours of sunshine per day) associated with high levels of another variable (for example, the morale of employees in an office). There are specialist tests that have been developed for dealing with different kinds of relationship for a variety of types of variable.

Relationships and differences – what's the difference?　While the distinction we just described in pretty straightforward, it can actually be quite misleading. Consider the question above about whether there are more men than women on the boards of companies. We just stated this in terms of a difference between two groups, but we could just as easily have expressed it in the language of relationships: is there a relationship between gender and board membership. Those are just two ways of talking about the same thing.

There was a time when statistical work was done using a calculator or even pen and paper; and in those days researchers looked for the easiest way of doing their work. This led them to develop short-hand techniques, which were custom-made for each specific configuration of data. So, we have separate procedures in packages such as SPSS for looking at either group differences or relationships. However, statisticians have realized over the last 40 years or so that there are deep similarities between methods that were up to then regarded as quite different. Thus we now have methods called generalized linear models, which use a common language (albeit a rather inaccessible algebraic one) to express research hypotheses, whether they be relationships or group differences. We won't spend much time in this book on these general models, but it is useful to remember that any hypothesis about differences between groups can also be expressed as a relationship involving the concept that underlies the group distinction.

The rationale of hypothesis testing

Every piece of empirical management research involves analysis of data from a sample of some kind at two levels: first to identify patterns in that sample data, and second to use the conclusions drawn from those patterns to make claims that go beyond the sample itself. The greatest part of the craft of quantitative data analysis lies in defining the limits to which it is appropriate to generalize beyond a specific sample. The studies listed in Table 9.1 at the start of this chapter each used quantitative data to address important research questions. The authors of those studies presented their data, but their conclusions relate not just to the specific sample but to claims about theory based on the data. In general, scholars do not theorize on the basis of specific datasets alone; instead, theories are statements about relationships between concepts, about boundary conditions for when those relationships occur, and about causes and consequences. **Hypothesis testing** is about making inferences about populations based upon data drawn from samples. Because we want to go beyond a sample, there is always an element of judgement or guesswork involved, and mistakes can be made. Hypothesis testing allows the researcher to define how safe it is to go beyond a specific sample of data.

Bloom and van Reenen (2006) claim that family-owned firms are better run (and perform better) when the CEO is a professional manager and not chosen because he or she is a family member. Their claim is based on comparisons of management practice between groups of firms that differ in ownership and the status of the CEO. Having made statistical comparisons within their data, they go on to make broad statements about such things as the reasons for the rise of the United States in the early part of the twentieth century compared to the UK (something their data do not address directly).

As part of a long-lasting collaboration between one of the authors and a large pharmaceutical company, data from company bi-annual employee opinion surveys were made available for research. One of the regular questions in the surveys is about the speed of decision-making within the company (it isn't really surprising to find that snail-like bureaucracy is a concern in a big company). Here we take a look at what two groups of employees think: those who have been in the company less than two years and those with longer organizational tenure (more than two years).

In the survey questionnaire respondents were offered three response alternatives: 1 = too fast; 2 = about right; and 3 = too slow. The mean scores for the two groups are as follows:

Short tenure (< 2 years; $n = 802$):   mean = 2.40

Long tenure (2 or more years; $n = 6993$):   mean = 2.59

We can see that there is a higher mean score for longer-tenure employees, and this indicates that they are more likely to feel that decision–making is too slow. Taking another perspective, 44 per cent of short-tenure employees reported that decision-making is *too slow*, compared to a much higher proportion (64 per cent) of longer-tenure employees. It would appear that opinions about the speed of organizational decision-making differ according to how long employees have been within the company. But how confident can we be about that claim? The purpose of hypothesis testing is to enable the researcher to draw conclusions like that.

Formal steps in hypothesis testing

Whatever the statistical procedure that is applied, the underlying logic is the same. This chapter concentrates on the **univariate test** (taking one dependent variable at a time) while the next chapter looks at the **multivariate test** (where many variables are considered at once). However complex the dataset, the steps are the same. We spell out the five steps using the decision-making data as an example, and then set out in more general form what choices the researcher has in setting out to test hypotheses with data.

Step 1 – defining a research hypothesis to be tested   The initial research question reflects the purpose of the study – to explore sample differences in speed of organizational decision-making as reported by company employees. The researchers had reason to believe that the two samples of employees might see decision-making speed differently, but observation of the data alone does not allow any firm conclusion to be drawn. In general, we are interested in two states of affairs: what the data would look like if there is a real difference between the two samples, and if there really is no difference between the samples. The research hypothesis, called H_1, is that there is a real difference between the two samples in reputation ratings. Note that making a decision about whether to accept this hypothesis or not does nothing to explain *why* such a difference might occur.

Step 2 – defining a null hypothesis   In the absence of any evidence to the contrary, the simplest starting point is to assume that it makes no difference how the data were collected. This defines a **null hypothesis** (called H_0) that the responses for short tenure employees are generated by the same process as the responses from long tenure employees. If the evidence in favour of the **alternative hypothesis** (H_1) is inconclusive, then the reasonable conclusion to draw is the starting position (H_0). On the other hand, strong evidence of a difference in decision-making speed scores between the two samples would allow the researcher to modify this initial position. It is important to note the logic here. The null hypothesis has nothing to do with what the researcher *wants* to be true, and neither is it anything to do with a specific theory. Instead, it reflects a simple agnostic position that the data from the two samples were generated by the same process unless there is strong evidence otherwise.

Step 3 – deriving a summary measure of a characteristic of interest   Having defined a null hypothesis, the third step is to calculate a summary index based on the characteristic of interest. In this case, the natural way to express the hypotheses is in terms of summary measures of the location of the data on the decision-making speed measurement scale. Earlier in this chapter we described three summary measures of location, which could be used to test the research hypothesis: the median, the mean and the mid-mean. Whichever summary measure is chosen, the null hypothesis is that the difference between the location measures for the two samples is zero, while the alternative research hypothesis is that the difference is not zero. Thus the hypothesis test is expressed in terms of the group difference in a measure of location. The previous section showed that the mean decision-making speed scores for the two groups are 2.40 and 2.59, with a group difference of 0.29. Of course, it is unrealistic to expect a difference of precisely zero in a specific study even if it can be guaranteed that the method of collecting data makes no difference. Repeated studies with the same structure would be expected to show differences in means (or medians or mid-means) between samples; but the differences would be expected to be small most of the time and very different only infrequently. The problem that the researcher faces is: what does similar mean? How different is very different? For these data, is a mean difference of 0.29 a large or a small difference? Addressing this problem is the job of the reference distribution in the next step.

Step 4 – choosing a reference distribution and calculating a test statistic   The logic of hypothesis testing is that convincing evidence is needed from the study data before the researcher is prepared to move away from the null hypothesis in favour of an alternative. If the null hypothesis were true, how likely is the outcome observed in the study data? Quantifying the answer to this question requires the use of a **reference distribution**, which summarizes the alternatives available if the null hypothesis were true. Text books often refer to this as a **sampling distribution**, but we prefer the more general term to reflect the process of calibrating a result from one study against a reference standard. The reference distribution is not the distribution of the observations in a dataset, but rather it is the distribution of the hypothesis summary index for all possible outcomes, of which the one from a specific study is just one.

Sources of reference distributions   Selecting a reference distribution involves either using extra data (over and above that from a sample) or making assumptions about the data and the process that generated it. There are four different sources of reference distributions:

1   *Standard reference distributions* are drawn from statistical theory, and choosing them is the commonest way of testing hypotheses. There are many families of reference distributions derived from theorizing about different kinds of idealized situations. For example, the **normal distribution** is the distribution of the sum of independent measures where the standard deviation of the reference distribution is known. The **t-distribution** is the same as the normal distribution, but differs only in that the standard deviation of the reference distribution is estimated from sample data. The **binomial distribution** is the distribution of entities that are binary (present/absent, success/failure). These distributions are used for testing hypotheses about differences in location. The **chi-square distribution** is the distribution not of means but of variances, and is used for testing hypotheses about spread. The **F-distribution** is the distribution of ratios of variances, and is used for testing hypotheses about group differences in the spread of mean scores. All standard reference distributions share a number of characteristics:

   a   *They are mathematically well defined* – their shape reflects a few features called parameters (this is the reason why tests using standard reference distributions are called **parametric tests**). For example the precise form of the normal distribution depends only upon just two quantities, the mean and standard deviation.

b *Their theoretical properties are well worked out.* For example, the normal distribution is symmetrical and bell-shaped. For a normal distribution with a mean of zero and a standard deviation of one, two thirds (68 per cent) of the area under the curve lies in the range between -1 and +1 on the measurement scale: 34 per cent on either side of the mean. A further 13 per cent of the area under the curve lies either side of the mean in the range between -1 and -2 and between +1 and +2 on the measurement scale.

c *They are theoretical entities* that do not exist in the real world, but researchers can use them as approximations to their own data. Thus, many of the tests described below (see Tables 9.4 and 9.7) are said to assume normally distributed data. Since real data never follow precisely any of the standard reference distributions, this assumption is almost never valid. However, the practical issue is whether the approximation to normality is close enough to allow reliable inference. Statisticians agree that most statistical tests that use standard reference distributions are robust in the face of departures from the ideal assumptions provided that sample sizes are more than about 50 and that the distribution of sample data is approximately symmetrical.

2 *Permutation distributions* are reference distributions formed by finding all possible **permutations** of ranked data. For example, consider tossing two dice. Overall, there are six different outcomes for each die, making 36 outcomes in all; and the distribution of all of these 36 alternatives is the permutation distribution. There is only one way of achieving a total score of 12, by throwing two sixes; similarly there is only one way of achieving a score of 2, by throwing two ones. However, there are six ways of achieving a score of 7 (1+6, 2+5, 3+4, 4+3, 5+2, 6+1), and this is the commonest total score from throwing two dice.

As the dice example shows, permutation distributions are derived by taking all possible alternative outcomes for a specific setting, and they do not rely on assuming anything about an underlying theoretical parametric distribution for data. As a result, tests using them are called **non-parametric tests**. Examples include the Mann-Whitney U test and the Kruskal-Wallis test for differences between groups, and Kendall's rank order correlation test of association (see Tables 9.4 and 9.7).

3 *Bootstrap distributions* are reference distributions formed by treating the available data as all there is, and drawing repeated samples from it. The **bootstrap** procedure requires heavy use of computational resources, and is only used when there is no real alternative. We will not go into details here, although an example of how it works is given by Jackson (1986).

4 *Using archive data to form reference distributions* treats archive data as all there is, and derives the reference distribution from it. If there is a lot of information available about how data are distributed, it is sometimes appropriate to make use of that information. Again we do not go into detail, but Box, Hunter and Hunter (2005) show how it is done.

The next step in the hypothesis testing process is to calculate the difference between the two summary measures – either medians or means – for the two samples.

Step 5 – drawing a conclusion   What is the probability of getting a difference as big as this if the null hypothesis were true? If the probability is small enough (the conventional criterion that is used is 1 in 20, equivalent to 5 in 100 or 5 per cent), then the researcher can conclude that the observed outcome is too surprising for the null hypothesis to be true, or stated another way, that the evidence from the data is convincing enough to modify the starting position. This is usually stated as: reject the null hypothesis at the 5 per cent level, or the difference between the groups is significant at the 0.05 level.

When someone makes a claim about how the world is on the basis of data, there are two kinds of mistakes that can be made, which are shown in Table 9.3. In the case of the example of the two sets of data collected for short- and long-tenure employees, there are two conclusions that could be drawn: either that there is a difference between the two groups in how employees see the speed of organizational decision-making, or that there is no difference. If there really is no difference between the groups but the researcher uses sample data to make the false claim that there is a difference, this is called a **type I error**. A type I error is made when someone claims a difference where none exists. On the other hand, if there really is a difference between the groups but the researcher falsely concludes that there is none then this is called a **type II error**.

The convention is that type I errors are more serious than type II errors, since the type II error is the same as retaining the initial starting point before the data were collected. The type I error amounts to changing the initial state of affairs in falsely claiming something new about the world based on data. After all, it is possible to correct an error of omission by gathering more data, while making false positive claims on the basis of a single sample is altogether different. From time to time, there are dramatic examples of such type I errors reported in the press. These include claims of finding so-called 'cold fusion' (offering potential for unlimited free energy for the world), emissions from PC screens as harmful to unborn babies, the triple MMR vaccine as a cause of autism. All of these claims were subsequently found to be false, but each one was a source of confusion for researchers and sometimes alarm for members of the public.

Selecting the right kind of statistical test   So far, we have set out the general principles of hypothesis testing, using as an example the case of comparing the means of two samples of data. We next turn our attention to deciding how to choose the right significance test for a given situation.

TABLE 9.3   Options in drawing conclusions from data

Conclusion from Data	True State of Affairs	
	Groups do not differ	Groups are different
Data shows no difference between groups	Correct conclusion from sample data	Type II error
Data shows a difference between groups	Type I error	Correct conclusion from sample data

TABLE 9.4 Selecting the right kind of test for group differences

Purpose	Measurement Scale	Characteristic of Data	Test	Null Hypothesis	Test Statistic	Reference Distribution
Compare 2 groups	Continuous	Location: means	t-test	Groups are from a single population	t-value	t
	Ordered category	Location: medians	Mann-Whitney U test	Groups are from a single population	U statistic	All combinations of ranks
Compare 3 or more groups	Continuous	Location: means	Analysis of variance (ANOVA)	Groups are from a single population	F-ratio	F
	Ordered category	Location: medians	Kruskal-Wallis test	Groups are from a single population	W statistic	All combinations of ranks

For each type of test, two versions are listed: a parametric test which assumes that the variables are measured on continuous scales, and also that the data are at least approximately bell-shaped, like the normal distribution, and a non-parametric test which makes the simpler assumption that the variables are measured on ordinal category scales. Thus, the choice between tests depends on what the researcher is prepared to assume about the measurement scale for the variables involved (see Chapter 8). Sometimes the answer is very straightforward. When a study asks whether there are more men than women employed at top level in a company, gender cannot be anything but measured on a **category scale**: male versus female. At other times, the issue is more a matter of judgement about the quality of measurement. When measurement quality is high, the researcher will probably be confident to think of the measurement scale as *continuous* and use the mean as a measure of location (choosing the mean because it is very efficient). This leads to choosing a parametric test such as the *t*-test or ANOVA for testing group differences. When there is more uncertainty about measurement quality, it is probably wiser to treat the scores as no more than ranked (an *ordinal* scale) and then rely on the median as a measure of location. This then leads to choosing non-parametric tests, which are more robust (because the summary measures they use are less influenced by extreme scores) but less efficient (because they throw away information that is in the data).

Testing for group differences – comparing groups

Table 9.4 lists procedures that can be used to test hypotheses about group differences in location. We distinguish between tests for comparing two groups, and tests for more complex datasets involving three or more groups. Table 9.5 picks out research questions that involve comparing groups from some of the studies listed in Table 9.1. Where there are only two groups to compare, the choice is between the **t-test** for comparing means and the **Mann-Whitney U test** for ranked data. For each, the table sets out how the groups were defined and what variable was involved in the group comparison. The second two examples concern hypotheses about differences between three groups, and the appropriate choice here is between the **analysis of variance** (ANOVA) for comparing means and the **Kruskal-Wallis test** based on ranked data. We illustrate the process of using the *t*-test for testing for differences between two groups; though the general principles apply to analysis of variance too.

Worked example of the *t*-test for the speed of decision-making data   The data for this example come from the collaborative project described, which is looking at ways of promoting innovation in a pharmaceutical company. Here we use the *t*-test to make a more precise inference about whether the two groups of employees differ in their view of the speed of organizational decision-making. The null hypothesis is that there is no difference, such that two groups could have been defined by splitting the sample randomly into two groups. The null hypothesis is accepted unless there is sufficient evidence from the data to discard it in favour of the alternative that the two sets of observations are drawn from different populations.

The appropriate summary index that captures the relevant feature of the data is the difference between the group means. Table 9.6 shows that the mean (M_1) for the short-tenure

TABLE 9.5 Examples of research questions that involve comparing groups

Study	Groups to Compare	Dependent Variable
a) Testing for group differences – comparing two groups		
B2B relationships (Dyer and Hatch, 2006)	Two car companies – Toyota versus US	quality of supplier products
Locating your HQ (Birkinshaw et al., 2006)	Two types of HQ – business unit versus corporate	satisfaction of stakeholders
b) Testing for group differences – comparing three or more groups		
SOEs in China (Ralston et al., 2006)	Three categories – privately-owned versus foreign-owned versus state-owned	culture
MNEs' marketing strategies (Katsikeas, Samiee and Theodosiou, 2006)	Three groups of MNEs – US versus German versus Japanese	marketing strategies

TABLE 9.6 Summary statistics of speed of decision-making scores for two samples

	Short-tenure employees ($n = 802$)	Long-tenure employees ($n = 6993$)	t-value ($df = 7793$)
Speed of decision-making	2.40 (SD = 0.55)	2.59 (SD = 0.58)	8.70 **

** $P < .01$.

group is 2.40 ($n = 802$) and the mean (M_2) for the long-tenure group is 2.59 ($n = 6993$). The difference in group means is 2.59 – 2.40 = 0.19 and the null hypothesis is that this group difference is zero. The formula for the t-test is a ratio:

$$t = M_1 - M_2 \, / \, SE \, (\text{diff})$$

The top line is the difference between the group means (0.187), and the bottom line (which makes it possible to judge how big a difference this is) is the standard error of the difference (0.021). The standard error is calculated from the standard deviation and the sample size in each group. The smaller the spread of scores around the group mean and the larger the sample size, the smaller is the standard error. Applying this formula gives a t-value of $0.187 / 0.021 = 8.703$.

If the null hypothesis (H_0) is true, the difference in means will be close to zero most of the time, and far from zero seldom. If the alternative hypothesis (H_1) is true, the difference in means will be far from zero most of the time and close to zero seldom. Where there is prior expectation about the direction of difference between the groups, the test is called a **2-tailed test**; and where one group is expected to have a higher mean than the other, the test is called a **1-tailed test**.

In order to get an idea of how big the observed difference actually is, it is necessary to locate it on the t-distribution. The shape of the t-distribution is defined by two parameters: the mean as an estimate of location and the standard deviation as an estimate of spread. The mean of the reference distribution is estimated from the difference between the group means under the null hypothesis. The standard deviation of the reference distribution, also called the **standard error** (SE) of the difference in group means, forms the bottom line of the t-test formula. It is a scaling factor that allows us to say whether a given difference is large or small. The size of the standard error depends on the sample sizes in the groups and on the spread of scores around the mean in each of the groups. The standard error is inversely related to the total number of observations in the study, and this makes sense because most people would have more confidence in means based on large samples. It also depends on the spread around the group means in the observed data (as measured by the standard deviations of the two groups); and this too makes sense. If data points are widely dispersed around their respective group means, then the mean is a less precise indicator of where the data in each group lie on the measurement scale. Overall then, the size of the t-value obtained depends upon three things:

1 The difference in group means.

2 The spread around group means.

3 The sample size in each group.

In general, convincing evidence about whether groups differ comes from big differences between means, small spread around those means (thus increasing their precision) and large sample sizes.

The bigger the t-value obtained, the more convincing is the evidence from the data that the initial starting position of two samples from a single population is incorrect, and needs to be modified in the light of evidence from the data. The final step is to select a significance level (conventionally $p < .05$), and find in the test tables the value of t that would be necessary to achieve the desired significance level. If the researcher finds that the actual t-value is greater than the tabulated value, then he or she will reject the null hypothesis that the groups are random samples from a single population at that level of significance, in favour of the alternative hypothesis that they are sampled from different populations.

The shape of the reference distribution depends on a quantity called **degrees of freedom** (or *df*). For the two-sample t-test, this is calculated as the total sample size (7795) minus the number of groups (2), giving the value of 7793 shown in Table 9.6. The probability

TABLE 9.7   Selecting the right kind of test for association

Purpose	Measurement Scale	Characteristic of Data	Test	Null Hypothesis	Test statistic	Reference Distribution
Association in a contingency table	Two nominal category scales	Co-variation of scores on two variables	Chi-square test	Independence – overall distribution applies to all groups	χ^2 (chi-square)	χ^2 distribution
	Two binary category scales (0 / 1)	Co-variation of scores on two variables	Phi coefficient	Independence – overall distribution applies to all groups	Φ (phi)	R distribution
Correlation between variables	Two continuous scales	Co-variation of scores on two variables	Pearson product-moment correlation	Independence	r	R distribution
	One continuous scale and one binary category scale	Co-variation of scores on two variables	Point bi-serial correlation	Independence	r	R distribution
		Consistency of ranking on two variables	Rank-order correlation (Kendall);	Independence	τ (tau)	τ distribution
	Two ordered category scales		Rank-order correlation (Spearman)	Independence	ρ (rho)	R distribution

of achieving a *t*-value as big as 8.70 if the null hypothesis were really true is 1 in 1,000, shown in the table as *p* < .01. This is a small probability, and the conclusion is that the null hypothesis is very unlikely to be true and is rejected in favour of the alternative that the groups really do differ. Expressed in the language of the study, the short-tenure group have a more positive view of the speed of organizational decision-making than the long-tenure group. Most people would be very confident about this conclusion from these data, because the test statistic is so large. However, it is possible that the conclusion is wrong and the null hypothesis may actually be true. In that case, the claim that the two groups differ would be a type I error.

Testing association between variables

If there is an **association** between two variables, then knowing how someone responds on one variable carries information that can be used to predict their response on the other. There is a *positive* association between two variables when high scores on one tend to occur with high scores on the other, and similarly for low scores. A *negative* association is shown by people responding with high scores on one variable but low scores on the other. A *zero* association indicates that knowing about one variable does not help in telling us anything about the other. Table 9.8 shows examples of association between variables from the studies in Table 9.1.

Different kinds of association between variables can be illustrated using artificial data for ten people. Figure 9.6 shows a strong *positive association* between two variables, labelled as Var1 and Var3. Along the bottom of the plot is the scale for Var1, with high scores to the right and low scores to the left. Along the side of the plot is the scale for Var3, with high scores to the top and low scores to the bottom. The data points tend to congregate along the diagonal of the plot – top right and bottom left. This is what would be expected of a strong positive association, and knowing an individual's score on one of the variables would allow

TABLE 9.8 Examples of research questions that involve testing association between variables

Study	Association Between:	
Influencing companies on environmental issues (Eesley and Lenox, 2006)	Different stakeholder actions	Positive corporate responses
MNEs' marketing strategies (Katsikeas, Samiee and Theodosiou, 2006)	Standardization of marketing strategy	Market environment
Locating your HQ (Birkinshaw et al., 2006)	HQ – business unit/corporate	Satisfying stakeholders
Is CSR smart as well as good? (Luo and Bhattacharya, 2006)	CSR activities of companies – cash donations/employee volunteering	Market value of company/customer satisfaction

a reasonable guess about that person's score on the other. Figure 9.7 shows a strong *negative association* between two variables, labelled as Var1 and Var2. Once again, the scale at the bottom shows Var1, with high scores to the right and low scores to the left. Along the side of the plot is the scale for Var2, and high scores are to the top and low scores to the bottom. This time, the data points tend to congregate along the opposite diagonal of the plot – top left

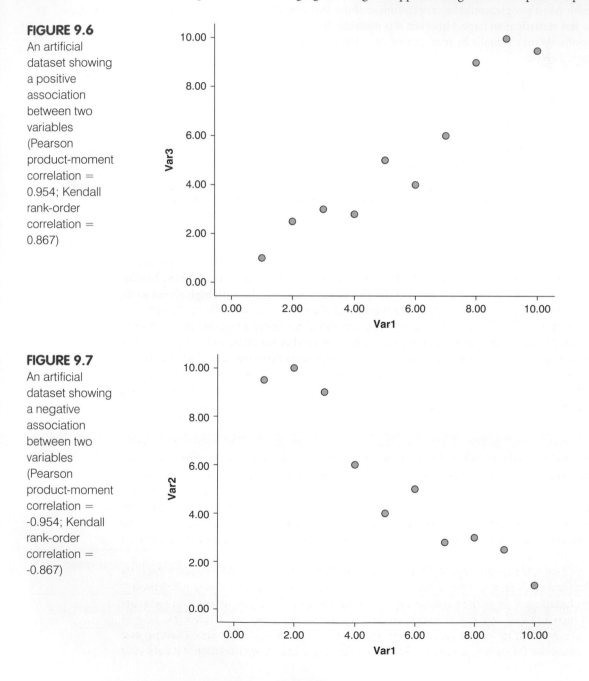

FIGURE 9.6

An artificial dataset showing a positive association between two variables (Pearson product-moment correlation = 0.954; Kendall rank-order correlation = 0.867)

FIGURE 9.7

An artificial dataset showing a negative association between two variables (Pearson product-moment correlation = -0.954; Kendall rank-order correlation = -0.867)

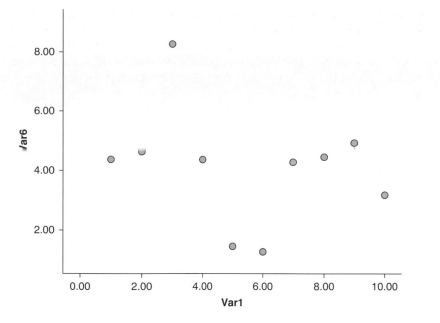

FIGURE 9.8
An artificial dataset showing no association between two variables (Pearson product-moment correlation = -0.264; Kendall rank-order correlation = -0.156)

and bottom right. This is what would be expected of a strong negative association. Finally, Figure 9.8 shows two variables with no obvious pattern of association to suggest a relationship between the two, and the correlation coefficient is zero.

The specific test for association between two variables depends on the measurement scale. For variables measured on nominal category scales the **chi-square test** (χ^2) is appropriate. Where the measurement scale is either ordinal or continuous association between variables is assessed by a *correlation coefficient*. The correlation coefficient for continuous scales is the Pearson **product-moment correlation**. For data measured in the form of ranks, the Kendall **rank-order correlation** is used.

Testing association for category measurement scales: the chi-square test   While it is possible to draw a scatterplot for looking at association between variables measured on category scales, it is generally more convenient and informative to use a contingency table to show how a sample is divided up according to each person's score on the two variables we are interested in. Contingency tables do not have to be two-way, but they get much harder to read when we use more than two variables to divide up the sample. The chi-square test is used to test association between two category variables measured on nominal scales.

An example of a contingency table is shown in Table 9.9, which is taken from a study by a doctoral student. She carried out a worldwide survey (18 countries) of over 3,000 professional managers (both men and women) who had been made redundant by their company and then enrolled in a career transition programme to help them get another job. One of the things that the student looked at was the effect of job loss on family relationships, and she asked the following question: *What is the effect of job loss on your relationship with your*

TABLE 9.9 Contingency table showing frequencies of men and women according to the reported effect of job loss on the relationship with their partner

	Effect of Job Loss on Relationship			
	Brings closer	No difference	Causes difficulties	Total
Men	952 (43%)	874 (39%)	406 (18%)	2232 100%
Women	223 (35%)	276 (44%)	130 (21%)	629 100%
Total	1175 (41%)	1150 (40%)	536 (19%)	2861 100%

NOTE: PERCENTAGES ARE BASED ON THE ROW TOTALS

partner/spouse? They could select from three responses: *bringing you closer together*, *having no effect at all* and *causing relationship difficulties*. She wondered whether unemployed men and women would answer this question differently, and the contingency table below shows the two variables together. The table shows the counts, and also the row percentages: each count as a percentage of the row total. The first row shows how men answered the question, and the second row shows responses for women.

The bottom right-hand corner of the table shows that 2,861 people answered the relationship question and also reported their gender. The right-hand column with the row totals shows that there are 2232 men in the analysis, and 629 women. The bottom row of the table shows how people answered the question about the effect of job loss on their relationship, and the effect seems to be mostly either positive or neutral. About four out of ten people (1,175 out of 2,861, 41 per cent) say that the experience has brought them closer together, and about the same number (1,150 out of 2,861, 40 per cent) say it has not affected their relationship. Only a minority (536 out of 2,861, 19 per cent) say that job loss has caused relationship difficulties.

One of the key questions that Johnson asked was whether the effect of the experience was different for men and women. In other words, is there an association between gender and the effect of job loss on the quality of the relationship with partner? An initial step in addressing this question is to look at the pattern of responses for men and women separately, using the row percentages. For men, 43 per cent say that job loss has brought them closer together compared to 35 per cent for women – so men tend to be more positive about how job loss has affected the relationship with their partner. Corresponding to this, 18 per cent of men say that job loss has caused relationship difficulties, compared to 21 per cent of women – men are again more positive, or less negative, than women. Overall then, there does seem to be an association between gender and impact of job loss on partner relationship.

Interpreting this result is quite complicated. It could be that losing a job is really more damaging to the family relationships of women than it is for men; but it could also be that harm is equally strong for both sexes, but that women are more aware of it than men. From semi-structured interviews that Johnson carried out she suspected that the second interpretation was more likely. These tended to show that men are less aware of their own feelings and those of their partner than are women, and so do not notice when relationship problems exist.

Having looked at the data, it would appear that there is an association between gender and the effect of job loss on the relationship, but this can be tested formally using the chi-square (χ^2) test of association. The null hypothesis for the chi-square test of association is that there is no relationship between the two variables. For a contingency table this means that the distribution of responses for the total sample (shown by the percentages in the bottom row of the table) applies equally to both men and women. The alternative hypothesis is that the distribution of responses is different for men and women; and that seems to be the case for these data.

Just as with any significance test, the purpose is to estimate how likely would be the pattern observed in the data if the null hypothesis were true; and the test statistic, χ^2, for this table is 10.52. The degrees of freedom for the test with these data are 2 (for χ^2 this is calculated as (number of rows – 1) times (number of columns – 1) = 2. The probability of getting a distribution of data like this if there really is no association between gender and the effect on relationship is 0.005, or five in a thousand. This is a small number, so the odds of the null hypothesis being true are small; and the null hypothesis is rejected at the 0.005 level. Johnson concluded that there is a gender difference in how people see the effect of job loss on the relationship with their partner.

Testing association for continuous and ordered category scales: correlation between variables

For variables measured on scales that are at least ordered, association can be tested using a correlation coefficient. For continuous scales (whether interval or ratio), the test of choice is the Pearson product-moment correlation (r); while the test of choice for ordinal category scales is a rank-order correlation coefficient developed by Kendall (Kendall's *tau*) though there is another one developed by Spearman (Spearman's *rho*), which is less commonly used. Pearson's r is the extension of the variance to cover the co-variance between two variables: the extent to which variation in one variable is associated with variation in the other. Spearman's *rho* is the product-moment correlation of the ranked scores for two variables. Kendall's *tau* is an index of consistency of the two sets of ranked scores – how many swaps of scores are necessary to bring the two into consistency.

Figure 9.9 shows the scatterplot for two artificial variables and the Pearson product-moment correlation coefficient is 0.516, suggesting a positive relationship. But this is nonsense for the dataset as a whole as the scatterplot clearly shows: all the data points bump along at the bottom of the plot, apart from a single extreme score in the top right-hand corner. The Kendall rank-order correlation coefficient uses information only about the ranked scores for each variable and its value is much lower (0.116).

Figure 9.10 shows the scatterplot for two more artificial variables, this time with a perfect positive association between the variables on the left-hand side and a perfect negative association on the right-hand side. The value of both correlation coefficients is zero, and the researcher would conclude that there is no relationship between the two variables. However, this conclusion is misleading because there clearly is a relationship – as Var1 increases, the other variable first goes up and then goes down, but it is not a straight-line

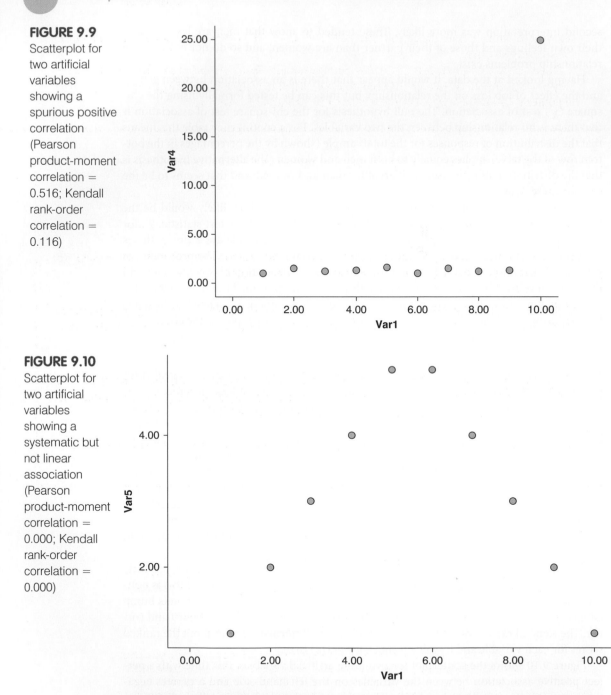

FIGURE 9.9
Scatterplot for two artificial variables showing a spurious positive correlation (Pearson product-moment correlation = 0.516; Kendall rank-order correlation = 0.116)

FIGURE 9.10
Scatterplot for two artificial variables showing a systematic but not linear association (Pearson product-moment correlation = 0.000; Kendall rank-order correlation = 0.000)

relationship. This form of relationship is called **curvilinear**; and it is not easy to summarize such complex relationships with a single measure of association. Instead, it often makes sense to divide the data into segments and calculate correlation coefficients for each segment separately. Here the correlation coefficient is +1 for the first five cases of Var1 and -1 for the second five cases.

There are two lessons to learn from this simple example. First, correlation coefficients summarize only **linear** forms of association between variables. Second, while it is tempting to rush straight into hypothesis testing there is real value in looking at graphical displays first.

CONCLUSION

The material we have covered in this chapter is:

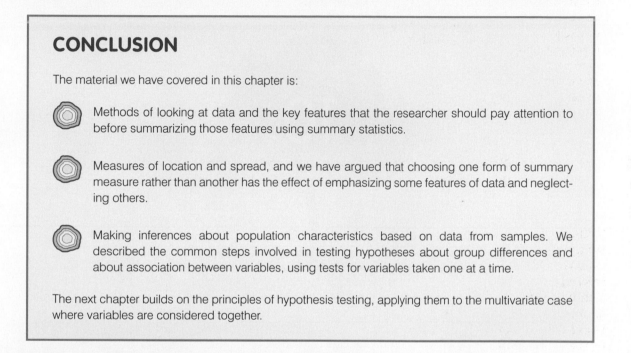

Methods of looking at data and the key features that the researcher should pay attention to before summarizing those features using summary statistics.

Measures of location and spread, and we have argued that choosing one form of summary measure rather than another has the effect of emphasizing some features of data and neglecting others.

Making inferences about population characteristics based on data from samples. We described the common steps involved in testing hypotheses about group differences and about association between variables, using tests for variables taken one at a time.

The next chapter builds on the principles of hypothesis testing, applying them to the multivariate case where variables are considered together.

FURTHER READING

Field, A. (2009) *Discovering Statistics Using SPSS*, 3rd edn. London: Sage.
The focus of this book is getting the statistical work done rather than the dry statistical theory itself. It is accessible (provided you can tune into the author's sense of humour), and covers much of the material in this chapter and the next, plus a lot more.
Howell, D. (2009) *Statistical Methods for Psychology* (international edn). Belmont, CA: Wadsworth.
Howell, D. (2010) *Fundamental Statistics for the Behavioral Sciences*, 7th edn. Broadman and Holman Publishers.
Both books go into more detail on the logic of hypothesis testing and describe a much more extensive set of statistical tests for comparing groups or testing association between variables. The strengths of the author's approach are that he emphasizes the importance of looking at data intelligently before making decisions about forms of analysis, and he also explains clearly the conceptual underpinnings of the methods that are covered.

MULTIVARIATE ANALYSIS

10

INTRODUCTION

The domain of multivariate analysis

The social world that we all live in is a complex system, and cannot really be understood just by looking at one thing at a time: causes interact with each other in complex ways; effects are not always simple to measure. Table 10.1 lists studies from the management literature which use **multivariate methods** to test theoretical propositions.

The complication arises because most of the interesting things researchers want to look at are correlated with each other. The tools and methods that we considered in the previous chapter are basic ones for working with quantitative data, but they are not enough to deal with the complexities of the world of work. This chapter on multivariate analysis builds on the previous two, but it is more advanced because it deals with analytical methods for looking at complex data, and these are intrinsically more difficult than the univariate methods that were considered in the previous chapter.

The purpose of multivariate analysis is to find a way of summarizing the relationship between variables, which is simpler than the original data but also captures the essence of that relationship. In that respect, working with quantitative data is no different from working with research evidence in any other form (see Chapter 7): research seeks out a conceptual model that is both simpler and richer. Simplicity is desirable so that the model is understandable; richness is desirable so that the model can stimulate new ways of thinking about the world. The models that are used in multivariate analysis are mathematical models, and a full understanding of multivariate statistics requires a fair amount of facility with matrix algebra. However, in this chapter we give a conceptual introduction to some of the methods, which can then be built on in a more advanced way.

TABLE 10.1   Examples of studies using multivariate statistical methods

Coyle-Shapiro and Kessler (2000): Commitment of employees to the organization (DV) as a function of fulfilment of the psychological contract (PV).
Brouthers and Brouthers (2003): Mode of entry into foreign markets (DV) by service and manufacturing organizations (PV).
Thompson (2004): Decline in national competitiveness (DV) as a function of cost factors or institutional arrangements (PV).
Filatotchev (2006): The entry of forms into public ownership (DV) according to the characteristics of executives and involvement of venture capital (PV).

Forms of interdependence in management research

There are many kinds of interdependency among concepts within the domain of manage-ment research. The first kind of interdependence is **interaction effects** where variables have different effects depending on the context, and these have been examined in the form of **contingency theories**. Examples of contingency theories can be found in cross-cultural management (for example, what works well in a US business negotiation would cause deep offence among Arabs), in organizational design (different forms of organizing are needed to deal with rapidly changing markets compared to the stable bureaucracies that most people work in (Brown and Eisenhardt, 1998)), and in guidance on how organizations can effec-tively manage worker stress (Jackson and Parker, 2001).

The second kind of interdependency is that of **synergy**, one of the favourite buzz words of the management change consultant. The idea is a simple one: plant a seed, give it both warmth and water and it will grow. Water alone will make it rot, warmth alone may lead the seed to become dormant; but both together can achieve the miracle of making a new plant. This is the logic behind many organizational mergers where the capabilities of differ-ent partners are brought together with the intent of making a step change in performance.

The third kind of interdependency is that *influences on performance tend to occur together*, either because they affect each other or because they have common causes. Several of the studies in Table 10.1 share the same feature, i.e. that they control for organizational size in their analysis (for example, Brouthers and Brouthers, 2003; Filatotchev, 2006). Looking at the Brouthers and Brouthers study first, their logic was simple – they were not directly interested in differences between large and small firms but they know that size makes a difference to lots of things, so ignoring it would probably bias answers to questions they were interested in. They wanted to study how service and manufacturing firms went about their internationalization through entering new foreign markets. If the service firms in their sample were smaller (or larger) on average than the manufacturing ones then conclusions based on a comparison between the two sectors would be confounded by differences in size. As a result, including the size of the firm in statistical analysis makes sense. Filatotchev used the same logic in his efforts in explaining what happens when entrepreneurial firms first go into public ownership through IPOs.

Ways of dealing with interdependence within quantitative analysis

In this section, we consider four ways of dealing with inter-related influences (see Table 10.2). Three of them involve simplification: through design, through selecting sub-samples and through statistical control. The final method is multivariate analysis, and this forms the main focus of this chapter. While all four methods are useful, most people develop a prefer-ence to suit their own style or the options open to them in their research area.

Simplification through design   The first way of dealing with inter-related influences is to design the study so that relevant causal factors are made independent of each other through the design itself. Consider the case of age and salary level: as people get older their

TABLE 10.2 How to deal with inter-related factors

Method	Action
1 Simplification through design.	Sampling – select equal numbers within sub-groups.
2 Simplification through selecting sub-samples.	Restrict sample to one level of a key variable.
3 Simplification through statistical control.	Take variables two at a time, and use partial correlations to achieve statistical control.
4 Multivariate analysis.	Use multiple predictors and consider their joint influence.

experience grows and their salary level tends to go up. Thus there is an association between age and salary, which can be summarized by a positive correlation (see Chapter 9). If a researcher picks employees at random then the sample will be likely to reflect this association. However, another approach would be to divide the potential sample into groups based on age, and then select equal numbers of people at a number of salary levels within each age range. Even though age and salary may be correlated within the organization as a whole, the effect of this sampling strategy would be to create a sample of respondents where the two are independent of each other. The linkage between the two variables would not then be present in the sample.

The craft of research design (Shadish, Cook, and Campbell, 2002) is about developing imaginative ways of achieving simplicity of inference through creating a study design within which factors are orthogonal, where they are not independent of each other in the world at large. Such study designs are linked to statistical methods called *analysis of variance*, and designs with multiple factors are called factorial designs. Because they make analysis and inference simple even in research areas with many inter-related complicating factors, they have developed a strong appeal for some kinds of people. Experimental approaches based on structured research designs are widely used particularly in work psychology, marketing and information systems research.

Simplification through selecting a sub-sample   The second way of dealing with inter-related influences is through selecting samples to be equal on potentially confounding factors. It is common to find that women are paid less than men, and one of the reasons is that men and women tend to do different jobs, which in turn command different pay levels. In random samples of men and women at work then, there will be different mixes of jobs for the two groups as well as differences in pay levels; and it is difficult to disentangle the relative influence of gender and job type. However, restricting a study sample to people doing the same job would mean that any gender difference cannot be attributed to job type but must be due to something else. The same logic was used by Hofstede (1991) in his research on national culture, where he gathered data only from IBM employees working in many countries across the world rather than by drawing random samples in each country. The differences he found led him to conclude that there were four basic dimensions of national culture: power distance, masculine-feminine, individual-collective and uncertainty avoidance (he later added long-term orientation). Relying on samples drawn from only one company means that he is controlling for differences in labour markets across the world.

Simplification through statistical control   The third way to deal with inter-related influences is through a form of **statistical control** called **partial correlation**. We have already seen in Chapter 9 that a correlation is a way of summarizing the extent to which people respond to two variables in consistent ways. A partial correlation is a correlation between two variables (we call them A and B) where the value of a third variable (we call this S) is adjusted statistically as if it were equal to the sample mean for everybody (this is usually referred to as *holding constant* a third variable). The correlation between A and B is written as r_{AB}. The symbol for the partial correlation is $r_{AB|S}$. The method of partial correlation allows the researcher to see how much of an observed correlation, say between A and B, can be accounted for by the relationship that both variables have with a third variable, S.

Table 10.3 presents three possible patterns for r_{AB} and $r_{AB|S}$. We will use an example to explain the three patterns. Social media technologies such as blogs (Scoble and Israel, 2006) are rapidly becoming popular, and it would not be surprising to find correlations between willingness to use blogs for external marketing (B) and both age (A) and salary level (S). A correlation between age and blogging (r_{AB}) could be interpreted in terms of the conservatism of older people when it comes to embracing new technologies. A correlation between blogging and salary (r_{BS}) could be interpreted in terms of more senior people in the organization having fewer direct links with customers. We have already suggested that a correlation between age and salary is plausible (r_{AS}); and so all three variables are likely to be correlated. The partial correlation of age and blogging with salary held constant identifies that part of the total correlation which is independent of salary. Pattern 1 shows a high AB correlation and also a high AB|S partial correlation, and here the S variable has not altered the correlation between A and B. Pattern 2 shows a high AB correlation but a zero AB|S partial correlation, and in this case the researcher would conclude that A and B are not really correlated at all. The relationship suggested by the AB correlation is spurious. Finally, pattern 3 shows an unusual but interesting case, where the AB correlation is zero suggesting that A and B are not related at all. However, a high partial correlation implies that there really is a relationship between the two, but one that has been masked by the third variable S.

TABLE 10.3   Example of possible relationships between correlation and partial correlation

Pattern	Interpretation
1 r_{AB} is high; $r_{AB|S}$ is high	A and B are related; and S is irrelevant to both
2 r_{AB} is high; $r_{AB|S}$ is zero	A and B are not really related at all; but S has contributed to the appearance of a relationship between A and B
3 r_{AB} is zero; $r_{AB|S}$ is high	S is masking the 'real' relationship between A and B

Multivariate analysis   The final way of dealing with many inter-related factors builds on this logic of statistical control but extends it to many variables and also to predictive relationships rather than simple associations as measured by correlations. Multivariate statistical methods are designed to allow researchers to include many variables in a single analysis and to assess the separate contribution of each variable within an overall model. These methods are the focus of the rest of this chapter. Their main feature is the specification of a conceptual model that expresses the researcher's hypotheses about the relationships among variables. The variables to be included in a model will be defined by the focus of the research. Researchers in business and management get excited in their work by very different things. For example, in some of the studies considered already in this chapter, the size of the firm is treated as a 'nuisance' factor, which gets in the way of finding clear answers to interesting questions. However, there are other scholars for whom understanding the factors that make firms grow is the very focus of their work, and the size of the firm is not a nuisance factor at all.

Once a decision is made about which variables to include in a model, the next step is to specify what role each variable has in the model, usually as a cause (a predictor variable) or as an effect (a dependent variable). Making a decision about whether something is a dependent variable or a predictor variable is really a decision about how a variable is treated in the researcher's thinking. It is not an intrinsic characteristic of a variable, but instead a function of how it is used in a particular circumstance. This will depend to a large extent on the focus of a specific research project. Note that the role that a variable plays in statistical analysis reflects its position in the researcher's thinking, not something about the variable itself. The role that a variable plays in a researcher's model may even change within a study. Thus the paper by Coyle-Shapiro and Kessler (2000) reports one analysis where perceived organizational support is treated as a dependent variable; and later in the paper the authors use the same variable as a predictor of organizational commitment. So, its role changes from dependent variable to predictor variable.

Multivariate models can be specified using matrix algebra, for those with a strong mathematical training, and also represented graphically for those without such a background. We will use the graphical representation in this chapter for the sake of simplicity (see Figure 10.1). Variables are shown by boxes, which may be either rectangular or elliptical; and relationships among variables are shown by either single-headed or double-headed arrows. The variables used in multivariate models may be of two kinds: those which are measured directly by the researcher, called **observed variables**, and **latent variables** which are not measured directly but are inferred from observed variables. Observed variables are shown by rectangular boxes, and latent variables are shown by elliptical boxes.

Figure 10.1(a) shows a model for observed variables, with a single dependent variable to the right (DV1) and two predictor variables (PV1 and PV2). The assumed causal relationship between the PVs and the DV is indicated by the single-headed arrows. The double-headed arrow connecting the two PVs indicates an association between them, which may or may not reflect a causal relationship (this relationship is called **exogenous**, because the specified model does not concern itself with its origins: it is taken as a given). Figure 10.1(b) shows a model with two observed variables (DV1 and DV2) and one latent predictor variable (LV). The LV is assumed to be a cause of both DV1 and DV2.

The next sections give an introduction to two kinds of multivariate analysis methods: methods for analysing measurement models and methods for analysing **causal models**.

FIGURE 10.1

Graphical representation
of multivariate models

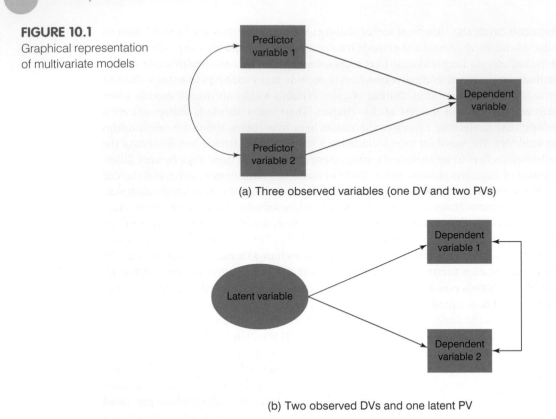

(a) Three observed variables (one DV and two PVs)

(b) Two observed DVs and one latent PV

Measurement models explore the relationship between observed variables and latent variables. Causal models are of two kinds: those that involve only observed variables and those that involve both observed and latent variables.

MULTIVARIATE ANALYSIS OF MEASUREMENT MODELS

Rationale for measurement models

It is often not possible to measure directly the characteristic that a researcher is interested in, and it may be necessary to rely on indirect indicators of it. This is very common in studies using secondary data sources (see Chapter 8) where variables that are present in a dataset are often used as *proxies* for constructs that are the main focus of interest but are not themselves available directly. For example, the success of a company entering into a new market could be shown through a number of different ways of defining success (e.g. market share, speed of growth, cost of capital to fund the expansion, satisfaction of new customers, profitability, share price), and looking at just one of them would probably be misleading.

Where a construct cannot be observed directly, it is common practice to select a set of items that are assumed to reflect the construct. A **measurement model** is then the relationship between a set of observed variables and the construct that they are intended to measure. Then answers are combined together to form a composite variable to represent the construct (Spector, 1992). The rationale behind this approach is that many of the characteristics that management researchers are interested in are complex (particularly in marketing and work psychology), being made up of different elements. A simple-minded approach to measurement would take the following view: if we want to measure how people see the reputation of an organization, then just ask them, 'Does company X have a good reputation?'. While this approach has some appeal on grounds of simplicity, it scarcely does justice to the complexity of the concept of corporate reputation (Davies et al., 2002). Individuals' attitudes, motivation and commitment are all impossible to observe directly, but understanding them is key to explaining why consumers buy what they do, and why workers stay in a job or leave it. In such circumstances, the researcher is faced with the choice of whether to select a single variable for analysis or to combine several variables together into a single index. The latter approach has many advantages: it allows greater richness in measurement, capturing nuances of a construct, and it also allows the researcher to assess how reliably the construct has been measured.

EXAMPLE
10.1

A hot topic among HR and communications professionals is that of employee engagement and its possible link to business success. Investigating this relationship would require great care, and involves a number of steps:

1   The sentence above proposes a causal relationship between two variables (let us call them EE for employee engagement, and BS for business success). EE is a predictor and BS is the dependent variable in this relationship: EE ➔ BS.

2   Next we consider both variables in turn, and it quickly becomes pretty clear that we cannot measure either of them in a direct way. The success of a business could be assessed in a variety of ways, and the same applies to employee engagement. So both EE and BS are really latent variables, and for each one we need to specify a number of observed variables, which can be used to indicate the value of the latent variable. For example, the kinds of behaviours we might associate with an engaged employee are: putting effort into work over and above what is required; staying in the organization despite offers of better pay elsewhere; taking the initiative to solve work-related problems; praising the organization as a good place to work.

The structure of measurement models

The basic logic here is that items that reflect features of an underlying construct will show common patterns of answering. For example, a manager who feels good about his or her job will tend to respond in a consistently favourable way to questions about different aspects of that job. Consistency in responses from study participants will produce correlations among items, and these correlations are the starting point for identifying patterns that reflect underlying constructs. In a measurement model (e.g. Figure 10.2), the *observed* variables are those that are measured directly by the researcher, and the *latent* variables are the constructs that the researcher assumes are causal factors influencing how sample members respond to the observed variables.

Figure 10.2 shows a measurement model for six measured variables and two unmeasured latent variables. The model distinguishes between two influences on how respondents answer for each observed variable:

1   Those that reflect common features of the constructs being assessed, indicated by the two **common factors**. The first common factor is what respondents are assumed to have in mind when they respond to variables 1–3, while the second common factor is assumed to influence answers for variables 4–6. The stronger the influence of the common factors (this is the value attached to each of the paths in Figure 10.2, and is called a **factor loading**), the higher will be the correlations among the observed variables.

2   Those that are idiosyncratic to the wording of each variable, indicated by the **specific factors**, one for each observed variable. These are unique to that question and will not influence answers to other questions.

FIGURE 10.2

Measurement model for six observed variables and two latent variables

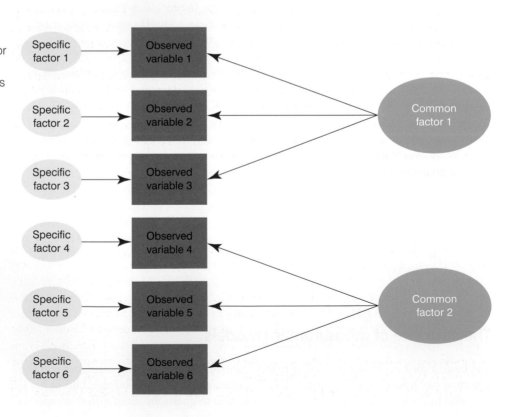

TABLE 10.4 Hypothetical correlation matrix showing the pattern of correlations for six observed variables and two latent variables

	1	2	3	4	5	6
1	–					
2	.36	–				
3	.36	.36	–			
4	0	0	0	–		
5	0	0	0	.36	–	
6	0	0	0	.36	.36	–

The **reliability** of a composite scale depends on the average correlation among the observed variables and is measured by the **Cronbach's alpha coefficient** (a value greater than 0.70 indicates an acceptable level of reliability).

Table 10.4 shows what the pattern of correlations would look like if the factor loadings for all observed variables were set at 0.60. Taking the correlation between observed variable 1 and observed variable 2 as an example, the value of 0.36 for the correlation between them is calculated by tracing the paths linking the two variables in the figure and multiplying the loadings for each path. Thus, 0.6 * 0.6 = 0.36. The first three observed variables are all correlated with each other, shown by the shading, reflecting the fact that they share loadings on the first common factor; and the second three observed variables, again shown by shading, are also correlated reflecting the influence of the second common factor. Furthermore, the bottom left un-shaded area of the correlation matrix contains only zero correlations because the two blocks of variables (1–3 and 4–6) do not share loadings on a common factor with each other.

Analysis methods for measurement models – CFA and EFA

Sometimes, the researcher has a set of questionnaire items with no clear idea of what constructs might underlie them, and here the method of choice for analysing the measurement model is **exploratory factor analysis** (EFA). More commonly, though, researchers know what constructs they are trying to measure and design their questionnaires to do just that. In that case, the aim is not to explore what constructs there might be but rather to confirm (or otherwise) a structure that has been designed into a study. This leads to **confirmatory factor analysis** (CFA) as the method of choice. Both types of model share a distinction between common factors and specific factors. Where the methods differ is in the prior specification of a measurement model. EFA analyses can be carried out by many general purpose statistical packages, such as SPSS (Bryman and

Cramer, 2004; Blunch, 2008; Field, 2009); while CFA requires one of the specialist SEM programmes, which we consider later.

In the EFA method, there may be as many common factors as there are observed variables; and all the observed variables have loadings on all the common factors. Two methods are common factor analysis and **principal components analysis**, and both methods derive estimates for the factor loadings of each of the common factors and the specific factors, and give summary indices (called **eigenvalues**) of the importance of each of the common factors, shown by how much of the covariation among the observed variables each one accounts for. The researcher uses these estimates to select a subset of common factors, usually retaining only the largest. The size of the loadings for the common factors determines the correlations among the observed variables. The size of the loadings for the specific factors determines the reliability of the common factors.

In the CFA method, the researcher defines in advance how many common factors are expected and the pattern of predicted loadings for observed variables. The common factors represent the latent variables that the researcher is interested in measuring: one factor for each latent variable. Observed variables are selected specifically to measure each of the latent variables; and so these observed variables are usually assumed to load on only one factor. The method derives estimates for each of the factor loadings for common factors and for specific factors, and gives an overall test statistic for how well the measurement model fits the data. Ullman (2006b) gives a readable introduction to CFA with particular reference to personality assessment, and shows how measurement models can be fitted and tested using SEM software.

EXAMPLE
10.2

Measurement models for measures of work design characteristics: EFA and CFA results

This example takes six variables from the dataset used by Sprigg and Jackson (2006) in their study of the impact of work design on the health of call handlers in UK call centres. The variables fall into two groups: three items measuring timing control, the extent to which call handlers had control over work timing (TC) and skill utilization (SU), how much their work enabled them to use the skills they had. The sample was large, over 1,000 people drawn from a large number of call centres throughout the UK.

The matrix of correlations is shown in Table 10.5(a), and the high correlations are shaded. It is clear that they form two groups reflecting the constructs that the items were designed to measure. The factor loadings from exploratory factor analysis are shown in Table 10.5(b). The first thing to note is that there are two factors, as would be expected, and that all six variables have loadings on both factors. The second thing to note is that the loadings of the three timing control items are very high on the first factor, but very low on the second factor; while the reverse is true for the skill utilization items (again the high values are shaded). It

(Continued)

TABLE 10.5 Measurement model for measures of work design characteristics: EFA and CFA results

(a) *Matrix of correlations among variables*

	TC1	TC2	TC3	SU1	SU2	SU3
TC1	–					
TC2	.40	–				
TC3	.48	.45	–			
SU1	.16	.16	.14	–		
SU2	.16	.18	.15	.52	–	
SU3	.16	.15	.13	.55	.56	–

(b) *Factor loadings from exploratory factor analysis*

	Timing control	Skill utilization
TC1	.78	.10
TC2	.76	.11
TC3	.82	.06
SU1	.09	.82
SU2	.12	.82
SU3	.09	.84

(c) *Factor loadings from confirmatory factor analysis*

	Timing control	Skill utilization
TC1	.61	0
TC2	.67	0
TC3	.63	0
SU1	0	.78
SU2	0	.73
SU3	0	.71

(Continued)

would be reasonable to label the two factors according to the content of the times that load on them, and that is what we have done in the table. However, this is an inference on our part; the statistical analysis is agnostic about what these latent variables are called.

Table 10.5(c) gives the factor loadings for confirmatory factor analysis, and the major difference is that each item is constrained to load onto one factor. The values of zero are called fixed values because they were constrained as part of the input specification for CFA. The reason is that we hypothesized that the first three items would measure a timing control construct and the second three items would measure a skill utilization construct. The factor loadings from CFA are not identical to those given by the EFA analysis, because the models that were fitted to the data are different; but the conclusion is broadly the same. Finally, the measurement model from CFA is shown diagrammatically in Figure 10.3.

FIGURE 10.3

Measurement model for measures of work design characteristics: CFA results

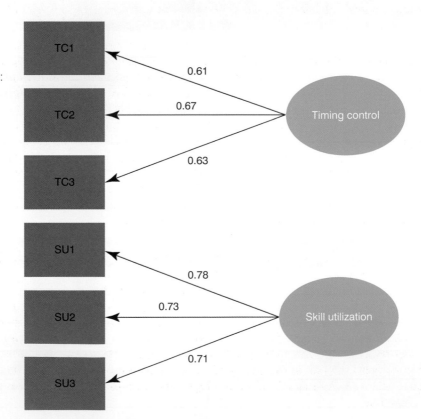

MULTIVARIATE ANALYSIS OF CAUSAL MODELS

Rationale for causal models

Causality cannot be proved   Using multivariate statistical methods to test causal models is a very powerful technique that is widely used within management research. Its major value is that it forces the researcher to define very precisely both the variables to be included and the way in which they relate to each other. In return, the statistical methods offer specific tests of hypotheses that can allow the researcher to judge how good those models are. However, what causal modelling methods cannot do is prove a causal relationship. Instead, they allow decisions to be made about whether a given model is consistent with observed data. The plausibility of a particular model needs first to be established conceptually from theory, and then quantitative evidence can be used to assess whether the model is consistent with data. Consider again the study by Coyle-Shapiro and Kessler (2000) from Table 10.1. In their article, they developed a theoretical rationale for treating employee commitment as a dependent variable and psychological contract fulfilment as a predictor variable. Unless they have longitudinal data, with variables measured on more than one occasion, it is impossible for them to prove that this assumption is correct. Instead, all they can do is assess whether the conceptual model that they formulated is consistent with their data.

Defining what variables to include in the model   This step is important because any causal model will estimate the best values that it can for the contribution of each variable that is included. However, the estimation procedure can only take into account the information it has available to it. If the researcher leaves out (by accident or by design) a factor that is critically important, then the modelling procedure cannot find it, and the results obtained can be misleading. Studies that leave out important variables are very likely to produce misleading conclusions. Almost every week, some survey is reported in the newspapers showing that red wine is good/bad for health, or that chocolate/chips help you diet. Such studies almost always suffer from small and idiosyncratic samples; and their big failing is that the true causal factors behind good health or weight loss were not even included in the study. For the most part, the findings are either chance results that cannot be replicated, or are the spurious consequence of some other more important variable.

Specifying causal models   Research propositions should be translated into formal causal models that can be tested statistically; either as a single model or as a sequence of models of increasing complexity. Comparing a simple model with a more complex one is a powerful way of testing research hypotheses, but it is important to remember that a more complex model, one that includes more variables or has more complex relationships among them, will always give a better fit to a given dataset. So, **goodness of fit** alone is not the most important criterion in selecting the best model. Instead, the researcher needs to take into account what the gain in the quality of the model is relative to the added complexity needed to achieve it. An example of the development of a series of causal models is shown in Example 10.3.

EXAMPLE
10.3

Stakeholder relationship management and corporate financial performance: formulating alternative causal models

This example considers different accounts of how stakeholder relationship management links to corporate strategy and to the performance of the organization (Freeman et al., 2010; Cornelissen, 2011). Berman et al. (1999) propose two kinds of model, the normative model and the instrumental model, and show how they can be tested empirically. The *normative* model states that looking after the interests of stakeholders is the right thing to do, and that the strategic goals set by senior management will be determined by a need to protect and promote the interests of their stakeholders. So principles of stakeholder relationship management guide how the organization formulates its corporate strategy, and strategy in turn has some influence on financial performance. Figure 10.4 expresses the normative model using blocks for the key variables and arrows to show the hypothesized causal relationships among them.

FIGURE 10.4

The normative model of stakeholder relationship management and corporate financial performance

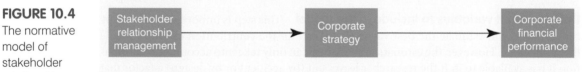

SOURCE: ADAPTED FROM BERMAN ET AL. (1999)

The *instrumental* model (Figure 10.5) states that organizations should pay attention to their stakeholders because they will benefit financially; and thus the model proposes that both stakeholder relationship management and corporate strategy influence corporate financial performance. Berman et al. propose two variants of the instrumental model: the direct effects model shown in Figure 10.5(a) and the moderation model shown in Figure 10.5(b). The direct effects model differs from the normative model in that there is no path between corporate strategy and stakeholder relationship management but there is a direct path from stakeholder relationships to financial performance. The moderation model is a more sophisticated version of the direct effects model, which proposes a different mechanism for the role of stakeholder relationship management, as modifying the link between strategy and performance. The logic behind this form of the model is that companies will find it easier to put their strategic goals into practice and benefit from them if they foster good relationships with their stakeholders.

(Continued)

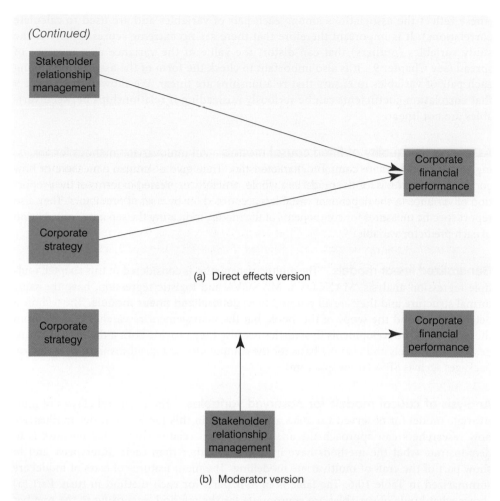

(Continued)

Sample size The trustworthiness of a model depends on how stable it is, and that means the sample size needs to be large enough to give confidence that the results could be replicated in new samples. Analyses based on small samples tend to give quirky results that may not be repeatable. The adequacy of a sample depends on the complexity of the model that is fitted to the data: complex models need larger samples. As a useful rule of thumb, multiplying the number of observed predictor variables by ten gives a minimum sample size (though this really is a minimum, and other factors such as the reliability of measurement would lead us to recommend larger samples than this).

Assessing the appropriate form of a causal model Once the researcher has defined the conceptual model in a form that can be tested statistically, the next step is to check that the data available are expressed in a form which is appropriate for the assumptions required by the statistical method. This involves assessing both measurement quality and that the form of the statistical model is appropriate. The input for all multivariate analysis methods is a matrix containing the variances of each variable (indicating the spread of scores: see Chapter 9) and the **covariances** among them (these reflect the associations among each pair of variables and are used to calculate correlations). It is important therefore that there are no extreme scores on any of the study variables (outliers) that can distort the value of the variance as a measure of spread (see Chapter 9). It is also important to check the form of the association among each pair of variables to ensure that relationships are linear. We showed in Chapter 9 that correlation coefficients can be seriously misleading if relationships between variables are not linear.

Assessing the quality of fitted causal models   All multivariate methods for analysing causal models share common characteristics. They give a summary measure of how good the prediction is for the model as a whole, generally expressed in terms of the proportion of variance in the dependent variable/s accounted for by a set of predictors. They also report specific measures for components of the model, indicating the separate contribution of each predictor variable.

Generalized linear models   The multivariate methods considered in this chapter, multiple regression analysis, MANCOVA, MANOVA and logistic regression, have the same formal structure and they are all referred to as **generalized linear models**. The technical details are beyond the scope of this book; but the management researcher benefits from these theoretical developments in statistics because they provide both a theoretical 'cleanness' to the models and also the basis for the computational algorithms used by statistical packages such as SPSS (www.spss.com).

Analysis of causal models for observed variables   Three general classes of multivariate model for observed variables are described in this section in order to illustrate how researchers can approach the analysis of causal relationships. Our purpose is to demonstrate what the methods have in common rather than their differences, and to show part of the craft of multivariate modelling. The main features of class of model are summarized in Table 10.6. The table is in four parts for each method in turn. Part (a) shows what kinds of variables are appropriate for the method, according to the number of dependent variables used and the measurement scale for both DVs and PVs. Part (b) describes how the quality of the model as a whole is assessed in that method; and part (c) lists how the individual elements of the model are represented in the model. Finally, part (d) outlines alternative options that are available within each method. First, we consider the multiple regression and analysis of covariance models whose characteristics are shown in column 1.

Multiple regression analysis (MRA)   The basic **multiple regression model** consists of a single dependent variable measured on a continuous scale and a set of predictor variables, which may be measured on continuous or category scales (see Table 10.6(a)). The model for two predictor variables can be expressed algebraically like this:

$$Y = a + b_1 X_1 + b_2 X_2 + e$$

TABLE 10.6 Multivariate methods for analysis of causal models for observed variables

	MRA / ANCOVA	MANOVA / MANCOVA	Logistic Regression Analysis
(a) Variables	DV – a single continuous variable. PVs – • MRA – one or more continuous variables. • ANCOVA – one or more category variables and one or more continuous variables.	DVs – two or more continuous variables. PVs – • MANOVA – one or more category variables (factors). • MANCOVA – one or more category variables and a one or more continuous variable (covariates).	DV – a single dichotomous category variable. PVs – one or continuous and/or category variables.
(b) Assessing quality of the model as a whole	Multiple R shows the validity of the model as a whole; multiple R^2 shows the proportion of variance in the DV accounted for. An F-ratio tests whether the multiple R is significantly different from zero.	Wilks' Lambda – multivariate test for each effect (category and continuous variable) shows the significance level for all DVs jointly. An F-ratio tests the significance of Lambda.	Model χ^2

(Continued)

TABLE 10.6 (Continued)

	MRA / ANCOVA	MANOVA / MANCOVA	Logistic Regression Analysis
(c) Contribution of individual elements of the model	Regression weights show the independent contribution of each PV; beta weights are regression weights standardized onto the same measurement scale for all variables. A *t*-test assesses whether a regression weight is significantly different from zero.	Separate tests for each dependent variable: ● Univariate tests (which ignore correlations among the dependent variables). ● Stepdown tests (which partial out the effects of dependent variables entered according to a pre-determined sequence).	Regression weights and odds ratios for each predictor variable
(d) Options available	● Simultaneous entry of all predictors. ● Hierarchical regression – entry of variables in a sequence determined the researcher. ● Stepwise regression – sequential entry of variables determined by the predictive value of variables.	● Stepdown tests require a pre-determined sequence for the dependent variables. ● Tests could be performed with and without covariates in the model.	● Simultaneous entry of all predictors. ● Hierarchical logistic regression – entry of variables in a sequence determined by theory. ● Stepwise logistic regression – sequential entry of variables according to their predictive value.

where the symbol Y is used for the dependent variable; while the symbol X is used for each predictor variable; *a* is called the intercept or the constant (it is the value of Y when each X is zero); *b* is called a **regression weight**; *e* is a **residual** (or error term). On the predictor side of the model above, there are two kinds of variables. The PVs (shown here by X_1 and X_2) are the systematic part of the model chosen by the researcher. All other factors that influence the spread of scores on the DV are combined together into the residual term, *e*. The graphical form of this regression model is shown in Figure 10.6.

The quality of the regression model as a whole (Table 10.6(b)) is summarized by the **squared multiple correlation**, R^2, whose value varies between 0 and 1 and shows how much of the spread in DV scores can be accounted for by the predictors in the model. In MRA, the measure of spread that is used is the variance (see Chapter 9), and the R^2 measure is the proportion of variance in the DV accounted for by the PVs collectively. It is often multiplied by 100 to give a percentage of variance accounted for, from 0 per cent to 100 per cent. R^2 indicates the relative importance of the PVs and the residual term, which is shown to the right in Figure 10.6. Thus where a set of predictors account for 20 per cent of the variance in a DV, this means that 80 per cent of the variance is accounted for by all other causal factors combined into the residual term. An *F*-test (see Chapter 9, Table 9.4) is used to test the null hypothesis that the proportion of variance accounted for by the PVs is zero against the alternative hypothesis that it is greater than zero. The individual components of the model are summarized in Table 10.6(c). The regression weights indicate the size of the independent contribution that each PV makes to predicting the spread in scores on the DV. When predictor variables are measured on different scales, the relative size of regression weights for different variables cannot be compared. So it is usual to transform each of the variables in MRA to a common measurement scale (this is called **standardizing**), and then the regression weights are referred to as either **standardized regression weights** or β **(beta) weights**. The significance test for regression weights gives a *t*-value; and the null hypothesis tested is that the regression weight is zero against the alternative that it is different from zero.

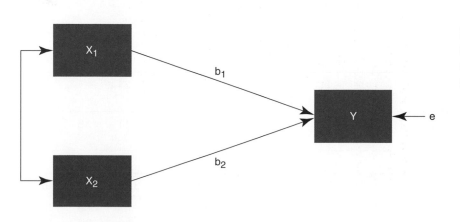

FIGURE 10.6

Graphical representation of a multiple regression model

SOURCE: JACKSON, 2004

EXAMPLE
10.4

Multiple regression analysis of predictors of quality commitment

Jackson (2004) reported a study of one aspect of employees' commitment to the values of their organization, their commitment to quality. There were three stages to the research: defining the concept of quality commitment itself, formulating a way of measuring it, and developing and testing a conceptual model of how quality commitment relates to both personal and organizational variables. Here, we focus on the third stage where a sequence of regression analyses were used to test the conceptual model.

Table 10.7 shows a matrix of correlations for quality commitment, demographic variables (age, company tenure and gender) and a number of measures of work design. Row 10 of the table shows the correlation between quality commitment and each of the other variables in the study. There is a strong relationship with age ($r = 0.30$, $p < .001$), indicating that older workers show higher quality commitment; and the relationship with company tenure is much lower but also significant ($r = 0.14$,

(Continued)

TABLE 10.7   Correlations among study variables

		1	2	3	4	5	6	7	8	9	10
1	Organization	–									
2	Age	.13	–								
3	Gender	−.43	−.09	–							
4	Company tenure	.02	.48	−.11	–						
5	Individual timing control	.28	.26	−.23	.23	–					
6	Individual method control	.29	.19	−.28	.24	.67	–				
7	Monitoring demands	−.08	.11	−.03	.17	.16	.28	–			
8	Problem-solving demands	.09	.00	−.22	.21	.20	.34	.52	–		
9	Production responsibility	.00	.02	−.11	.05	.02	.15	.42	.34	–	
10	Quality commitment	.02	.30	.09	.14	.21	.24	.23	.11	.16	–
Mean		.22	30.78	.78	5.74	2.83	3.09	3.85	3.00	3.19	3.97
Standard deviation		.62	11.12	.41	6.16	1.21	.93	.84	.88	1.06	.51

(Continued)

p < .001). Gender differences are significant but small in size ($r = 0.09$, $p < .05$), with women showing higher quality commitment. Table 10.7 also shows, not surprisingly, that age and company tenure are correlated: those who have been employed longer with their company tend to be older. There are also consistently strong correlations between quality commitment and work design characteristics. Workers with more control over the timing and methods aspects of their jobs report higher quality commitment ($r = 0.21$, $p < .001$ and $r = 0.24$, $p < .001$ for timing and method control respectively); workers whose jobs are more mentally demanding in terms of problem-solving ($r = 0.11$, $p < .001$) and system monitoring ($r = 0.23$, $p < .001$) also report higher quality commitment; and quality commitment is correlated with production responsibility ($r = 0.16$, $p < .001$): workers reporting more expensive consequences if they make a mistake have higher quality commitment.

TABLE 10.8 Hierarchical regression analysis for predicting quality commitment from demographic and work design variables

	Step 1	Step 2
Organization	.04	.02
Demographics		
Age	.30 **	.27 **
Gender	.14 **	.19 **
Company tenure	.01	−.05
Work design		
Individual timing control		.07
Individual method control		.15 **
Monitoring demands		.12 **
Problem-solving demands		.00
Production responsibility		.10 **
Multiple R^2	.10	.18
Change in Multiple R^2	.10	.08
F-ratio for test of change in R^2	36.03 **	18.47 **

SOURCE: ADAPTED FROM JACKSON (2004)
** P < .01

(Continued)

(Continued)

However, interpreting these relationships is not simple, because the table shows that there are strong correlations among many of the study variables. For example, people who have been employed in the company for longer tend to report higher levels of the work design variables, presumably because they have jobs with more responsibility. We have also seen that age and company tenure are correlated. Testing the conceptual model means that it is necessary to tease out these relationships and that is the purpose of multiple regression analysis.

In the analyses reported in Table 10.8, the DV is quality commitment, and the predictors are the demographic and work design variables. Two steps in hierarchical regression analysis are shown in the table. In the first step, column 1, the demographic variables are used as PVs and the results show that both age and gender are significant predictors of quality commitment, while company tenure is not. This suggests that the correlation between company tenure and quality commitment arises because both variables are correlated with age: it would appear that quality commitment reflects a person's age rather than the length of employment with the employer. The second step (column 2) adds the work design predictors in order to test how much each one adds independently to predicting quality commitment, but also how important work design factors are relative to demographic factors. The regression weights shown here give a different picture from the correlations. Although all five work design variables were significantly correlated with quality commitment (Table 10.7), only three of the five regression weights are significant. Interpreting how important each individual work design variable is on the basis of how strongly it correlates with quality commitment is clouded by the correlations among the work design variables themselves. The difference in interpretation between pairwise correlation analysis and multiple regression analysis in this example shows how important it is to consider variables together.

An example application of multiple regression analysis is shown in Example 10.4. It illustrates the basic elements of MRA, but also shows the value of a variant of MRA called **hierarchical regression** (see Table 10.6d) where predictors are entered sequentially in more than one block. Hierarchical regression allows the researcher to test hypotheses not just about the importance of individual predictors but also about variables entered into a model as groups. Table 10.8 (bottom row) shows that it is possible to compare the overall fit of a model to another one with one or more predictor variables added. Each model has an R^2 value and the same F-test that was used to assess each individual R^2 can be used to test the change in R^2 between models.

Figure 10.7 shows two versions of a hypothetical regression model for three observed variables. In both models, the variable PV1 is assumed to be a cause of PV2, shown by the single-headed arrow between them, and PV2 in turn is assumed to be a cause of DV. The difference between the models lies in how PV1 relates to DV: in (a) there is a direct path between the two, while in (b) there is no path and any causal influence of PV1 on DV would

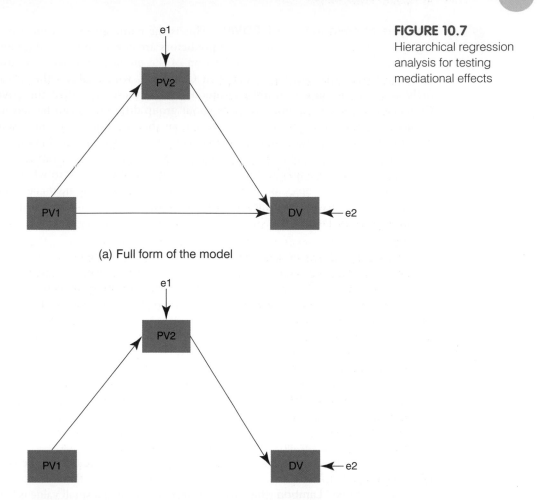

FIGURE 10.7
Hierarchical regression analysis for testing mediational effects

(a) Full form of the model

(b) Reduced form of the model with one path removed

have to work through PV2. Such a causal influence would make PV2 a mediator between PV1 and DV; and the model is called a **mediational model**. Hierarchical regression analysis could be used to test the mediational model as follows. First, model (a) is tested using both PV1 and PV2 as predictors of DV. The multiple R^2 shows what proportion of the variance in DV is accounted for by both predictors. Second, model (b) is tested by dropping PV1 from the set of predictors of DV, and again multiple R^2 is calculated. The only difference between model (a) and model (b) is the removal of PV1, so the difference between the two values of R^2 shows whether PV1 is a significant predictor of DV and therefore the path between them in Figure 10.7(a) is necessary.

There are other forms of regression analysis, called **stepwise regression**, which involve an automatic process of adding or subtracting variables according to how well they contribute to predicting the dependent variable. However, they rely on a blind search among predictors in order to identify those that make the greatest contribution to predicting the dependent variable; and such methods rarely have a place in management research.

Analysis of covariance (ANCOVA)   This is the name given to a form of multiple regression analysis where some of the predictors are continuous variables and others are category variables. It is a generalization of the methods for assessing differences between groups that were considered in Chapter 9, which allows the researcher to include predictors measured on continuous scales (these are called the **covariates**). Conclusions based on hypothesis tests about group differences can be seriously misleading if groups differ on variables other than the dependent variable. **Analysis of covariance** adjusts the dependent variable scores to what they would have been had the treatment groups been equal on the covariate. ANCOVA achieves a statistical matching between treatment groups, by adjusting groups means on the DV to what they would have been had the groups scored the same on the covariates. The next class of methods that we consider are **multivariate analysis of variance** (MANOVA) and **multivariate analysis of covariance** (MANCOVA) and their characteristics are listed in column 2 of Table 10.6.

MANOVA/MANCOVA   These methods bring together a number of methods that we have already considered, generalized to the situation where the researcher is interested in assessing the predictability of more than one dependent variable. MANOVA is used for comparing groups that are classified on the basis of one or more category variables. MANCOVA is the multivariate generalization of ANCOVA, which includes one or more continuous variables as covariates as well as at least one category variable.

The practical problem addressed by this class of methods is that of interpreting the causal influences of predictors on dependent variables that are correlated among themselves. Taking correlated dependent variables singly can be misleading because each one carries not just information about the thing it measures but also something of what it shares with other dependent variables.

The quality of the model as a whole is shown by a multivariate test for the whole set of DVs taken together. There are several test statistics available, but the one most frequently used is called **Wilks' Lambda** (this varies between 0 and 1 and a small value is better), and an F-ratio tests the significance of Lambda. Having looked at each of the effects for the set of DVs taken together, the next step is to explore individual components of the model, and there are two options here. The first option is the **univariate F-test** and this is the same test as if the analysis had been performed for each DV separately, but with an adjustment in significance level made to take account of the number of dependent variables in the model. The univariate F-test thus ignores correlations among the DVs, and so its usefulness depends on how high those correlations are. Another option is a **stepdown F-test**, where the DVs are tested in a sequence decided upon by the researcher. In effect it is a form of analysis of covariance, which holds constant previous DVs. The first test is carried out ignoring the others DVs; the second test adjusts for the first DV; and so on. Stepdown tests are preferable to univariate tests because they take into account the correlations among the DVs, but their value is dependent on whether the researcher can give a justifiable ordering of the dependent variables. While the results from the univariate tests will be the same regardless of which order the DVs are listed, this is not true of stepdown tests. Univariate tests and stepdown tests will only give the same answers when the DVs are completely uncorrelated with each other.

Worked example of MANOVA

EXAMPLE
10.5

This example uses the same data as Example 10.4 from a developmental study of employees' commitment to quality (Jackson, 2004). Earlier, we used gender and a number of work design characteristics as predictors of individuals' quality commitment; and this example tests the hypothesis that there are gender differences in work design. Table 10.7 shows that there are correlations among the work design variables, so it may be misleading to ignore these relationships by taking each variable alone. Table 10.9 gives the main results from MANOVA with gender as a category variable predictor and five work design characteristics as dependent variables.

TABLE 10.9   Results of multivariate analysis of variance: gender differences in five work design characteristics ($n = 967$)

	Male (n = 209)	Female (n = 758)	t-test
(a) Univariate tests for each variable separately			
Individual timing control	3.37	2.69	7.24 **
Individual method control	3.60	2.96	9.25 **
Monitoring demands	3.89	3.84	0.76
Problem-solving demands	3.37	2.89	7.16 **
Production responsibility	3.41	3.12	3.51 **
(b) Multivariate test for all variables together			
Wilks' Lambda = 0.87, F = 27.73 **			

** INDICATES SIGNIFICANT AT .01 LEVEL

The mean scores for males and females on each work design variable are shown in Table 10.9(a), together with the results of univariate *t*-tests (ignoring the correlations among the DVs). This shows that women report significantly lower scores on four out of the five work design characteristics: they have less control over work timing and methods, the problem-solving demands on them are lower, and their responsibility for production mistakes is lower. These results would suggest that women's jobs in this sample are more routine and undemanding than those of the men in the sample.

However, the individual tests ignore the fact that there are correlations among the work design variables, and the multivariate test of the gender effect is shown

(Continued)

(Continued)

in Table 10.9(b). This shows the Wilks' Lambda coefficient and its associated significance test, an *F*-ratio. The null hypothesis being tested is that there is no gender difference in the set of DVs taken together, and this is rejected with a high level of confidence. There is clear evidence for a gender difference in work design in general, confirming what was observed for the analysis of the individual DVs.

Follow-up analyses could go in a number of directions, depending on the interests of the researcher. One direction would be to examine in more detail what job titles the men and women in this sample actually hold in order to determine whether men have higher grade jobs in this sample or whether the observed effects reflect gender differences among people doing the same jobs. A different avenue to explore is whether there is a common factor underlying the work design variables (see the earlier section on measurement models), which might give a greater conceptual clarity to this analysis. Finally, we focused here on gender, but there may be other influential demographic differences between men and women, such as age or organizational tenure, which have been ignored. If so, any interpretation that focuses purely on gender would be misguided.

The final class of multivariate methods that we consider for causal analysis of observed variables is logistic regression analysis.

Logistic regression analysis This addresses the same questions as multiple regression analysis except that the DV is a dichotomous category variable rather than a continuous variable (Table 10.6, column 3). Like MRA, predictor variables may be continuous or category variables or any mix of the two. Examples of dependent variables that might be used in **logistic regression** analysis include: the presence or absence of a risk factor for stress; the success or failure of a merger; the survival or not of a joint venture partnership. The dependent variable in logistic regression analysis is based on an **odds ratio**, which expresses the relative likelihood of the two possible outcomes. For example, if 20 per cent of mergers in a dataset of companies succeed while 80 per cent do not, then the odds of success are 4:1 against (20 per cent/80 per cent). It is the log of these odds that is used as the DV in logistic regression:

$$\log p / (1\text{-}p)$$

where p is the probability of succeeding and $1\text{-}p$ is the probability of failing. The model is used to assess the independent contribution of several predictor variables to the prediction of these odds.

Because the DV in logistic regression is a complex function of the probability of being in one category rather than another, the method used to fit the model is different from that used in multiple regression. This method gives a different test statistic for the quality of the model as a whole, a **likelihood ratio chi-square**. Despite this difference from multiple regression, the significance test tells the same story: whether the set of predictors as a whole account for significant variation in the DV. The individual components of the model are also evaluated by their regression weights; and each is tested by comparing its size relative to the standard error. In logistic regression, the result is called a **Wald test**; but its meaning is the same as in multiple regression. A worked example of logistic regression analysis is shown in Example 10.6.

EXAMPLE
10.6

A worked example of logistic regression analysis

This example uses data from the study by Sprigg and Jackson (2006) of stress in call centre staff. The DV is whether or not the respondent had experienced musculoskeletal disorder (MSD) caused by his or her work in the previous seven days (this includes back pain, aches in the wrist or shoulders, and so on). Logistic regression is appropriate because the DV is a category variable with two levels. The two predictors that we focus on here are: workload, a continuous variable assessing aspects of the demands of the job, and scripting, a three-point ordered category variable assessing to what degree call handlers followed a strictly worded script when they answered calls. The sample size for this analysis was 836, and of these 520 (62 per cent) reported MSD in the previous seven days. MSDs are thus relatively common in this sample of call handlers. The odds in favour of MSD are 62 relative to 38, and the odds ratio is calculated as:

Odds ratio $= p / (1 - p) = .622 / .378 = 1.65.$

Logistic regression takes the log of this odds ratio as the DV, and the hypothesis being tested is whether the predictor variables either increase or decrease the risk of experiencing MSD while working as a call handler.

Table 10.10 shows the results of logistic regression. The quality of the model as a whole is shown by a chi-square test statistic, and its value is 5.46, with 2 degrees of freedom (because there are two predictors). This is statistically significant, so we conclude that the two predictors together do account for a difference in the relative risk of MSDs.

The separate contribution of each predictor variable is shown by the standardized regression weights (labelled as **beta weights** in Table 10.10), just as in multiple

TABLE 10.10 Results of logistic regression analysis for MSD as a function of workload and following a set script

Overall fit of the model: chi-square = 5.46 (df = 2), p <.01		
Variable	Beta weight	Wald statistic
Workload	.50**	29.90
Script	.28*	5.31

(Continued)

(Continued)

regression. The hypothesis that the beta weight is zero is tested by a Wald statistic rather than a *t*-value for testing significance, but otherwise the interpretation of the coefficients is the same as for multiple regression. Both beta weights are positive in sign and statistically significant, indicating that higher workload is associated with an increased risk of MSDs and more use of a set script is also associated with an increase in risk. These influences are independent, so that someone who has high workload *and* greater use of a set script will tend to experience greater risk of MSD than someone who is high on only one predictor.

The options available to the researcher within logistic regression are exactly the same as for multiple regression analysis (see Table 10.6(d)). Predictor variables may be entered in a single block, or the researcher may have theoretical reasons for defining a sequence of models to be fitted hierarchically. Finally, stepwise logistic regression can be used to enter predictor variables purely on the basis of how well they predict the dependent variable. Just as for stepwise options in multiple regression analysis, we see limited scope for this within management research.

Analysis of observed and latent variables – structural equation modelling

Structural equation modelling (SEM) (Blunch, 2008; Hair et al., 2008; Tabachnick and Fidell, 2012) brings together the two kinds of multivariate methods that we have considered so far in this chapter: *measurement models* for assessing hypotheses about relationships between observed and latent variables, and *structural models* of the causal relationships among both observed and latent variables. As such, they provide within the same framework a way of expressing and estimating many of the different kinds of model that are used by management researchers. There are several statistical packages available for fitting structural equation models, and the best known are: LISREL (www.ssicentral.com), EQS (www.mvsoft.com), Mplus (www.statmodel.com) and AMOS (www-01.ibm.com/software/analytics/spss/products/statistics/amos/). While the detailed characteristics differ among them, they all share the same underlying models and the graphical interface used to develop the model. AMOS has a reputation for being easier to use than the others, but, according to Ullman (2006a), the craft of SEM involves the same five steps whatever software is used (see Table 10.11).

TABLE 10.11 Steps in structural equation modelling

1 Define model hypotheses
2 Specify the model
3 Estimate model parameters
4 Evaluate the quality of the model
5 Consider alternative models

The first step in SEM is to *define model hypotheses*, specifying what variables are included within the model (both measured and latent variables), and what the relationships are among them. Any model fitting procedure will use the relationships among the variables that are included to estimate the parameter in the hypothesized model. There is no substitute for careful consideration of which variables to include in a model: leave out something important and the model obtained can be seriously biased and misleading. Furthermore, the use of latent variable models places the responsibility onto the researcher to think carefully about what indicators to use for each latent variable and to ensure that they are measured reliably. The most sophisticated of statistical treatment cannot overcome the deficiencies introduced by sloppy thinking or poor measurement practice.

The second step in SEM is to *specify the model*, including either fixed or free parameters. Free parameters are those elements of the model whose values are to be estimated from data; while fixed parameters have a pre-defined value allocated to them (usually, but not always, zero). Fixed parameters are usually necessary to make a model identifiable, and they also give the basis for testing theoretical propositions by comparing different models where fixed parameters are set free. The full structural equation model has both measured variables and latent variables, and may also include causal relationships among the latent variables. The model in Figure 10.8 looks quite different from the ones considered so far in this chapter, but it is almost the same as the model in Figure 10.2. Both models have three kinds of variable: observed variables shown in rectangles, latent variables (we called these common factors earlier) and specific factors both shown in ellipses. Apart from a cosmetic change in layout, the only difference is that there is a causal arrow linking the two latent variables in the centre of the model.

The left hand side shows the measurement model for the latent variable labelled as PV (see the earlier section of this chapter). This model hypothesizes that the PV is a common factor that accounts for the correlations among observed variables 1-3, while the specific factor associated with each of the observed variables captures all influences on observed variable scores which are specific to that variable. The right-hand side shows the equivalent measurement model for the DV. At the centre of the figure is the structural model showing the hypothesized causal link between the two latent variables.

Each of the arrows in the figure represents a path between two variables and also a parameter to be estimated from the data. For measurement models, these parameters are called factor loadings; while for causal models, they are called regression weights or path coefficients. Since (by definition) latent variables cannot be measured directly, the only information the researcher has about them comes from the observed variables. For a structural equation model, there are two kinds of parameter that need to be defined.

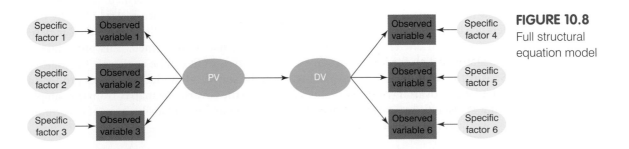

FIGURE 10.8

Full structural equation model

The first is the covariance among the latent and observed variables. The second is the variance of each latent variable, so that its measurement scale is defined. The variance of an observed variable indicates the spread of scores around the mean on its measurement scale and thus defines the scale, and the same is true of the variance of a latent variable. However, the scale of a latent variable is unobservable and so it has to be defined in another way. One common option is to assume that the measurement scale of a latent variable is the same as that of one of its indicator variables (it does not matter which one), and another is to assume that the scale is a standardized one with a variance of one. For each parameter, the researcher can either define a fixed value for a parameter (as shown in the CFA example earlier in the chapter), or estimate a value from data. The commonest fixed values are zero for paths between variables, and one for variances of latent variables.

The input to a model fitting procedure consists of:

- The variances of the observed variables, which define their measurement scale.
- The covariances among the observed variables.

If there are p observed variables, then the number of items of information available for model fitting is p variances and $p*(p-1)/2$ covariances. The model in Figure 10.8 contains six observed variables, so the number of items of information available is $6 + 6*5/2 = 21$. There are three possibilities for the relationship between the number of parameters to be estimated and the information available to do it, and together they define the **identifiability** of a model:

1 *Just identified* – there are the same number of parameters to estimate and information available. A just-identified model will always fit the observed data perfectly. Unique values for the parameters of the model can be estimated and their significance tested, but the model is as complex as the original data.

2 *Under-identified* – there are more parameters to be estimated than information available to define unique values for them, and it is then impossible to fit a model.

3 *Over-identified* – there are fewer parameters to be estimated than items of information. Here, the fitted model is simpler than the original data, and it is possible to calculate a significance test for the model as whole as well as unique values for the individual parameters.

The third step in SEM is to *estimate model parameters*. All the programmes work broadly in the same way. First, starting values for model parameters are formed, and these are used to calculate the initial estimate of the population covariance matrix (Σ). The difference between this and the sample covariance matrix (**S**) is called the *residual matrix*. The initial parameters are modified, and a new Σ matrix is formed. This procedure is repeated until no further improvements in goodness of fit can be achieved. The logic of SEM is to find estimates of the parameters in the statistical model in order to produce a population covariance matrix that is a close fit to the covariance matrix from the sample data. A close fit indicates that the hypothesized model is a plausible way of describing the relationships within the sample data. The goal of SEM therefore is to achieve a good fit between hypothesized model and the data – shown by a small and non-significant index of goodness of fit.

Evaluate the quality of the model   A goodness of fit index is calculated based on the estimated population covariance matrix (Σ) and the sample covariance matrix (**S**). A common estimation method is called maximum likelihood, and the goodness of fit index that is minimized is called chi-square (χ^2). The value of χ^2 depends on a function of the **S** and Σ matrices and on the sample size. This means that large values of χ^2 reflect either poor model fit or a large sample size, or both. Studies with large samples (e.g. over 1,000 participants) will almost always shows significant χ^2 values regardless of how good the fitted model is. As well as indices for the model as a whole, it is also important to look at the individual parameters within the model. A significance test for each parameter is reported by all of the programmes, testing the null hypothesis that the population value of the parameter is zero.

The fourth step is to *assess the fit of a model*. The quality of the overall fit between a hypothesized model and the data can be assessed in a variety of ways: indeed one version of AMOS has 24 different fit indices, and most published papers report three or four different indices (see Jaccard and Wan, 1996). They fall into three broad categories:

- *Discrepancy-based indices*. The commonest index is the chi-square value, which is reported by every SEM programme. It indicates the goodness of fit between the observed covariance matrix from the data and the predicted covariance matrix from the hypothesized model. A small value of chi-square indicates a close fit between the two, and suggests that the hypothesized model is a good one. However, there are problems with the chi-square index since a large value need not mean that the model is poor because chi-square varies with sample size.

- *Relative fit compared to a null model*. As well as the hypothesized model, most of the SEM programs also fit a **null model**, which assumes that all the covariances among the observed variables are zero (this is often called the independence model). A number of fit indices have been developed that adjust the chi-square value for a specific model according to how much better it is than the null model and also take into account the complexity of the model (the number of parameters needed to achieve fit). One of these is the **non-normed fit index** (NNFI), whose values can vary between 0 and 1, and a value above 0.95 is regarded as acceptable (Bentler and Dudgeon, 1996).

- *Relative fit adjusted for the complexity of the model*. Complex models will fit data better than simple models, and some indices assign a cost to this extra complexity: in other words, they reward **parsimony**. On these criteria a model that achieves a reasonable fit with few parameters is better than a model that gives a marginally better fit achieved at the cost of a large increase in complexity. One of these measures is **RMSEA** (the root mean squared error of approximation), which adjusts chi-square according to the degrees of freedom of the model and the sample size.

The fifth step in SEM after examining the fit of a particular model is to *consider alternative models*, and it is most unusual to fit only a single structural equation model to a set of data. Almost all SEM work involves modifying the model in some way, either to improve the fit of an initial model or to test hypotheses derived from theory. The logic of SEM is strictly confirmatory, since the method requires that the researcher define a set of observed and latent variables together with a hypothesized model for the relationships among them. However, many tests of theoretical propositions involve comparisons between models rather than fitting a single model. We have already considered two examples in this chapter. Example 10.3 presented three models of the impact of stakeholder relationship management on corporate financial performance. Testing these alternatives involves fitting a sequence of models. Similarly, mediational models (see earlier section) can most effectively be tested by comparing a model including direct paths with a model that fixes the value of all these paths to zero. Model comparison tests like these are done by chi-square difference tests, the difference in goodness of fit between two models, in exactly the same way that we have seen already in hierarchical regression.

However, most researchers find that their *a priori* model does not fit the data to an acceptable degree and so they often undertake an exploration of alternatives using **modification indices**. The **Lagrange multiplier (LM) test** corresponds to forward stepwise regression, and tests what would happen if each one of the fixed parameters in the model were to be set free. The second type of index is called the Wald test and this corresponds to backwards stepwise regression. It tests which parameters currently included in the model have a value so small that they could be dropped from the model. The logic behind these procedures is similar to that used in the stepwise options available in the methods for multivariate analysis of causal models among observed variables (e.g. multiple regression and logistic regression). They involve a search through fixed parameters to see what the effect would be if fixed parameters were allowed to be free.

For example, the CFA model in Figure 10.9 (repeated from Figure 10.2) has six free parameters representing the loading of each observed variable on a single latent common factor. However, there are also an additional seven fixed parameters, which are implied by the model in Figure 10.2. They are shown by dotted lines in Figure 10.9: six additional arrows linking observed and latent variables, and also a double headed arrow between the two common factors indicating a correlation between them. There are even more implied fixed parameters, because the model also assumes that the specific factors to the left of the diagram are uncorrelated with each other. We have not drawn the double headed arrows for those because it would complicate the diagram considerably.

If the hypothesized CFA model does not fit the data well, the researcher might decide that at least one of the items should load on both common factors, and thus relax the constraint of a fixed zero loading for that path. If this process is guided firmly by conceptual considerations, there could be a strong justification; but blind searching through multiple alternative models in the hope of finding one that is 'best' violates both the statistical requirements that underpin the SEM method and also the principles of sound research practice that we have described in this book. Theory development should be guided both by conceptual rigour and by the weight of evidence from data. Holding to theory regardless of what the data say is not good practice; but neither is blindly following data regardless of the theoretical justification.

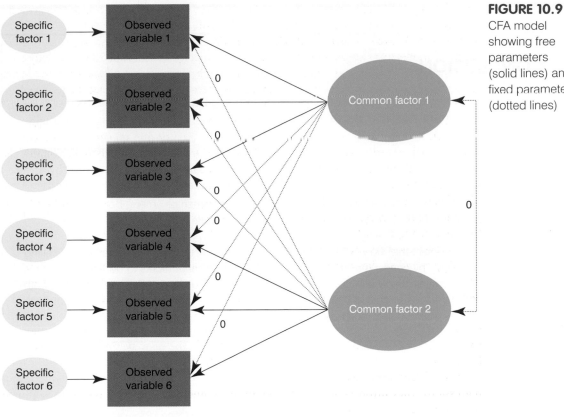

FIGURE 10.9
CFA model showing free parameters (solid lines) and fixed parameters (dotted lines)

NOTE: THE VALUE OF EACH OF THE FIXED PARAMETERS IS SET TO ZERO IN THIS MODEL.

Advanced features   The SEM area of statistics is developing rapidly, and each update of the programs adds features and options:

- New goodness of fit indices for assessing the quality of models.
- New estimation procedures for fitting the parameters in a hypothesized model.
- Additional methods for the preliminary assessment of data characteristics before fitting SEMs.
- New models, e.g. for analysing multiple groups, for longitudinal designs, for testing differences in the means of latent variables, for complex sampling designs.

Going further   Researchers interested in keeping up with developments in SEM can go to the software distributors' websites listed at the start of this section. There is also a journal *Structural Equation Modeling* published by Taylor and Francis, but be aware that the articles here tend to be quite technical.

CONCLUSION

This chapter has introduced a number of methods for analysing the complexity of the world of business and management using quantitative data:

 Methods for working with complex concepts which often cannot be measured directly but have to be inferred from observed variables.

 Conceptual introduction to ways of modelling causal relationships among both observed and latent variables, particularly using structural equation models.

The most important point that we would like to make is that the process of multivariate model fitting must be guided firmly by conceptual considerations. Fitting statistical models to quantitative data is not an automated process of blindly finding the 'best' model. Good quality models are grounded both in rigorous conceptualization guided by existing literature and also in an evidence base of data collected according to sound design and measurement principles.

FURTHER READING

Blunch, N.J. (2008) *Introduction to Structural Equation Modelling Using SPSS and AMOS*. London: Sage.
This is a readable book, which introduces both SEM but also key concepts underlying measurement models (such as reliability). The examples are based on the AMOS package, which is now an add-on to SPSS; but could easily be adapted for use with other software.

Hair, J. F., Black, B., Babin, B., Anderson, R. E. and Tatham, R. L. (2008) *Multivariate Data Analysis*, 7th edn. Upper Saddle River, NJ: Prentice Hall.
This too is an excellent book on the use of multivariate methods in social science. The strength of the book is the applications it uses as illustration of the methods covered, and the focus on preparatory work to examine the properties of the data first before embarking on complex multivariate analysis.

Tabachnick, B.G. and Fidell, L.S. (2012) *Using Multivariate Statistics*, 6th edn. Boston, MA: Pearson Education.
This is an excellent and thorough text on multivariate statistical methods for social science researchers. Its approach is practical rather than theoretical, and the authors cover all of the methods described in this chapter as well as others not covered here. For each method, they give its rationale, practical guidelines about how to use it, worked examples using a variety of statistical packages, and show how to present the results of analysis.

WRITING MANAGEMENT AND BUSINESS RESEARCH

11

LEARNING OBJECTIVES

- To develop personal strategies for writing.
- To appreciate different structures for writing.
- To recognize the needs and interests of different audiences.
- To develop awareness of the requirements of different forms of output.
- To develop skills in publishing and disseminating research.

INTRODUCTION

This book has examined the various ways of designing and conducting research: it has looked at how to choose and use the methods that will provide the relevant data; it has considered how to analyse, interpret and use data; and it has offered insights into the political and ethical sides of doing research. This last chapter, then, focuses on how to write up research findings, and how and where to disseminate research.

There are many potential audiences, including tutors, clients, academics, policy-makers and the general public, and these audiences correspond roughly to the stakeholders that we discussed in Chapter 4. However, as there are many ways of effecting dissemination, we think it is important to consider communication early in the research process, preferably at the design stage. Although the written word dominates in the form of reports, articles and books, there are other important ways of getting the message across including presentations, videos and media interviews. A dissemination strategy, therefore, may include the use of different media at different points of time during the research, and after it has been completed.

We start the chapter with writing, and argue that there are generic skills that apply to any context. We then look at different forms of output, concentrating on how evaluative criteria vary, and discuss the stylistic differences between, for example, positivist and constructionist forms of research. Third, we provide guidance on the main elements of a report or dissertation, including literature reviews; fourth, we consider different audiences and the media available for communication; and finally we draw the threads together by looking at dissemination strategies.

THE SKILLS OF WRITING

The main aim in writing about research is to communicate with an audience, and to persuade them that the research is serious, important and believable. This means that it is important to be clear about the potential *readership* to which the paper or report is aimed. One technique used by a number of successful authors is to hold two or three 'typical' readers in mind while writing something. Gerry Johnson, the lead author of a best-selling book on corporate strategy (Johnson, Scholes and Whittington, 2008), writes his books with two imaginary individuals in mind: a lecturer at Kingston University called Theresa, and a third year student called Charles who is bright but more interested in rugby than his studies. These imaginary people help him to focus on the potential readership and also to communicate with co-authors about the appropriateness of new material in new editions (personal communication).

A second point is that readers will be more interested in the document if it relates to their ongoing concerns and this is where Huff (1999) stresses the importance of trying to link into an existing 'conversation'. Thus it is important to start a journal article with a summary of the main debate that has appeared up to that point, and upon which the current paper intends to build. Here the researcher needs to be aware of who are the main contributors in the field. Similarly, when writing a client report it is important to start with a brief statement of how the client has articulated the problem.

Third, in order to increase the credibility of the research there are a number of rhetorical strategies that may be used in written accounts. Positivist authors often write in the third person so that the researcher seems distanced from the research, and this gives an impression of greater objectivity; they may cite papers by famous authors in order to give credibility to the present research; and present the research as a linear process that was designed in advance and executed precisely to plan. On the other hand, constructionist authors often go to great lengths to be reflexive, indicating their engagement with the research setting and their influence on the research material; they often write up the research as it actually happened, indicating the problems that they encountered along the way, and how they tackled (sometimes heroically) these problems.

Writing as a habit

Woody Allen, the American comedian, director and author, has remarked that 90 per cent of the success in writing lies in getting started and finished on time, and the bit in the middle is easy. There is a key implication: don't wait until the end before starting to write. Get into the writing habit from the beginning, and sustain it throughout the research. Normally, reviews of the literature and research designs should be written up in the early stages of the research and 'banked' for later use. Of course they will have to be edited and rewritten later on, but they provide critical foundations upon which other parts can build. This ability to edit material is one of the joys of computers – which were not available when the authors of this book wrote their doctoral theses in longhand!

Most people experience writing blocks at some stage or another: the blank page can be exhilarating or intimidating. Many different strategies can be adopted to overcome writing blocks. The American author John Steinbeck (1970) adopted an interesting strategy when writing *East of Eden*. He always began his daily sessions by writing a letter to his editor about what he planned to say that day. The letters were written on the left-hand pages of a large note book (and not sent); on the right-hand pages he wrote the text of the book. He found this a useful way of starting his thought processes, and overcoming his own writing block.

Various academic authors offer advice on how to get into the flow of writing, including creating sufficient time and space for writing, setting modest goals on a daily basis and providing rewards for oneself, such as coffee breaks or Liquorish Allsorts after the next paragraph or section is completed (Saunders, Lewis and Thornhill, 2009). Murray and Moore (2006) emphasize the need to take time out from writing for exercise or social activities: it's fine if the writing is flowing, but if not, take a break and do something completely different for an hour or so.

Developing structures

It is also important to develop an appropriate structure for the report or thesis, which can be done in a number of ways. First, an *emergent* structure comes from writing anything in order to get started, and once you have worked out what you are trying to say, deleting the initial paragraphs that may be a lot of rubbish. A *patchwork* structure comes from writing self-contained chunks of text and then starting to stitch them together into a coherent narrative. A *planned* structure involves trying to work out all the main sections and paragraphs in advance.

A good way of starting the planning process is to develop a 'mind-map'. This has the advantage that no commitments to linearity are required: one can simply type in ideas and then experiment to see how they group together. We used this in an early plan for this chapter (see Figure 11.1).

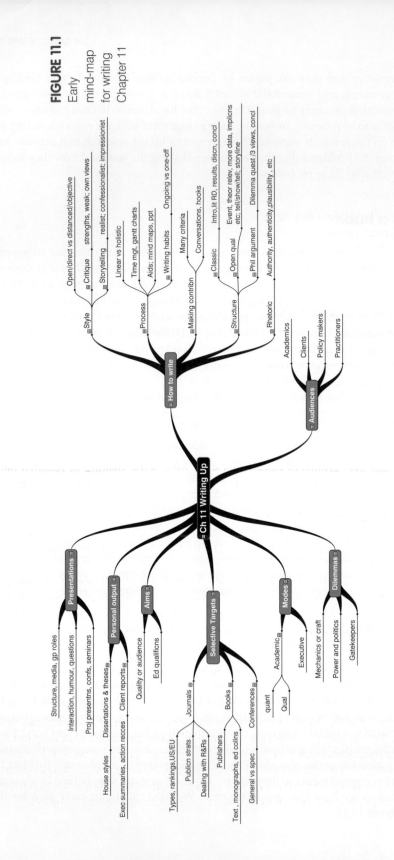

FIGURE 11.1
Early mind-map for writing Chapter 11

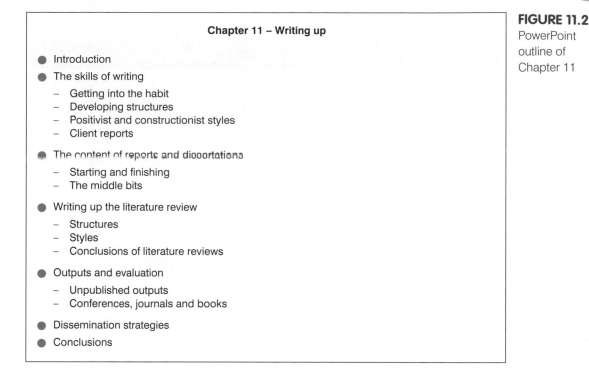

FIGURE 11.2
PowerPoint outline of Chapter 11

Mind-maps can help groups of researchers share their sense-making of research data, and they are also useful for authors when planning books and reports. But there is a limit to the amount of information that can be displayed on one page, and so it is generally best to move to PowerPoint in order to work out the details of a report. Figure 11.2 shows a PowerPoint slide that provides the overall structure for the current chapter. The first slide summarizes the main subheadings, and then later slides (not shown) provide further detail on each of the sections.

It should be noted that this PowerPoint screen performs an intermediate stage between the mind-map and the final version of the chapter, because once we started to write we realized that we needed to make some further changes both to the subheadings and the content in order to make the argument flow. This flexibility is important; it is also a good way of communicating when you are trying to write with other people.

Generic structures for writing papers and research reports

Although research papers and reports conducted under different traditions may look quite different, there is much consistency in the basic issues and topics that they need to cover. The main differences come in the style and language used. In Table 11.1, we have therefore summarized the main questions that need to be answered in academic research in column 1. In the other two columns we summarize the way each of these questions gets operationalized, respectively in positivist or constructionist research reports.

TABLE 11.1 Typical report structures

Principle	Positivist Research	Constructionist Research
What is the research about?	Abstract.	Abstract.
What is already known?	Review of literature and previous studies.	Review of literature and relevant theories.
What is new about this study?	Statement of aims and hypotheses.	Identify the gap or research question(s).
How was the research done?	Description of procedures, samples and methods used.	Research design and methods.
What did it find out?	Data tables and summary of results.	Descriptions of data and interpretations.
What are the implications?	How far the hypotheses are supported.	How the data adds to existing theory.
Next steps?	Limitations and suggestions for future research.	Limitations and suggestions for future research.
Addenda	References, questionnaires, etc.	References, sample transcripts and analytic process.

As can be seen, there is much similarity in the earlier and later parts; the main differences come in the articulation of the central research questions and in the handling of data. Although most positivist studies follow the list of subheadings in column 2, there is often more flexibility in how qualitative reports and client reports are presented, especially in the presentation of qualitative data. In this case there is an opportunity for the researcher to exercise some creativity depending on the needs of the situation, the actual research and the audience. Hence we provide further comment below on ways of presenting qualitative data.

Where the research makes deliberate use of mixed methods the normal solution is to structure the outer parts of the report according to whichever method is dominant, and then to present the data in two separate sections. Alternatively, where qualitative data is used to explain *why* various quantitative results are obtained, then it may be appropriate to present some qualitative data in relation to each of the quantitative hypotheses. However, as we said in Chapter 3, it is important to articulate in the research design/methodology section how the qualitative and quantitative data are supposed to be supporting each other.

Client reports

Reports of projects conducted for clients usually have a different structure to the more academic reports and dissertations. Essentially, these need to be shorter, with more emphasis

TABLE 11.2 Generic structure for a client report

Sections of Client Report	Contents
Executive Summary	Aims, conclusions and recommendations.
Introduction	What is the problem, and what are the potential solutions? How will this study help?
Methodology	What data was gathered, and from what sources?
Results	Tabulations and presentation of data.
Discussion and Conclusions	Using the results to evaluate alternative actions.
Recommendations	List of practical recommendations.
Appendices	References and background data.

on the identification of the problem and the practical courses of action to be taken. There needs to be some explanation of methodology because this has a bearing on the quality of evidence underpinning the recommendations; but there is much less need for a literature review, which might be restricted to half a dozen references that have informed both the focus and methods of the study. In Table 11.2 we summarize the elements that will typically feature in a client report.

THE CONTENT OF REPORTS AND DISSERTATIONS

Following Woody Allen's comment, we will begin with 'starting and finishing', and then move on to discuss how to craft the middle bits of research reports.

Starting and finishing

Most experienced writers and editors agree that the start and end of a report or article are crucial. Reviewers, examiners and editors often form provisional judgements by reading the first and last pages, on the assumption that if the authors are able to communicate their message clearly in the first page, the rest of the document will be of similar quality; but if the initial page is unclear or confusing this bodes badly for the rest of the document.

Locke and Golden-Biddle (1997) provide a very interesting analysis of the way successful academic authors structure their introductory paragraphs. They conducted an analysis of 82 papers that had appeared in two leading journals (*AMJ* and *ASQ*) over the 20 preceding years and identified two factors that were always present. First, the authors provided a coherent overview of the previous literature using one of three strategies: they either produced *progressive coherence*, showing how concepts and literature developed cumulatively over time; or *synthesized coherence*,

TABLE 11.3 Academic introductions (after Golden-Biddle and Locke, 1997)

		Finding the new niche		
		New data	New theory	New methods
	Progressive coherence	13	18	3
Past research	Synthesized coherence	11	11	3
	Non-coherence	6	13	2

where they identify links between streams of research or theory that have not been spotted before; or *non-coherence*, where the field is characterized by arguments, debates and general fragmentation. Second, authors try to identify a new niche that demonstrates how they can add to previous research. Again, three methods appeared to be most commonly used, either through introducing new data, or new theory or new research methods.

In Table 11.3 we show the frequency with which different strategies were adopted in the 82 papers. As can be seen, the most common way of developing a new niche was to claim that new theory was being introduced, and the least common way was through introducing new methods. Progressive coherence was the most common way of characterizing past research, and this was most likely to be linked to the introduction of new theory.

It is possible to summarize the four key elements that need to be in the introduction of an academic paper as follows:

1 Establish the *theoretical field* and why this particular topic is important.
2 Summarize *previous research*.
3 Identify the *niche*. What is the problem/question that is to be addressed?
4 State what the present study will *contribute* to this problem/question, and how it is tackled in this paper.

Exercise 11.1 provides an opportunity to test out skills in writing a credible academic introduction. This can be done either individually, or as a small group exercise.

EXERCISE
11.1

Writing academic introductions

The following text was written on the back of a bottle of **pesto**.[1] Try to rewrite this piece of text as if it is the introduction of an academic article. You will have to use your imagination with regard to references. Use the four key elements listed above as the basic structure, and limit the introduction to a maximum of two paragraphs.

(Continued)

---

[1]Thanks to Nickie Hedge for drawing our attention to this example.

(Continued)

Think about how you are going to characterize the past research and establish your niche using the categories in Table 11.3. Add a title that in your view encapsulates the essence of the paper. Present the finished product on a flip chart or computer projector for critique by tutors and colleagues!

Pesto is a mainstay of Italian cooking; yet surprisingly it is little known in the UK. The inviting ease with which *Sainsbury's Pesto* can be used belies the difficulty with which it is made. The fresh basil that gives the sauce its distinctive colour and flavour is by far the most troublesome ingredient.

It occupies some of the most desirable real estate in Europe: the Ligurian hills that frame the Italian Riviera. Here, a unique mix of soil and sea breezes infuse the herb with an aroma and texture unmatched in any other part of Italy. Throughout June and July the farmers brave the summer sun to survey the maturing crop. They wander from bush to bush, sniffing and chewing the young leaves until the day they are deemed to be perfect. Then, to ensure the leaves are harvested at their aromatic peak, the whole crop is picked within the space of a few days.

In the above exercise we suggested writing a title that captured the essence of the paper. Good titles are short and memorable. In academic work it is very common to write a title in two parts, separated by a colon. The first part summarizes the topic of the research, and the second part indicates the argument that the paper is taking, or the question that it is addressing. Sample titles for the example in Exercise 11.1 might be: 'The marketing of exotic foods: the role of image and metaphor', or 'The globalization of food products: can local production methods survive?' Once you have a good title the rest should be easy! Conversely, lengthy and convoluted titles usually indicate that the author is unclear about the central topic and main message of his or her document. Given the importance of the title we would recommend developing a provisional title very early in the writing process. This should evolve as the work develops, but at any point in time it provides a point of reference against which to check the coherence of what has already been written.

Then we have the conclusions. As we have indicated in Table 11.1, the precise form of the conclusions may vary with different kinds of work: essentially they need to summarize the nature of the research, the main findings or contributions, provide an indication of the limitations of the work, and make suggestions for future research directions. Once again, they need to be clear and reasonably succinct (three or four paragraphs is enough for an academic paper, and 10 to 12 pages is enough for a doctoral thesis).

The middle bits

One recurrent dilemma with constructionist studies is about how to achieve a balance between qualitative data in the form of quotations, and discussions of the theoretical implications. Golden-Biddle and Locke (2007) suggest different strategies for combining data and theory. They distinguish between 'showing' the data/evidence and 'telling' what it means. Although some authors might be tempted to show large amounts of data, there is a limit to how far it will hold the attention of the reader without being put into the context of the wider narrative. Consequently one of the preferred strategies is to start with a theoretical point, then illustrate it with a quote, and then explain further what it all means (tell-show-tell). Another way of grabbing the imagination of readers is to provide a sneak preview of the data right at the start of the paper followed by setting the theoretical context, and then adding more sections of quotations and discussions (show-tell-show-tell).

WRITING UP THE LITERATURE REVIEW

Literature reviews have many features in common with other forms of writing, plus some features that are distinct, and hence there is some justification for considering the writing of literature reviews as the distinct art. In this section we cover five features of literature reviews that are often regarded as problematic: selection of material, different ways of structuring literature reviews, styles of presenting literature, the issue of criticality, and the endpoint of a literature review. In doing this we also build from Chapter 5 on conducting literature reviews.

Selection of source material

In most topics the quantity of existing literature is almost limitless, and the problem for the researcher is to decide which bits to include, and which bits to leave out. We have two main criteria that can determine the selection of literature for the review: importance and relevance. By *importance*, we mean the extent to which a particular book or article is regarded as central to the particular field you are working on. A quick search on GoogleScholar, using the title or central topic of your work as the search item, will normally yield a list of the key books and some of the main articles that have been cited by others. Similarly, searches through ISI Web of Science using the same search terms will yield the primary journal articles that have addressed the topic. Since these indexes accumulate over time, the books and articles that come to the top of the list will be the older classical works. A few of these will have to be mentioned, but not too many, because they will not take account of more recent developments in the field.

For example a search within GoogleScholar using the term 'absorptive capacity' leads immediately to the paper by Cohen and Levinthal (1990) with over 12,000 citations. So the work of Cohen and Levinthal would need to be mentioned in any literature review of absorptive capacity, perhaps with a few other foundational works on the subject. But the issue of whom else to include depends very much on the *relevance* to the line of argument that you are trying to develop in your work. If you consider that the foundational works on absorptive capacity pay too little attention to the inner processes of knowledge absorption and transformation, then you would need to continue through the work of Zahra and George (2002) and Todorova and Durisin (2007), and then follow up on more recent work that has cited these authors.

There is always a dilemma in deciding how many sources to quote in a literature review, and this partly depends on the depth versus breadth of coverage decision. In general, dissertations and theses need to demonstrate a wide coverage of literature so that you can demonstrate to tutors and examiners that you are fully aware of the breadth and range of the field, and the more focused coverage comes towards the latter end of the review. If you are seeking to publish an article in a journal then it is less important to demonstrate that you know everything about the field, because a general level of familiarity will normally be assumed by the reader, and unless you have anything especially new to say about the traditional literature it is likely that it will be seen as boring to have to wade through material that is familiar to everybody.

Structures

Structures refer to the way that you decide to marshal your literature, and the logic behind different ways of grouping the material. Although the framework of Locke and Golden-Biddle (1997) was derived from analysis of how the literature was presented in academic papers, the principles are still relevant to literature reviews conducted in dissertations. The idea of progressive coherence implies that literature should be organized within a timeline in order to demonstrate how the particular field evolved chronologically. Within the overall timeline there may be additional structures, such as characterizing different periods of time (for example, decades), or organizing discussion of the literature around a few key works or turning points.

With synthesized coherence you may try to demonstrate how two or three different perspectives on the subject may be combined because they are able to make up for the weaknesses of each other. On the other hand, non-coherence is most often associated with broad mapping exercises, which show, for example, that different disciplines have tackled a particular topic without demonstrating much awareness of what each other has been doing.

Stephen Allen was reviewing the literature on sustainability for his PhD. He identified seven main bodies of literature that had tackled the topic of sustainability, and which he characterized as follows: history; engineering; social movements; philosophy; economics; corporate social responsibility; and natural science (including ecology and botany). Since these were rooted in distinct disciplines with their own languages and internal debates, which paid minimal attention to writings in the other disciplines, this represented the literature as being non-coherent. He therefore decided to structure his review around the concepts of complexity, production of knowledge and scale – which enabled him to cut across the seven disciplinary areas.

EXAMPLE
11.1

Styles

With regard to style, there are still a few dilemmas, but there is a reasonable amount of agreement between authors and experts regarding what is desirable or less desirable in the writing of a literature review (see Table 11.4). First, it is important to avoid producing an 'annotated bibliography'. This usually takes the form of a series of paragraphs each of which starts with the names of the authors of the works cited, then summarizes the main points made by those authors, possibly with a brief critique of what they have said. Then in the next paragraph another author is introduced, and so on. The problem here is that there is rarely any clear linkage between successive paragraphs, and it is very difficult for the readers to identify the thread or argument that the author might be wishing to make. This is where a thematic structure to the literature review is preferable because it enables the links and relationships between the contributions to be identified.

Second, the references cited in the text need to be selected on the grounds of relevance. In other words each reference needs to make a distinct contribution to the general argument. It is generally best for authors/references to be mentioned in the middle of sentences, rather than being added at the end of a sentence to provide 'decoration' and an air of authority over what has just been said. In particular, when trying to develop an argument, it adds precision if you indicate the page numbers of the book or article where the particular elements of the argument are being made.

Third, and especially with constructionist research, we think it is important for the *author's voice* to be heard. In general it is better to summarize what you think other writers are saying, rather than simply dropping quotations from these writers into your text. There is no problem with the occasional quote, if it is central to your argument; but there is a danger if there are lots of short quotes from other authors that the review will seem like a patchwork quilt. There is also a dilemma here between depth and breadth. A good literature review will contain some of both. In other words, it will pay considerable attention to the more important and relevant works, but it will also demonstrate a reasonable awareness of related literature. Thus in a journal article one might expect to see five or six major pieces of work discussed in some depth, but with brief reference made perhaps to 50 or 60 other pieces of work. Of course, in longer documents such as dissertations or theses these numbers could be doubled or tripled.

Fourth, the literature review needs to demonstrate *criticality*. This does not mean being negative about everything that has previously been written. Far from it. It means demonstrating discernment about what is good and bad about the previous literature, and explaining why

TABLE 11.4   Stylistic features in literature reviews

Stylistic Features	Incorporate	Avoid
Framework for literature review	Thematic structure; progressive coherence.	Annotated bibliography; no links between paragraphs.
Selection of references	Clear relevance; functional; focused on argument development.	Decorative use; long strings that are vaguely linked.
Voice	Focus on key works; paraphrase others' arguments.	Patchwork of quotes from other authors.
Criticality	Explain what you like/dislike about other authors' work; build on others' critiques.	Sweeping dismissal of others' work.

you have reached these judgements. This is where the voice of you, the author, is particularly important. One dilemma with regard to critical literature reviews is where the critique should be placed within the overall structure. For example, if you have divided your topic into five major themes, then it might make sense to summarize the views and contributions of the main contributors to each theme, and then provide a critique at the end. But if there are major works contained within that overall theme, it may be better to interleave summaries of each work, with the main critiques produced by other people of that work, and then give your own view.

Conclusions of literature reviews

Sometimes, when a student or author gets to the end of the literature, they are often so exhausted, or short of time, that they simply present material and then move on to the next chapter. But the whole point of the literature review, other than demonstrating that you have in-depth knowledge of the field you are investigating, is to provide a platform for the work that is yet to come within the research project. This normally requires two elements. First, there needs to be a summary of the main features and arguments covered in the literature review, which may take the form of a diagram, a model, a table, a set of propositions, or hypotheses. Second, it is essential to identify some sort of gap, or weakness, or limitation in the previous work – which provides a justification for the work that you will be describing in the following chapters.

OUTPUTS AND EVALUATION

What, then, are the different forms of output that can be generated by research, and how may they be evaluated? To some extent, the answer builds upon the discussion of political issues in Chapter 4. Here we can distinguish three main types of output: *unpublished outputs*, such as reports and dissertations, which are generally targeted at a very small number of people, such as clients and examiners; *published outputs*, such as articles and books, which are intended to be widely disseminated; and *presentations*, which will be more ephemeral, mainly verbal, but probably backed up by PowerPoint slides.

Unpublished outputs: reports, dissertations and theses

Reports and dissertations are initially aimed at a small number of people, and although some may eventually get published, this is the exception rather than the rule. The immediate audience are often involved in the evaluation of the work (possibly supplemented by a presentation), and this will result in the award of grades and educational qualifications. We will start with research reports, and then discuss dissertations and theses.

Client reports   Projects are increasingly being incorporated into undergraduate and postgraduate degree schemes where small groups of students tackle a real problem located in a company or other organization. Normally a senior manager will act as the client and will make arrangements or appropriate access to people and documents. Since the client project is being conducted as part of an educational qualification, those working on the project will face two different kinds of evaluation. First, they must come up with results or recommendations that satisfy the client, and second, they must produce a written document that satisfies the academic tutors and examiners.

The written output from the project can seek to resolve the potential tension of expectations in three ways: (a) as a single report for the client, which has sufficient elements of reflection and critical thought to pass academic muster; (b) as a distinct consultancy report, which can be sandwiched within a more academic commentary that reflects on choices made, evaluates experiences, and develops relevant theoretical insights; or (c) as two completely separate documents tailored to the distinct needs of the client and the academic assessors. The first two options are pedagogically appealing, since they require integration between academic and practical discourse; and they are more feasible nowadays since a growing proportion of 'clients' are former students of business and management courses, and therefore have a greater understanding of the mutual contribution of theory and practice. Nevertheless, the third option is increasingly appealing since it provides greater clarity for students uncomfortable with ambiguous evaluation criteria.

Funded research projects   These are normally carried out by small teams of established academics working with research associates employed on fixed-term contracts. All of these projects require full reports at the end, which describe the conduct of the research, any problems encountered in doing it, and give an overview of the theoretical and practical contributions provided by the project. Research reports are sent out to external referees with expertise in the area of the project for evaluation, and who will be expected to comment on the degree to which the project achieved its original objectives, whether any departures from the original proposal have been adequately justified, and the quality of the public academic output. In general the academic output needs to include conference papers, journal papers (at least under submission), and perhaps an edited book.

Dissertations   For BBA and Masters' courses the required dissertations are often longer than research reports (perhaps 10,000 to 20,000 words), and are the product of individual rather than group efforts. In most cases they are written solely for academic evaluation, and therefore do not have the potential competing objectives of project reports. In general it is worth following the suggested report structure in Table 11.1, although there is less of a requirement to demonstrate theoretical contribution than in the case of a doctoral thesis (see below). Evaluative criteria will depend both on the nature of the dissertation, and on the formal expectations of tutors and examiners. A general guide to criteria is given in Table 11.5, which summarizes seven features that should normally be present in a good dissertation. The list is based on Bloom's taxonomy of educational objectives (Bloom and Krathwohl, 1956) and is organized hierarchically in terms of the increasing complexity of each feature. Thus, demonstrating knowledge of the field and comprehension of the problem to be addressed are relatively basic elements; the evaluation of literature and ideas, and clear argumentation are regarded as more complex processes, which will therefore gather more brownie points when the dissertation is being evaluated.

There is some uncertainty at the moment about whether it is more important for management dissertations to demonstrate evidence of application or analysis. As we noted in

TABLE 11.5 Hierarchy of evaluative elements

7) *Quality of argumentation*
6) *Evaluation of concepts*
5) *Synthesis of ideas and concepts*
4) *Analysis of data and evidence*
3) *Application of theories/ideas to practise*
2) *Comprehension of the problem addressed*
1) *Knowledge of the field*

Chapter 1 there is a long-standing debate in the UK about whether management education should emphasize practical or academic training (Whitley, Thomas and Marceau, 1981), and this has translated into the debate between mode 1 and mode 2 forms of research (Tranfield and Starkey, 1998; Huff, 2000). The rise of the MBA puts greater emphasis on practical relevance and application; while academics are likely to value the analytic and evaluative elements of the dissertation. Since most degrees are awarded by academics, it is prudent to include some elements of analysis and synthesis in the work submitted.

Doctoral theses These are similar to Masters' dissertations in that they require a synthesis of ideas and data. In addition they must provide critical evaluation of relevant work, and demonstrate some kind of original *contribution* to the field. This contribution can be provided in three main forms: as new knowledge about the world of management (**substantive contribution**), as new theories and ideas (**theoretical contribution**), or as new methods of investigation (**methodological contribution**). In each case the contribution needs to be stated explicitly in the conclusions, and there also needs to be a clear link back to the early part of the thesis where the existing theories and methods were reviewed and evaluated. The theoretical contribution is most important, although it may be supplemented by each of the others.

The final award of a doctorate depends on the judgement of independent examiners (though practice in this respect varies surprisingly widely across Europe and North America), and it is very important that the right choices are made. Not only do the examiners need to be conversant with the field of study, but they should also be sympathetic to the worldview and methodology of the researcher. In this context it is worth developing a provisional list of examiners early on in the period of study, which gets refined and updated as the theoretical and empirical work develops. If the candidate has done sufficient networking through conferences and learned societies (such as the BAM or the AoM), he or she should be clear about who the best examiners would be.

Published outputs: conferences, journals and books

Nowadays it is essential for aspiring academics to get their research into the public domain. It is advisable to attempt publication from doctoral research while the work is being conducted, and occasionally it is possible to publish results from Masters' dissertations. In each of these cases the evaluation takes place before the final copy of the work is produced, and this acts as a filter on the quality of work that appears in public. In general, it is easier to get a paper accepted for a conference than for a journal, although significant hierarchies exist within both categories. Hence many researchers will take an incremental approach, submitting the results of their work to a conference, and then on the basis of feedback rewriting the paper and submitting it to a journal.

With some conferences it is possible to submit extended abstracts, which are evaluated by two or three referees, and the feedback from the referees can be incorporated into the paper before the conference takes place. Other conferences, such as the Academy of Management, will only accept submission of full papers, but in these cases the feedback from referees can be more focused, and this can be combined with discussion and feedback at the conference itself in helping the authors revise the paper for submission to a journal. As we have mentioned earlier, participation at conferences is very important for publishing contacts and building up research networks. However, conference papers *per se* have limited value for academics wishing to build up their careers or to gain tenure. The 'gold standard' is acceptance of papers in academic journals, and preferably the more highly rated ones.

As we noted in Chapter 4, there are very clear hierarchies in the reputation of different journals. Most countries have their own journal ranking systems,[2] and internationally the ISI Impact Factor and the Financial Times (FT) list are the most widely recognized indicators of quality. There are a number of factors that help to sustain the position of the top journals: they get large numbers of submissions and are therefore able to be very selective; people will usually only submit their very best work to the top journals; and the reviewing process is conducted with such rigour that the finally published paper is often significantly better than the initial submission. Our general advice regarding publication strategies is to aim for good journals wherever possible, and perhaps seek to submit papers with others (supervisors, examiners, people met at conferences) who have already been successful in getting published in the target journal.

It is important to understand the decision-making process for most journals, especially the role of referees. In Figure 11.3 we summarize the decision-making process of a typical journal. In this figure the numbers indicate the percentage of the original submissions that move to each of the successive stages. A number of papers (perhaps 60 per cent) will be rejected by the editors without being sent to the referees, a further number will be rejected after receipt of referees' reports, and most of the remainder will be sent an offer to revise and resubmit (R&R). It is extremely rare for a paper to be accepted outright by a good journal. For those lucky enough to have been sent an R&R, they then move into the critical stage of responding to the criticisms/recommendations of reviewers and the editors. Frequently the reviewers will provide conflicting advice, and a good editor will notice the conflicts and provide guidance on which lines to follow.

The resubmitted paper needs to be accompanied by a letter to the editor (and referees) explaining how recommendations have been implemented and providing a rationale where the authors feel that the recommendations are not appropriate. Sometimes these letters can

---

[2]The dominant system in the UK is provided by the Association of Business Schools (the ABS List). It rates over 2,000 journals from 1 up to 4, and the list is updated biennially in April.

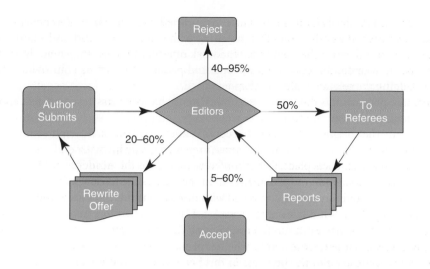

FIGURE 11.3
Flowchart of journal decision-making

get very lengthy, perhaps 10 to 20 pages, but long letters can irritate editors and make it difficult for referees to see how their suggestions have been implemented – so the advice is to deal with every point the editors and reviewers have made, but only discuss the critical issues at any length.

Finally there is the possibility of publishing a book. Although in some subjects, such as history, it is quite normal to turn theses into books, this is relatively rare in the management field. Publishers have a preference for textbooks and handbooks because they have more general and sustained appeal than research monographs. In order to develop a book proposal with broad appeal, it is generally necessary to collaborate with other scholars who can provide complimentary perspectives, and this may not be a sensible option until several years after the PhD is completed. In the short term there are few academic credits for publishing books in the management field. Nevertheless, in the longer term they can contribute substantially to personal reputation and visibility, and this can also be measured in terms of 'hits' in the ISI index, or Google Scholar.

Peters and Waterman (1982) are reputed to have received royalties of $1.8 million in the first year of their book's publication, and Mintzberg (1973) did well out of his book (unusually, based on his PhD thesis). But these are the exception: for most people the direct financial rewards are not great. Fortune is most likely to follow the fame of being a published author, and academic careers depend on both the reputation of the publisher and the quality of the reviews that ensue. The nice thing about books is that it is usually possible to develop ideas over a period of time with the help of the publisher. Once again contacts with publishers are most easily established at conferences, where more of the relevant firms are represented.

PLAGIARISM

It is important to be aware of plagiarism, because over the years there has been a steady growth in cases of, and discussions about, plagiarism among students, which often reveal uncertainty and doubt about its significance. Acknowledging work and referencing sources means that the student or researcher knows his or her topic, has read and searched for sources, and knows how to acknowledge the work of others. Plagiarism generally involves presenting the work and ideas of other people and passing them off as your own, without acknowledging the original source of the ideas used.

Although plagiarism is not a new issue, its existence has been less easy to detect and it is only through the advent of information technology and packages such as Turnitin (www.turnitin.com) that plagiarism can be detected. While Internet search engines may make information easier to acquire, they also serve to provide students with endless sources of material from which to 'cut and paste'. What were once cases of minor infringements have become a problem of epidemic proportions (Duggan, 2006). Similarly, while there may be naïve use and sloppy referencing, Leask (2006) observes that there is a growth in deliberate plagiarism, especially as it relates to the Internet. He draws attention, however, to ambiguities that can exist between interpretations, arguing that plagiarism has different meanings, depending on the context; for example, whether plagiarism relates to research in the context of a report or an exam. For the progress of this book, discussions on plagiarism centre on conscious attempts by individuals to steal the work of others. Also under this heading are those without due recognition or reference, researchers who memorize ideas that originate from other sources, and after a degree of assimilation then go on to make the same very ideas their own and as a consequence fail to add an appropriate acknowledgement (Park, 2003). A screenshot of how Turnitin works is illustrated in Figure 11.4.

FIGURE 11.4

Turnitin
software

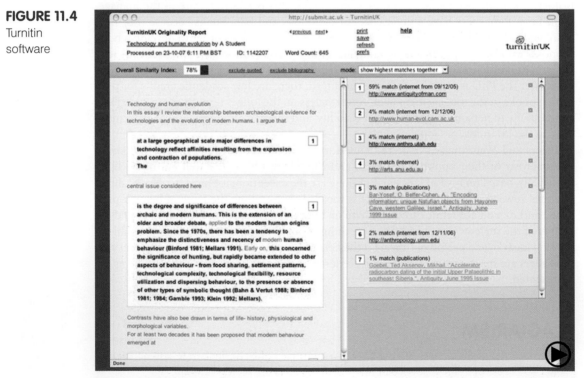

Examples of plagiarism

The recurring themes as to what constitutes plagiarism include, as we have already identified, copying another person's material without proper acknowledgement or reference, paraphrasing others without acknowledgement, thereby giving others the impression that the work represents your own original formulation, and of course buying ready-made material from professional writers. There is an increasing number of websites that offer such services and some of those being offered are extremely sophisticated. Payment relates to the level of degree but individual topics can be specific. Of course for those who have to undergo oral defence of their work the fact they are not attached to the literature soon means they are caught out, while references that are not in the university libraries also raise suspicion. In preparing this book use has been made of the work of others but references or acknowledgement will be seen in the text. Where researchers have provided data or material for incorporation or critical feedback obtained from colleagues they have been acknowledged by name at the front of the book. Park (2003: 475) synthesized four different forms of plagiarism found to be common among students:

1 Stealing material from another source and passing it off as their own, e.g.

- Buying a paper from a research service, essay bank or term paper mill (either pre-written or specially written).

- Copying a whole paper from a source text without proper acknowledgement.

- Submitting another student's work, with or without that student's knowledge (e.g. by copying a computer disk).

2 Submitting a paper written by someone else (e.g. a peer or relative) and passing it off as their own.

3 Copying sections of material from one or more source texts, supplying proper documentation (including the full reference) but leaving out quotation marks, thus giving the impression that the material has been paraphrased rather than directly quoted.

4 Paraphrasing material from one or more source texts without supplying appropriate documentation.

In order to avoid plagiarism students should ensure that they have clearly referenced where others' words and concepts have been used but also where others' ideas have influenced their thought process. This involves keeping up-to-date and precise references about where you have accessed material from, as even accidental plagiarism is considered a serious issue. Given the increase in plagiarism, universities are employing a zero-tolerance policy and students are increasingly being penalized over this issue. In an attempt to combat this problem, institutions are beginning to run courses that aim to educate students' to ensure that they are aware of what constitutes plagiarism. Given that plagiarism is a difficult and confusing area, it may be worthwhile checking if any such courses are available at your institution, where you will be most likely given clear examples of both deliberate and accidental plagiarism to ensure you are aware of the potential perils of careless referencing.

DISSEMINATION STRATEGIES

In the previous section we concentrated on dissemination mainly to academic audiences, and here we focus on other audiences, especially policy-makers and practitioners. We start with some general comments on making public presentations (although this applies equally to client and conference presentations), then discuss publishing in practitioner journals and making the best use of the public media.

We hesitate to provide much advice on the technicality of presentations since most of our students nowadays are very expert and professional at structuring and presenting data using PowerPoint. However, a common mistake is to provide too much material, especially in the form of slides, which puts the presenters under considerable time pressure and makes it extremely difficult for them to introduce any kind of interaction into the presentation. Our preference is to use a minimal number of slides (four or five for a ten minute presentation) to provide a basic structure, and then provide stories and vignettes to illustrate the points that are being made. If it is a team presentation, then people can take different roles according to their strengths: providing introductions, telling stories, making jokes, encouraging interaction and dealing with questions. If the presentation is being made by an individual, it is often worth recording the session because you may be so focused on providing answers to questions that you do not listen to what people are really saying!

Publications in practitioner journals are also important because they reach much wider audiences and demonstrate that you are engaging with potential 'users'. However, it can be very difficult to get into the famous practitioner journals, such as *Harvard Business Review*, *Sloan Management Review* or *California Management Review*, because the majority of papers are written by established academics, who may have been invited by the editors to submit because they have recently published some interesting material in a top academic journal. So, there is a virtual cycle operating, and it may be quite difficult to break in.

Another way to increase the exposure of one's research results is to approach the media. This can most easily be done through a press release, which is circulated to relevant newspapers and radio stations. Most universities and learned societies have considerable experience in dealing with the media and should be able to provide advice on whom to contact. In Example 11.2 we provide some general guidance on writing press releases.

EXAMPLE

11.2

Guidance on writing press releases

Press releases should be quite short, with a maximum of 600 words printed on two sides of a single sheet of paper. From the outset, you have to convince the reader that you have something interesting to say, perhaps a new fact about the world or a new way of looking at an important issue that has topical relevance. The press release should start with the conclusions, and then provide the supporting evidence – which is opposite to the normal way of writing academic papers, which end with the conclusions. In summary:

- Begin with a catchy headline.
- Provide a general statement that sums up the main finding.
- Distil into three or four points the essence of the research.

(Continued)

(Continued)

- Back up these points with facts and figures.
- Finish with the main policy implications or the 'way forward'.
- Add your contact details including e-mail address and phone numbers.
- Above all, keep the language intelligible and jargon-free.

Source: Personal communication from Romesh Vaitilingam: mailto:romesh@compuserve.com

Naturally there is much competition about getting access to the media and those academics who excel in this respect generally build up excellent relationships over time with journalists and make themselves available 24/7. There are also wider political implications of building up reputations: credit for research should not be taken for granted; it depends very much on how much the researcher is able to exploit his or her work through contacts, publications and other forms of dissemination. In Chapter 1 we used the story of Fleming's discovery of penicillin to illustrate some of the factors that underlie scientific discoveries. There is a sequel to that story, which relates to capitalizing on research (see Example 11.3).

The politics of reputations

EXAMPLE
11.3

Fleming discovered penicillin in 1923, but after undertaking only one experiment when he injected penicillin into a mouse and found that it disappeared from the blood stream within 30 minutes, he concluded that it would have little therapeutic application. Ten years later, Howard Florey and Ernest Chain, working with a team at Oxford, uncovered Fleming's description of penicillin following a systematic review of the literature (Macfarlane, 1985). Although the paper ignored previous literature on bacteriological inhibition and was vague about the chemical properties, it did note that the therapeutic potential might be worthy of further investigation. Florey and Chain concentrated on penicillin and eventually produced sufficient quantities to be able to demonstrate its life-saving properties. The results were published in a leading article in *The Times*. Following this, Sir Almroth Wright, the head of Fleming's department, saw an opportunity to increase charitable contributions to St Mary's, and wrote a letter to the editor claiming credit for penicillin for Fleming. The upshot was that Fleming was given the major credit in the form of 25 honorary degrees, 15 civic freedoms and 1140 major honours, despite the fact that he had conducted no further research during the 11 years following his experiment with the mouse.

It is important to develop a dissemination strategy at the outset of any funded research projects, and perhaps halfway through doing a doctoral thesis. This should normally include two or three conferences with a brief synopsis of the possible paper in each case, and potential target journals for the next phase of each paper. It is also worth thinking about potential media strategies, including developing press releases towards the end of the research period. As with all forms of publishing it is important to believe that you have something worth saying.

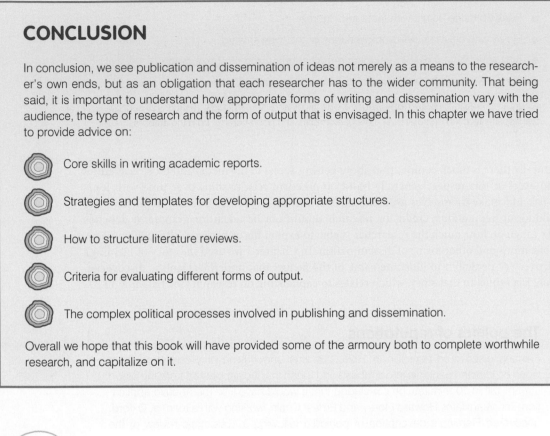

CONCLUSION

In conclusion, we see publication and dissemination of ideas not merely as a means to the researcher's own ends, but as an obligation that each researcher has to the wider community. That being said, it is important to understand how appropriate forms of writing and dissemination vary with the audience, the type of research and the form of output that is envisaged. In this chapter we have tried to provide advice on:

- Core skills in writing academic reports.

- Strategies and templates for developing appropriate structures.

- How to structure literature reviews.

- Criteria for evaluating different forms of output.

- The complex political processes involved in publishing and dissemination.

Overall we hope that this book will have provided some of the armoury both to complete worthwhile research, and capitalize on it.

EXERCISE
11.2

A Map out the ideas for your current research project using a computer programme such as MindGenius.

B Develop a short press release for either (1) the research project you are currently engaged upon, or (2) the piece of research that you developed for the *pesto* example above. Share the results with colleagues for critique and suggestions.

C Debate the proposition that: 'The public dissemination of social science results is harmful to the integrity and progress of research'. This can be done with different groups taking the *pro* or *anti* line.

FURTHER READING

Golden-Biddle, K. and Locke, K. (2007) *Composing Qualitative Research*, 2nd edn. London: Sage.
    A delightful book that looks at strategies for presenting qualitative research. It also provides good examples from the authors' own experiences of how to handle the complex politics of the review process when submitting papers to journals.

Hart, C. (1998) *Doing a Literature Review: Releasing the Social Science Research Imagination*. London: Sage.

The final chapter provides guidance on writing up literature reviews, with an emphasis on how to develop arguments and guidance on the elements that need to be included.

Murray, R. (2002) *How to Write a Thesis*. Milton Keynes: Open University Press.

This book provides lots of advice and guidance on the technicalities of writing including grammar, style and structure. It is also very helpful on the more strategic and emotional aspects of academic research and writing.

Phillips, E.M. and Pugh, D.S. (2005) *How to Get a PhD: A Handbook for Students and their Supervisors*, 4th edn. Maidenhead: Open University Press.

This is a thoughtful and practical book with lots of advice on how to manage and complete research work, especially at the doctoral level. Lots of examples and good humour from the authors.

ANSWERS TO EXERCISES

Chapter 1

Exercise 1.1
Classical: mapping organizational structures, observing and analysing physical work.
Human relations: talking to managers/employees about their likes and dislikes at work.
Decision theory: combining external and internal data to predict most favourable courses of action.
Work activity: observing what managers do, under different circumstances.
Competencies: comparing behaviours of supposedly good and bad managers to determine successful patterns.
Critical: concentrating on the maintenance of elites or the experiences of less powerful organizational members.
Process: focusing on episodes where learning takes place; following innovations over time.

Exercise 1.4
Here are some possibilities: systems view; management by walking about; delegation; participative management; management by objectives; just in time management; operations management ...

Chapter 2

Exercise 2.1
1 Positivist: 'empirically validating'.
2 Constructionist: 'holistic model'; 'perspectives'.
3 Constructionist: 'drawn from a longitudinal study'.
4 Positivist: 'has a stronger influence on'.
5 Positivist: 'when both LMX quality and empowerment were low'; 'both variables were high'; 'positive outcomes resulted'.

6 Constructionist: 'our longitudinal, inductive study'.
7 Strong constructionist: 'a discussion of the credibility performance'; 'the very structure of a corporation can be seen as ...'

Chapter 3

Exercise 3.1
Q1 What are the physical working conditions that contribute to increasing productivity of workers?
Q2 Research design includes incremental changes to supposed key variables; continual comparisons against predicted variable; and continuous observation.
Q3 The selection of workers is not random; there is no parallel control group; open observation takes place throughout, including interaction with the subjects.

Exercise 3.2
Q1 *History* and *maturation* threats were excluded in the design by repeated measurement, in the Greenfield site (condition A) and in the conventional site (condition C), over the period during which autonomous group working was introduced in condition B. Another potential threat to internal validity is that workers on the two sites might have competed with each other, but the researchers believed that this was unlikely due to the distance between the sites (250 miles apart), and the lack of contact between them.
Q2 In a design where random allocation to groups cannot be achieved, problems of *selection* may arise. The researchers checked for differences in production processes, in the ratio of men to women, and in length of service. Where differences

were noted they conducted supplementary analyses with sub-samples selected to be equivalent on these dimensions. There was also a danger that labour turnover could lead to missing values over time, and therefore to threats of *mortality*. Full inclusion or exclusion of leavers and joiners could be misleading because leavers and joiners may be different from those who stay throughout the study. To address this issue, the authors performed analyses to compare leavers and joiners to the group of those ever-present through the study. No differences were found; and the threat of mortality was therefore excluded.

Q3 A simple effect of work design would be shown by a pattern of results corresponding to the existence of autonomous workgroups, and unaffected by other factors such as site, shift or time. If autonomous group working is associated with higher job satisfaction, we would expect employees in conditions A_1, A_2, A_3, B_2 and B_3 to report higher job satisfaction than their counterparts in conditions B_1, C_1, C_2 and D_1.

Q4 More specific patterns of predictions are also possible. The first three patterns relate to cross-sectional comparisons between conditions at each of the three measurement occasions; while the second set of three patterns relate to predicted change or no change over time for conditions A, B and C where longitudinal data were available.

Time$_1$ comparisons: $A_1 > (B_1, C_1, D_1)$. Lack of difference between C_1 and D_1 would help to discount shift differences; while lack of difference between B_1 and D_1 would help to discount site differences. Full support for this predicted pattern would strengthen the case that differences between A_1 and the other conditions is attributable to autonomous group working.

(ii) *Time$_2$ comparisons: $(A_2, B_2) > C_2$.* An effect of autonomous group working would be shown by C_2 different from A_2 and B_2; while a lack of difference between A_2 and B_2 helps to rule out a shift effect.

(iii) *Time$_3$ comparisons: (A_3, B_3).* Similarly no difference between A_3 and B_3 would be expected if the only influence on job satisfaction is the form of work design.

(iv) *Change for condition A: (A_1, A_2, A_3).* No change over time in job satisfaction scores would be

expected, since autonomous group working was introduced in condition A at the outset of the study.

(v) *Change for condition B: $B_1 < (B_2, B_3)$.* Since autonomous group working was introduced in condition B after the first measurement occasion, an increase in scores would be predicted from B_1 to B_2 with no change subsequently.

(vi) *Change for condition C: (C_1, C_2).* Finally, autonomous group working was never introduced in condition C, and no change in scores would be expected from C_1 to C_2.

Exercise 3.3

Q1 The study involved gathering data from multiple sources over a period of time, and this was appropriate to studying the complex interrelationships and processes within the company. But also the feedback to key actors in the company also added to the validity of the conclusions we drew.

Q2 Because this is a unique study, the findings can only be generalized theoretically. That is, the case study needs to be able to demonstrate something about dynamic capabilities, knowledge management, or the relationship between the two of them, which supports, contradicts, challenges or adds to current theories in the literature.

Q3 They do make sense if you want to publish the results of the study in an academic journal. However, there are plenty of stories that came out of the study which can provide useful anecdotes to illustrate decision-making processes, group dynamics, etc. – which we had not expected in the first place, but which made good stories in their own right.

Exercise 3.4

Q1 This depends on whose version of grounded theory she follows. She uses open coding, which leads to a central category (see Chapter 7), but, there is no theoretical sampling, nor saturation. The interplay between external theory/literature and data is more complex than as outlined in Glaser and Strauss.

Q2 We think this deviation is quite appropriate, provided she is able to articulate what and why. Reasons include the constraints of the research setting/access, the nature of the theory she is looking at, and the conscious combination of theory development and deduction.

Exercise 3.5

	Ontology	Epistemology	Methodology	Method
Grounded theory	*	***	**	*
Unobtrusive measures		*		***
Narrative	*	*	**	*
Case method		*	***	*
Ethnography	*	**	**	
Critical realism	***	**	*	
Participant observation			**	*
Experimental design		***		
Falsification		***		
Theoretical saturation		*	**	**

Chapter 4

Exercise 4.2

Q1 Persist, ask for the manager; start observation of departments; phone your tutor; find the administrative head; say that you will return next morning.

Q2 Sign it; try to renegotiate; refuse to sign.

Q3 The dilemma is whether your commitment to confidentiality over-rides everything, or whether you have a duty to expose wrong-doing? How confident would you be in the quality of data?

Q4 Choices include full, partial or zero disclosure; buy time by arguing that you will need to reflect on this rather than giving an off-the-cuff opinion.

Q5 Confront him as soon as it first happens, or later on? Work with others to apply group pressure? Shop him to the tutor?

Chapter 11

Exercise 11.1

An example of a response that ticks most of the boxes!

Can English Basil be Romantic?

Supermarket shelf space is limited and merchandizers only select products based on brands they believe will sell. The field of consumer behaviour is important because it contributes significantly to understanding how product selection is made from the shelf in the supermarket. Early research has shown that the romantic association of characteristics of the country of origin influences consumer behaviour (Romeo and Juliet, 1574). More recently, it has been argued by Berlusconi (2010) that romantic associations are linked to linguistic origins. But the evidence to support this claim is thin, and furthermore, as pointed out by Sarkozy (2011), it is not clear which language provides a romantic association with which product.

This study focuses on the case of pesto because of its association with basil production, which takes place both in the romantic Ligurian hills of Italy and in the lesser-known valleys in the South Downs of England. Using matched English and Italian focus groups, we examine perceptions and stereotypes of basil quality in both countries. The study reported in this paper contributes to the field of consumer behaviour by identifying the interactions between product origin, language and romantic associations in both countries, and thus resolves the limitations in the work of Berlusconi (2010) and Sarkozy (2011).

Based on initial draft by: Andrei Kovacs, Fionnuala Runswick and Paula Higson on the Executive Doctorate, Cranfield Management School.

GLOSSARY

1-tailed test refers to a directional alternative hypothesis relative to the null hypothesis; a prediction of a positive association between variables, or that one group mean will be bigger than another

2-tailed test refers to a non-directional alternative hypothesis relative to the null hypothesis; association between variables may be either positive or negative, or that the means of two groups will differ in either direction

academic theory explicit ideas developed through exchanges between researchers to explain and interpret scientific and social phenomena

action research an approach to research that seeks understanding through attempting to change the situation under investigation

alternative hypothesis (H_1) position adopted during hypothesis testing if the evidence from data is strong enough to reject the null hypothesis (see also null hypothesis)

analysis of covariance (ANCOVA) a form of test of group differences on a continuous dependent variable which also includes continuous variables as predictors (covariates)

analysis of variance (ANOVA) a form of hypothesis test for comparing the means of two or more groups which may be classified on the basis of other variables

analytic theory a conceptual framework that seeks to explain why things happen

applied research studies that focus on tackling practical problems in organizations where the desired outcome will be knowledge about how to solve the problem

archival research collection and analysis of public documents relating mainly to organizational or governmental strategies

argument analysis an approach to the analysis of natural language data that identifies the data used in making claims, the premises made and the conclusions drawn by individuals about issues of relevance

association two variables are associated where knowing a value on one variable carries information about the corresponding value on the other; can be measured by a correlation coefficient

ATLAS.ti a software package that assists in the building and testing of theories through the creative assembly of qualitative analysis of textual, graphical and audio/visual data. Available from www.atlasti.com

auto-ethnography a form of insider research often conducted by those studying in the organization in which they work

axial codes codes that specify categories or sub categories where the dimensions are specified

bar chart a form of graphical summary for category scales, with bars whose length indicates the frequency of responses for each category

best practice research this seeks to identify practices in the most successful companies, which might be adopted in other companies.

beta weight see standardized regression weight

bias in sampling design, a biased sample is one that does not represent the features of the population from which it is drawn (see representativeness)

binomial distribution a form of reference distribution; the distribution of entities that are binary (present/absent, success/failure)

bootstrap a way of forming a reference distribution by repeated sampling from a specific dataset; used in hypothesis testing

CAQDAS computer assisted qualitative data analysis software

case method a research design that focuses in depth on one, or a small number of, organizations, events or individuals, generally over time

category scale a form of measurement scale where responses are recorded in a small number of discrete units, for example, makes of car purchased (cf. continuous scale)

causal model a class of multivariate models of the causal relationships among a set of variables which can be fitted to data

chi-square distribution a form of reference distribution; the distribution of variances used for testing hypotheses about spread

chi-square test a form of hypothesis test for testing association between two variables measured on nominal category scales

classical management theory a normative view of management, which stresses the key organizational functions that managers need to consider: forecasting and planning; organizing and increasing structure and capital; commanding and coordinating personnel and organizational efforts; ensuring control, such that personnel and activities conform to organizational protocol.

cluster analysis a general term for a range of statistical methods that serve to group data with similar properties into categories

cluster sampling a modification of random sampling where the population is first divided into convenient units, called clusters, and then all entities within a cluster are selected

cognitive mapping a method of spatially displaying data in order to detect patterns and by so doing better understand their relationship and significance

common factors a class of latent variables in a measurement model, which are assumed to account for the covariances among a set of observed variables (see also specific factors)

confirmatory factor analysis (CFA) a multivariate method for testing measurement models of the relationship between a set of observed variables and a hypothesized set of latent variables (see also exploratory factor analysis)

content analysis a relatively deductive method of analysis where codes (or constructs) are almost all predetermined and where they are systematically searched for within the data collected

contingency theory theoretical models which propose that variables have different effects depending on the context

continuous scale a form of measurement scale where responses are recorded in a large number of discrete units, for example, age recorded in months (cf. category scale)

convenience sampling a form of non-probability sampling design where entities are included in a sample on the basis of their ease of access

conversation analysis an analysis of natural language data used with naturally occurring conversations to establish linguistic patterns through the detailed examination of utterances

co-operative inquiry a form of action research where the research 'subjects' not only play a part in sense-making, but also are encouraged to determine the main questions to be researched

covariance a measure of association between two continuous variables expressed in the units of the measurement scales of the variables; its square root is the correlation coefficient

covariates variables measured on continuous scales, which are included as predictors in analysis of group differences

critical action learning a group-based inquiry that takes account of the viewpoint and feelings of members within a social and political context. The agenda and process are determined largely by members, rather than by academics

critical discourse analysis the analysis of natural language data, which emphasizes the power relations and ideologies that are both created and conveyed

critical incident technique a method of teasing out information often employed within interviews, which goes to the heart of an issue about which information is sought

critical management study a perspective on management research that concentrates on power relations, and particularly on the less powerful members of organizations

critical realism an approach to social research with an explicit ontological position, which combines features of both positivism and constructionism

critical theory a philosophy that critiques the structures and outcomes of capitalist society, and examines how powerful members of society maintain their dominance over the less powerful members

Cronbach's alpha coefficient an index of the internal consistency of a composite variable formed by combining a set of items; a common measure of reliability

cross-sectional surveys these usually involve selecting different organizations, or units, in different contexts, and investigating the relationships between a number of variables across these units

curvilinear relationship a relationship between two variables whose form changes according to the level of values on one variable; usually used to describe relationships that are positive in one part of the range and negative in another part (cf. linear relationship)

Decision Explorer a software program for collecting, conveying and managing ideas and other kinds of qualitative information that surround complex and uncertain situations. It is available from Banxia software (www.banxia.com)

decision theory a rational theory of management which assumes that optimum (if not ideal) decisions can be made through analysis of factual data, and this will lead to corporate success

degrees of freedom (*df*) the value that defines the shape of a standard reference distribution in hypothesis testing; for example, in testing association, *df* = sample size minus one

dependent variables the factors that research is trying to predict (see independent variables)

descriptive theory seeks to provide an accurate view of what actually takes place in organizations and the work that managers do

discourse analysis the analysis of natural language data that takes into account the broader social context in which the interview takes place

efficiency the extent to which a summary measure captures all the information within the data which is relevant to what is summarized

eigenvalues the term used in exploratory factor analysis for the summary measure of the amount of variance in the observed variables accounted for by a factor

embedded case a case within a larger case, for example, the Accident and Emergency Department within a hospital that was the primary case

emic insights into communities, societies or organizations as seen from the perspective of insiders

engaged research involves close collaboration between academics and practitioners in determining the research aims, its implementation, and the practical implications

enlightenment model an approach to social policy formulation, which engages those likely to be affected by the policy both in the research process and in determining its consequences

epistemology views about the most appropriate ways of enquiring into the nature of the world

ethnography approaches to research and data collection that emphasize gaining access to the perspectives and experiences of organizational members

etic insights into communities, societies or organizations as seen from the perspective of outsiders

everyday theory the ideas and assumptions we carry round in our heads in order to make sense of everyday observations

exogenous variables those variables that are part of a multivariate model, but whose causal influences are taken as given and do not form part of the model itself

experimenter effect the idea that the act of observing or measuring any social process actually changes that process

exploratory factor analysis (EFA) a multivariate method for fitting measurement models, which describes the covariances among a set of observed variables in terms of a set of latent variables (see also confirmatory factor analysis)

exploratory surveys these are similar to cross-sectional surveys, but tend to focus on identifying patterns within the data through the use of factor analysis or principal components analysis (see Chapter 10)

external validity whether the results of the research can be generalized to other settings or contexts

factor loading the weight allocated to the path between a latent variable and an observed variable in a measurement model

factual surveys involve collecting and collating relatively 'factual' data from different groups of people

falsification a research design that seeks evidence to demonstrate that the current assumptions or hypotheses are incorrect

F-distribution a form of reference distribution; the distribution of ratios of variances used for testing hypotheses about group differences in means

feminism a philosophy that argues that women's experiences and contributions are undervalued by society and by science; also an emancipatory movement to rectify these inequalities

financial databases archives of records about companies or other entities, which contain financial data, such as income data, cash flow, profit and loss, share prices

focused codes codes that are directed, conceptual and analytical

frequency distribution a summary representation of a sample of data containing the number of responses obtained for each alternative on the measurement scale

generalizability the extent to which observations or theories derived in one context can be applicable to other contexts

generalized linear models a class of multivariate statistical models within which the relationships between DVs and PVs are linear, and DVs can be expressed through a transformation called a link function; it includes multiple regression analysis, ANOVA and logistic regression

goodness of fit a summary measure of the discrepancy between observed values and the fitted values derived from a hypothesized model

grand theory a coherent set of assumptions intended to explain social or physical phenomena. May or may not be empirically testable

grounded analysis the linking of key variables (theoretical codes) into a more holistic theory that makes a contribution to knowledge in a particular field or domain

grounded theory an open (and inductive) approach to analysis where there are no *a priori* definitional codes but where the structure is derived from the data and the constructs and categories derived emerge from the respondents under study

hermeneutics a philosophy and methodology about the interpretation of texts. Stresses that textual materials should be understood in the context within which they are written

hierarchical regression a form of multiple regression analysis, which involves entering predictor variables sequentially in blocks

histogram a form of bar chart for continuous scales, where scale points are first grouped together and the length of bars indicates the frequency of responses for each category

human relations theory assumes that performance of both individuals and organizations is dependent on the commitment and involvement of all employees, and hence managers need to foster positive relationships with, and between, employees

hypothesis testing the process of making inferences about populations based upon data drawn from samples

identifiability the characteristic of a hypothesized model defined by the relationship between the number of parameters in a model to be estimated and the information available to do it; a model is identified if there are fewer parameters to be estimated than there are items of information available

independent variables the factors that are believed to cause the effects that are to be observed; also called predictor variables (see dependent variable)

in-depth interview an opportunity, usually within an interview, to probe deeply and open up new dimensions and insights

inference drawing conclusions about a population based on evidence from a sample

inferential surveys surveys that are aimed at establishing relationships between variables and concepts

interaction effects where the effect on a variable depends on the context defined by another variable

internal realism a philosophical position which assumes that reality is independent of the observer, but that scientists can only access that reality indirectly

internal validity assurance that results are true and conclusions are correct through elimination of systematic sources of potential bias

interquartile range see mid-range

interval scale a form of continuous scale that has no true zero point, so that ratio calculations are not meaningful, for example, temperature (cf. ratio scale)

interview bias occurs when the process of questioning influences the interviewee's response

Kruskal–Wallis test a form of hypothesis test for comparing two or more groups that uses rank-order data

Lagrange multiplier test a form of modification index in SEM that indicates the value of a fixed parameter if it were to be set free

latent variables a class of variables within a multivariate model, which are not measured directly but are inferred from observed variables

leading question a form of wording of a question that leads the respondent to give the answer preferred by the questioner

likelihood ratio chi-square an index of the overall quality of a model fitted by the maximum likelihood method; used in logistic regression analysis

Likert scale a form of ordinal category scale for measuring attitudes from very positive to very negative

linear relationship a relationship between two variables where, as values on one variable increase, there is a proportional increase in values on the other (cf. curvilinear relationship)

local knowledge ideas and principles that are relevant to the setting of a particular organization or social setting, but which may not apply in other contexts

location a characteristic of a set of data that summarizes where the data are located on the measurement scale; measured by the mode, median, mid-mean or mean

logistic regression a form of multivariate analysis of causal relationships among observed variables where the dependent variable is measured on a binary category scale

Mann–Whitney U test a form of hypothesis test for comparing two groups that uses rank-order data

mean a summary measure of location that uses all the values in a dataset in its calculation; the sum of all data points divided by the sample size

measurement model a multivariate model for the relationship between observed variables and latent variables

median a summary measure of location that uses the ranks of all the values in a dataset in its calculation; the middle value in an ordered set of data points

mediational model a form of causal model in which the causal influence of a predictor variable on a dependent variable is indirect, operating through an intermediary variable (called a mediator)

methodological contribution this is achieved where an academic report or paper develops new methods of inquiry, or extends existing methods into new contexts

methods and techniques the instruments and processes for gathering research data, analysing it and drawing conclusions from it

middle-range theory a set of ideas and concepts relevant to explaining social or physical phenomena within relatively specific contexts. Normally empirically testable

mid-mean a summary measure of location; the mean of the middle half of the data

mid-range a summary measure of spread; the range of the middle half of the data (also called the interquartile range)

mode 1 research the generation of theoretical knowledge through detached scientific research

mode 1½ research the generation of useful knowledge through combining scientific research methods with practical engagement

mode 2 research the generation of practical knowledge through direct engagement with practice

mode a summary measure of location; the most frequently occurring value in a dataset

modification index an estimate in SEM of the change in goodness of fit of a fitted model if a fixed parameter were allowed to become free

multiple regression model a multivariate method that includes a single dependent variable measured on a continuous scale and a set of predictor variables that may be measured on continuous or category scales

multi-stage sampling a process of dividing up a population into hierarchical units, such as countries, regions, organizations, work groups, and applying random sampling at each level

multivariate analysis of covariance (MANCOVA) a class of statistical methods for testing group differences for two or more dependent variables simultaneously, which also includes one or more continuous variables as predictors

multivariate analysis of variance (MANOVA) a class of statistical methods for testing group differences for two or more dependent variables simultaneously

multivariate methods a class of statistical methods that analyses the covariances among a number of variables simultaneously

multivariate test a test of a study hypothesis that involves consideration of several dependent variables simultaneously

narrative methods ways of conducting research that concentrate on collecting the stories told among organizational members

nodes these represent ideas or concepts linked to passages of text. Nodes can be recognized and reorganized during analysis without affecting the coding structure

nominal scale a form of category scale where the scale units have no natural ordering, for example, makes of car purchased (cf. ordinal scale)

nominalism an ontological view that objects in the world are 'formed' by the language we use and the names we attach to phenomena

non-experimental designs positivist research conducted through comparing groups for which the members have not been assigned at random. Similar to quasi-experimental designs

non-normed fit index an incremental index in SEM of the goodness of fit of a hypothesized causal model relative to the null model

non-parametric test a form of hypothesis test that uses a reference distribution derived from all possible permutations of study outcomes using the ranking of data (cf. parametric test)

non-probability sampling designs sampling designs where the likelihood of each population entity being included in the sample cannot be known

non-proportional stratified random sampling a form of sampling where the population is divided into subsets (called strata) and different sampling proportions are used for each stratum for selecting a sample

normal distribution a form of standard reference distribution; the distribution of the sum of independent measures where the standard deviation of the reference distribution is known (its shape is sometimes called the bell-curve)

normative theory describes how organizations should be structured and managed

null hypothesis (H$_0$) the initial position adopted during hypothesis testing, which may be modified on the basis of evidence from data; for tests involving comparing groups, the null hypothesis is that the groups are nothing but random samples from a single population (see also alternative hypothesis)

null model a model within structural equation modelling which assumes that all the covariances among the observed variables are zero; used as the baseline for calculating incremental fit indices

NVivo a software package that assists in the building and testing of theories by classifying, sorting and arranging information. Available from QSR International, www.qsrinternational.com

observational methods ways of collecting data that involve direct sampling of aspects of behaviour

observed variables a class of variables in a multivariate model that are directly measured; they can be used to estimate latent variables

observer effects influences on behaviour that result from study participants knowing that they are being observed

odds ratio the relative likelihood of the two possible outcomes for a binary category variable; used to form the dependent variable in logistic regression analysis

ontology views about the nature of reality

ordinal scale a form of category scale where the scale units have a natural ordering, for example social class (cf. nominal scale)

paradigm a consensual pattern in the way scientists understand, and inquire into, the world

parametric test a form of hypothesis test that uses a standard reference distribution derived from probability theory whose form is defined by a small number of parameters (cf. non-parametric test)

parsimony the extent to which a fitted model in SEM can account for observed data with fewer parameters

partial correlation a correlation between two variables that is adjusted to remove the influence of a third variable

participant observation a form of ethnography where there is close involvement in the organization in order to gain a detailed understanding of other people's realities

permutations all possible ways of rearranging a set of entities; used in forms of non-parametric testing of hypotheses

phi coefficient a test of association between two variables measured on binary category scales

population the set of entities about which a researcher wishes to draw conclusions

positivism the key idea of positivism is that the social world exists externally, and that its properties should be measured through objective methods

postal questionnaire survey a form of survey distribution that involves postal distribution, and relies on respondents to complete a survey themselves and return it to the researcher

postmodernism a collection of philosophies that are opposed to realism, and are generally critical of scientific progress

pragmatism a philosophical position that argues that knowledge and understanding should be derived from direct experience

precision the level of confidence that the researcher has in estimating characteristics of the population from evidence drawn from a sample; it depends on sample size but not on the sampling proportion

predictor variables the factors that are believed to cause the effects that are to be observed; also called independent variables (see dependent variable)

primary data new information that is collected directly by the researcher

principal components analysis a mathematical procedure that assists in reducing data and by so doing indicates possible relationships between a number of uncorrelated variables. The first principal component accounts for as much of the variability in the data as possible, successive components (of which there may be two, three or four) account for as much of the remaining variability as possible

probability sample designs sampling designs where the likelihood of each population entity being included in the sample is known

probe a device used as an intervention technique to improve and sharpen the interviewees' response

process theory stresses the idea that management is about making sense of, and acting on, fluid and changing situations

product-moment correlation a test of association between two variables measured on continuous scales

proportional stratified random sampling a form of sampling where the population is divided into subsets (called strata) and within strata the same sampling proportion is used for selecting a sample

pure research research for which the primary objective/output is the development of theory

purposive sampling a form of non-probability sampling design where the criteria for inclusion in a sample are defined, and entities are first screened to see whether they meet the criteria for inclusion; those entities that meet the criteria are included in the sample

quasi-experimental design the use of multiple measures over time in order to reduce the effects of control and experimental groups not being fully matched

quota sampling a form of non-probability sampling design where the population is divided into units and a target sample size (quota) is defined for each unit; entities that meet the criteria for a specific unit are added to the sample until the target sample size for the unit is achieved

random assignment where the objects of the experiment (e.g. people) are assigned at random to either the experimental treatment or to the control (non-treatment) groups

range a summary measure of spread; the difference between the largest and smallest data values

rank-order correlation a test of association between two variables measured on ordered category scales

ratio scale a form of continuous scale that has a true zero point, so that ratio calculations are meaningful, for example, height (cf. interval scale)

realism an ontological position which assumes that the physical and social worlds exist independently of any observations made about them

reference distribution the distribution of all alternative values of a test statistic based on the assumption that the null hypothesis is true; used in hypothesis testing

reflexivity where researchers think about the effects they have had or may have on the outcome and process of research

regression weight the value of the independent contribution of a predictor variable to predicting a dependent variable in multiple regression analysis

relativism an ontological view that phenomena depend on the perspectives from which we observed them. Also an epistemological position that observations will be more accurate/credible if made from several different perspectives

reliability the consistency of measurement in a composite variable formed by combining scores on a set of items; can be measured by Cronbach's alpha coefficient

repertory grid a tool for uncovering an individual's (or group's) view of the world based on the constructs they develop and hold

representativeness in sampling design, this refers to how much the characteristics of a sample are the same as the characteristics of the population from which the sample is drawn

residual the value of that portion of the variance of a dependent variable that cannot be accounted for by a set of predictor variables

RMSEA (root mean squared error of approximation) an index in SEM of the goodness of fit of a hypothesized causal model adjusted for the complexity of the fitted model

robustness the extent to which a summary measure is sensitive to disturbances in data quality

sample a subset of the population from which inferences are drawn based on evidence

sample size the number of entities included in a sample

sampling distribution a form of reference distribution derived from probability theory based on repeated sampling from a theoretical population; used in hypothesis testing

sampling frame the list of all of those eligible to be included in a sample

sampling proportion the size of a sample relative to the size of a population

scholarship this is a term given to the development of high levels of knowledge about a particular issue or topic, largely on the basis of secondary data

search engine a program that will find text relating to the word(s) input

secondary data research information that already exists in the form of publications or other electronic media, which is collected by the researcher

semi-concealed research a form of ethnography where there is negotiated access with research agendas that the researchers are not always willing to reveal to all those they meet

semi-detached design a mixed methods design where there are no direct linkages between the two parts of the study

simple random sampling a form of sampling where every entity in the population has an equal chance of being included in the sample

snowball sampling a form of non-probability sampling design where the criteria for inclusion in a sample are defined; entities that meet the criteria are included in the sample and then asked whether they know others who also meet the criteria

Social Sciences Citation Index provides access to current and retrospective bibliographical information in the social sciences in the world's leading journals

social constructionism the idea that 'reality' is determined by people rather than by objective and external factors, and hence it is most important to appreciate the way people make sense of their experience

social desirability where people adjust their answers to a survey in order to project a positive image of themselves to the interviewer

social engineering model an approach to social policy formulation that relies on the research and analysis of expert scientists to determine the best course of action

specific factors a class of latent variables in a measurement model, which is assumed to account for idiosyncratic aspects of an observed variable (see also common factors)

spread a characteristic of a set of data that summarizes how much the data vary around a measure of location; measured by the range, mid-range or standard deviation

squared multiple correlation an overall measure of the quality of a multiple regression model; the proportion of variance in a dependent variable accounted for by a set of predictor variables

standard deviation a summary measure of spread; based on the average deviation of scores around the mean

standard error the standard deviation of a sampling distribution used in hypothesis testing; estimated from the standard deviations and the sample size within groups in a sample

standardization the process of transforming a variable in order to express it on a scale with a mean of zero and a standard deviation of one; often carried out for variables measured on interval scales (with no true zero point) so that regression weights can be compared between predictor variables

standardized regression weight the value of the independent contribution of a predictor variable to predicting a dependent variable in multiple regression analysis after the predictor and dependent variables have been standardized; also called a beta weight

statistical control a way of simplifying inference about the relationships among variables by adjusting for their covariance with another variable

stepdown F-test the test statistic in a multivariate analysis of variance of group differences, where the DVs are tested singly in turn in a sequence decided upon by the researcher holding constant DVs earlier in the sequence

stepwise regression a form of multiple regression analysis where predictor variables are automatically entered or dropped sequentially on the basis of the extent of their independent contribution to predicting the dependent variable

stratified random sampling a form of sampling where the population is divided into subsets (called strata) and within strata every entity in the population has an equal chance of being included in the sample

structural equation model a multivariate model of the hypothesized causal relationships among a set of variables, which may include both observed and latent variables

structuration theory an epistemology that assumes that social structure and individual behaviour are interlinked, and that each is produced and reproduced by the other

structured interview surveys a form of survey where an interviewer locates each participant, and completes the survey face-to-face by asking structured questions

structured interviews where the interviewer follows a prescribed list of questions each of which may have predetermined response categories

substantive contribution this is achieved when the research throws new light onto the subject of study, whether it is a particular kind of organization or aspects of employee or managerial behaviour

summarizing describing a characteristic of a dataset such as location or spread based on aggregating data from all respondents

survey feedback the collection of opinions about the management of an organization, which is then fed back to all employees to stimulate change and improvements

symmetry a balanced distribution of data points around a central value

synergy a form of interaction between variables, where their joint effect is different from the sum of their individual effects

systematic random sampling a process of random sampling where every nth entity from the population is selected

systematic review a means of synthesizing research on a topic or within a field in such a way that is both transparent and reproducible

t-distribution a form of standard reference distribution; a form of the normal distribution where the standard deviation of the reference distribution is estimated from sample data

telephone interview surveys a form of survey where an interviewer locates each participant, and completes the survey by telephone by asking structured questions

testing effect where changes observed in individual behaviour or attitudes over time are caused by the measures having been made in the first place

theoretical codes codes that derive from an understanding of how substantive codes relate one with another

theoretical contribution this is achieved when new concepts are developed, or existing concepts are extended, in order to understand or explain behaviour and organizational phenomena

topic guide a prepared list of areas (rather than specific questions) that need to be covered during the course of an interview

transcendental realism a philosophical position which assumes that the objects of scientific inquiry exist and act independently of the observer

triangulation using different kinds of measures or perspectives in order to increase the confidence in the accuracy of observations

trimmed mean a family of summary measures of location where a proportion of the largest and smallest values are ignored in calculating a mean; the mid-mean is a 25 per cent trimmed mean, the median is a 50 per cent trimmed mean

t-test a form of hypothesis test for comparing mean scores of two groups

type I error a false conclusion from a hypothesis test involving a claim that an effect exists (an association between variables or a group difference) when there is no such effect in the population

type II error a false conclusion from a hypothesis test involving a claim that no effect exists (an association between variables or a group difference) when there is an effect in the population

unit of analysis the main level at which data is aggregated: can be individuals, groups, events, organizations, etc. Within relativist studies researchers look for relationships between attributes that vary across different units of analysis

univariate *F*-test the test statistic in multivariate analysis of variance for group differences in a single dependent variable ignoring others

univariate test a test of a study hypothesis, which involves consideration of a single dependent variable

universal theories theories that may be derived in one social organizational setting, and which are applicable in any other setting or context

validity the extent to which measures and research findings provide accurate representation of the things they are supposed to be describing

variance a summary measure of spread used in calculating the standard deviation; the average deviation of scores around the mean

verification a research design that seeks evidence to demonstrate that the current assumptions or hypotheses are correct

visual metaphors an approach to eliciting the views of individuals or groups with the notion of metaphors in order to get individuals (or groups) to draw and describe issues or events as they currently see them or would like to see them in the future

Wald test the test statistic in logistic regression analysis expressing the independent contribution of a predictor variable

Web of Knowledge a database that provides a single route to journals in the Social Sciences Citation Index

web-based surveys a form of survey where a website link is sent to each potential participant, respondents complete the survey by recording their answers on online; answers may be checked for consistency and then stored on a database for analysis

Wilks' Lambda the test statistic in multivariate analysis of variance for group differences in a set of two or more dependent variables

work activity school this describes the nature of managerial work in practice. Although it does not assume that these work patterns are desirable, or undesirable, it does imply that training programmes need to prepare managers to cope with this 'reality'

Zetoc a current awareness service for higher education institutions in the United Kingdom. The service gives access to the British Library's table of contents database and a Zetoc alert can provide users with information on the contents of new journals as soon as they are issued

BIBLIOGRAPHY

Abrahamson, M. (1983) *Social Research Methods*. Englewood Cliffs, NJ: Prentice Hall.

Ackroyd, S. and Fleetwood, S. (2000) 'Realism in contemporary organizational and management studies', in S. Ackroyd and S. Fleetwood (eds), *Realist Perspectives on Management and Organizations*. London: Routledge, pp. 3–25.

Agar, M.H. (1986) *Speaking of Ethnography*. Beverly Hills, CA: Sage.

Ahmed, S. (1998) *Differences that Matter: Feminist Theory and Postmodernism*. Cambridge: Cambridge University Press.

Ahuja, G. (2000) 'Collaboration networks, structural holes, and innovation: a longitudinal study', *Administrative Science Quarterly*, 45: 425–55.

Aiken, H.D. (1956) *The Age of Ideology*. New York: Mentor.

Alvesson, M. (1990) 'Organization: from substance to image', *Organisation Studies*, 11: 373–94.

Alvesson, M. (1998) 'Gender relations and identity at work: a case study of an advertising agency', *Human Relations*, 51 (8): 969–1005.

Alvesson, M. (2003) 'Beyond neopositivists, romantics, and localists: a reflexive approach to interviews in organisation research', *Academy of Management Review*, 28 (1): 13–33.

Alvesson, M. and Deetz, S. (2000) *Doing Critical Management Research*. London: Sage.

Alvesson, M. and Kärreman, D. (2011) 'Decolonializing discourse: critical reflections on organizational discourse analysis', *Human Relations*, 64 (9), doi: 10.1177/0018726711408629.

Alvesson, M. and Sköldberg, K. (2000) *Reflexive Methodology: New Vistas for Qualitative Research towards a Reflexive Methodology*. London: Sage.

Amis, J. and Silk, M.L. (2008) 'The philosophy and politics of quality in qualitative organizational research', *Organizational Research Methods*, 11: 456–80.

Anderson, L.M. (2008) 'Critical action learning: an examination of the social nature of management learning and development', unpublished PhD thesis, University of Leeds, Leeds University Business School, April.

Anderson, L. (2008) 'Participant observation', in R. Thorpe and R. Holt (eds), *The Sage Dictionary of Qualitative Management Research*. London: Sage, pp. 150–2.

Anderson, M.L. (1993) 'Studying across difference: race, class and gender in qualitative research', in J.H. Stanfield and R.M. Dennis (eds), *Race and Ethnicity in Research Methods*. London: Sage, pp. 39–52.

Ashton, D.J.L. and Easterby-Smith, M. (1979) *Management Development in the Organisation*. London: Macmillan.

Astley, W.G. and Zammuto, R.F. (1992) 'Organisation science, managers, and language games', *Organisation Science*, 3: 443–60.

Austin, J.H. (1978) *Chase, Chance and Creativity*. New York: Columbia University Press.

Ayer, A.J. ([1936] 1971) *Language, Truth and Logic*. Harmondsworth: Pelican.

Back, L. (2006) *ESRC Research Development Initiative Conference*. London: Royal College of Physicians.

Baker, S. (1996) 'Consumer cognitions: mapping personal benefits relating to perfume purchase in the UK and Germany', 207th ESOMAR Seminar, Capturing the Elusive Appeal of Fragrance: Techniques, Experiences, Challenges. Amsterdam.

Baker, S. and Knox, S. (1995) 'Mapping consumer cognitions in Europe', in M. Bergadaa (ed.), *Marketing Today for the 21st Century*. Proceedings of 24th EMAC Conference, Cergy-Pontoisse, France, 1: 81–100.

Bales, R.F. (1950) *Interaction Process Analysis*. Cambridge, MA: Addison-Wesley.

Bales, R.F. (1970) *Personality and Interpersonal Behavior*. New York: Holt, Rinehart & Winston.

Bales, R.F. (1988) 'A new overview of the SYMLOG system: measuring and changing behavior in groups', in R.B. Polley, A.P. Hare and P.J. Stone (eds), *The SYMLOG Practitioner*. New York: Praeger, pp. 319–44.

Bales, R.F., Cohen, S.P. and Williamson, S.A. (1979) *SYMLOG: A System for the Multiple Level Observation of Groups*. New York: The Free Press.

Banks, M. (1995) 'Visual research methods', *Social Research Update*, 11: 1–6.

Banks, M. (2008) *Using Visual Data in Qualitative Research*. London: Sage.

Bannister, D. and Fransella, F. (1971) *Inquiring Man: The Theory of Personal Constructs*. Harmondsworth: Penguin.

Barley, S.R. (1986) *The Innocent Anthropologist: Notes from a Mud Hut*. Harmondsworth: Penguin.

Barry, C.A. (1998) 'Choosing qualitative data analysis software: Atlas/ti and Nudist compared', *Sociological Research Online*, 3 (3). Available at www.socresonline.org.uk/3/3/4.html (last accessed 27 October 2008).

Barry, L.R. (2004) 'NVivo 2.0 and ATLAS.ti 5.0: a comparative review of two popular qualitative data-analysis programs', *Field Methods*, 16: 439–64.

Bartunek, J.M. and Louis, M.R. (1996) *Insider/Outsider Team Research*. Thousand Oaks, CA: Sage.

Barwise, P., Marsh, P., Thomas, K. and Wensley, R. (1989) 'Intelligent elephants and part-time researchers', *Graduate Management Research*, Winter: 12–33.

Bazeley, P. (2007) *Qualitative Data Analysis with NVivo*. London: Sage.

Bell, E. and Bryman, A. (2007) 'The ethics of management research: an exploratory content analysis', *British Journal of Management*, 18 (1): 63–77.

Bennis, W.G. and O'Toole, J. (2005) 'How business schools lost their way', *Harvard Business Review*, 83 (5): 1–9.

Bentler, P.M. and Dudgeon, P. (1996) 'Covariance structure analysis: statistical practice, theory and direction', *Annual Review of Psychology*, 47: 563–92.

Berger, P.L. and Luckman, T. (1966) *The Social Construction of Reality*. London: Penguin.

Berger, R. and Rosenberg, E. (2008) 'The experience of abused women with their children's law guardians', *Violence Against Women*, 14: 71–92.

Berghman, L., Matthyssens, P. and Vandenbempt, K. (2006) 'Building competences for new customer value creation: an exploratory study', *Industrial Marketing Management*, 35 (8): 961–73.

Berman, S.L., Wicks, A.C., Kotha, S. and Jones, T.M. (1999) 'Does stakeholder orientation matter? The relationship between stakeholder management models and firm financial performance', *Academy of Management Journal*, 42 (5): 488–506.

Bessant, J., Binley, S., Cooper, C., Dawson, S., Gernard, J., Gardiner, M., Gray, A., Jones, P., Mayer, C., Magee, J., Pidd, M., Rowley, G., Saunders, J. and Stark, A. (2003) 'The state of the field in UK management research: reflections of the Research Assessment Exercise (RAE) Panel', *British Journal of Management*, 14: 51–68.

Bettis, R.A. and Prahalad, C.K. (1995) 'The dominant logic: retrospective and extensions', *SMJ*, 16 (1): 5–14.

Beynon, H. (1973) *Working for Ford*. Harmondsworth: Penguin.

Beynon, H. (1988) 'Regulating research: politics and decision making in industrial organisations', in A. Bryman (ed.), *Doing Research in Organisations*. London: Routledge, pp. 21–33.

Bhaskar, R. (1978) *A Realist Theory of Science*. New York: Harvester Press.

Bhaskar, R. (1989) *Reclaiming Reality: A Critical Introduction to Contemporary Philosophy*. London: Verso.

Billig, M. (1988) 'Review of: *Murderous Science: Elimination by Scientific Selection of Jews, Gypsies and Others in Germany, 1933–1945* [B. Muller-Hill, Oxford: OUP]', *The Psychologist*, December: 475–6.

Billig, M. (1991) *Ideology and Opinions: Studies of Rhetorical Psychology*. London: Sage.

Birkinshaw, J., Braunerhjelm, P., Holm, U. and Terjesen, S. (2006) 'Why do some multinational corporations relocate their headquarters overseas?', *Strategic Management Journal*, 27 (7): 681–700.

Blaikie, N. (2007) *Approaches to Social Enquiry*, 2nd edn. Cambridge: Polity Press.

Bloom, B.S. and Krathwohl, D.R. (1956) *Taxonomy of Educational Objectives*. London: Longman.

Bloom, N. and van Reenen, J. (2006) 'Measuring and explaining management practices across firms and countries'. CEP Discussion Paper No. 716. London School of Economics.

Blunch, N.J. (2008) *Introduction to Structural Equation Modelling Using SPSS and AMOS*. London: Sage.

Boissevain, J. (1974) *Friends of Friends*. Oxford: Blackwell.

Boje, D.M. (1991) 'The storytelling organization: a study of storytelling performance in an office supply firm', *Administrative Science Quarterly*, 36: 106–26.

Boje, D.M. (1995) 'Stories of the story-telling organization: a postmodern analysis of Disney as "Tamara-land"', *Academy of Management Journal*, 38 (4): 997–1035.

Boje, D.M. (2001) *Narrative Methods for Organizational and Communication Research*. London: Sage.

Boje, D.M. (2003) 'Using narratives and telling stories', in D. Holman and R. Thorpe (eds), *Management and Language*. London: Sage.

Boje, D. (2008) 'Storytelling in management research', in R. Thorpe and R. Holt (eds), *The Sage Dictionary of Qualitative Management Research*. London, Sage, pp. 213–15.

Borgatti, S.P. (2006) 'Identifying sets of key players in social network', *Computational and Mathematical Organisation*, 12 (1): 21–34.

Borgatti, S.P., Everett, M.G. and Freeman, L.C. (2002) *Ucinet for Windows: Software for Social Network Analysis*. Harvard, MA: Analytic Technologies. Available at: www.analytictech.com (last accessed 24 November 2011).

Borgatti, S.P., Mehra, A., Brass, D.J. and Labianca, G. (2009) 'Network analysis in the social sciences', *Science*, 323: 892–95.

Bouty, I. (2000) 'Interpersonal and interaction influences on informal resource exchanges between R&D researchers across organizational boundaries', *Academy of Management Journal*, 43: 50–65.

Bowey, A.M. and Thorpe, R. (1986) *Payment Systems and Productivity*. Basingstoke: Macmillan.

Box, G.E.P., Hunter, S.J. and Hunter, W.G. (2005) *Statistics for Experimenters: Design, Innovation, and Discovery*, 2nd edn. John Wiley & Sons.

Boyacigiller, N.A. and Adler, N.J. (1991) 'The parochial dinosaur: organizational science in a global context', *Academy of Management Review*, 16: 262–90.

Boyatzis, R.E. (1982) *The Competent Manager: A Model for Effective Performance*. New York: Wiley.

Brandi, U. and Elkjaer, B. (2008) 'Pragmatism', in R. Thorpe and R. Holt (eds), *Sage Dictionary of Qualitative Management Research*. London: Sage, pp. 169–71.

Brass, J.B., Galaskiewicz, J., Greve, H.R. and Tsai, W. (2004) 'Taking stock of social networks and organizations: a multi-level perspective', *Academy of Management Journal*, 47 (6): 795–817.

Brewer, J.D. (2000) *Ethnography*. Buckingham: Open University.

Brouthers, K.D. and Brouthers, L.E. (2003) 'Why services and manufacturing entry mode choices differ: the influence of transaction cost factors, risk and trust', *Journal of Management Studies*, 40(3): 1179–204.

Brown, S.L. and Eisenhardt, K.M. (1998) *Competing on the Edge: Strategy as Structured Chaos*. Boston, MA: Harvard University Press.

Bryman, A. and Bell, E. (2003) *Business Research Methods*. Oxford: Oxford University Press.

Bryman, A. and Bell, E. (2007) *Business Research Methods*, 2nd edn. Oxford: Oxford University Press.

Bryman, A. and Cramer, D. (2004) *Quantitative Data Analysis with SPSS 12 and 13: A Guide for Social Scientists*. London: Routledge.

Buchanan, D.A. (1980) 'Gaining management skills through academic research work', *Personnel Management*, 12 (4): 45–8.

Buchanan, D.A. (1999) 'The role of photography in organisation research: a re-engineering case illustration', *Journal of Management Inquiry*, 10: 151–64.

Buchanan, D.A. and Badham, R. (2008) *Power, Politics and Organizational Change: Winning the Turf Game*, 2nd edn. London: Sage.

Buchanan D.A., Boddy, D. and McCalman, J. (1988) 'Getting in, getting on, getting out, getting back: the art of the possible', in A. Bryman (ed.), *Doing Research in Organisations*. London: Routledge, pp. 53–67.

Buchanan, D.A. and Bryman, A. (2007) 'Contextualizing methods choice in organizational research', *Organizational Research Methods*, 10 (3): 483–501.

Bulmer, M. (1988) 'Some reflections upon research in organization', in A. Bryman (ed.), *Doing Research in Organizations*. London: Routledge, pp. 151–61.

Burgess, R.G. (1982) *Field Research: A Source Book and Field Manual*. London: Allen and Unwin.

Burgoyne, J. and James, K. T. (2006) 'Towards best or better practice in corporate leadership development: operational issues is Mode 2 and design science research', *British Journal of Management*, 17: 303–16.

Burgoyne, J. and Stuart, R. (1976) 'The nature, use and acquisition of managerial skills and other attributes', *Personnel Review*, 15 (4): 19–29.

Burkhardt, M.E. (1994) 'Social interaction effects following a technological change: a longitudinal investigation', *Academy of Management Journal*, 37: 869–98.

Burrell, G. (1993) 'Eco and the Bunnymen', in J. Hassard and M. Parker (eds), *Postmodernism and Organizations*. London: Sage, pp. 71–82.

Burrell, G. and Morgan, G. (1979) *Sociological Paradigms and Organisational Analysis*. London: Heinemann.

Buzan, T. (2004) *Mind Maps: How to Be the Best at Your Job and Still Have Time to Play*. New York: Plume.

Calder, A. and Sheridan, D. (1984) *Speak for Yourself: A Mass-Observation Anthology 1937–49*. London: Cape.

Calhoun, M.A., Starbuck, W.H. and Abrahamson, E. (2011) 'Fads, fashions and the fluidity of knowledge: Peter Senge's *The Learning Organization*', in M. Easterby-Smith and M. Lyles (eds), *Handbook of Organizational Learning and Knowledge Management*, 2nd edn. Chichester: Wiley, pp. 225–48.

Castells, M. (2000) *The Rise of the Network Society*, 2nd edn. Oxford: Blackwell.

Charmaz, K. (2000) 'Grounded theory: objectivist and constructivist methods', in N.K. Denzin and Y.S. Lincoln (eds), *Sage Handbook of Qualitative Research*, 2nd edn. Thousand Oaks, CA: Sage, pp. 509–35.

Charmaz, K. (2006) *Constructing Grounded Theory: A Practical Guide Through Qualitative Analysis*. London: Sage.

Chia, R. (2008) 'Postmodernism', in R. Thorpe and R. Holt (eds), *Sage Dictionary of Qualitative Management Research*. London: Sage, pp. 162–3.

Chouliaraki, L. and Fairclough, N. (2010) 'Critical discourse analysis in organisational studies: towards an integrationist methodology', *Journal of Management Studies*, 47 (6): 1213–18.

Churchill, J. (1990) 'Complexity and strategic decision making', in C. Eden and J. Radford (eds), *Tackling Strategic Problems: The Role of Group Decision Support*. London: Sage, pp. 11–17.

Clarke, J. (2007) 'Seeing entrepreneurship: visual ethnographies of embodied entrepreneurs', unpublished PhD thesis, University of Leeds, Leeds University Business School, June.

Clarke, J. (2011) 'Revitalizing entrepreneurship: how visual symbols are used in entrepreneurial performances', *Journal of Management Studies*, 48 (6), doi: 10.1111/j.1467-6486.2010.01002.x.

Coch, L. and French, J.R.P. (1948) 'Overcoming resistance to change', *Human Relations*, 1: 512–33.

Coffey, A. and Atkinson, P. (1996) *Making Sense of Qualitative Data*. London: Sage.

Cohen, W.M. and Levinthal, D.A. (1990) 'Absorptive capacity: a new perspective on learning and innovation', *Administrative Science Quarterly*, 35: 128–52.

Coleman, J.S. (1988) 'Social capital in the creation of human capital', *American Journal of Sociology*, 94: S95–S120.

Collier, J. and Collier, J. (1986) *Visual Anthropology: Photography as a Research Method*. Albuquerque, NM: University of New Mexico.

Collins, H.M. (1983) 'An empirical relativist programme in the sociology of scientific knowledge', in K.D Knorr-Cetina and M. Mulkay (eds), *Science Observed: Perspectives on the Social Study of Science*. London: Sage, pp. 3–10.

Collinson, D.L. (1992) *Managing the Shop Floor: Subjectivity, Masculinity, and Workplace Culture*. New York: de Gruyter.

Collinson, D.L. (2002) 'Managing humour', *Journal of Management Studies*, 39: 269–88.

Comte, A. (1853) *The Positive Philosophy of Auguste Comte* (trans. H. Martineau). London: Trubner and Co.

Cook, S.D.N. and Brown, J.S. (1999) 'Bridging epistemologies: the generative dance between organizational knowledge and organizational knowing', *Organization Science*, 10 (4): 381–400.

Cooper, R. (1992) 'Formal organization as representation: remote control, displacement and abbreviation', in M. Reed and M. Hughes (eds), *Rethinking Organization*. London: Sage, pp. 254–72.

Cooper, R. and Burrell, G. (1988) 'Modernism, postmodernism and organizational analysis: an introduction', *Organization Studies*, 9 (1): 91–112.

Cornelissen, J.P. (2011) *Corporate Communications: A Guide to Theory and Practice*, 3rd edn. London: Sage.

Cotterill, P. (1992) 'Interviewing women: issues of friendship, vulnerability and power', *Women's Studies International Forum*, 15 (5/6): 593–606.

Cotterill, S. and King, S. (2007) 'Public sector partnerships to deliver local e-government: a social network study', *Sixth*

International EGOV Conference, Regensburg (Germany), 3–7 September. Available at: www.springerlink.com/content/a646737037n18g70/ (last accessed 24 November 2011).

Couper, M.P. (2008) *Designing Effective Web Surveys*. Cambridge: Cambridge University Press.

Couper, M.P., Traugott, M.W. and Lamias, M.J. (2001) 'Web survey design and administration', *Public Opinion Quarterly*, 65 (2): 230–53.

Coyle-Shapiro, J. and Kessler, I. (2000) 'Consequences of the psychological contract for the employment relationship: a large scale survey', *Journal of Management Studies*, 37 (7): 903–30.

Crawford, S.D., Couper, M.P. and Lamias, M.J. (2001) 'Web surveys: perceptions of burden', *Social Science Computer Review*, 19 (2): 146–62.

Creswell, J.W. (2003) *Research Design: Qualitative, Quantitative and Mixed Methods Approaches*, 2nd edn. Thousand Oaks, CA: Sage.

Crotty, M. (1998) *The Foundations of Social Research: Meaning and Perspective in the Research Process*. London: Sage.

Cryer, P. (2000) *The Research Student's Guide to Success*. Buckingham: Open University Press.

Cunliffe, A.L. (2001) 'Managers as practical authors: reconstructing our understanding of management practice', *Journal of Management Studies*, 38: 351–71.

Cunliffe, A.L. (2002a) 'Reflexive dialogical practice in management learning', *Management Learning*, 33 (1): 35–61.

Cunliffe, A. L. (2002b) 'Social poetics as management inquiry: a dialogical approach', *Journal of Management Inquiry*, 11 (2): 128–46.

Cunliffe, A.L. (2003) 'Reflexive inquiry in organizational research: questions and possibilities', *Human Relations*, 56 (8): 983–1003.

Cunliffe, A.L. (2008) 'Discourse analysis' in R. Thorpe and R. Holt, *The Sage Dictionary of Qualitative Management Research*. London: Sage.

Cunliffe, A.L. (2010) 'Retelling tales of the field: In search of organizational ethnography 20 years on', *Organizational Research Methods*, 13 (2): 224–39.

Cunliffe, A.L. (2011) 'Crafting qualitative research: Morgan and Smircich 30 years on', *Organizational Research Methods*, 14 (4): 647–73.

Curran, J. and Downing, S. (1989) 'The state and small business owners: an empirical assessment of consultation strategies', paper presented at the 12th National Small Firms Policy and Research Conference, Barbican, London.

Cyert, R.H. and March, J.G. (1963) *A Behavioral History of the Firm*. Englewood-Cliffs, NJ: Prentice Hall.

Czarniawska, B. (1998) *A Narrative Approach to Organization Studies*. London: Sage.

Daft, R.L. and Lengel, R.H. (1986) 'Organisational information requirements, media richness and structural design', *Management Science*, 32: 554–71.

Daiute, C. and Lightfoot, C. (2004) *Narrative Analysis: Studying the Development of Individuals in Society*. Thousand Oaks, CA: Sage.

Dalton, M. (1959) *Men Who Manage: Fusion of Feeling and Theory in Administration*. New York: Wiley.

Dalton, M. (1964) 'Preconceptions and methods in *Men Who Manage*', in P. Hammond (ed.), *Sociologists at Work*. New York: Basic Books, pp. 50–95.

Davies, G., Chun, R., Da Silva, R. and Roper, S. (2002) *Corporate Reputation and Competitiveness*. London: Routledge.

Davies, J. and Easterby-Smith, M. (1984) 'Learning and developing from managerial work experiences', *Journal of Management Studies*, 21: 169–82, doi: 10.1111/j.1467-6486.1984.tb00230.x

Davila, C. (1989) 'Grounding management education in local research: a Latin American experience', in J. Davies, M. Easterby-Smith, S. Mann and M. Tanton (eds), *The Challenge to Western Management Development: International Alternatives*. London: Routledge, pp. 40–56.

Deem, R. and Brehony, K. (1997) 'Research students' access to research cultures: an unequal benefit?', paper presented at Society for Research in Higher Education Conference, University of Warwick.

Denzin, N.K. and Lincoln, Y.S. (eds) (2006) *Sage Handbook of Qualitative Research*, 3rd edn. Thousand Oaks, CA: Sage.

Derrida, J. (1978) *Writing and Difference*. London: Routledge and Kegan Paul.

Detert, J.R. and Edmondson, A.C. (2011) 'Implicit voice theories: taken-for-granted rules of self-censorship at work', *Academy of Management Journal*, 54 (3): 461–88.

Dewey, J. (1916) *Democracy and Education*. London: Collier Macmillan.

Dhanaraj, C., Lyles, M.A., Steensma, H.K. and Tihanyi, L. (2004) 'Managing tacit and explicit knowledge transfer in IJVs: the role of relational embeddedness and the impact on performance', *Journal of International Business Studies*, 35 (5): 428–43.

Dillman, D.A. (2000) *Mail and Internet Surveys: The Tailored Design Method*, 2nd edn. New York: John Wiley & Sons.

Ditton, J. (1977) *Part-time Crime*. London: Macmillan.

Dobson, A.J. (2001) *Introduction to Generalized Linear Models*, 2nd edn. London: Chapman and Hall.

Douglas, J.D. (ed.) (1976) *Investigative Social Research*. Beverly Hills, CA: Sage.

Drisko, J.W. (2004) 'Qualitative data analysis software: a user's appraisal', in D. Padgett (ed.), *The Qualitative Research Experience*. Belmont, CA: Wadsworth, pp. 193–209.

Duggan, F. (2006) 'Plagiarism: prevention, practice and policy', *Assessment & Evaluation in Higher Education*, 31 (2): 151–4.

Dyer, J.H. and Hatch, N.W. (2006) 'Relation-specific capabilities and barriers to knowledge transfers: creating advantage through network relationships', *Strategic Management Journal*, 27 (8): 701–19.

Easterby-Smith, M. ([1986] 1994) *Evaluation of Management Education, Training and Development*. Aldershot: Gower.

Easterby-Smith, M. (1997) 'Disciplines of organizational learning: contributions and critiques', *Human Relations*, 51 (9): 1085–116.

Easterby-Smith, M. and Ashton, D. (1975) 'Using repertory grid technique to evaluate management training', *Personnel Review*, 4 (4): 15–21.

Easterby-Smith, M., Graca, M., Antonacopoulou, A. and Ferdinand, J. (2008) 'Absorptive capacity: a process perspective', *Management Learning*, 39 (5): 483–501.

Easterby-Smith, M. and Lyles, M. (2011) *Handbook of Organizational Learning and Knowledge Management.* Oxford: Blackwell.

Easterby-Smith, M. and Malina, D. (1999) 'Cross-cultural collaborative research: toward reflexivity', *Academy of Management Journal,* 42 (1): 76–86.

Easterby-Smith, M., Thorpe, R. and Holman, D. (1996) 'The use of repertory grids in management', *Journal of European Industrial Training,* 20 (3): 1–30.

Easterby-Smith, M., Thorpe, R. and Holman, D. (2010) 'Using repertory grids in management', in F.B. Birks and T. Macer, *Marketing Research* (Vol. 2). London: Routledge, pp. 448–90.

Eden, C. (1990) 'Strategic thinking with computers', *Long Range Planning,* 23 (6): 35–43.

Eden, C. and Ackermann, F. (1998) *Making Strategy: The Journey of Strategic Management.* London: Sage.

Eden, C. and Huxham, C. (1995) 'Action research for the study of organisations', in S. Clegg, C. Hardy and W. Nord (eds), *Handbook of Organisation Studies,* Beverley Hills, CA: Sage.

Eden, C. and Huxham, C. (1996) 'Action research for management research', *British Journal of Management,* 7 (1): 75–86.

Eden, C. and Huxham, C. (2002) 'Action research', in D. Partington (ed.), *Essential Skills for Management Research.* London: Sage, pp. 254–72.

Eden, C. and Huxham, C. (2007) 'Action research and the study of organisations', in S. Clegg, C. Hardy and W. Nord (eds), *Handbook of Organisation Studies.* London: Sage, pp. 526–42.

Eden, C., Jones, S. and Sims, D. (1983) *Messing About in Problems: An Informal Structured Approach to Their Identification and Management.* Oxford: Pergamon Press.

Eesley, C. and Lenox, M.J. (2006) 'Firm responses to secondary stakeholder action', *Strategic Management Journal,* 27 (8): 765–81.

Eisenhardt, K.M. (1989) 'Building theories from case study research', *Academy of Management Review,* 14 (4): 532–50.

Eisenhardt, K.M. and Graebner, M.E. (2007) 'Theory building from cases: opportunities and challenges', *Academy of Management Journal,* 50 (1): 25–32.

Engeström, Y. (1999) 'Activity theory as a framework for analysis and redesigning work', *Ergonomics,* 43 (7): 960–74.

Engeström, Y. (2000) 'Activity theory and the social construction of knowledge: a story of four imports', *Organisation,* 7 (2): 302–10.

Ernst, P. (1996) 'The nature of mathematics and teaching'. *Philosophy of Mathematics Education Journal,* Volume 9.

ESRC (2009) *Postgraduate Training and Development Guidelines.* Swindon: Economic and Social Research Council.

Evers, F.T. and Rush, J.C. (1996) 'The bases of competence: skill development during the transition from university to work', *Management Learning,* 27 (3): 275–300.

Fairclough, N. and Hardy, G. (1997) 'Management learning as discourse', in J. Burgoyne and M. Reynolds (eds), *Management Learning: Integrating Perspectives in Theory and Practice.* London: Sage, pp. 144–60.

Fairhurst, E. (1983) 'Organisational rules and the accomplishment of nursing work on geriatric wards', *Journal of Management Studies,* Special Issue, 20 (3): 315–32.

Fayol, H. ([1916] 1950) *Administration Industrielle et Generale.* Paris: Dunod.

Field, A. (2009) *Discovering Statistics Using SPSS,* 3rd edn. London: Sage.

Fielding, N.G. and Fielding, J.L. (1986) *Linking Data.* Beverly Hills, CA: Sage.

Filatotchev, I. (2006) 'Effects of executive characteristics and venture capital involvement on board composition and share ownership in IPO firms', *British Journal of Management,* 17, 75–92.

Finch, J. (1986) *Research and Policy: The Uses of Qualitative Methods in Social and Educational Research.* London: The Falmer Press.

Firth, J.R. (1957) *Papers in Linguistics, 1934–1951.* London and New York: Oxford University Press.

Flanagan, J.C. (1954) 'The critical incident technique', *Psychological Bulletin,* 1: 327–58.

Foucault, M. (1979) *Discipline and Punish.* Harmondsworth: Penguin.

Fournier, V. and Grey, C. (2000) 'At the critical moment: conditions and prospects for critical management studies', *Human Relations,* 52 (1): 7–32.

Freeman, R.E. (1984) *Strategic Management: A Stakeholder Approach.* London: Pitman.

Freeman, R.E, Harrison, J.S., Wicks, A., Parmar, B. L. and de Colle, S. (2010) *Stakeholder Theory: The State of the Art.* Cambridge: Cambridge University Press.

Gadamer, H.-G. (1989) *Truth and Method,* 2nd rev. edn (trans. J. Weinsheimer and D.G. Marshall). New York: Crossroad.

Gash, S. (2000) *Effective Literature Searching for Research.* Aldershot: Gower.

Geary, L., Marriott, L. and Rowlinson, M. (2004) 'Journal rankings in business and management and the 2001 Research Assessment Exercise in the UK', *British Journal of Management,* 15: 95–141.

Gergen, K.J. (1995) 'Relational theory and discourses of power', in D.-M. Hosking, H.P. Dachler and K.J. Gergen (eds), *Management and Organization: Relational Alternatives to Individualism.* Aldershot: Avebury, pp. 29–49.

Gergen, K.J. (1999) *An Invitation to Social Construction.* London: Sage.

Ghauri, P. and Grønhaug, K. (2010) *Research Methods in Business Studies.* Essex: Prentice Hall.

Gibbons, M.L., Limoges, C., Nowotny, H. Schwartman, S., Scott, P. and Trow, M. (1994) *The New Production of Knowledge: The Dynamics of Science and Research in Contemporary Societies.* London: Sage.

Gibbs, G.R., Friese, S. and Mangabeira, W.C. (2002) 'The use of new technology in qualitative research'. Introduction to *Forum Qualitative Sozialforschung/Forum: Qualitative Social Research,* 3 (2), Art. 8, http://nbn-resolving.de/urn:nbn:de:0114-fqs020287 (last accessed 29 October 2008).

Giddens, A. (1984) *The Constitution of Society: Outline of the Theory of Structuration.* Cambridge: Polity Press.

Glaser, B.G. (1978) *Theoretical Sensitivity.* Mill Valley, CA: Sociological Press.

Glaser, B.G. (1992) *Basics of Grounded Theory Analysis: Emergence versus Forcing.* Mill Valley, CA: Sociology Press.

Glaser, B.G. (1998) *Doing Grounded Theory: Issues and Discussions.* Mill Valley, CA: Sociology Press.

Glaser, B.G. and Strauss, A.L. (1967) *The Discovery of Grounded Theory: Strategies for Qualitative Research*. New York: Aldine.

Gold, J., Hamblett, J. and Rix, M. (2000) 'Telling stories for managing change: a business/academic partnership', *Education through Partnership*, 4 (1): 36–46.

Gold, J., Holman, D. and Thorpe, R. (2002) 'The role of argument analysis and story telling in facilitating critical thinking', *Management Learning*, 33 (3): 371–88.

Gold, J., Thorpe, R. and Holt, R. (2007) 'Writing, reading and reason: the "Three Rs" of manager learning', in R. Hill and J. Stewart (eds), *Management Development. Perspectives from Research and Practice*. Abingdon: Routledge, pp. 271–84.

Goldacre, M.J., Davidson, J.M. and Lambert, T.W. (2004) 'Country of training and ethnic origin of UK doctors: database and survey studies', *British Medical Journal*, 329 (11): 597–600.

Golden-Biddle, K. and Locke, K. (1993) 'Appealing work: an investigation of how ethnographic texts convince', *Organisation Science*, 4 (2): 595–616.

Golden-Biddle, K. and Locke, K. (2007) *Composing Qualitative Research*, 2nd edn. London: Sage.

Granovetter, M. (1973) 'The strength of weak ties', *American Journal of Sociology*, 78: 1360–1380.

Green, S. and Li, Y. (2011) 'Rhetorical institutionalism: language, agency and structure in institutional theory since Alvesson 1993', *Journal of Management Studies*, 48 (7): 1662–97.

Grey, C. (2005) *A Very Short, Fairly Interesting and Reasonably Cheap Book about Studying Organizations*. London: Sage.

Guba, E.G. and Lincoln, Y.S. (1989) *Fourth Generation Evaluation*. London: Sage.

Gubrium, J.F. and Silverman, D. (eds) (1989) *The Politics of Field Research*. London: Sage.

Gummesson, E. ([1988] 1991) *Qualitative Research in Management*. Bromley: Chartwell-Bratt.

Gummesson, E. (1992) *Case Study Research in Management: Methods for Generating Qualitative Data*. Stockholm: Stockholm University.

Gunn, H. (2002) 'Web-based surveys: changing the survey process', *First Monday*, 7 (12). www.firstmonday.dk/issues/issue7_12/gunn/#note3 (last accessed 24 November 2011).

Habermas, J. (1970) 'Knowledge and interest', in D. Emmett and A. Macintyre (eds), *Sociological Theory and Philosophical Analysis*. London: Macmillan, pp. 36–54.

Habermas, J. (1971) *Towards a Rational Society*. London: Heinemann.

Hair, J.F., Black, B., Babin, B., Anderson, R.E. and Tatham, R.L. (2008) *Multivariate Data Analysis*, 7th edn. Upper Saddle River, NJ: Prentice Hall.

Hales, C.P. (1986) 'What do managers do? A critical review of the evidence', *Journal of Management Studies*, 23 (1): 88–115.

Handy, C. (1996) *Beyond Certainty: The Changing Worlds of Organizations*. London: Arrow Books.

Hanneman, R.A. and Riddle, M. (2005) *Introduction to Social Network Methods*. Riverside, CA: University of California. Available at: http://faculty.ucr.edu/~hanneman/ (last accessed 24 November 2011).

Hansen, M.T. (1999) 'The search-transfer problem: the role of weak ties in sharing knowledge across organization subunits', *Administrative Science Quarterly*, 44: 82–111.

Hardy, C. (1996) 'Understanding power: bringing about strategic change', *British Journal of Management*, 7 (Special Issue): S3–S16.

Harper, D. (1989) 'Visual sociology: expanding sociological vision', in G. Blank, J. L. McCartney and E. Brent (eds), *New Technology in Sociology: Practical Applications in Research and Work*. New Brunswick, NJ: Transaction Books, pp. 81–97.

Harper, D. (1994) 'On the authority of the image: visual methods at the crossroads', in N.K. Denzin and Y.S. Lincoln (eds), *Handbook of Qualitative Research*. Thousand Oaks, CA: Sage, pp. 403–12.

Harris, K.J., Wheeler, A.R. and Kacmar, K.M. (2009) 'Leader–member exchange and empowerment: Direct and interactive effects on job satisfaction, turnover intentions, and performance', *Leadership Quarterly*, 20: 371–82.

Hart, C. (1998) *Doing a Literature Review: Releasing the Social Science Research Imagination*. London: Sage.

Harvey, C., Morris, H. and Kelly, A. (eds) (2007) *Association of Business Schools Academic Journal Quality Guide*. London: The Association of Business Schools.

Harzing, A.-W. (ed.) (2007) *Journal Quality List*, 27th edn. Available at: www.harzing.com (last accessed 24 November 2011).

Hassard, J. and Parker, M. (eds) (1993) *Postmodernism and Organizations*. London: Sage.

Hatch, M. J. (1996) 'Irony and the social construction of contradiction in the humor of a management team', *Organization Science*, 8 (3): 275–388.

Hayano, D.M. (1979) 'Auto-ethnography paradigms, problems and prospects', *Human Organisation*, 38: 99–104.

Hayes, R.H. and Abernethy, W.J. (1980) 'Managing our way to economic decline', *Harvard Business Review*, 58: 67–77.

Heath, C. and Hindmarsh, J. (2002) 'Analyzing interaction: video, ethnography and situated conduct', in T. May (ed.), *Qualitative Research in Action*. London: Sage, pp. 99–122

Heisenberg, W (1927) 'Über den anschaulichen Inhalt der quantentheoretischen Kinematik und Mechanik', *Zeitschrift für Physik*, 43: 172–98. [English translation: J. A. Wheeler and H. Zurek (1983) *Quantum Theory and Measurement*. Princeton, NJ: Princeton University Press, pp. 62–84.]

Heron, J. (1996) *Co-operative Inquiry: Research into the Human Condition*. London: Sage.

Herzberg, F., Mausner, B. and Snyderman, B.B. (1959) *The Motivation to Work*. New York: Wiley.

Hickson, D.J. (1988) 'Ruminations on munificence and scarcity in research', in A. Bryman (ed.), *Doing Research in Organizations*. London: Routledge, pp. 136–50.

Hobday, M. and Rush, H. (2007) 'Upgrading the technological capabilities of foreign transnational subsidiaries in developing countries: the case of Thailand', *Research Policy*, 36: 1335–55.

Hofstede, G. (1980) *Culture's Consequences: International Differences in Work-Related Values*. Beverly Hills: Sage.

Hofstede, G. (1991) *Cultures and Organizations: Software of the Mind*. Maidenhead: McGraw-Hill.

Holman, D. (1996) 'The experience of skill development in undergraduates', PhD thesis, Manchester Metropolitan University.

Hong, J., Easterby-Smith, M. and Snell, R. (2006) 'Transferring organizational learning systems to Japanese subsidiaries in China', *Journal of Management Studies*, 43 (5): 1027–58.

Howell, D. (2001) *Statistical Methods for Psychology*, 5th edn. Belmont, CA: Wadsworth.

Howell, D. (2007) *Fundamental Statistics for the Behavioral Sciences*, 6th edn. Belmont, CA: Wadsworth.

Hsiu-Fang, H. and Shannon, S.E. (2005) 'Three approaches to qualitative content analysis', *Qualitative Health Research*, 15 (9): 1277–88.

Huczynski, A.A. (1996) *Management Gurus: What Makes Them and How to Become One*. London: International Thomson Business Press.

Huff, A.S. (1999) *Writing for Scholarly Publication*. Thousand Oaks, CA: Sage.

Huff, A.S. (2000) 'Changes in organizational knowledge production', *Academy of Management Review*, 25 (2): 288–93.

Huff, A. (2009) *Designing Research for Publications*. London: Sage.

Humphreys, M. and Brown, A.D. (2002) 'Dress and identity: a Turkish case study', *Journal of Management Studies*, 39 (7): 927–52.

Humphreys, M. and Brown, A.D. (2008) 'An analysis of corporate social responsibility: a narrative approach', *Journal of Business Ethics*, 80 (3): 403–18.

Huxham, C. (2003) 'Action research as a methodology for theory development', *Policy and Politics*, 31 (2): 239–48.

Hyder, S. and Sims, D. (1979) 'Hypothesis, analysis and paralysis: issues in the organisation of contract research', *Management Education Development*, 10: 100–11.

Ibarra, H. (1992) 'Homophily and differential returns: sex differences in network structure and access in an advertising firm', *Administrative Science Quarterly*, 37: 422–47.

Irwin, A. (1994) 'Science's social standing', *The Times Higher Educational Supplement*, 30 September: 17–19.

Jaccard, J. and Wan, C.K. (1996) *LISREL Approaches to Interaction Effects in Multiple Regression*. Thousand Oaks, CA: Sage.

Jackson, P.R. (1986) 'Robust methods in statistics', in A.D. Lovie (ed.), *New Developments in Statistics for Psychology and the Social Sciences*. London: The British Psychological Society and Methuen, pp. 22–43.

Jackson, P.R. (1989) 'Analysing data', in G. Parry and F.N. Watts (eds), *Behavioural and Mental Health Research: A Handbook of Skills and Methods*. London: Lawrence Erlbaum Associates, pp. 55–79.

Jackson, P.R. (2004) 'Employee commitment to quality: its conceptualisation and measurement', *International Journal of Quality & Reliability Management*, 21 (7): 714–30.

Jackson, P.R. and Parker, S.K. (2001) *Change in Manufacturing: Managing Stress in Manufacturing*. London: HSE Publications.

James, W. ([1907] 1979) *Pragmatism*. Cambridge, MA: Harvard University Press.

Jansen, J.P., Van den Bosch, F.A.J. and Volberda, H.W. (2005) 'Managing potential and realised absorptive capacity: how do organizational antecedents matter?', *Academy of Management Journal*, 48 (6): 999–1015.

Jarzabkowski, P., Balogun, J. and Seidl, D. (2007) 'Strategizing: the challenges of a practice perspective', *Human Relations*, 60 (1): 5–27.

Jick, T. D. (1979) 'Mixing qualitative and quantitative methodologies: triangulation in action', *Administrative Science Quarterly*, 24 (4): 602–11.

Jobber, D. and Horgan, I. (1987) 'Market research and education: perspectives from practitioners', *Journals of Marketing Management*, 3 (1): 39–49.

Johnson, G., Scholes, K. and Whittington, R. (2008) *Exploring Corporate Strategy*, 7th edn. London: Prentice Hall.

Jones, O. (2006) 'Developing absorptive capacity in mature organizations: the change agent's role', *Management Learning*, 37 (3): 355–76.

Jones, S. (1985) 'The analysis of depth interviews', in R. Walker (ed.), *Applied Qualitative Research*. Aldershot: Gower, pp. 56–70.

Kalaitzidakis, P., Mamuneas, T.P. and Stengos, T. (2001) *Ranking of Academic Journals and Institutions in Economics*. Available at: www.le.ac.uk/economics/ research/rankings/econ-rankings.html (last accessed 24 November 2011).

Katsikeas, C.S., Samiee, S. and Theodosiou, M. (2006) 'Strategy fit and performance consequences of international marketing standardization', *Strategic Management Journal*, 27(9): 867–90.

Kelly, G.A. (1955) *The Psychology of Personal Constructs*. New York: Norton.

Kilduff, M. and Brass, D.J. (2010) 'Organizational social network research: core ideas and key debates', *The Academy of Management Annals*, 4 (1): 317–57.

King, N. (1998) 'Template analysis in qualitative methods and analysis', in G. Symon and C. Cassell (eds), *Organizational Research: A Practical Guide*. London: Sage.

King, N. (2004) 'Using templates in the thematic analysis of text', in C. Cassell and G. Symon (eds), *Essential Guide to Qualitative Methods*, 2nd edn. London: Sage, pp. 118–34.

Knorr-Cetina, K.D. (1983) 'The ethnographic study of scientific work: towards a constructivist interpretation of science', in K.D. Knorr-Cetina and M. Mulkay (eds), *Science Observed: Perspectives on the Social Study of Science*. London: Sage, pp. 115–40.

Koenig, T. (2008) 'CAQDAS comparison'. www.lboro.ac.uk/research/mmethods/research/software/caqdas_comparison.html (last accessed 29 October 2008).

Kolb, D.A. (1984) *Organisational Psychology: An Experimental Approach to Organisational Behaviour*. Englewood Cliffs, NJ: Prentice Hall.

Kolb, D.A. (1986) *Experiential Learning*. Englewood Cliffs, NJ: Prentice Hall.

Konopásek, Z. (2008) 'Making thinking visible with ATLAS.ti: computer assisted qualitative analysis as textual practices', *Forum Qualitative Sozialforschung/Forum: Qualitative Social Research*, 9 (2), Art. 12, http://nbn-resolving.de/urn:nbn:de:0114-fqs0802124 (Last accessed 29 October 2008).

Kotter, J. (1982) *The General Managers*. Glencoe, IL: Free Press.

Krech, D., Crutchfield, R.S. and Ballachey, E.L. (1962) *Individual in Society*. London: McGraw-Hill.

Kuhn, T.S. (1962) *The Structure of Scientific Revolution*. Chicago, IL: University of Chicago Press.

Kvale, S. (1996) *InterViews*. London: Sage.

Kwon, W., Clarke, I. and Wodak, R. (2009) 'Organizational decision-making, discourse, and power: integrating across contexts and scales', *Discourse and Communication*, 3 (3): 273–302.

Labov, W. (1972) *Language in the Inner City*. Oxford: Blackwell.

Latour, B. (1988) 'The politics of explanation; an alternative', in S. Woolgar (ed.), *Knowledge and Reflexivity: New Frontiers in the Sociology of Knowledge*. London: Sage, pp. 155–77.

Latour, B. and Woolgar, S. (1979) *Laboratory Life: The Social Construction of Scientific Facts*. Beverly Hills, CA: Sage.

Law, J. (1994) *Organizing Modernity*. Oxford: Blackwell.

Lawrence, P.R. (1986) *Invitation to Management*. Oxford: Blackwell.

Lawrence, P.R. and Lorsch, J.W. (1967) *Organisational Environment: Managing Differentiation and Integration*. Boston, MA: Division of Research, Graduate School of Business Administration, Harvard University.

Lawrence, T. B., Dyck, B., Maitlis, S. and Mauws, M. K. (2006) 'The underlying structure of continuous change', *MIT Sloan Management Review*, 47 (4): 59–66.

Lawrence, T.B., Mauws, M.K., Dyck, B. and Kleysen, R.F. (2005) 'The politics of organizational learning: integrating power into the 4I framework', *Academy of Management Review*, 30 (1): 180–91.

Leask, B. (2006) 'Plagiarism, cultural diversity and metaphor – implications for academic staff development', *Assessment & Evaluation in Higher Education*, 31 (2): 183–99.

Lee, F.S. (2007) 'The Research Assessment Exercise, the state and dominance of mainstream economics in British universities', *Cambridge Journal of Economics*, 31: 309–25.

Lee, R.M. (2000) *Unobtrusive Methods in Social Research*. Buckingham: Open University Press.

Legge, K. (1984) *Evaluating Planned Organisational Change*. London: Academic Press.

Leitch, S. and Palmer, I. (2010) 'Analysing texts in context: current practices and new protocols for critical discourse analysis in organisational studies', *Journal of Management Studies*, 47 (6).

Lewin, K. (1948) 'Frontiers in group dynamics', *Human Relations*, 1: 5–41.

Lewins, A. (2008) 'CAQDAS: Computer Assisted Qualitative Data Analysis', in N. Gilbert, *Researching Social Life*, 3rd edn. London: Sage.

Lewins, A. and Silver, C. (2007) *Using Software in Qualitative Research: A Step-by-Step Guide*. London: Sage.

Lewins, A. and Silver, C. (2009a) *QSR NVivo 8 Distinguishing Features and Functions*. Working Paper No. 004, 1–5.

Lewins, A. and Silver, C. (2009b) *ATLAS.ti 6 Distinguishing Features and Functions*, NCRM Working Paper. Guildford: University of Surrey.

Lewins, A. and Silver, C. (2009c) *Choosing a CAQDAS Package*, NCRM Working Paper. Guildford: University of Surrey.

Liebow, E. (1993) *Tell Them Who I Am: The Lives of Homeless Women*. New York: Penguin.

Locke, K. (1997) 'Re-writing the discovery of Grounded Theory after 25 years?', *Journal of Management Inquiry*, 5: 239–45.

Locke, K. (2001) *Grounded Theory in Management Research*. London: Sage.

Locke, K. and Golden-Biddle, K. (1997) 'Constructing opportunities for contribution: structuring intertextual coherence and "problematizing" in organization studies', *Academy of Management Journal*, 40 (5): 1023–62.

Lowe, A. (1998) 'Managing the post merger aftermath by default remodelling', *Management Decision*, 36 (2): 102–10.

Lu, Y. and Heard, R. (1995) 'Socialised economic action: a comparison of strategic investment decision-making in China and Britain', *Organization Studies*, 16: 395–424.

Luff, P., Hindmarsh, J. and Heath, C. (eds) (2000) *Workplace Studies: Recovering Work Practice and Informing System Design*. Cambridge: Cambridge University Press.

Luo, X. and Bhattacharya, C.B. (2006) 'Corporate social responsibility, customer satisfaction, and market value', *Journal of Marketing*, 70 (4): 1–18.

Lupton, T. (1963) *On the Shop Floor: Two Studies of Workshop Organization and Output*. New York: Macmillan.

Lyles, M.A. and Salk, J.E. (1996) 'Knowledge acquisition from foreign parents in international joint ventures: an empirical examination in the Hungarian context', *Journal of International Business Studies*, Special Issue, 27: 877–903.

Lyotard, J.-F. (1984) *The Postmodern Condition: A Report on Knowledge*. Manchester: Manchester University Press.

Macfarlane, G. (1985) *Alexander Fleming: The Man and the Myth*. Oxford: Oxford University Press.

Mackinlay, T. (1986) 'The development of a personal strategy of management', Master of Science Degree, Manchester Polytechnic, Department of Management.

Maclean, D., Macintosh, R. and Grant, S. (2002) 'Mode 2 management research', *British Journal of Management*, 13: 189–207.

Macmillan, K. (2005) 'More than just coding? Evaluating CAQDAS in a discourse analysis of news texts' [57 paragraphs], *Forum Qualitative Sozialforschung/Forum: Qualitative Social Research*, 6 (3) Art. 25, http://nbn-resolving.de/urn:nbn:de:0114-fqs0503257 (last accessed 29 October 2008).

Macpherson, A. (2006) 'Learning to grow: the evolution of business knowledge in small manufacturing firms', PhD thesis, Manchester Metropolitan University.

Macpherson, A., Kofinas, A., Jones, O. and Thorpe, R. (2010) 'Making sense of mediated learning: cases from small firms', *Management Learning*, 41 (3): 303–23.

Mangham, I.L (1986) 'In search of competence', *Journal of General Management*, 12 (2): 5–12.

Marshall, C. (2000) 'Policy discourse analysis: negotiating gender equity', *Journal of Education Policy*, 15 (2): 125–56.

Marshall, S. and Green, N. (2007) *Your PhD Companion: A Handy Mix of Practical Tips, Sound Advice and Helpful Commentary to See You Through Your PhD*, 2nd edn. Oxford: Cromwell Press.

Mason, J. (1996) *Qualitative Researching*. London: Sage.

Mauch, J.E. and Birch, J.W. (1983) *Guide to the Successful Thesis and Dissertations: A Handbook for Students and Faculty*. New York: Marcel Dekker.

Mayo, E. (1949) *The Social Problems of an Industrial Civilisation*. London: Routledge and Kegan Paul.

McClelland, D.A. (1965) 'Achievement and enterprise', *Journal of Personal Social Psychology*, 1: 389–92.

McClellend, D.A. (1967) *The Achieving Society*. Princetown: Van Nastrand.

McCullagh, P. and Nelder, J. (1989) *Generalized Linear Models*. London: Chapman and Hall.

McLaughlin, H. and Thorpe, R. (1993) 'Action learning – a paradigm in emergence: the problems facing a challenge to traditional management education and development', *British Journal of Management*, 4: 19–27.

Mehra, A., Kilduff, M. and Brass, D.J. (1998) 'At the margins: a distinctiveness approach to the social identity and social networks of underrepresented groups', *Academy of Management Journal*, 41: 441–52.

Mehrabian, A. (1981) *Silent Messages: Implicit Communication of Emotions and Attitudes*, 2nd edn. Belmont, CA: Wadsworth.

Miles, M.B. and Huberman, A.M. (1984) *Qualitative Data Analysis: A Sourcebook of New Methods*. London: Sage.

Miles, M.B. and Huberman, A.M. (1994) *An Expanded Sourcebook Qualitative Data Analysis*, 2nd edn. London: Sage.

Miller, D. (1993) 'The architecture of simplicity', *AMR*, 18 (1): 116–38.

Mintzberg, H. (1973) *The Nature of Managerial Work*. London: Harper and Row.

Mintzberg, H. (2005) *Managers Not MBAs: A Hard Look at the Soft Practice of Managing and Management Development*. San Francisco: Berrett-Koehler.

Moeran, B. (2005) 'Tricks of the trade: the performance and interpretation of authenticity', *Journal of Management Studies*, 42: 901–22.

Moingeon, B. and Edmondson, A. (1997) *Organizational Learning and Competitive Advantage*. London: Sage.

Moreno, J.L. (1934) *Who Shall Survive?* Washington, DC: Nervous and Mental Disease Publishing Company.

Morgan, G. and Smircich, L. (1980) 'The case for qualitative research', *Academy of Management Review*, 5: 491–500.

Moser, C.A. and Kalton, G. (1971) *Survey Methods in Social Investigation*, 2nd edn. London: Heinemann.

Murray, R. (2002) *How to Write a Thesis*. Milton Keynes: Open University Press.

Murray, R. and Moore, S. (2006) *The Handbook of Academic Writing: A Fresh Approach*. Maidenhead: McGraw-Hill.

Nguyen, P. (2005) 'Public opinion polls, chicken soup and sample size', *Teaching Statistics*, 27 (3): 89–91.

Nonaka, I. (1988) 'Toward middle-up-down management: accelerating information creation', *Sloan Management Review*, Spring: 9–18.

Nonaka, I. and Takeuchi, H. (1995) *The Knowledge-Creating Company: How Japanese Companies Create the Dynamics of Innovation*. Oxford: Oxford University Press.

Nor, S.M. (2000) 'Privatisation and changes in organization: a case study of a Malaysian privatised utility', PhD thesis, Lancaster University.

Norman, M. (2006) 'Student teachers' perceptions of becoming teachers and their experiences of confidence during their transition to teaching', PhD thesis, University of Manchester.

Obstfeld, D. (2005) 'Social networks, the tertius iungens orientation, and involvement in innovation', *Administrative Science Quarterly*, 50: 100–30.

O'Reilly, D. and Reed, M. (2010) '"Leaderism": an evolution of managerialism in UK public service reform', *Public Administration*, 88 (4): 960–78.

Padgett, D.K. (2008) *Qualitative Methods in Social Work Research*. Thousand Oaks, CA: Sage.

Padgett, K. (ed.) *The Qualitative Research Experience*. Belmont, CA: Wadsworth, pp. 193–209.

Park, C. (2003) 'In other (people's) words: plagiarism by university students – literature and lessons', *Assessment & Evaluation in Higher Education*, 28 (5): 471–88.

Patriotta, G. (2003) *Organizational Knowledge in the Making*. Oxford: Oxford University Press.

Pears, D. (1971) *Wittgenstein*. London: Fontana.

Peters, T.J. and Waterman, R.H. (1982) *In Search of Excellence: Lessons from America's Best Run Companies*. New York: Harper and Row.

Petticrew, M. and Roberts, H. (2006) *Systematic Reviews in the Social Sciences: A Practical Guide*. Malden, MA: Blackwell.

Pettigrew, A.M. (1985a) *The Awakening Giant: Continuity and Change in Imperial Chemical Industries*. Oxford: Blackwell.

Pettigrew, A.M. (1985b) 'Contextualist research: a natural way to link theory and practice', in E.E. Lawler (ed.), *Doing Research that Is Useful in Theory and Practice*. San Francisco, CA: Jossey Bass, pp. 222–48.

Pettigrew, A.M. (1990) 'Longitudinal field research on change: theory and practice', *Organization Science*, 1 (3): 267–92.

Phillips, E.M. (1984) 'Learning to do research', *Graduate Management Research*, 2 (1): 6–18.

Phillips, E.M. and Pugh, D.S. (2005) *How to Get a PhD: A Handbook for Students and their Supervisors*, 4th edn. Maidenhead: Open University Press.

Pike, K.L. (1954) *Language in Relation to a Unified Theory of the Structure of Human Behavior*. Glendale, CA: Summer Institute of Linguistics.

Pink, S. (2001) *Doing Visual Ethnography: Images, Media and Representation in Research*. London: Sage.

Platt, J. (1976) *Realities of Social Research: An Empirical Study of British Sociologists*. Brighton: Sussex University Press.

Popper, K. (1959) *The Logic of Scientific Discovery*. London: Hutchinson.

Porter, L.W. and McKibbin, L.E. (1988) *Management Education and Development: Drift or Thrust into the 21st Century?* New York: McGraw-Hill.

Potter, J. and Wetherell, M. (1987) *Discourse and Social Psychology Beyond Attitudes and Behaviour*. London: Sage.

Potter, J. and Wetherell, M. (1988) *Social Psychology and Discourse*. London: Routledge.

Prieto, I.M. and Easterby-Smith, M. (2006) 'Dynamic capabilities and the role of organizational knowledge: an exploration', *European Journal of Information Management*, 15: 500–10.

Pugh, D.S. (1983) 'Studying organisational structure and process', in G. Morgan (ed.), *Beyond Method*. Beverly Hills: Sage, pp. 45–55.

Pugh, D.S. (1988) 'The Aston research programme', in A. Bryman (ed.), *Doing Research in Organisations*. London: Routledge, pp. 123–35.

Pugh, D.S. and Hickson, D.J. (1976) *Organisation Structure in its Context: The Aston Programme*. Farnborough: Saxon House.

Punch, M. (1986) *The Politics and Ethics of Fieldwork*. Beverly Hills, CA: Sage.

Punch, K.F. (1998) *Introduction to Social Research: Qualitative Approaches*. London: Sage.

Putnam, H. (1987) *The Many Faces of Realism*. La Salle: Open Court.

Ralston, D.A., Terpstra-Tong, J., Terpstra, R.H., Wang, X.L. and Egri, C. (2006) 'Today's state-owned enterprises of China: are they dying dinosaurs or dynamic dynamos?', *Strategic Management Journal*, 27 (9): 825–43.

Ram, M. and Trehan, K. (2010) 'Critical action learning, policy learning in small firms: an inquiry', *Management Learning*, 41(4): 414–28.

Rappoport, R.N. (1970) 'Three dilemmas in action research', *Human Relations*, 23 (4): 499–513.

Reason, P. (1988) *Human Inquiry in Action*. London: Sage.

Reason, P. and Bradbury, H. (2001) *Handbook of Action Research: Participative Inquiry and Practice*. London: Sage.

Rerup, C. and Feldman, M. (2011) 'Routines as a source of change in organizational schemata: the role of trial-and-error learning', *Academy of Management Journal*, 54 (3): 577–610.

Ricoeur, P. (1981) 'What is a text? Explanation and understanding', in J.B. Thompson (ed.), *Paul Ricoeur, Hermeneutics and the Human Sciences*. Cambridge: Cambridge University Press, pp. 145–64.

Roberts, K.A. and Wilson, R.W. (2002) 'ICT and the research process: issues around the compatibility of technology with qualitative data analysis' [52 paragraphs], *Forum Qualitative Sozialforschung/Forum: Qualitative Social Research*, 3 (2), Art. 23, http://nbn-resolving.de/urn:nbn:de:0114-fqs0202234 (last accessed 29 October 2008).

Roethlisberger, F.J. and Dickson, W.J. (1939) *Management and the Worker*. Cambridge, MA: Harvard University Press.

Rouleau, L. (2005) 'Micro-practices of strategic sensemaking and sensegiving: how middle managers interpret and sell change every day', *Journal of Management Studies*, 42 (7): 1413–41.

Roy, D. (1952) 'Quota restriction and goldbricking in a machine shop', *American Journal of Sociology*, 57: 427–42.

Roy, D. (1954) 'Efficiency and "the fix": informal intergroup relations in a piecework machine shop', *American Journal of Sociology*, 60 (3): 255–66.

Roy, D. (1970) 'The study of southern labour union organising campaigns', in R. Haberstein (ed.), *Pathway to Data*. New York: Aldine, pp. 216–44.

Rugg, G. and Petre, M. (2004) *The Unwritten Rules of PhD Research*. Maidenhead: Open University Press.

Ryave, A.L. and Schenkein, J.N. (1974) 'Notes on the art of walking', in R. Turner (ed.), *Ethnomethodology: Selected Readings*. Harmondsworth: Penguin, pp. 265–74.

Said, E. (1978) *Orientalism*. London: Routledge and Kegan Paul.

Sapsford, R. (2006) *Survey Research*, 2nd edn. London: Sage.

Saunders, M.N.K., Lewis, P. and Thornhill, A. (2003) *Research Methods for Business Students*, 3rd edn. Harlow: FT Prentice Hall.

Saunders, M., Lewis, P. and Thornhill, A. (2006) *Research Methods for Business Students*, 4th edn. Harlow: Pearson Education.

Saunders, M., Lewis, P. and Thornhill, A. (2009) *Research Methods for Business Students*, 5th edn. London: FT Prentice Hall.

Sayer, A. (2000) *Realism and Social Science*. London: Sage.

Scarbrough, H. (ed.) (2008) *The Evolution of Business Knowledge*. Oxford: Oxford University Press.

Scarbrough, H. and Swan, J. (1999) 'Knowledge management and the management fashion perspective', Proceedings of British Academy of Management Conference, Manchester, Vol II: 920–37.

Schmitt, N. and Stults, D.M. (1985) 'Factors defined by negatively keyed items: the results of careless respondents?', *Applied Psychological Measurement*, 9 (4): 367–73.

Schon, D.A. (1983) *The Reflective Practitioner: How Professionals Think in Action*. London: Maurice Temple Smith.

Schyns, B. Kiefer, T., Kerschreiter, R. and Tymon, A. (2011) 'Teaching implicit leadership theories to develop leaders and leadership – how and why it can make a difference', *Academy of Management Learning and Education*, 10 (3): 397–408.

Scoble, R. and Israel, S. (2006) *Naked Conversations: How Blogs Are Changing the Way Businesses Are Talking to Customers*. Hoboken: NJ: John Wiley & Sons.

Scott, M. (1997) 'PC analysis of key words – and key key words', *System*, 25 (1): 1–13.

Scott, M. (2001) 'Comparing corpora and identifying key words, collocations, and frequency distributions through the WordSmith Tools suite of computer programs', in M. Ghadessy, A. Henry and R.L. Roseberry (eds), *Small Corpus Studies and ELT: Theory and Practice*. Amsterdam: Benjamins, pp. 47–67.

Scott, M. (2002) 'Picturing the key words of a very large corpus and their lexical upshots – or getting at the *Guardian*'s view of the world', in B. Kettemann and G. Marko (eds), *Teaching and Learning by Doing Corpus Analysis*. Amsterdam: Rodopi, pp. 43–50 (see also CD-rom).

Scott, M. (2010) 'What can corpus software do?' in A. O'Keeffe and M.J. McCarthy (eds), *Routledge Handbook of Corpus Linguistics*. London: Routledge, pp. 136–51.

Seale, C. (2000) 'Resurrective practice and narrative', in M. Andrews, S.D. Sclater, C. Squire and A. Treacher (eds), *Lines of Narrative*. London: Routledge, pp. 36–47.

Seale, C. (2000) 'Using computers to analyse qualitative data', in D. Silverman (ed.), *Doing Qualitative Research: A Practical Handbook*. London: Sage, pp. 154–74.

Secrist, C., Koeyer I., de Bell, H. and Fogel, A. (2002) 'Combining digital video technology and narrative methods for understanding infant development', *Forum: Qualitative Social Research*, 3 (2). Available at: www.qualitative-research.net/fqs-texte/2-02/2-02secristetal-e.htm (last accessed 24 November 2011).

Selvin, H.C. and Stuart, A. (1966) 'Data-dredging procedures in survey analysis', *American Statistician*, 20: 20–3.

Senge, P. (1990) *The Fifth Discipline: The Art and Practice of the Learning Organization*. London: Century.

Shadish, W.R., Cook, T.D. and Campbell, D. T. (2002) *Experimental and Quasi-Experimental Designs for Generalised Causal Inference*. Boston, MA: Houghton Mifflin.

Shotter, J. (1993) *Conversational Realities*. London: Sage.

Shotter, J. (1995) 'The manager as a practical author: a rhetorical-responsive, social constructionist approach to social-organizational problems', in D. Hosking, H.P. Dachler and K.J. Gergen (eds), *Management and Organization: Relational Alternatives to Individualism*. Aldershot: Avebury, pp. 125–47.

Shrader, C.B., Lincoln, J.R. and Hoffman, A.N. (1989) 'The network structures of organizations: effects of task contingencies and distributional form', *Human Relations*, 42: 43–66.

Siggelkow, N. (2007) 'Persuasion with case studies', *Academy of Management Journal*, 50 (1): 20–4.

Silver, M. (1991) *Competent to Manage*. London: Routledge.

Silverman, D. (1993) *Interpreting Qualitative Data: Methods for Analysing Talk, Text and Interaction*. London: Sage.

Silverman, D. (2000) *Doing Qualitative Research: A Practical Handbook*. London: Sage.

Simon, H.A. (1959) *Administrative Behaviour*, 2nd edn. London: Macmillan.

Simpson, B. (1995) 'A university: an organisation for learning … but a learning organisation?', unpublished MSc dissertation, Manchester Metropolitan University.

Sims, D. (1993) 'Coping with misinformation', *Management Decision*, 3: 18–21.

Sims, D. (2003) 'Between the millstones: a narrative account of the vulnerability of middle managers' storying', *Human Relations*, 56: 1195–211, doi: 10.1177/00187267035610002.

Slater, D. (1989) 'Corridors of power', in J.F. Gubrium and D. Silverman (eds), *The Politics of Field Research*. London: Sage, pp. 113–31.

Smeyers, P. and Verhessen, P. (2001) 'Narrative analysis as philosophical research, bridging the gap between the empirical and the conceptual', *International Journal of Qualitative Studies in Education* (QSE), 14 (1): 71–84.

Snell, R.S. (1993) *Developing Skills for Ethical Management*. London: Chapman and Hall.

Spector, P.E. (1992) *Summated Rating Scale Construction: An Introduction*. Newbury Park, CA: Sage.

Sprigg, C.A. and Jackson, P.R. (2006) 'Call centers as lean service environments: well-being and the mediating role of work design', *Journal of Occupational Health Psychology*, 11 (2): 197–212.

Stake, R.E. (2006) 'Qualitative case studies', in N.K. Denzin and Y.S. Lincoln (eds), *Sage Handbook of Qualitative Research*, 3rd edn. Thousand Oaks, CA: Sage, pp. 443–66.

Starbuck, B. (2004) *Journals Ranked by Citations per Article*. Available at: http://pages.stern.nyu.edu/~wstarbuc/ (last accessed 24 November 2011).

Starkey, K. and Tiratsoo, N. (2007) *Business Schools and the Bottom Line*. Cambridge: Cambridge University Press.

Steenkamp, J.-B.E.M. and Geyskens, I. (2006) 'What drives the perceived value of web sites? A cross-national investigation', *Journal of Marketing*, 70 (3): 136–50.

Steers, R.M., Bischoff, S.J. and Higgins, L.H. (1992) 'Crosscultural management research: the fish and the fisherman', *Journal of Management Inquiry*, 1 (4): 321–30.

Steinbeck, J. (1970) *Journal of a Novel: The East of Eden Letters*. London: Pan Books.

Stewart, R. (1967) *Managers and their Jobs*. Maidenhead: McGraw-Hill.

Stewart, R. (1982) *Choices for the Manager: A Guide to Managerial Work and Behaviour*. London: McGraw-Hill.

Stewart, V., Stewart, A. and Fonda, N. (1981) *Business Applications of Repertory Grid*. Maidenhead: McGraw-Hill.

Stokes, D. and Bergin, R. (2006) 'Methodology or "methodolatry"? An evaluation of focus groups and depth interviews', *Qualitative Market Research: An International Journal*, 9 (11): 26–37.

Strauss, A.L. (1987) *Qualitative Analysis for Social Scientists*. Cambridge: Cambridge University Press.

Strauss, A.L. and Corbin, J. (1990) *Basics of Qualitative Research: Grounded Theory Procedures and Techniques*. Thousand Oaks, CA: Sage.

Strauss, A.L. and Corbin, J. (1998) *Basics of Qualitative Research: Techniques and Procedures for Developing Grounded Theory*, 2nd edn. Thousand Oaks, CA: Sage.

Tabachnick, B.G. and Fidell, L.S. (2012) *Using Multivariate Statistics*, 6th edn. Boston, MA: Pearson Education.

Tashakkori, A. and Teddlie, C. (eds) (2003) *Handbook of Mixed Methods in Social and Behavioral Research*. Thousand Oaks, CA: Sage.

Taylor, B. (1999) 'Patterns of control within Japanese manufacturing plants in China: doubts about Japanisation in Asia', *Journal of Management Studies*, 36 (6): 853–73.

Taylor, F.W. (1947) *Scientific Management*. London: Harper and Row.

Taylor, S.J. and Bogdan, R. (1984) *Introduction to Qualitative Research Methods*. New York: Wiley-Interscience.

Teagarden, M.B., von Glinow, M.A., Bowen, D.E., Frayne, C.A., Nason, S., Huo, Y.P., Milliman, J., Arias, M.E., Butler, M.C., Geringer, J.M., Kim, N.M., Scullion, H., Lowe, K.B. and Drost, E.A. (1995) 'Toward a theory of comparative management research: an ideographic case study of the best international human resources management project', *Academy of Management Journal*, 38: 1261–87.

Tesch, R. (1990) *Qualitative Research, Analysis Types & Software Tools*. New York: Falmer Press.

Thomas, W.I. and Thomas, D.S. (1928) *The Child in America: Behavioural Problems and Progress*. New York: Knopf.

Thompson, E.E. (2004) 'National competitiveness: a question of cost conditions or institutional circumstances?', *British Journal of Management*, 15: 197–218.

Thorpe, R. (1980) 'The relationship between payment systems, productivity and the organisation of work', MSc thesis, Strathclyde Business School.

Thorpe, R. and Cornelissen, J. (2003) 'Visual media and the construction of meaning', in D. Holman and R. Thorpe (eds), *Management and Language: The Manager as Practical Author*. London: Sage, pp. 67–81.

Thorpe, R. and Danielli, A. 'Oldham Town Park', unpublished study conducted for Oldham Borough Council.

Thorpe, R. and Holloway, J. (2008) *Performance Management: Multidisciplinary Perspectives*. Houndsmill: Palgrave Macmillan NC.

Thorpe, R. and Holt, R. (2009) *The Sage Dictionary of Qualitative Management Research*. London: Sage.

Thorpe, R., Holt, R., Macpherson, A. and Pittaway, L. (2005) 'Knowledge within small and medium-sized firms: a review of the evidence', *International Journal of Management Reviews*, 7 (4): 257–81.

Tilly, C. (2006) *Why?* Princeton: Princeton University Press.

Todd, D.J. (1979) 'Mixing qualitative and quantitative methods: triangulation in action', *Administrative Science Quarterly*, 24: 602–11.

Todorova, G. and Durisin, B. (2007) 'Absorptive capacity: valuing a reconceptualization', *Academy of Management Review*, 32 (3): 774–86.

Toulmin, S. (2001) *The Uses of Argument*. Cambridge: Cambridge University Press.

Tranfield, D. (2002) 'Formulating the nature of management research', *European Management Journal*, 20 (4): 378–82.

Tranfield, D., Denyer, D. and Marcos, J. (2004) 'Co-producing management knowledge', *Management Decision*, 42 (3/4): 375–86.

Tranfield, D., Denyer, D. and Smart, P. (2003) 'Towards a methodology for developing evidence-informed management knowledge by means of systematic review', *British Journal of Management*, 14 (3): 207–22.

Tranfield, D. and Starkey, K. (1998) 'The nature, social organization and promotion of management research: towards policy', *British Journal of Management*, 9: 341–53.

Tsai, W. and Ghoshal, S. (1998) 'Social capital and value creation: The role of intrafirm networks', *Academy of Management Journal*, 41(4): 464–76.

Tsang, E.W.K. (1997) 'Learning from joint venturing experience: the case of foreign direct investment by Singapore companies in China', PhD thesis, University of Cambridge.

Tsang, E.W.K. (1999) 'Internationalisation as a learning process: Singapore MNCs in China', *Academy of Management Executive*, 13 (1): 91–101.

Tsang, E.W.K. (2002) 'Acquiring knowledge by foreign partners from international joint ventures in a transition economy: learning-by-doing and learning myopia', *Strategic Management Journal*, 23: 835–54.

Tsoukas, H. and Hatch, M.J. (1997) 'Complex thinking, complex practice: the case for a narrative approach to organisational complexity', paper presented to the American Academy of Management.

Turner, B.A. (1988) 'Connoisseurship in the study of organisational cultures', in A. Bryman (ed.), *Doing Research in Organisations*. London: Sage, pp. 108–21.

Ullman, J.B. (2006a) 'Structural equation modeling', in B.G. Tabachnick and L.S. Fidell (eds), *Using Multivariate Statistics*. Boston, MA: Allyn & Bacon, pp. 653–771.

Ullman, J.B. (2006b) 'Structural equation modeling: reviewing the basics and moving forward', *Journal of Personality Assessment*, 87 (1): 35–50.

Uzzi, B. (1997) 'Social structure and competition in interfirm networks: the paradox of embeddedness', *Administrative Science Quarterly*, 42: 35–67.

Van de Ven, A. H. and Johnson, P. E. (2006) 'Knowledge for theory and practice', *Academy of Management Review*, 31 (4): 802–21.

Von Bertalanffy, L. (1962) 'General systems theory – a critical review', *General Systems*, 7: 1–20.

Walker, G.B. and Sillars, M.O. (1990) 'Where is argument? Perelman's theory of values', in R. Trapp and J. Schuetz (eds), *Perspectives on Argumentation*. Illinois: Waveland Press, pp. 121–33.

Walker, R. (1985) *Applied Qualitative Research*. Aldershot: Gower.

Wall, T.D., Jackson, P.R. and Davids, K. (1992) 'Operator work design and robotics system performance: a serendipitous field experiment', *Journal of Applied Psychology*, 77: 353–62.

Wall, T.D., Kemp, N.J., Jackson, P.J. and Clegg, C.W. (1986) 'Outcomes of autonomous workgroups: a long-term field experiment', *Academy of Management Journal*, 29 (2): 282–304.

Walsh, G. and Beatty, S.E. (2007) 'Customer-based corporate reputation of a service firm: scale development and validation', *Journal of the Academy of Marketing Science*, 35 (1): 127–43.

Walsh, G., Mitchell, V.-W., Jackson, P.R. and Beatty, S.E. (2009) 'Examining the antecedents and consequences of corporate reputation: a customer perspective', *British Journal of Management*, 20 (2): 187–203.

Warr, P.B., Cook, J.D. and Wall, T.D. (1979) 'Scales for the measurement of some work attitudes and aspects of psychological well-being', *Journal of Occupational Psychology*, 52: 129–48.

Watford, A.J. (1980–87) *Watson's Guide to Reference Material. Volume 2 – Social and Historical Sciences, Philosophy and Religion*. London: Library Association.

Watson, T.J. (1994) *In Search of Management: Culture, Chaos and Control in Managerial Work*. London: Routledge.

Watzlawick, P. (ed.) (1984) *The Invented Reality*. London: Norton.

Weick, K.E. (1995) *Sense-making in Organisations*. London: Sage.

Weick, K.E. (2001) 'Theory construction as disciplined imagination', *Academy of Management Review*, 14 (4): 516–31.

Weitzman, E.A. (1999) 'Analyzing qualitative data with computer software', *Health Services Research*, 34 (5/2): 1241–63.

Wertsch, J.V. (1991) *Voices of the Mind: A Socio Cultural Approach to Mediated Action*. Cambridge, MA: Harvard University Press.

Whitley, R., Thomas, A. and Marceau, J. (1981) *Masters of Business?* London: Tavistock.

Winter, S.G. (2003) 'Understanding dynamic capabilities', *Strategic Management Journal*, 24: 991–5.

Wittgenstein, L. (1953) *Philosophical Investigations*. Oxford: Blackwell.

Wright, R.P. (2006) 'Rigor and relevance using repertory grid technique in strategy research', *Research Methodology in Strategy and Management*, 3: 295–348.

Yin, R.K. (2002) *Case Study Research: Design and Methods*, 3rd edn. Thousand Oaks, CA: Sage.

Zahra, S. A. and George, G. (2002) 'Absorptive capacity: a review, reconcepualisation, and extension', *Academy of Management Review*, 27 (2): 185–203.

INDEX

Tables and Figures are indicated by page numbers in bold.

QUALITATIVE ORGANIZATIONAL RESEARCH

Core Methods and Current Challenges

Edited by **Gillian Symon** *Birkbeck College, University of London* and
Catherine Cassell *University of Manchester*

This comprehensive text brings together in one volume both consideration of the core methods available for undertaking qualitative data collection and analysis, and discussion of common challenges faced by all researchers in conducting qualitative research.

Qualitative Organizational Research: Core Methods and Common Challenges contains 27 chapters, each written by an expert in the area. The first part of the volume considers common challenges in the design and execution of qualitative research, examining key contemporary debates in each area as well as providing practical advice for those undertaking organizational research. The second part of the volume looks at contemporary uses of core qualitative methods in organizational research, outlining each method and illustrating practical application through empirical examples.

Key features:

- Coverage of all the key topics in qualitative research
- Chapters written by experts drawing on their personal experiences of using methods
- Introductory chapters outlining the context for qualitative research and the philosophies which underpin it

READERSHIP

Students and researchers on courses in organization studies, management research and organizational psychology

March 2012 • 536 pages
Hardback (978-0-85702-410-7) • £90.00
Paperback (978-0-85702-411-4) • £32.99

ALSO FROM SAGE

CASE STUDY RESEARCH FOR BUSINESS

Jillian Dawes Farquhar *University of Bedfordshire*

The only case study research textbook written exclusively for students of Business and related disciplines.

Using a step-by-step approach, **Case Study Research for Business** takes you right through the case study research process from research design and data collection using qualitative and quantitative methods, to research analysis, writing up and presenting your work.

Key features:-

- Takes a multidisciplinary approach to case study research design by drawing on research philosophies to improve student understanding of these critical research traditions and hence provide firmer theoretical foundations for their research
- Coverage of contemporary topics such as research ethics and access
- Packed with practical examples from all areas of business - Pedagogical features include vignettes, exercises and 'cases' which directly relate to business research

Case Study Research for Business will prove a valuable resource for undergraduate, postgraduate and research students of business and related disciplines.

CONTENTS

What Is Case Study Research? \ Philosophical Assumptions of Case Study Research \ Developing Your Case Study Research Strategy \ Access and Ethics in Case Study Research \ Data Collection \ Managing and Analyzing Data \ Quality in Case Study Research \ Writing and Presenting Your Research

READERSHIP

Undergraduate and postgraduate students studying business or business-related disciplines

February 2012 • 144 pages
Hardback (978-1-84920-776-8) • £75.00
Paperback (978-1-84920-777-5) • £24.99

ALSO FROM SAGE